THE HUMANITY OF MAN

THE
HUMANITY
OF MAN

EDMOND BARBOTIN

Translated by Matthew J. O'Connell

ORBIS BOOKS
MARYKNOLL NEW YORK

Originally published by Editions Aubier, Paris, France, 1970.

Copyright © 1975, Orbis Books, Maryknoll, N.Y. 10545
Library of Congress Catalogue Card Number: 74-21108
ISBN: 0-88344-183-7

Manufactured in the United States of America

CONTENTS

46455

THE HUMANITY OF MAN

INTRODUCTION

*. . . at least I expected to find many associates
in the study of man because it is the true
study and is proper to him. I was mistaken;
there are even fewer who study man than study
mathematics.* PASCAL, *Pensées.*

The humanity of man: this unusual title is anything but a meaningless redundancy, for the attempt to penetrate to the specific nature of man is as old as culture itself. It is through self-questioning that the rational animal lays hold upon and transcends nature: the nature around him and the nature he carries within himself.

The question is always relevant, then, but the conditions of contemporary civilization give it a new bearing and a genuine urgency. On the one hand, the unequal development of the northern and southern hemispheres of the world has given rise to two diverse but equally dangerous kinds of alienation. In the southern hemisphere, persistent economic stagnation deprives men of the material means

3

required for legitimate self-development. In the northern, increasing technological rationalization threatens to submerge the person, to enslave him to the production and consumption of means, and to divert him from raising questions about ends. In one part of the world there is no provision for the "how?"; in the other, no vision of the "why?"

On the other hand, the development of the positive sciences, whatever its advantages, exposes man to a number of "reductions" which are death-dealing to all that defines him most radically and specifically as man. Through the continual application of quantitative measurement we have been led to believe that thanks to diagrams and statistics man has finally been delimited, seized, pinned down: "Here is what man is!" Indeed, what it amounts to is crying, *"Ecce homo*—behold man!"* Seen within this exclusive perspective, what remains is measurable man—that is, man disfigured, downgraded, made into an object. The humanity of man in its irreducible original-ity is missing. The medievals, on the contrary, were well aware of the difference between *actus hominis* (the actions of a man) and *actus humani* (specifically human actions). The sciences of man will really serve humanity only if the scholar maintains a keen awareness of the limitations of his methods.

Philosophical thought, in the broad sense of this term, is not innocent of similar oversimplifications. In former times idealism and a false spiritualism reduced man to a disembodied *cogito* (I think) with no real relationships to the world. The existentialism of a Sartre reduces man to an absolute freedom, emancipated both from any link with ideal values and from limitation by any determining forces. Positivism, especially for the last century, tends to reduce man to various empirical conditions which surround his life and his activity. In a more or less radical way, Marxism makes man a sum-total of economic and social relations, Freudianism a complex of instincts, and structuralism a plaything in the hands of impersonal and oppres-sive systems. At the extreme, the human subject is devalued as is his meaning; he ceases even to be a problem. Man, once "reduced" and "objectified," is dead or in process of dying to himself.[1]

All these currents of thought have the indisputable merit of clarify-ing one or other aspect of the human phenomenon. All of them err through exclusivism and oversystematization and through infidelity to experience, which bears manifold witness to the complexity and specificity of the datum being examined. This book proposes that we return to man as he really is, a subject and not a mere object, situated within the world but nonetheless an original source of meaning.

The attempt would deserve no hearing if it proceeded from one or other initial philosophical postulate. Nor is our intention to develop a new conception of man by way of a critical examination and refutation of the positions mentioned above. An interpretation can claim value for itself only if it is based on the data of immediate experience. We shall try here to observe and describe man as we find him in his concrete existence, in the small and numberless details of his daily life.

Such an examination of experience calls for constant attention to the language of word and gesture. That is where meaning is manifested and man expresses himself in his relations to things; where the "lived" universe shows itself as distinct from the universe as thought by science; where, without yielding anything to romanticism, the human most evidently refuses to submit to objectification and a reduction to the purely rational. We shall clarify our general purpose by first recalling the nature, requirements, and limits of scientific objectivity.

Explanation and Understanding

Strict scientific method demands, to begin with, that the scientist put aside all prejudices, passions, and biases and remain scrupulously faithful to the "given." This rule of objectivity is the source both of the paradox and the greatness of rational knowledge. The paradox, because the subject who takes the initiative in research tries to disappear more and more completely behind his object. The greatness as well, because such a strict asceticism adds to the value of the knowledge attained the moral merit of a purifying self-sacrifice.

In the sciences that study inanimate and animate matter, objectivity is, however, not simply a matter of intellectual and moral discipline. The objectivist attitude, at a deeper level, defines the mind's epistemological stance in the scientific situation. For the physicist or biologist, the object is what "lies there in front of one" (*ob-jectum*) as a norm that knowledge must respect. The scientist detaches himself, puts a certain distance between himself and the object, sets it before him as a point of concentration. But the datum here is unconscious, opaque to itself. This other is not another person. No intersubjective reciprocity links the knowing mind to the reality it tries to take possession of. Objectification acknowledges and perpetuates this irreducible duality. The scientific task is then to "explain": it orders facts according to relations of priority and posteriority, causality and mutual conditioning; it attempts to express these relations in the most precise and rational of languages, that of mathematics. Science makes the universe intelligible by bringing out objective meanings.

The study of a "human" fact—historical, religious, sociological, etc.—cannot, however, be content with such a purely objectivist attitude. No analysis of the internal components or the external conditions of the fact is enough to grasp its full intelligibility. Far from it. The reason is that an historical event, for example, brings into play not only physical, biological, psychic, economic, social, and cultural determinisms but also the free initiative of human subjects. An event is the point of convergence at which numerous blind forces and deliberate choices criss-cross, confront each other, and are inextricably interwoven; natural phenomena and human intentions meet. An historical fact, consequently, is inexhaustible. Consequently, too, scientific history is never definitive but must always be revised, since men will never stop trying to interpret the meanings which the actors willy-nilly give to the events in which they are involved. This is to say that history, more than any other science, recognizes no such thing as raw facts;[2] that historical facts, and social ones too (*pace* Durkheim), are not things; and that objectivity in the human sciences cannot be of the same kind as in physics. Consideration of the event must be impartial and objective, of course, but it cannot be objectivist except at the cost of reducing the historical event to its material components and of annihilating the very reality it wishes to investigate. The proper approach to an event involves not only "explanation" but "understanding" as well.

This distinction, derived from Dilthy and widely used by contemporary psychologists and characteriologists, opposes the objective study of phenomena—desire, thought, or free decision—to the understanding of their meaning for the subject. To take an example from the historical sphere, let us consider three ways in which one could approach the history of philosophy. One might consider a given philosophical system as a cultural, or even a sociological, phenomenon; explain it by other antecedent or concomitant phenomena of the same type, and determine its proximate or remote influence on other cultural phenomena. Or one might analyze the author's work as to its elements, a careful study for the purpose of determining its sources. Finally, one might transcend the objectivist viewpoint in an effort to attain an intuitive grasp of the original intention behind the system, to get inside the creative aim which makes use of such diverse materials and influences and reenact the effort which must have been involved in turning a heterogeneous multiplicity into a new totality with an original meaning of its own. In the first two approaches the historian seeks to "explain"; in the last, his aim is to "understand." In the former modes of approach, the mind assumes an objectivist attitude in the presence of a cultural fact; in the latter mode, the historian puts himself in the presence of the philosopher as one thinking subject in the presence of another. In the former cases one puts oneself outside the system; in the latter, one moves inside the other's thought and tries to "live" it from within in order to adopt the other's viewpoint and follow along in the course of his thinking. Here the method is no longer deduction but rather a kind of induction, communing with a living intention and illumining an intellectual process through its ends, not its "causes." The consciousness of the historian goes out to an encounter with another consciousness, aware of interaction with it; seeks to discern an intention it knows to be in control of the materials used and present in the totality of the system as well as in all its details without, perhaps, manifesting itself as such at any point. This effort of understanding becomes a process conducted in the first and second person: the author is no longer a "he"; he is a "you" facing my "I." The procedure is no longer one of examination but has become a dialogue and an exchange.[3]

Understanding and Objectivity

Can the effort of understanding, thus defined, claim to be scientific? If you let the intentions of one or several *subjects* play a role in a piece of research, do you not necessarily fall short of the ideal of *objective* knowledge?

We must here avoid being ensnared by words and therefore considering such an effort of understanding to be alien to the scientists's way of dealing with reality. It is a scientific task to try to penetrate to the original intuition behind an artistic or literary work, a philosophical or religious movement. This point emerges clearly from the distinction just drawn between the three ways of approaching a system of thought: understanding completes explanation and gives it its real significance. A textual analysis concerned only with the component parts of a work can proceed with complete scientific strictness and bring a wealth of philological, historical, and literary erudition to bear, and yet fail to get at the essential object of study: the meaning and intention of the author. Whatever some kinds of positivism may hold, *meaning is part of the datum*, and the spirit of a text is inseparable from its letter. You may dismember a text into sentences, the sentences into propositions, the propositions into words, the words into linguistic elements: root, prefix, ending. If you are content with this kind of analysis, all you have done is to dissect a living whole and destroy it. Beyond the letter there is the spirit, beyond the vocable (*le mot*) the word (*la parole*). The author's meaning, the "spirit," the "word" cannot be grasped except in the text as a living totality. After having, in numerous strictly conducted procedures, analyzed the external elements of intelligibility (historical circumstances, influences at work, cultural milieu) and the internal elements of intelligibility (genre and literary themes, images, style, and vocables), there still remains the effort at synthesis: the effort to reunify the multiplicity of parts and to grasp in a single act of the mind the living meaning of the organism which a text is. After I have explained, I must still understand.[4]

The interpreter's task, in brief, is to *relive the intellectual experience* of the author, to adopt for a while his historical, moral, and religious outlook. It cannot be too much insisted on that men (whether they are scientists or not) meet and understand each other not so much through the exchange of pure ideas as through the sharing of common experiences. Ideas have no chance of leading to true understanding unless they tend to foster the encounter of personal experiences. I understand an ancient or contemporary text or a living person with whom I am conversing only if I discover myself in it or him. The experience of another person awakens no echo in me if nothing in my life gives me access to it—the advice of old men is rarely helpful to the young. This is exactly the situation in the human sciences (taking this latter term in its broadest interpretation). Contrary appearances notwithstanding, the scholar who is attuned to the social, moral, and religious convictions of another will be more likely to interpret them accurately than one to whom they are alien. In this sense, there is a true understanding of secular or sacred texts, rites, customs, and myths which can be attained only within the religious faith or ethnic group of their origin. At least the interpreter must keep himself as open and available as possible to the experience of others, if he is to re-experience it himself and penetrate into it as a vital process. Such openness and availability are precisely what are sought in setting aside all prejudices, passions, and biases; they constitute the effort at *scientific objectivity*. Despite the verbal contradiction which might seem to be involved, to be objective in the human sciences consists largely in a capacity for receiving and reliving the experiences of another subject. There can thus be no question of attaching greater importance either to explanation or to understanding: they are equally necessary and call for each other. Objective explanation seeks understanding of a subject's living thought. Understanding finally summarizes, completes, justifies, and illumines in turn the patient analysis which has prepared the way for it.[5]

Objective and Subjective

The essential connection between explanation and understanding is an example of the larger and deeper connection between the objective and the subjective. Karl Jaspers has shown how the "subject-object dichotomy" ceaselessly arises at the heart of being, of the "Comprehensive,"[6] and Gabriel Marcel has stressed the impossibility, for any thought that raises the questions of being as such, of totally objectifying this being which envelops and grounds thought itself.[7] In short, neither the objective point of view nor the subjective can claim to exhaust being in its totality; each approach calls for and complements the other. The subject-object dichotomy sets up an unalterable rhythm; but since the dichotomy is situated within being and contains the whole weight of being, it is not in danger of becoming a purely dialectical opposition; rather, it expresses a radical requirement of the given.

This duality of viewpoints occurs again in man himself and, consequently, in his self-knowledge. I can be studied as an organism by the biologist; my psyche can be scrutinized by the psychologist; I can be treated as mentally ill by the psychiatrist; in a word, I can be objectified by science and technology. But if anyone claims thereby to reduce me to the status of pure object, I feel violated and, as it were, annihilated. The best part of my being is my "I," my subjectivity. That is what gives meaning to my bodily appearance, my thought, and my free actions. These two aspects of my being, objectivity and subjectivity, are equally real and are coextensive. The man who I am is entirely object and entirely subject. Each of these two perspectives embraces my whole being, but neither exhausts it, neither is total.

We must beware, moreover, of dividing the two aspects, objective and subjective, between body and soul, as if the former were conceived as pure object and the latter as pure subject. This has been the error of every dualism throughout history, whether Platonic, Cartesian, or any other; it necessarily ends in the denial of man in his specificity. My body is neither thing nor machine; it is subjective, it is mine and it is I myself; the unique significance which "I" possess compenetrates it and gives its matter its incommunicable meaning. On the other hand, my consciousness is not reducible to a transcendental ego: it presents a certain objectivity which is able to become the basis of the psychological sciences and, beyond that, a metaphysics of the soul and spirit. But even as I present myself to science as an object, I simultaneously elude its grasp because I am a subject and yet forbid it—paradoxical though the prohibition is—to lose sight of my subjectivity. The biologist, for example, has no right to experiment on my body as though I were a plant or an animal. Medical ethics and the limits it imposes on the objectivist attitude of the practitioner have their basis in this ambiguity of my being. I possess myself, therefore, insofar as I am this particular "I," but because of my objectivity I also elude myself and run the risk of being possessed by others. My existence as a man is reducible, in a measure, to this ceaseless interior debate; I cannot resolve it by rejecting one or other term but only by assuming my own objectivity in an ever freer way. Thus the subject-object dichotomy is always at work and always being overcome in my own being. I separate and reunify myself in the very act by which I exist. It is to this ontological depth that we must penetrate if we are to grasp the distinction and the necessary collaboration of explanation and understanding in the human sciences.

Understanding Man

Our effort then will be to understand man, to encounter the subject at that secret core of his being which can never be defined nor adequately described. The attempt is to be made at the level of the immediate, the everyday, the data to which one can point, so as to grasp the most evident implications as fully as possible. There is no question of scholarly or bookish knowledge. I am a man and do not cease for a single moment to live my humanity. My truth as a man is inseparable from my existence and it is entirely up to me to try to discover it. Thus each day I experience in one or other way my situation in time or in space. Furthermore I am in search of myself as I exercise my expressive functions: speech, gestures, actions of every kind. Self-expression, self-discovery, and self-fulfillment go together.

This effort at understanding must not lead me into the morbid deviations of autism or introversion, for it will achieve its goal only in communication with others. There is no genuine speech or gesture except those which bind me to my fellows. The distinction between expression and communication must therefore not be made too clear-cut. Although two studies in this book will be devoted to especially significant interpersonal encounters—the visit and the meal—the relation to others will in fact be an integral element in every problem to be studied.

If then I am to learn and understand what man is, I must observe myself in my relations with the world, myself, and others. I must recognize with clarity what I am and do and say; become aware of the concrete meaning of my attitudes, gestures, and actions; discover that I am a sign ceaselessly offered to myself and others; try to decipher this living sign by a constant and appropriate effort at interpretation; and exercise the greatest of human privileges, which is to be not simply pitched into the world like the insentient stone, but able to take hold of myself by reflection and to become fully aware of what, too often, I do in the dim light of habit.

Since we are concerned to see ourselves as we live in daily life, we shall exclude, without denying its great value, any study of differential anthropology.[8] This science restricts its field of observation to a particular social or ethnic group, and thus would turn us away from the universality proper to the human phenomenon as such. If any allusion is made to a cultural milieu far removed from our own, it will be in order to confirm or illustrate amid the very play of variations the constant meanings we have discovered. Some elements of biblical anthropology to which we refer are to be taken simply as cultural data. In any case, we have felt it necessary to limit such cultural comparisons. Highly interesting though they are, they could not be multiplied without overburdening the book.

It is immediately evident, on the other hand, that our approach must be the phenomenological method of describing facts themselves and their meaning. Without claiming to exhaust the significance of the human activities under consideration, we shall try to recognize the direction of the many orientations which the slightest word or the least perceptible gesture contains, wherein the intentionality of consciousness itself finds expression.

Having deliberately established and maintained our inquiry at the level of lived experience, we shall avoid alliance with any system whatsoever and shall even refrain from the metaphysical development of our ideas. Let us be clear on this point, however: we are not claiming that metaphysical investigation is of little importance; on the contrary it is the essential philosophical procedure. A phenomenology that regarded description as the ultimate goal of the philosophical undertaking would end up in an incoherent phenomenalism and would evade the basic problems: the ontological status of man, the radical principle of his being, the meaning of his destiny. Whatever the objections that may be raised against the metaphysical enterprise and the difficulties inherent to it, we consider it unavoidable—and possible as well. Indeed the effect of the description of the data of experience is to show the inescapable necessity of metaphysics. But to take that step is beyond the scope of this book.

Obstacles and Opportunities

If we reflect on the difficulties of the procedure we have elected, we see at once that it will meet with an obstacle in the ignorance of self from which man suffers unawares. Today as in Socrates' time, man is "absent" from himself: in the course of his daily round he passes by himself, brushes himself in passing the way one anonymous pedestrian does another; but he does not "encounter" himself. The individual lives in his own vicinity, with himself, but not very much in himself. There is the odd effect of a division into two selves, unperceived yet fatal, which keeps us on the surface of ourselves, separated from our own depths. We live, act, and think at the level of our outward appearance and our social personality, which is like a mask interposed between us and our self, between us and others. We live like a "double" of ourself rather than as our true self. Habit alienates us from ourselves, blind reflexes guide us. I am aware of what I do and how I do it, but the why of it escapes me. I hear myself addressed and I reply; but what do address and dialogue mean for two concrete human subjects? I stretch out my hand: have I ever reflected on the full meaning of this gesture, so commonplace and yet always so fresh in its implications? I come across countless faces, I admire a portrait, I photograph my neighbors: but what is the deeper meaning of the face and the whole bodily appearance, what is their role in interpersonal relations? I pay visits and receive them, share my meal with another, bear witness to some truth: but what is the deeper significance of each of these behaviors? What do they teach me about myself and about man? Too often, these questions themselves will sound odd. Thus alienation is a fact, and it has always existed despite the constant reaction of great minds against it.

But this strange ignorance of self, explainable as it is in terms of indolence of the mind and the attraction of "distraction," is complicated today by a number of epistemological obstacles. On the one hand, urban and collective life do violence to man's self-possession or hinder his self-mastery. The person and the home are robbed of their intimacy, which would allow man to "apperceive" himself, in the Leibnizian sense of the word, and take charge of his own destiny.[9] On the other hand, development of the physical sciences and of technology, in the absence of a concern for man himself sufficient to redress the balance, has formed a positivist and materialist mentality from which the sense of man's mystery has gradually withdrawn. In a civilization wherein everything receives a rational explanation, is verified by experience and expressed in mathematical terms, wherein technology robs man of the sense of his own limitations even as it reduces the person to his functions and evaluates him in terms of his product, the humanity of man is in danger of being maimed.

It is a happy circumstance that the difficulties we have just pointed out are balanced by a cultural factor which favors the approach we are taking. The interest of existentialist thought in concrete reality is of great assistance in recovering our hold on the significance of day-to-day reality. It is not an abstract man, a pure essence, which our contemporaries are examining, but a being of flesh and blood, involved in space and time and confronted with the necessity of giving a *meaning* to his life and his death, his personal fate and the fate of humanity. The fruitfulness of existentialist philosophy is too well known for us to insist on it here. But we must once again avoid misunderstanding. There is no question, for us, of minimizing the need of explanation and of the objective perspective in approaching man. This kind of knowledge is and will continue to be indispensible; the subjective perspective is its helper and complement. All the positive elements in culture must be used if we are to reach a better knowledge of man.

Anthropological Categories

Our approach to the human phenomenon demands special attention to the concrete categories of thought and language. For language is full of man and of his experiential relationships to things.

Philosophical reflection has always taken as one of its tasks the establishment of the most general schemata of knowledge. Whether these are conceived, with Aristotle, as the supreme classes of being, or, with Kant, as the *a priori* concepts of the understanding, the fact is that knowledge is ordered according to some latent organizing principles: the categories. The paradox of the categories is that they are always present but never grasped as such, everywhere operative but recognized only by reflective thought.

It is well known that the lists of categories drawn up by the classical philosophers are of an abstract kind. The effort was made to establish the most general aspects of being, the universal modalities according to which thought is structured, or, since thinking means judging, the modalities according to which a predicate is attributed to a subject.

The end result is necessarily an inventory of abstract relations, valid only for objective knowledge as we described it above. Consequently the man in the street is greatly surprised if one of these lists of categories happens to fall into his hands; he is ignorant of the basic role of these relations in the organization of science and even of his own empirical knowledge and fails to recognize his own lived experience in these lists of technical terms which apparently have no content at all. If the constant relations which bind ideas together are thus listed in such tables, the thousand ways in which each man experiences the universe, himself, and others are excluded from them. Hamelin's table of categories in the *Essai* does not avoid these limitations, even if movement, starting from the relation, terminates at the person; he is presenting an *a priori* dialectic which operates between pure ideas.[10]

My world, however, is not identical with the universe of science. The latter is thought out, the former experienced; the latter is explained, the former understood. One world excludes any consideration of the subject, the other exists only for the subject. Yet, even before any effort of reason, the world in which I live is not a chaos, and the immediately given is not the indistinct. The universe of my daily life, along with the everyday language which expresses it, is highly structured not only by the ideas and principles of causality and finality which are at work in my subconscious, but also by a number of concrete categories. There is need, then, to inquire into the existence, nature, and role of the concrete principles by which my experience is organized. Without trying here to draw up a full table of such categories, we would like to stress their importance and to point out some of them.

Things most familiar to our senses furnish language with its most obvious tools. Bachelard's work has made it brilliantly clear that the most general symbols provided by experience—namely, the elements —are genuine concrete categories, always operative in the functions of thought and language.[11]

The characteristic of a symbolic term is that it presents several degrees or forces of meaning. Taken in the first force—that is, in the literal sense—a symbolic term designates a concrete thing: "fire" means the element that burns, illumines, and heats. But in the second force—that is, in the figurative sense—the same term acquires an almost limitless plurality of meanings; somewhat like an algebraic symbol, it becomes polyvalent and able to express very varying meanings, even while the unbroken connection with the literal sense acts as regulator. Thus I speak of the fire of passion, of charity, of eloquence, of action. In speaking thus, I have given the initial meaning a kind of elasticity so that it can cover an indefinite multitude of relations and receive all the inventions of talent and genius. "Fire" is then a concept and an image; it speaks to reason, imagination, and the senses themselves.

Our purpose here is not to study the symbolism of things or their relations to man, but man—situated in the world, endowed with a body, and in reciprocal relation with other men—as creator of meanings.

My existence as an embodied subject is measured by the two dimensions of the universe itself: space and time. But the space in which I move is not the geometer's space. Geometric space is homogeneous and undifferentiated, while real space is heterogeneous, filled with things, animals, and men, and enriched by my body and my awareness with a thousand original meanings.[12] I introduce into it a number of basic divisions: high and low, before and behind, right and left. In the same way the mathematicians's objective time, with its regular and irreversible course, is not the time in which I live, for the rhythm of the latter sometimes accelerates in a dizzying way, sometimes slows to the point of making me despair. The literary work of a Marcel Proust, the philosophical reflections of a Bergson, a Minkowski, or a Merleau-Ponty, have shown the irreducible originality of lived time. It seems, nonetheless, that descriptive analysis and the consultation of language allow a new approach to subjective space and time. These two categories are *anthropological*, or, if you prefer a weightier word, *cosmo-anthropological*.[13]

In this book we would like to explicate the existence of *somatic categories* and show how deeply certain organizing principles of language and thought are rooted in the body.

There can be no question here of a deeper metaphysical study of the signifying function. It is enough for us to recall that only a being constituted of body and spirit can and must use sensible signs to express itself. Between the system of organs which the body is and the system of signs which make up language there is a deep and active continuity. What we are interested in here is the *stuctures* of languages and thought; some of them are provided for my use by my body and constitute a set of basic imaginative or symbolic categories.

In all this we are saying, of course, that the body is, epistemologically, not an obstacle but a medium. Harking back to the dualist tradition that originated in Plato, Descartes considers the body to be a pure hindrance to intellectual knowledge. The illusions to which the senses are subject lead the author of the *Meditations* to suppose that there are "no hands, no eyes, no flesh, no blood. . . ."[14] The *cogito* is the act of a thought which desires to be free of the body. In fact, even if I am not always thinking *of* my body, it is nonetheless true that at no moment can I think *without* my body. Even when the latter ceases to be the object of my knowledge, it does not cease to be its necessary condition. I can think only as an embodied person. But, beyond this, we must say that the body is not only the support of thought but is also, in a degree, an epistemological instrument. On the one hand, the abstract categories and corresponding principles of reason are provided by an embodied consciousness; as Maine de Biran has shown, I owe my idea of causality to the experience of muscular effort. On the other hand—and this is what we want to stress here—my body provides me with schemata for interpreting reality, with genuine concrete categories.

It is really a remarkable fact that in some languages the distinction between the sexes is also applied to the world of things. The arbitrariness shown in the attribution of grammatical genders and the limitation represented by the existence of a neuter gender do not lessen the significance of the fact. Men divide up the countless details of the universe according to a duality which differentiates mankind itself. Furthermore, if we consult a dictionary of any language whatsoever and read the articles on the major parts of our anatomy, we will find that these terms are constantly applied to things: the foot and head of the tree, the façade (face) of the house, the brow of the temple. The phenomenon is perhaps especially striking in geographical terminology. Numerous compound names use "head" for the tops of mountains. Topographical science studies the gorge (throat), pass (Latin, *passus*: step), the brow, breast, and flank or side of a hill, the coast (Latin, *costa*: rib, side, border, edge), the hump, and the serrated (toothed) mountain range. We also speak of an arm of the sea, a tongue of land, the mouth of the river, and the face of the earth. We like to speak of the capital as the country's heart, and some languages speak of an important place as the navel of the world.[15]

In addition to these linguistic inventions, the animist imagination, especially in the primitive, the child, and the poet, discovers countless original and even inspired correspondences and names. But we need not look only to poetic language, for the expression of my empirical relationships is itself structured by my own bodily organization. My body and each of my principal organs are privileged points at which countless irreducible ways of apprehending the world come into existence, intermingle, and meld into a unity. The world manifests itself to me and I move towards it not only through my sensory apparatus but also through my stature and its configuration and through my morphology, even through such internal organs as the heart. Taken figuratively, anatomical terms make it possible for me to express many different relations to things and other people, because I have first lived these relations "bodily." In raising a term like "head" or "hand" or "heart" to the second force, I turn it into a concrete or imaginary category, which is both symbol and polyvalent concept and suitable for expressing an indefinite number of meanings.[16] It is evident, then, what importance attaches, if not to a table of concordances, at least to research into the equivalences between abstract and concrete categories of language.

My body thus plays an interpretive role of primordial importance; it is an interpretive key which I apply to reality: an organism, it also organizes the universe; always requiring interpretation, it is itself interpretive; it is structured and structuring, measuring but also the measure of everything else. In short, I *read, think,* and *say* the world with the help not only of rational categories but of my lived body, taken as form and principle of concrete organization. My everyday language is thus the language of an easily accessible *empirical phenomenology.*

This "in-forming" of the world, the pre-understanding of it by my body, has two inverse and complementary aspects. In a first movement, I project my own bodily structure outside of myself and look at and interpret the world through it. If I am at home in the world, it is because at every moment I am imposing my own image on it. Even before any effort at transforming the world through labor and technology, my way of looking at it humanizes the universe, sets up landmarks in it, and discovers orientations there for myself. In expressing the world to my self "bodily," I take possession of it, remake and refashion it. The human world is thus my "larger body." Perhaps we may discern here the roots of hylozoist theories which attribute life to all matter and a soul to the world.

On the other hand, this projection of my own bodily structure onto things is completed by an inverse movement. At the same time that I impose my bodily image on the world, I draw the world to myself, appropriate it, and domesticate it. It can even be said that in speaking of the foot and head of a mountain, tree, or plant, I assimilate the latter to myself and "incorporate" them into myself, if the expression is not too strong. Henceforth I carry within myself the world reduced to my own scale. If the universe is my larger body, then my body is a smaller universe. My concrete life consists of this ceaseless to-and-fro movement between macrocosm and microcosm, and this vital flow is at the service of both the intentionality and the interiority of consciousness. Thanks to anthropomorphic language and its basic categories, man can adapt himself to the world and take his place in it, and, in return, humanize the world. This is why the symbolic language of anthropomorphism will always be an essential tool of culture and of every form of authentic humanism.

We are touching here the very root of a phenomenon which the essays of this book will be searching out and illustrating: the *circulation of meaning*. Thanks to the figurative usage of certain terms, countless exchanges of meaning are continuously occurring between me and the world. I project onto things a meaning which I have experienced bodily; this meaning is reflected in the mirror of the world, returns to me, is further enriched, and departs again in countless subtle and complex interchanges which can be discerned at the various levels of language. My *body* plays the part of *switchboard* in this *circulation of meaning*.

Let us note briefly the characteristics common to these somatic categories. They are innate in their foundation, since to be a man is to be a bodily being. Their universality is beyond question: wherever you find a man you find head, heart, and hand and the thousand meanings which they convey. With variants of meaning which are valuable in themselves, such concepts are common to all cultures —ancient and modern, traditional and industrial—and are present in all cultural products—folkloric, literary, artistic, intellectual, moral, and religious. Moreover, these categories come into play so spontaneously that I do not even perceive their unifying role in my language, whether the most empirical or the most abstract. They are not consciously worked out but are lived before—and usually without —being clearly thought. If you ask how, and with what justification, I pass from the literal to the figurative and categorical sense in using, for example, the word "hand," I answer that the transition is immediate—or rather, that there is no point of transition at all. When an executive asks to be given "a free hand," I do not grasp at once that his language is figurative, but only after an effort of reflection. The reason is that my living and lived hand is the privileged tool of my causality and my freedom. I live both my hand and my power of initiative in a single simple act, which I then analyze only to accomodate my thought processes. There is no distance I must traverse in going from my hand to my freedom any more than in going from my body to my mind and soul. *The unity of the literal and the figurative senses is established in my very being, which is an ensouled body, and embodied spirit.* The critical justification of symbolic language is contained in the spiritual character of the earthy and the earthy character of the spiritual, to use the terminology of Charles Péguy.

This means that such categories do not wrest me out of the concrete real. Despite what is too often thought, the categories of cause, substance, and the like, do not lead me into unreality; on the contrary, like a relief drawing showing the terrain or a geographical map, they seek to eliminate insignificant detail and thus to disengage the structure of a concrete totality. The abstract is not the unreal; it is the real grasped in depth. Abstract concepts thus can and should ceaselessly refer back to experience for correction and adaptation to its requirements. All the more, then, are somatic categories close to experience; their privilege is to be *both concept and symbol.* If taken figuratively, the terms *heart, hand,* and *head* are images. When these categories are applied to a great diversity of relations, their connection with the concrete is in no way lessened. If someone speaks to me of "the head of state" or "the heart of the problem," I understand his meaning because I project onto the realities in question my own anatomical structure.

It is possible, therefore, that concrete categories should become technical terms, that is, terms which through usage acquire precise and strict meanings. In everyday language, "to be someone's right hand" means, without any possible ambiguity, to be his principal agent in carrying out orders; "to be at the head" of an undertaking means to assume the main responsibility for it. We need to do away with the prejudice that all accurate language is necessarily abstract.

Interpersonal relations also furnish me with a number of categories for structuring my experience. Existentialist and personalist thinkers have, to our great profit, analyzed such *interpersonal categories* as encounter, presence, fidelity, and dialogue. These analyses represent a permanent contribution to philosophical thought. We need not insist here, therefore, on the categorical use of such terms, which can bring into firm but flexible unity a countless number of lived relationships. By passing from the literal to the figurative sense, I can say that I have encountered misfortune or history; that I have been visited by a neighbor but also by opportunity.

We shall end this classification of anthropological categories with some general remarks. For one thing, it cannot be maintained that the adjective "categorical" is simply a synonym of "conceptual" or "abstract."[17] There are *concrete categories* whose critical justification is of the existential, not the reflective order; the always present norm for applying such categories is a lived relation to the world, to oneself, or to others. Lévi-Strauss has shown this for the categories of the raw, the cooked, and others.[18]

What emerges here is a certain relativism of knowledge and language, for it is through such categories that I initially know and express the world. But such relativism is not a sign of inferiority. Scholars have noted how certain tools of knowledge and expression originated; but the use of such tools, as Lévi-Strauss has demonstrated, does not signify the kind of "pre-logical" thinking which Lévy-Bruhl defended in his early work. The symbol, no less than although differently from the concept, is essentially "open" and invites the mind to transcend it. In any event, should it disturb us to discover that man knows and expresses himself in a human way? The critical problem is not being tackled here at its deepest level, for I am not claiming to measure the being of things by my knowledge of them when I establish that some means of expression are connected with my condition as an embodied spirit, situated within the world and in mutual interaction with other persons. A Thomas Aquinas proposes a much more radical relativism when he measures the scope of our knowledge by our ontological structure as embodied subjects: the proper object of an embodied intelligence is the intelligibility contained within the sensible and not, as Augustine maintained, a pure intelligibility.[19]

A final consequence of what we have said is that *language is essentially "open."* This is an important consideration in the debate about structuralism. The conception of language as a purely formal and closed system may be legitimate as a working hypothesis, but it cannot be taken as deriving from observed fact. The play of "differences" and semantic derivation—the circulation of meaning within the system—are inseparably connected with the exchange of meanings that takes place between man and the world. The two circles are interlocked and the movement of each ceaselessly stimulates and enriches the other.

Practical Requirements and Possible Extensions

An approach to man which establishes some anthropological categories can make a contribution to the *philosophy of daily life.* Given the object of the present study, a certain simplicity of expression is called for. Doubtless philosophy, like any scientific discipline, is justified in the use of technical terms indispensable to precision of thought and the development of specific perspectives. But an approach to man at the level of concrete existence itself demands a special fidelity to the language in which that existence finds expression. A further consideration is that we do not want to direct this book only to specialists in philosophy.

A final word on the order of exposition. In the first part of the book we shall study the measures applied to embodied existence: lived *space* and *time.* The second part aims at the discovery of man through his principal means of expression and communication: *word, hand, face,* and *gaze.* The third part will offer a study of two interpersonal behaviors wherein self-communication tends to be sought with special intensity in communion: the *visit* and the *meal.*

These descriptive studies of man's humanity are put to use in another work for an anthropological approach to the Christian mystery. But in the present book the autonomy of philosophical research is kept intact. The demands of reason have their own coherence, their own finality, their own specific methods. If for the Christian, revelation gives human questions a transcendent answer, it does not nullify the legitimate efforts of the mind in its search for truth: "Essential autonomy and essential connection" was Maurice Blondel's subtitle for his *La philosophie et l'esprit chrétien*.[20] After all, a theologian who endeavors to attain a reflective awareness of the revealed datum and to express it in an intelligible way could not fruitfully use these instruments of knowledge unless the philosopher had performed his own task in strict fidelity to his method. Thus, although the book *The Humanity of God* makes reference to the studies which follow, the present work is wholly self-contained. Obviously, however, the philosopher and the historian of religion will find in *The Humanity of God* abundant illustration of the religious use of anthropological categories.

NOTES

1. Against contemporary anti-humanism, Mikel Dufrenne, in his *Pour l'homme* (Paris: Editions du Seuil, 1968), defends "the idea of a philosophy concerned about man" (p. 9).
2. Even in the material sciences the idea of pure fact expresses an unattainable ideal, since no datum can be enunciated without at least a virtual interpretation being included in the statement.
3. Cf. Emile Bréhier, *La philosophie et son passé* (Paris: Presses Universitaires de France, 1950), pp. 53 ff.; Paul Ricoeur, *History and Truth*, trans. Charles A. Kelbley (Evanston: Northwestern University Press, 1965), pp. 57–62.
4. Cf. below, Chapter 3, section 2, "Word and Vocable."
5. Cf. Bréhier, *op. cit.*, p. 37.
6. Karl Jaspers, *Way to Wisdom: An Introduction to Philosophy* (New Haven: Yale University Press, 1954), pp. 29–30
7. Gabriel Marcel, *Positions et approches concrètes du mystère ontologique* (Paris: Vrin, 1949), pp. 56 ff.
8. The term "anthropology" can be ambiguous. Its first meaning, historically, is the philosophical knowledge of man; thus, in Kant, *Anthropologie in pragmatischer Hinsicht* (1798); Maine de Biran, *Nouveaux essais d'anthropologie*, in *Oeuvres*, Tisserand, ed., Vol. 14 (Paris: Presses Universitaires de France, 1949); Cardinal Désiré Mercier, *Origines de la psychologie contemporaine* (Paris: Alcan, 1937), pp. 292–295; Bernard Groethuysen, *Anthropologie philosophique*,

6th ed. (Paris: Gallimard, 1952); Jean-Yves Jolif, O. P., *Comprendre l'homme* 1: *Introduction à une anthropologie philosophique* (Paris: Editions du Cerf, 1967). Since the end of the nineteenth century anthropology has also signified that group of sciences which study the human races, or, in a more limited use of the term, those which study the anatomical characteristics of men. Today, the study of races, along with the study of societies and cultures, is regarded as the specific object of ethnology. However, Paul Mercier, *Histoire d'anthropologie* (Paris: Presses Universitaires de France, 1966), would like to replace "ethnology" with "anthropology" (p. 1). Finally, Georges Gusdorf, *Traité de métaphysique* (Paris: Colin, 1956), would include under "anthropology" all the "human sciences": psychology, history, sociology, etc. (p. 161).

9. There is no hope of supplying for this deficiency by cultivating what is called, by an abuse of language, "mass culture." It is necessary, of course, that everything possible be done to allow every man, whatever his ethnic or social origins, to reach that culture which is the common possession of mankind. Literature aimed at the masses can help to this end, but it is not enough, because culture begins only with the awakening of personal reflection. Consequently the very idea of "mass culture" is a contradiction in terms and in reality. The goal of culture is to emancipate man from the forces—physical, psychic, or sociological—which alienate him, from the anonymity of the crowd, from the "they" and the "anyone at all," so that he may be helped to become fully himself. Such "personalization" must successfully overcome the two opposite forms of alienation represented by the crowd on the one side and individualism on the other. Genuine culture is neither anonymous nor egotistic: it opens man to other persons by giving him access to the best in himself. It is to be noted, furthermore, that there is more than one kind of humanistic culture. Along with an intellectualist culture which reaches man by way of ideas (for example, Greco-Latin culture in the West), there is a genuine culture, a deep understanding of man, to be gotten from life and from reflection on life; such a humanism is universal in time and space, a wisdom within the reach of all men yet very intimately personal, with men of the most humble origins often providing outstanding examples of it. A prudent use of the means of social communication could and should cultivate this basic wisdom throughout society.

10. Octave Hamelin, *Essai sur les éléments principaux de la représentation*, 3rd. ed. with notes and references by A. Darhon (Paris: Presses Universitaires de France, 1952).

11. Gaston Bachelard, *The Psychoanalysis of Fire*, trans. Alan C.M. Ross (Boston: Beacon, 1964); *La flamme d'une chandelle*, 2nd ed. (Paris: Presses Universitaires de France, 1962); *L'eau et les rêves* (Paris: Corti, 1942); *L'air et les songes*, 3rd ed. (Paris: Corti, 1959); *La terre et les rêveries de la volonté* (Paris: Corti, 1948); *La terre et les rêveries du repos* (Paris: Corti, 1948).

12. Gaston Bachelard, *The Poetics of Space*, trans. Maria Jolas (New York: Orion, 1964).

13. Jolif, *op. cit.*, writes: "Philosophical anthropology is . . . in the first place a *critical undertaking:* it aims at bringing out into the open the *a priori*

conditions for all human manifestations" (p. 133); "We propose . . . to present and analyze, in their most abstract form, the fundamental categories which philosophical anthropology must use" (pp. 134–135). Such an undertaking obviously differs wholly in purpose, object, and method from our descriptive and concrete approach. In another context, the Heideggerian "existentials" *(Existenzialien)*—that is, structures or modes of being proper to human existence *(Dasein)*—are genuine anthropological categories (even if Heidegger reserves the term "categories" for the modes of being of realities apart from man). Our own descriptions in this book will amount to a concrete investigation of the structures of human existence: being-in-the world, temporality, etc.

14. Descartes, *Meditations on First Philosophy I*, 12, in *The Philosophical Works of René Descartes*, trans. Elizabeth S. Haldane and G.R.T. Ross (Cambridge: Cambridge University Press, 1911), Vol. 1, p. 148.

15. Psychological categories, too, require attention: anger and serenity, for example, are applied to the very elements.

16. On the symbolism of the heart, which we cannot take up in this book, cf. Bruno de Sainte-Marie, ed. *Le coeur* (Bruges: Desclée de Brouwer, 1950). There is abundant illustration of the use of somatic categories in Edouard Dhorme, *L'emploi métaphorique des noms des parties du corps en hébreu et en akkadien* (Paris: Geuthner, 1923).

17. Cf. Paul Foulquié and Robert Saint-Jean, *Dictionnaire de la langue philosophique* (Paris; Presses Universitaires de France, 1962), *s.v.*

18. Claude Lévi-Strauss, *Introduction to a Science of Mythology:* (1) *The Raw and the Cooked* (New York: Harper, 1969); (2) *Du miel aux cendres* (Paris: Plon, 1967); (3) *L'origine des manières de table (ibid.,* 1968).

19. Thomas Aquinas, *Summa theologiae*, I, q. 84, a. 7; q. 85, a. 1.

20. Maurice Blondel, *La philosophie et l'esprit chrétien* I (Paris: Presses Universitaires de France, 1944).

PART I

THE DIMENSIONS
OF EMBODIED
EXISTENCE

Space and time: these two dimensions of the universe also measure my fragile existence. But, through an activity which originates ever anew within my consciousness, these limits of space and time receive a meaning of which I am myself the measure. Things situated in space and time manifest, in turn, a meaning which I ceaselessly create, grasp, and communicate. It does not detract at all from the value of that intelligibility which objective knowledge discovers in the universe, to say that I experience and "live" the universe before thinking it. I inscribe myself in the world not as a pure mind but as a being of flesh and blood. At the level of empirical knowledge my needs and aspirations make me the measure of things.

This circulation of meaning between myself and the universe reduces the opposition between objective and subjective in concrete experience. But I am not therefore dissolved into the world: if I impose meaning on space and time, it is because I am able to transcend them.

CHAPTER 1

HUMAN SPACE

To be born is to enter a three-dimensional world. My ego owes its being situated in space to my body; as material but also living and intimately my own, my body sets me in the world of things as their neighbor and makes me share in their spatial limitations. Like any material body mine has a local place defined by precise coordinates. To take my bearings on land with a compass or at sea with a mariner's compass or sextant, to figure out the right direction in a forest, even to recognize my room each morning when I awake,[1] are forms of determining, scientifically or empirically, my place in the material universe. In short, simply because I am a man I am never "nowhere" but necessarily "somewhere."

I. EXISTENCE AND SPATIALITY

Man and His Bodily Place

It is important to distinguish, right from the beginning, between the abstract space of the geometer and the concrete space of a living man. The medium in which the mathematician places the objects of his knowledge is conceived as limitless, homogeneous, and isotropic; that is, all the directions have the same properties, and there is no up or down, before or after, right or left. But that is not the kind of space in which I live, and the mathematician himself conducts himself concretely in quite a different medium: lived space. My real location is not abstract or reducible to a point. I exist as a subject in a heterogeneous space that is filled with a thousand things and peopled with animals and other men, and each direction has a vital meaning which requires analysis.[2]

In this lived space my body displaces a certain volume. Let us give the name of "bodily place" to the portion of space which I allocate to myself and in which I dwell as something contained in a perfectly adjusted container. By an act of the mind I can distinguish between the space I take up and my body which occupies it. But concretely, as Descartes observes, they are one and the same thing.[3] I move my place itself in all my "locomotive" movements. To go out from this internal space would mean leaving my body, becoming disembodied, ceasing to be in the world. Just as I am necessarily somewhere in the universe, so am I necessarily in my own place. When I come into the world, it is in this place that I am immediately and permanently put.

This bodily space is, for me, sharply distinguished from the rest of the universe: I know this space directly, from inside and by an experience that is inseparable from my embodied existence; I am not content to live in it, I live it. Applying Merleau-Ponty's distinction between the lived and the apperceived, I would say that my bodily place and my body itself are the lived and not apperceived place where I apperceive other places and other bodies without living them. My bodily volume manifests itself to me as an inside set over against the outside made up of the rest of space; my skin and secondarily my clothes are the dividing line. Here is where I am "at home" in the most specific and inalienable sense: I may be poor and a wanderer, without hearth or home in the world, but I carry this place with me; I shall leave it only at death when all "outside" like all "inside" will be destroyed.

The volume I thus have is not an empty space, but furnished with organs whose coenesthesia provides me with a global, undifferentiated knowledge. Through their functional rhythm the digestive and respiratory systems give me alternating sensations of relative emptiness and fullness; I thus become aware of my interior space. Numerous other phenomena—heartbeats, movements, efforts, postures, fatigue, pleasure and pain, hunger and thirst—instruct me by their localization in my own organic geography.[4] The awareness of my own volume becomes part of the image and idea I have of myself and gives rise to attitudes of extroversion or introversion, ease or malaise in my relations with the world and with other people.[5]

Social relations often give us a glimpse of how each person identifies himself with his bodily place. Is not "to make room" for someone on a bus seat a way of accepting one's own volume at the cost of a sometimes very meritorious embarrassement and of consenting to share the available space? To hold a place at table for someone still missing or to give up some of my comfortably large space when he arrives is to consent to his existence, to admit him as a partner, and to share myself by sharing my living space. The refusal to make room for another amounts to denying him, to suppressing his existence. Many drivers on the road apply the old saying: "Get out of the way or I'll kill you." And finally, assassination removes another person from human space as well as from human time.[6]

The movements of my limbs, my postures and attitudes, relax the contours of my bodily volume and give it various meanings. A sitting position bends the outline, curves it inward, concentrates it and hollows it out. When the mother sits down, a receptive space, the lap, is formed in which the child can nestle. The mother presses the infant to her heart; her impulse is to draw it even further into herself, to become one with it in a kind of return to the prenatal state. For the child the lap is a kind of external womb; here he receives nourishing milk, but it also represents a place of total security, peace, and tenderness. Among adults, extending a hand towards the hand of another, the mutual clasping in which each hand is not only taken but held, constitutes the most widely practiced form of physical compenetration. The embrace and hug are still more meaningful: my arms reach forward and open wide to enlarge my bodily place; I arrange a living space which is mine—is even I myself—and into which another is invited to come. The embrace, whose meaning reaches its climax in the conjugal union, expresses the essential desire of love: to coincide with the other, to create together a new unity. Every effort at communion between embodied subjects seeks coinherence in a single bodily place.[7] But materiality, which allows the assertion of this will to be one, also sets limits to the oneness.

Unity between persons cannot be accomplished in the empirical order, but must always be sought in a realm beyond bodily reciprocity. But it is nonetheless true that language cultivates the image of physical oneness with others. A sympathetic friend and a novelist or actor who is master of his art are said to put themselves "in the place" or "inside the skin" of another.

Objectivity and Subjectivity of the Body

Paradoxically, the person most adept at sympathizing with another and empathizing with his behavior, is never sure of what image he himself presents.

To put it more accurately, no one fully "recognizes" himself in the various images of himself which he knows exist; he is not quite able to match them up with himself in a way that fits. I have a lived and subjective image of my body derived from internal experience, and I add to it the intellectualized and objective image of the body provided by biology. The two images do not coincide; try as I will, I cannot reduce one to the other. The hand or the stomach I study about will never be the hand or stomach I use, feel, and ache in. Moreover, early in life a third image is added to these two disparate images of myself: the image in the mirror. There I discover myself as other people see me, as I am at the surface of my bodily being, and not as I am in that inside of which I have direct coenesthetic experience or that other inside which science claims to show me. The three images of my single self are partly overlapping and partly incongruent; they converge, criss-cross, mingle and separate and unite again in an interminable game of hide-and-seek. My ego tries to find itself in each image in turn: but the anatomical drawing, my mirrored image, my photograph, or my portrait will always seem strange and foreign in some respect or other—is *that* what I really am? I may want to believe it, since the mirror or science tells me it is so; but then belief, not evidence, is what I have. In the last analysis my ego feels fully "at home" only in the coenesthetic, subjective, and lived image of myself.[8]

These experiences contain a very important lesson: my bodily being, indeed my whole being, has two aspects, a subjective and an objective aspect. I can be known from two distinct, irreducible, and complementary points of view. No part of my being can claim to be inaccessible to either of the perspectives. Although they are not all equally expressive of my personality (we shall study later on the preeminent importance of hand and face), all the parts of my body are mine; my ego claims them all in a constantly renewed act which constitutes me as embodied subject. But this body is simultaneously an organism; it presents itself as an object to the gaze of others, as, for example, when I am stared at or undergo a medical examination. Both subjectivity and objectivity, therefore, apply to my being in its entirety, but neither one expresses it in its entirety; both are basic and constitutive properties. When one man looks at another (we shall return to this point later on), he is always faced with these alternatives and threatened with mental confusion. The worst temptation would be the wish to eliminate the ambiguity by settling for one or other perspective. The human reality with its radical complexity would then be deleted.[9]

Spatiality and Reality

Real space is the medium in which men and things are interrelated. Localization supposes a certain simultaneity; Leibniz saw this when he defined space as an order of coexistences. What we would like to stress here, however, is that this coexistence points to existence—that is, that for us as men, localization is a coefficient of being. The numerous relations which define our position in space constitute part of a person's reality both for himself and for others. We know how important the law regards the localization of people, for every official piece of paper must indicate place of birth, place of residence, and even place of work. The foreigner with no fixed residence in the country must note this fact on his papers and provide himself with legal residence.[10] If I happen to go astray in a forest, on a mountain, or at sea, I feel "lost." Once I do not know the geographical location of the place where I am and am perhaps in a place where I can't be found, I elude the grasp of others and of myself and am in a predicament which threatens to bring me to the definitive loss which is death. People have no hesitation in regarding as dead those who have disappeared—for example, the passengers of a ship or airplane whom no search efforts can situate in space. With all the more reason a historian treats as real only those events which can be localized. Any fact which cannot be fixed in space and time is by that very fact outside the scope of history.

At the level of everyday life, the phenomenon of *absence* enables me to grasp how much my awareness of other people's reality is connected with our coexistence in space. We can leave aside animals and things, although if my dog or my pen are not in the space familiar to me they are lost to me and, for practical purposes, nonexistent. Let us limit our consideration to persons, for presence or absence in the proper sense applies only to them. The man who is present is one who shares my "here"; the absent person is one whom I cannot meet in the space in which my daily life is carried on. Yet not everyone who is not here is automatically "absent." To be absent, another must be distant when he ought to be near: he is off yonder instead of being here; his being at a distance is opposed to the nearness which, in the eyes of friendship or love, ought to exist.

Furthermore, absence supposes that the other continues to exist away from me and that a return is always possible; someone who had wholly ceased to exist would not be absent, he simply would not be. Absence is therefore an anomalous situation to which a return puts an end; it is a time between times, a painful intermission between a presence now past and a presence still hoped for. But if absence is indeed suffering, the reason is that for me the separation cuts the other person off from part of his reality: to say good-bye is to die a little. From my standpoint the absent person is, as it were, lessened in his being, wounded, maimed, and so am I. Distance makes child or husband disappear, as far as the mother is concerned; they regain their full existential reality only if they return and once more share the domestic space, the family coexistence.

The definitive separation is death, in which the other withdraws forever, into inaccessible distance, from the space where the living are. If I reject the idea of any survival, the dead person is not simply absent, but deleted, annihilated. If, on the contrary, I think of the vanished person as having a mysterious life of some kind, then I hope to meet him again in the beyond and I speak of him as "absent," since his disappearance is only temporary. But in both cases the pain of separation is due to the injury which distance inflicts on the reality of the other. For me, as a man existing in space, beings can be fully real only in local proximity to me. Another person is most real when he is with me, here and now.

The hierophany, the magical rite, and the symbol provide valuable confirmation of what has just been said. The world of the gods and heroes is not ours, whether I believe the mythological tales or not. Although that world is represented with the help of elements taken from our universe, it refuses to be found, measured, and approached. Hence the reality of mythical personages is, even for the believer, of a different order from that of the believer's contemporaries who are localized within the space which he experiences. Let the sacred manifest itself, however, in a hierophany, or let man master it by magical rites and give it space preempted from the inhabited world, and the divine reality invades the human world. Such a breaking through of the "beyond" into the "here below" has two important consequences. On the one hand, the space consecrated by the divine manifestation or the magical rite is henceforth distinguished from the rest of space. Through a kind of restorative interpretation, the place is given a coefficient of radically new meaning, a higher ontological fullness which makes it a "center," even, in some cases, the center of the whole world.[11] On the other hand (and this is the more important consequence from our point of view here), the sacred takes its place within the world, is fully domesticated there, and acquires a wholly new realism: it becomes a fact for man and, by sharing his space, shares his existence as well.

The moral or religious symbol has an analogous function. Thanks to the emblem (a flag or a crucifix, for example), ideal values acquire a place in the space where human life is lived. On the one hand, they bestow a new dimension and a new meaning on our world. Whereas the everyday universe of work, interests, perception, observation, and even of science is necessarily limited when it comes to answering the basic human questions (why man? why life? why the inevitable limitation of death?), the world into which the symbol has been inserted becomes open, enlarged—an "expanding universe" is the way we might put it. The symbol produces a seemingly impossible lifting of our earthly horizon, so that the heavens no longer weigh down on our heads like a lid. An interpretive power thereupon develops which raises the level of the whole of visible reality, conferring on it a higher value.

On the other hand, and above all, the symbol reveals the power residing in the reality of the ideal: it enables me to resolve the irresolvable dilemma—transcendence or immanence—in which my thought is constantly in danger of being trapped when it applies itself to the consideration of the absolute. Since the ideal is now presented to me by a sign within the space in which I live, it is no longer unreal or inaccessible, as a false conception of transcendence would maintain. Yet the proximity of the ideal is not such as would permit it to be confused with the empirical—that is, become wholly immanent. By means of symbols, ideal values become important in my daily life, belong to my milieu. They become familiar and accessible without any blurring of their specific identity, manifest themselves without surrendering their independent existence. Thus the ideal becomes remote and yet near at hand—or rather, it is neither close nor distant, but is present to me as an absolute demand. Remaining itself intact whatever my infidelities, it is always within the grasp of my most intimate personal being. The symbol is the privileged sign which, through situating ideal values within human space, preserves them from the charge of unreality which is constantly leveled at them. Signified within my living space without permitting itself to be enclosed in it, the symbolized value acquires a wholly new fullness of being for me. For man, situated as he is in space, localization —insertion into this space—is an irreplaceable index of reality.

My Localized Body: Center of My World and Perspectival Focus

My body is the privileged place where I experience and bring into focus, as in a living center, the immense universe of matter and life. Men have always noted that the mineral, vegetable, and animal kingdoms, spread out through the cosmos, meet and are joined in a hierarchical order within man under the domination of the spirit, from which they receive a new meaning. My body is thus the uniquely special place where I undergo, experience, and sum up into unity the manifold influences that play upon me from the outer world. Cosmic radiations and magnetic and electrical forces pass through me. The rhythm of day and night, the succession of the seasons, the uncertainties of weather all punctuate my life and condition my health, my daily sense of well-being, and my very mood. Solar light and heat, food derived from the earth, the life-giving water and air—the whole universe, in short—sustains my existence. I become aware of it when I engage, for example, in breathing exercises: with the oxygen I inhale, the vast atmosphere enters my lungs and enlivens my whole being. Thus my bodily place is a focal point in which the universe is gathered up. I am the universe itself on a reduced scale, a miniature cosmos, a microcosm.

The same observation must be made apropos of my *position* in the world. My bodily place is a portion taken from the space in which I am immersed; it is part of that space and surrounded by it on every side. My localized body sets me in the midst of the world and of things and defines my position in relation to them. By an inherent necessity my body is the reference point in relation to which everything about me is situated; I am made the center of a vast circle, my "surroundings," each radius of which defines one of my "perspectives" and the circumference of which is my "horizon." Within the circle, any given thing becomes an ob-ject for me only if it remains there, lies there before my body, at a greater or lesser distance. My body is that for which and by which objects exist.

Wherever I am, therefore, as soon as I open my eyes I see the familiar objects which furnish my "home" as well as the heavens and stars all turning their face to me, or at least one of their possible faces (the moon, for example, always presents one and the same hemisphere to my gaze). My body is center and focus of my whole spatial universe, the geographical midpoint of the world from which I draw life; thanks to my localized body I draw into myself all the spatial dimensions, bring them to a focal point, sum them up, and interiorize them. But, inversely, I also move out from this position of mine towards every point on my horizon. Thanks to this rhythmic to-and-fro, the whole universe dwells in me and I have the whole universe for my dwelling. Contraction and expansion, systole and diastole: I am at the heart of the universe and am myself its heart.[12]

My body is for me the necessary reference point of the movement of things. I am present each day in the street as pedestrians and vehicles move about, and I define these movements by relation to myself: this person has crossed my path, passed me by, or met me; this automobile is moving away, that one approaching. But the reference point which is my body is itself mobile, so that my estimates are rendered inevitably relative. When seated aboard a train in a station, I sometimes think I am moving when in fact the neighboring train is starting out;

the two trains form a closed system, and I must set up an external point of reference—a nearby telephone pole, for example—in order to be sure.[13] This is, in part, the explanation and legitimate truth of geocentrism. It was inevitable that man, firmly set upon the terrestrial globe, should feel himself one with it and attribute to it his own seeming immobility at the center of the universe. I can say with complete accuracy that I see the sun rise and set, for I am describing, as I perceive it, the spectacle which the world presents to me. This is why even today a scientist who is fully aware of the real movement of the stars continues to use in conversation the geocentric language of perception. Lived experience is of a different order from reflective knowledge. Whatever the progress of science, my body continues to be for me the basic reference point of all movement.

My position in my place thus always sets up a unique and incommunicable perspective; every point in space is for me a possible "point of view," that is, a position from which I can see the world in an irreducibly personal way. Since my bodily place is strictly indivisible, if another is to see the landscape as I do, I must step away from my post of observation and "leave the place" to him. If it is a question of accurate perception, then sometimes I displace an object—the pen I am writing with, for example—within my range of vision by turning it around in my hand. At other times, as when I want to look at a monument, I keep walking around it; in other words, I keep changing my perspective in relation to the object. The twofold movement of things around my body and of my body around things is the basis for the limitless variability of my perspectives.

"Here" and "There"

I express this paradoxical situation of strict localization combined with limitless capacity for adopting new perspectives by the distinction of "here" and "there." "Here" designates that point in space at which I am, the place so close to my body that it is one with it and I wholly occupy it. "Here" is always mine; no one can expel me from it, because if I displace my body in space I carry my "here" with me. From this point of view the expression "Here we are," meaning "We have arrived," seems a pure truism, since from the very nature of spatiality we are always "here." But the phrase is in fact full of meaning, for it expresses a presence brought to pass at a point in space where we had already been in intention. The meaning is richer still if we are speaking of being "at home," which is the most important "here" for us.

If the place I occupy, my "here," is so privileged, what of the rest of space? The answer is simple: outside of "here," everything is "there." The "there" embraces the rest of the world, that whole extent of space where I am not at this moment and which in this sense is foreign to me. "Here" is the domain of the I; "there" is the domain of the other, whether person or thing; "here" is proximity, "there" is distance; "here" is familiar, "there" always more or less eludes me; I am master of "here," "there" besieges me on every side. "Here" is one and dense, for all space is concentrated in it; "there" is manifold and diluted, since space relaxes, as it were, and becomes extended. "Here" is one with the present moment, for "here and now" go together; "there" or "yonder" is future or possible. The "there" is not pure otherness or inaccessible distance for me, however: I can go "there"—"yonder," "up there," "under there"—and change the "there" into a new "here."

To this fundamental distinction of positions, to which every language bears witness, there corresponds the distinction of *going* and *coming* in the order of movement. I go only "there" where I am not, into the place which another has and which is his "here." Strictly speaking, as soon as I move, I always "go," whatever my route and destination. Inversely, the action of coming is that of whoever approaches me and whose destination I am in my "here." Strictly speaking, then, I can only go, and only another can come. Yet if another calls me and I agree to join him, I am surprised to hear myself saying: "I am coming." The usage is strange and seemingly illogical but in fact it is quite illuminating. In saying "I am coming," I am already putting myself in thought where the other person is, in his "here" which I straightway make my own, even from a distance. Having thus duplicated myself, as it were, and divided myself between one "here" in which my body situates me and another in which my intention puts me, I regard myself as "coming" from the point of view and through the eyes of the other. Intentional presence anticipates movement and actual presence.

In logic, every point within the all-inclusive "there" is a possible "here." In reality, however, any given point in the "there" hardly exists for me as long as it remains inaccessible; the ice-cap at the North Pole is only a geographical idea until such time as a journey to the Far East provides opportunity to fly over the region, and then the geographical idea becomes an experienced reality. But, apart from such borderline situations, "there" is contrasted with "here" on two counts. First, "here" strikes me by its extreme smallness, being almost infinitesimal in comparison with the immense world. Yet my corporeity keeps me in it, so that at times I have the feeling that I am a captive of this place and I try to escape it. Second, my "here" belongs to everyday, ordinary life. Being bound up with my work and my various obligations, it seems stale and worn-out, despite the comforts it brings me. "Yonder," on the contrary, appears new, original, even extraordinary, filled with adventure, leisure, and freedom. The places where I am not—that is, all points in the "there"—thus have a powerful attraction for me, for I spontaneously feel that "there" I would overcome my own limitations. In fact, of course, after the pleasant moments of initial discovery, I am disillusioned: however far I have traveled, I am forced to recognize that, like it or not, yesterday's "there" has become today's "here" and quickly becomes worn-out in turn, as it loses its seductive power by becoming ordinary and everyday. I carry with me my "here" and its inexorable limitations; indeed, the new "here" may even be an exile, a cruel captivity. Every point in the universe, then, can become the center of my world, a unique "here," a privileged perspectival standpoint towards which the whole immense universe gravitates; I assume this "here" and discover a new horizon. This is one possible meaning of Pascal's remark about "the reality of things . . . . an infinite sphere whose center is everywhere, whose circumference is nowhere."[14]

There is one especially privileged "here": the place where I am "at home," the point in the world where my existence is stabilized in a fundamental way, the vantage-point from which I look out to see the universe gravitating around me. The importance of this "here" is such that we will have to analyze it in detail later on in this book. But we must note that every human group of any importance—the tribe or nation, for example—marks out certain points in space which become focal points for social life; for example, the sacred center of the world in the various cosmogonies,[15] commercial, academic, cultural, religious, and political centers. The preeminent example is the national *capital*, where the main activities of the nation are ordinarily concentrated and find their highest expression. It would be easy to illustrate this basic sociological datum with countless examples from language and history. Let us note simply that the capital is a center and high point, the "head" (*caput* in Latin; cf. the German *Hauptstadt* or head-city), in which the national territory, the whole history, and the vital powers of a people are gathered up, as it were, and brought to fulfillment. The function of a "capital" is to "recapitulate." This is not simply a play on words; it is a wisdom embodied in language. Inversely, by a kind of centrifugal movement, the capital is present throughout the whole extent of the country. For from this central point spring a multitude of radii along which cities, towns, and hamlets are located; corresponding to the caprices of geography and history, these radii form the network of roads, railway lines, and waterways. The *urbs* (city) is present to the whole *orbs* (world) and contains it more than it is contained by it. The obstacles which hinder "decentralization" in so highly centralized a country as France —whereas in other countries such factors work against the creation of a national metropolis—show the "capital" role of such a metropolis and the complexity of the laws which govern all human space.

Psychological factors play a determining role here. History has consecrated a given place; generations of men have paid homage there to the trials and glories of their common past. The subtle web of memories and of those affective and moral elements every man carries within him, which make up patriotism, surrounds this unique center. As privileged point of native soil, it becomes the focus of the collective consciousness and subconsciousness, and an active principle of national unity. This explains the attraction which every capital, even a regional one, has for individuals. Western Christendom says: "All roads lead to Rome." In such a point of convergence life is lived more intensely than elsewhere. In the *orbs* (surrounding world), which is a kind of indefinite "there," existence seems diluted, slack, unstrung, because the inhabitants are spread out, but the *urbs* (city), which is the "here" beyond all others, manifests an unparalleled existential richness. The contemporary phenomenon of urbanization is to be understood in this perspective: men gather into the cities with the hope of a more intense kind of life. Too often, of course, they disappear into the "lonely crowd."[16]

Distance and Route

Between "here" and "there" lies distance. From my body, as center and primordial reference point, spring an infinite number of invisible radii along which men and things are located relative to me. This relationship is distance. Distance is an ambiguous reality, since at times it seems empty, at times full. It offers things to me but also refuses them, gives them to me and takes them away. It is enough—but necessary—that I accept and at the same time eliminate the distance in order to reach a given useful object. My moods and physical state confront and resolve the ambiguity; according to my dispositions at any time, distance seems either an obstacle or an open access route; the categories of "near" and "far" are thus as relative as those of "young" and "old." And do not diplomats say, depending on the political situation, that the Pyrenees or the Atlantic unite France to Spain and America or, on the contrary, separate her from them?

Distance is space that has simply been measured and put on a scale. The route, however, is distance crossed and mastered. A land without routes, a desert or a jungle, rejects man or swallows him up. A man without a route is "lost," that is, threatened with death. But let a pioneer set to work and hack his way through the thick jungle or set up roadmarks across the immense desert, then first a path, then a road, and finally a route comes into being. The route divides space and gives a new description to the two halves; the space to the right and the left is rejected and condemned as a place for blundering and going astray. It is a narrow ribbon, almost without width when compared to the surrounding immensity, but the route channels and directs all effort. It condemns stagnation and stimulates movement, plays down the "here" and wants only the "beyond." Every step effects my passage from past to present and draws me beyond, towards the future which waits for me. In the figurative sense, "to take a step" means to commit my future. Thus through the journey or the route—they are the same thing here—my body and my whole being obey the basic call to go further, to progress, that primordial drive which causes me to be and to be a man.

At the same time the route is an education in realism, for it reveals me to myself as I confront the world: bad weather, loneliness, accidents, hostile encounters force me to evaluate myself. I come to know my weakness or the limits of my strength, my laziness or my fear, my needs, my secret attachments to comfort and countless deceitful possessions. The route is also a school of total commitment: nothing in me is untouched by the effort needed. My feet leave no doubt about it; my arms, those natural balancing poles, give my movement its balance and rhythm; my senses, especially sight, direct and guide me; mind and body experience their radical unity more fully. The route is a school of life, for to live is to go forward, to be stopped neither by failure nor by success, always to move on: if my health is good and my business is prospering, "things are going well."

The route is a school of freedom: the route opens up the world to me with an intense feeling of being emancipated; the limitless horizon reveals to me my limitless liberty. The route is a school of detachment, for it defines a single perspective, thrusts towards a given point on the horizon to the exclusion of all others, and urges me to move towards it without delay. I learn that to accomplish is to choose; that to choose is to take very little and give up a great deal; that to pass from potential freedom to real and creative freedom there is no path but sacrifice. There can be a further experience of self-abnegation, for the difficult and dangerous route forces me at times to take a guide; to walk behind another is to surrender my own self-assurance and to entrust myself blindly to another for the goal to be reached and the road to be taken to it.

The paradox and deep mystery of the route is that it is found both at the point of departure and at the point of arrival. It is the same route which I "take" here and which awaits me there at the end. Through one of its extremities it is here, where I am; through the other, it is where I am not but wish to go, even if it be the other side of the world. The route unites the known and the unknown, the possessed and the hoped for, the present instant and the most improbable future, what is nearest and what is farthest off. The route acknowledges, measures, and does away with distance; it accepts it in order to swallow it up; it is movement, life, and mediation.

Thus, thanks to the route, while being here I am already yonder. I am held physically in this place by my materiality, but I am already at the goal by my intention, my hope, my project. The peasant's idiom brings this home to me: if I ask him where the next village is, he answers, "You're there!" even though I have a half-hour or more of walking still before me. As soon as I am on the right road, I am, virtually and intentionally, already at my destination. In this fashion I discover the radical principle, the genesis, and the justification of the route. It is because I conceive and will my presence in a distant place that I start from where I am to make my way to it. The route takes its origin from my presence, in intention, at some distant point in the world. The path originating in my mind is drawn by starting from where I want to go and moving towards where I am. But the path outside my mind starts from here and reaches to there: the mental order is first, and it is the inverse of the order of extra-mental accomplishment. But do not think, therefore, that the intention is a matter of pure thought! There can be a route, after all, only for an incarnated spirit. The same body whose mass keeps me at a distance from other things is structured by my project for the movement to be accomplished: it goes yonder in intention, and takes me with it, before the movement of actual transition takes place. The route is made for my body, no doubt, and will have to be adapted as far as possible to my body's needs. But, more radically still, the route is the projection into space and out upon the earth of this prior intentional movement, of which my body and my consciousness are the living and sole source.

My Body Measures Space

Such a project simultaneously creates my "field," that is, my vital space, that portion of the world towards which my body moves and which I intend to fill with my presence. But the field which distance opens up to me is differentiated according to my varied functions. There is a visual field, that portion of space over which my object-oriented sight ranges; an auditory field, the zone in which sounds are perceptible to me; the field of my gestures; the field of movement, strewn with landmarks and pathmarked in a thousand possible directions; I speak by analogy of my social field, my field of action, etc. But the reach of my senses and efforts is limited; it thus restricts the actual extent of my universe and of the various fields open to my intentions. Even when my eyesight is very keen, the world around me extends "out of sight." If I walk, the horizon keeps receding before me, but it also, and in the same degree, keeps closing in behind me. Heaven and earth meet at the horizon line and seem to be conspiring to enclose me within frontiers that vary in their outward appearance but are almost identical in extent. In addition, the keenness of my senses can decrease and narrow the world which I perceive. From infancy to middle age my vital field grows with me, then reaches its "acme" or highest point. With later years the field begins to narrow; death marks the irreversible return of the field of action, the perceptual field, and so on, to point zero. At this point the body ceases to transcend itself. Reduced to being only what it is in itself, the body becomes a corpse and disappears.

Another and even more fundamental indication of the relativity of my universe is that I spontaneously measure things and the distance which separates me from them by comparison with my own bodily dimensions. As a child I thought the table high, for it was taller than I. As an adult I look down with amused tolerance at the children whose age and size were once my own. I measure distance according to my stamina or the power of my vehicle. "Far" and "near" are values that vary greatly according to the individual, age, the size of the country, the temperature, and so on. The peasant, too, and the mountaineer like to express distance in anthropocentric terms: the hours it takes to walk it, stone's throws, or even, more delightfully (in a certain valley of the Roussillon) pipes—the distance the walker covers while smoking one pipe. The official system of measurement in the day before the metric system also made man the measure of things: lengths were calculated in spans, thumbs, feet, elbows, and arm's lengths.

But if it is natural for man spontaneously to make himself the measure of things, he also perceives how relative his estimates are. Swift expressed it vividly and humorously in *Gulliver's Travels:* if man becomes big, the universe becomes small, and if man becomes small, the universe grows big beyond believing. The aim of the metric system was to establish a set of fixed references which would not be subject to the accidents of time, place, and nationality; the unit of length was defined in relation to the earth's meridian. Yet today this geocentric point of reference seems insufficient in its turn, and the meter is given a value in terms of wavelengths. These definitions gain in scientific precision what they lose in "humanness." But at least I have daily experience of the meter, the kilogram, and so forth. On the contrary, sizes which are incommensurable with our physical being and must be expressed by mega- and micro- prefixes make the mind reel, lose all realistic meaning, and tend towards nothingness for me, that is, the nothingness of the infinitely small or the infinitely large.

What concrete conception do I have of the micron (the thousandth part of a millimeter) or the angstrom (one ten-billionth of a meter) or, at the opposite extreme, the light-year?

Let us hold on, then, to the basic, and more and more neglected, idea of the *human scale;* it expresses the need for an order of optimal sizes within which man can feel at ease and can develop his physical, spiritual, and social being. Whether it is a question of a family dwelling, a meeting hall, a city, a work program, or, in short, any reality which man is to use, man himself ought to be its center and its measure. It is indeed false to claim, with Protagoras and all the relativist philosophies, that man is absolutely the measure of all things: of truth and falsity, good and evil, for that would amount to making man his own prisoner, closing the door to any transcendence. Yet the world born of technology ought at least to retain human proportions! Only on this condition will man be able to survive his own conquests.

My Embodied "I" Modifies Space

If I am present to the world through my body, as Merleau-Ponty says, the converse is also true: the world is present to me through my body. I mean by that that my body is the unperceived but lived prism which refracts the perceived world for my "I." This double movement of consciousness, simultaneously centrifugal and centripetal, which links me with the world, transforms the latter in the process and gives it a new determination, a new qualification. Try to imagine a world from which man was wholly absent, a simple world of things; the dumbness of the brute, unconsciousness, opaqueness, "meaningless-ness" would hold sway in it, for there would be no subject to make signs or to perceive them. The silence of such a world would really be an alien emptiness, a sort of void, for silence has meaning only in relation to the word which at any moment can fill it.[17] If the world contains no gesture than can transform it, no gaze that can comprehend and order it—in short, if the world is stripped of any known or expressed meaning—is it not a world of nothingness?[18] Doubtless human thought here reaches the limits of its capacity to understand, and it is almost as difficult to think of a world without man as it is to conceive of absolute nothingness.

Yet there is a familiar idea which meets this difficulty: the notion of the *desert*. Concretely, and whatever the scientific definitions of the geographer, the desert is for me the place where there is no man, a "no man's land" in the fullest sense. I try to develop such a thought without fully succeeding, for I must try simultaneously to be present to this place myself mentally and yet exclude every human presence. I try to know it as the unknown, as the dwelling place where no one can dwell, as a place with no inhabitant; no voice echoes there, no hand leaves its mark upon it, no gaze surveys it. Worse still: this accursed space devours the man who tries to occupy it. The desert thus cannot be a "here," but only a forbidden "yonder," a pure and unqualified "there," a space without any meaning.

But let a hermit remove himself to the desert, and immediately the solitude comes to life and takes on meaning: the rock serves as shelter, the palm tree provides food and shade, the priceless spring in the oasis sustains the life-beat of the human heart. More surprising still is that the hermit comes to the desert to find there the absolute presence which fills all things, the presence of God; he finds it and is absorbed into it, lives by it and dies in it. But along with the divine presence other presences also manifest themselves, the hostile presence of evil spirits which attempt to rob the solitary of the absolute presence he seeks. The hermit is engaged in a ruthless conflict day and night, pitted alone against an invisible and elusive multitude; by his presence and on his account the solitude is now overpopulated. This is not all: in the degree to which he seeks and finds the Wholly Other, the hermit finds himself as well; he discovers his human wretchedness, his interior poverty, his powerlessness and—a far greater source of anguish than the terrifying emptiness of the desert—his hidden con-nivances with evil. But the height of irony is that other men are drawn by what is at stake in his struggle and join the solitary, to be his disciples and to share his efforts. Thus one man's presence turns the utter void into utter fullness; the place of total absence throngs with visible and invisible presences; the space without meaning overflows with significance; the solitude itself becomes the place of every kind of encounter, and indeed of the supreme encounter and the supreme meaning, since man there encounters God. By taking up his abode in the desert the ascetic or the mystic turns its meaning upside down.[19]

This boundary situation splendidly illustrates the power of the least human presence in even the most forgotten corner of the universe. The appearance of a human "I" in the world humanizes the world, tames and domesticates it like a great savage beast. *Terra incognita*—once the poorest hut, the rudest dwelling (*oikia*) is built there—becomes the *oikoumene*, or inhabited land. Each hitherto undifferentiated point in space becomes a place where now the word can be heard that utters the world, knows and expresses it; where the human gesture can unfold that remodels the universe; where the human gaze can at last take in the environing immensity. Such space is henceforth a field for word, for gesture, and for sight. The coming of man modifies space, gives it a radically new meaning, and makes of it a new *cosmos*—that is, a harmonious system.

This reciprocal influence, this mysterious relationship that links a man to his own place, needs analysis. Language shows an instinctive feeling for it when it distinguishes between earth and soil. The earth is initially the undifferentiated element which the ancient philosophers held to be one of the primordial and irreducibly simple realities. But let man put his hand to the earth, and the earth is immediately transformed, disciplined, and enriched. Once hostile, the ground becomes nourishing; once alien, it becomes familiar; once savage, it becomes a civilized country. It is transformed to meet the needs and wishes of man; it receives his mark and becomes his reflection. The earth now shows a new face put upon it by its master and lord. It becomes a living reality after the image of its master, whose very organs are projected upon it: do we not speak of the mountain's foot and crown and breast? Do men not distinguish white Africa and black Africa, thus communicating to the earth they live upon the very color of their skins?

The human inhabitant in turn takes his name from the continent, the country, the province, even the city: European, Frenchman, Burgundian, Dijonnais; and there was a time when the lord had no other name but that of his fief or manor. Moreover, man is transformed in his contact with the earth. In a wonderful exchange of meanings, I *cultivate* myself and become a particular kind of man by *cultivating* a particular portion of the land: the *genius loci*, or spirit of the place, marks me forever. If the soil is rich, it broadens its master's outlook and gives him assurance and ease; if the soil is poor and unrewarding, it makes him gloomy, dulls his sensitivity, narrows his outlook, and turns him into a stubborn man: compare a man from Touraine with one from the Auvergne or Brittany. A man's very language takes on the cast of the land, and a special, inimitable accent betrays the soil which has nourished the speaker. Even the works of the intellect itself reflect a sky and a climate. The strong, clear light of Athens radiates through the Platonic dialogues. As the sea makes the seaman, so does the mountain the mountaineer and the countryside the countryman. The soil is nothing but the humanized and humanizing earth. This fact lies behind both the worldwide myth of the Mother Earth[20] and the scientific idea (a curious one, when you reflect on it) of "human geography," both of them so expressive of our human roots.

At the term of his existence man is entrusted to the earth, and this inhumation, or earthing, has often been regarded as a return to the original source.[21] At least man thus brings to a climax the process of putting his own mark upon the earth, for here he makes the earth his very own and gives himself over to it in a supreme and irreversible encounter. The whole human group puts its roots down ever deeper into the soil as it entrusts its dead to it, and the earth becomes the "land of our fathers," the "fatherland." History is filled with dramatic scenes of man's passionate attachment, which is earthy and spiritual at the same time, to his native soil. The war in the trenches, when fighter and soil became incorporated, blended together with a view to the stronger defense of both—and Joffre's famous order, "Die on the spot rather than retreat"—are still among the most powerful expressions of this original oneness.[22]

Breaks in Space

In imposing various meanings on space, I introduce into it a series of decisive breaks. As soon as I claim a patch of ground for cultivation, for building a house or pitching a tent, I pull that portion of space out of the rest of the universe. A partition of some sort will often be produced to mark the line of the break which I want others to respect: a ditch, an embankment, a wall perhaps topped with spikes or the like, a hedge of thorns. Thus a village or town or entire city is made up of a collection of individual parcels of land, with or without buildings, each of which sets limits to the other, and you enter each by crossing the *threshold*—the significance of this point of radical division will be studied in connection with the notion of the visit. Outside these individual lots is the space common to all and intended for the free circulation of persons and things: the street and the road. The latter are the "public thoroughfare" in contrast to the private domain where each dweller is at home. There are, furthermore, enclosures with free access where people can gather to meet, converse, or take their leisure: the clubroom of a traditional-type society, plazas, meeting halls, roofed markets, and so forth. Every social activity has a definite place reserved more or less exclusively for itself: business streets, market places, town hall, hospital, museum, school library. There is another place marked by a decisive break: the cemetery, which is set apart from all profane use and all selfish activity as a place of recollection, remembrance, and peace (the *Friedhof* or peace-yard, as the Germans call it). There is, however, another place where these disinterested activities develop most fully: the *temple*. While men roundabout attend to their needs, their interests, and their pleasures, the temple enclosure is to be free of all activity for material profit; it is, in the strict sense, "useless," and its walls mark the division between profane space and sacred space. To the disinterestedness of the believer in his activities there corresponds the higest concentration of meaning. For the meaning of sacred space is the richest one conceivable, since a man goes there to encounter God. The threshold of the temple marks a radical break in the uniformity of space and gives access to a new world.

All these strictly ordered breaks in human space mirror a definite system of interpersonal and social relations, and their preservation is an expression of institutional stability and group cohesion. But if the latter unity is suddenly compromised, the whole distribution of social space is suddenly turned upside down. Places change their purpose and new dividing lines appear. The disaffected occupy the places of work and seize the town hall or the theater or other public places. The inviolability of the individual's home is contested or even denied outright. The temple is given over to the worship of a new divinity or converted into an arsenal or warehouse or dance-hall, for the sacred is denied and absorbed into the profane; it is "profaned." The university becomes a public meeting place or a hotel. The space hitherto open to the free movement of all the citizenry—the public thoroughfare—is broken up and fragmented by the erection of *barricades*. The latter introduce into the social field new dividing lines which the insurgents impose by main force. As a fortified structure, however inadequate, for offense and defense, the barricade sets up within the group a violent division between the forces of order and the forces of rebellion. It doesn't matter for our purposes here that the breastwork has lost its original strategic purpose as a hindrance to cavalry charges, for the barricade nonetheless retains an essential symbolic meaning. The break in social space expresses the break in human relations within the group. A moral crisis manifests itself in terms of a disruption in the structures of extended space. The health of society will always demand the disappearance of barricades (a first concern, in fact, of the insurgents if they achieve power) and a reintegration of space with a restored or newly found moral cohesion.

Beyond the limited groups of which we have been speaking, whole peoples are separated by territorial frontiers, customs stations, and even by fortified lines which divide up the area of the inhabited continents. International disputes always involve, even if they are not reducible to, questions about existing and future lines of national demarcation. In the second century after Christ the emperor Hadrian built his famous wall, and as early as the third century before Christ the Chinese empire embarked on the building of the Great Wall which was eventually to be 1,250 miles long. In our own day grim "walls" and "curtains" continue to rend space and humanity. The struggle for universal brotherhood and peace will therefore always seek to create a unified human space and a world without frontiers.

II. ORIENTATIONAL STRUCTURES

My Embodied "I" Is Orientated in Space

Whether I am out in the great open spaces of nature or inside the limited and highly organized space of my home, I am orientated: that is, each dimension of the world presents both a direction for movement (at least movement in mental intention) and an existential significance. The orientational structures which sustain all our behavior, from the most automatic to the most deliberate—individual or social, moral, magical, or religious—extend and transcend the structures found in the other beings of the natural world.

At first sight we might think that inert bodies are strewn about at random in the universe; this stone, for example, could just as well be there as here—or rather, since it lacks consciousness, it has neither "here" nor "there," its place is "just anywhere." But science informs us that the localization of such bodies is subject to laws; their weight impels them towards the center of the earth in quest of a delimited position in which perfect equilibrium would be achieved; avalanches and landslides manifest the working of this law. Water especially, with its astounding instability and mobility that make it look alive, is always moving, whether gently or furiously, towards a state of equilibrium that is never attained. The wind buffeting our bodies makes us aware of the extreme instability of the air, to such an extent, indeed, that it can arouse in us a psycho-physiological state of disquiet and insecurity. Without being animists or defenders of the ancient theory of "natural places" (each of the four elements naturally tends towards a determined place which is "its own proper place"),[23] we can see in the movements of inanimate bodies a distant foreshadowing of the "orientation" which living things have.

When we come to plants, we find in each, according to its kind, "movements" of desire and repulsion; these are the positive and negative "tropisms." These spontaneous vital movements turn vegetables towards the nourishing earth (geotropism) or water (hydrotropism) or the sun (heliotropism), or else turn them away from harmful influences. Instinct directs an organism, whether or not it is capable of locomotion, towards food and everything that is useful to it and turns it aside from what is harmful. For most people, the word "orientation" calls to mind above all the phenomenon of animals getting their bearings to return home from a distance, a capacity which is so notably developed in some domestic species and in the carrier pigeon.[24]

At a deeper level, it is significant to note that the very constitution of a living thing shows an orientational structure: its various relationships to surrounding space determine the differentiation of its organs and direct its growth. A plant artificially freed from gravitational pull loses its native élan: the stem writhes and curls up in a kind of dumb suffering, for a certain kind of relationship to space is required for a living thing to develop. On the other hand, the smallest shoot, with its roots provided for and its stalk growing in the opposite direction, will suffice to differentiate and structure the universe. Consider the oak with its roots thrust deep into the earth to find support, nourishing juices, and life-giving moisture. These organs and their deep plunge into the earth are what they are only to permit the bold soaring of the trunk in the opposite direction towards the light and warmth of the sun. The boughs and branches reach out to take in all the other directions of the horizon, surveying them, embracing them, summing them up. This twofold creative thrust, vertical and horizontal, whereby the tree absorbs into its own unity the immensities of the earth and the heavens, differentiates both its own organs and the surrounding space; it is likewise a basic constituent of its beauty and a marvellous manifestation of the dynamism of life.

But the phenomenon of orientation finds its full meaning in man. I am not situated in space like a pebble in a box or like any content you might name in any container you might think of. I am the center of a world-that-is-for me, and I give a meaning to each of its dimensions. The space which science describes is abstract, homogeneous throughout, but the space of the real world is rent when my body makes its appearance and is differentiated in relation to it. Up and down, before and behind, right and left are dichotomies I introduce into space and continuously maintain in it. My body divides up the universe after its own image and projects upon the universe meanings of which the body itself is the source. There is a primordial, innate intentionality in my body which ceaselessly flows out to the different parts of the universe. I am aware of this fact only in moments of giddiness and disorientation when the world spins around me because I have momentarily ceased to impose direction on it. My body is the privileged place at which the world is divided up, receives a multiplicity of meanings, and becomes the human universe.

Even as it divides up the universe, my body also continuously puts it back together into unity. In a simple act which is inseparable from its very being, my body constantly gathers up and reunites all that it constantly splits up, and creates a personal harmony between all the meanings which it assigns to the various parts of the world. Thanks to the body, up and down, before and behind, right and left are molded into an organic whole. My body determines where the center of the universe is; it is the indivisible point at which the analysis and synthesis of all reality take place; its coming

upon the scene is the coming of a new space and a new universe.
All this is not to say that the division of the universe has no basis
outside my body. On the contrary, the world as I experience it has an
order, it is a cosmos. The sun rises in the east and sets in the west; the
north pole is before me if the east is on my right; the heavens are above
me and the earth beneath me—these are all fixed points which condition my own orientation. Even on the opposite side of the earth I carry
my reference points with me. Similarly, the space familiar to me in
daily life is structured by a series of reference points by which I situate
myself: school, city hall, church, stores, friends' houses, the place
where I work. At home the things I am used to provide a reassuring
order, and thanks to them I can find my way even in darkness.

The structures which provide me with *direction*, however, are also
structures of *signification*, and both my movements and external
phenomena are rich in both elements.[25] Does not the wind, according
to the quarter it comes from, offer quite different values, desirable
and undesirable? We find exemplified here a truth already enunciated: my relation to the world is simultaneously objective and
subjective. If the world by its sheer extent contains me, I in turn
differentiate and interpret the world; I accept and submit to it, but I
also master it and take responsibility for it. My orientation in the
world is both adaptation and creative arrangement, submission and
initiative, a situation that is given and the imposition of a *meaning*. In
return, this meaning which originates in me reverberates from the
walls of the world, comes back to me like an echo, and enables me to
achieve a better awareness of myself. In one and the same movement,
I project myself, am reflected, and discover myself in the universe, for
cosmic structures and anthropological structures are both distinct and
correlative. As my days pass, I come to understand myself in an
uninterrupted dialogue with the world.

Up and Down

Man is the vertical animal, and upright stance is his privilege. The
structure of my body—feet on the ground, head raised towards the
sky—divides the universe into two halves: up and down. Whether I
am here or on the other side of the world, the whole adventure of my
"being in the world" develops between these two poles.[26]

At birth my body is too weak to stand upright; it is born recumbent and remains lying upon the earth on which it has just appeared and from which, some would say, it has come forth.[27] But as my limbs grow stronger I cease to recline on the earth's surface and attempt rather gradually to separate myself from it. After repeated tries I learn to sit and then to stand erect. Here I am on my feet, extended between above and below, master of heaven and earth, and thrusting towards both earth and zenith, the two poles which ceaselessly draw me and which I ceaselessly unite with one another. Thus the parallelism of man and tree is immediately obvious. My head is the pinnacle of my physical being, my summit where I point towards the heavens. Languages therefore contain numerous exchanges of nomenclature between man and tree; we speak of the trunk of the human body, and of the foot and head of the tree. We respect a man with "deep roots." The blind man in the gospel, as he was being cured, saw men like walking trees.[28] The yogis give the name *vrikâsana* or "tree position" to the position in which a man, balanced on one leg, stretches his arms vertically towards heaven. Thus the structure which tree and man have in common gives them the same symbolism; both of them recapitulate and signify, by their very being, the whole of the living cosmos.[29]

The earth, the "down," is my pole of stability and security. The surface which holds me up determines my "here" in the narrowest sense and is my firmest support. Before I begin any work or any rest, I always try to get into a well-balanced position on the ground. As I walk, each step breaks and restores this balance; it replaces the static balance of motionlessness and inertia with a dynamic balance. To learn to walk, to run, to dance, to climb mountains, to ski, or to walk a tightrope is to acquire new kinds of bodily balance. To have one's "sea legs" is to be sure-footed on a boat despite its pitching and rolling. In figurative language he alone has "both feet on the ground" who has good psychological balance and an accurate sense of reality.

While firmly set upon the earth, I carry my head raised towards heaven, the other pole of my embodied existence. The "up" of the universe is that part of the world which is situated above my eye-level. From above I receive the light of the sun, the air I breathe, and, with these, life itself and the exhilaration of living; from above there comes in the night the light of the stars which reassures and guides me. Thus it is that a spontaneous vital movement presses my body to develop upwards. For a child to grow is to rise upwards in space and achieve gradual and imperceptible bodily increase until the full stature of maturity is reached. If a tall and slender figure is an element of beauty, this is because it obeys and expresses the natural upward thrust of the human being. Even adults still dream at times of growing taller, and various methods claim they can add an inch to a man's height; and if this dream is delusory, men wear high heels.

The awareness each individual constantly has of his own stature thus plays an important, sometimes a decisive, part in his feeling of personal identity, of inferiority or superiority; for my stature provides the first standard for measuring myself against another. Strength, self-respect, arrogance all make me straighten up and carry my head high. But these situations also have strange reversals: if I am of gigantic size and aware that this extraordinary height disrupts the natural harmony of the human body and offends the eye of the observer, I can paradoxically develop a sense of inferiority.

Whatever its stature, the body's orientation upward brings to man, alone among all the animals, the privilege of standing erect. While the other higher living forms show a horizontal balance and the anthropoid apes approach verticality without quite reaching it (since the front limbs are still used for walking), man is the animal who stands up straight. This orientation is so essential that it need only be reversed for a while to cause death—in ancient Egypt some condemned men were simply hung head downward until death ensued. In contrast to the reclining position, an erect stance is for man the sign of life, health, alertness, and strength; "to be standing" or "to be on one's feet" are synonymous with being in good health, watchful, ready for action. It is also the sign and act of a full self-mastery: when I am erect, I triumph over gravity, am master of my bodily mass, and achieve a most improbable balance—vertical, supported by a minimal ground surface. It is the sign and act of personal unity, for when I am standing up, whether I am moving about or not, I coordinate my movements, unify body and spirit, am at one with my own physical being, and at the same time transcend it. It is the sign and act of my specific dignity: my upright stance expresses my superiority over the lower orders of life, especially over the animals, for my stance allows me to dominate them with my eyes.[30] In Germany, if someone wants to train a dog to stand on his hind legs and beg, he orders the dog to "play a little man" (*Männachen machen*). In social relationships, my vertical stance is the sign that I exist and expect to be recognized; I stand up for myself in standing up. The upright stance is a symbol of order; disorder in a man's affairs is expressed by saying "he has his feet in the air and his head to the ground." It is for the sentinal an attitude of alert attention to what may happen, for the soldier at attention an attitude of being fully at the disposal of another, and for the boy scout the expression of his "Always prepared." It is an attitude of respect and welcome, as when I rise to receive a visitor. It is the attitude suited to public speaking, and the leader or the prophet stands up to convince his hearers.

Thus rooted in the body, the importance of the heights, or the "up" is reflected in a good deal of social behavior. Groups of men like to exhibit their pride by building high towers: the Tower of Babel, the Eiffel Tower, the Empire State Building. Kings "ascend the throne." Those in authority make regular use of platforms and daises. The low-lying sections of a city are often where the poorest people live. It is instructive to note that in one industrial city which is built on the side of a hill, the hierarchy of jobs carries over very strictly to the physical level of the employees' homes. The street which runs around the lowest level of the hill is where the low-salaried manual laborers live; then in ascending order come the artisans, the skilled workers, the foremen, and finally the top-salaried engineers. Every promotion on the job is immediately translated into a move to the appropriate street. If every success tends to be expressed in terms of an ascent or exaltation or elevation, the very idea of social hierarchy is supported by the image of the ladder, the mountain to be scaled, or the pyramid which culminates in a summit where only one can stand. Whoever has a "high idea" of himself nourishes the hope that he may engage in the upward movement which is inseparable from his very life, and perhaps reach the first place. Then he is said to "aim high" and to want to "climb the ladder"; if he succeeds, he will be "highly placed."[31]

Even the moralist makes use of such expressions. To say a man is morally perfect he speaks of him as "highly conscientious" or as having "a lofty morality"; or he says that "a soul which raises itself up, raises up the world with it" and describes such a person's "moral ascent."

The universally accepted significance of the upward extreme explains and justifies the old idea that heaven is the dwelling place of the gods. In constrast to our earthly "here" in which gravity keeps us or even drags us constantly "further down," the inaccessible heavens appear as the "there" and the "up" beyond all others. The dialectic of "down here" and "up there," of the nearest place and the farthest place, provides a universally used thought-scheme. Man is in this "lower world," "down here," on the earth (*homo* [man] is derived from *humus* [earth]), while divinity is situated, by a very obvious anthropological necessity, at the zenith from our position, "up there," in the celestial hemisphere which is the realm of the sovereign, universally present cosmic powers, the region of solar light and life-giving air, and thus the place of blessedness, eternity, infinity, and immortality. It was natural that the idea of apotheosis (the placing of a human hero in the ranks of the gods) should be expressed as his elevation upon a very high throne, symbolic of his exaltation into the heavens (cf., for example, Ingres' *Apotheosis of Homer*); or that the Chinese Empire should be called the "Celestial Empire" and the emperor "the son of heaven"; or that the king of the Incas should call himself "Son of the Sun-god"; or that the mountain where heaven and earth seemed to meet—cf. Olympus or Horeb—should be considered as a dwelling place of the divinity and should become a religious "high place"; or that one or other hill should be "inspired"; or that the God of the Bible should be the "Most High."

It is with good reason, too, that even the most purified philosophical conceptions straightway launch into spatial language, as when Plato places the perfect, immutable, and eternal Ideas in the intelligible heaven, and Aristotle's god dwells in the celestial sphere most remote from our world. But this last example indicates not only the necessity but the danger as well in all spatial imagery: such images can be a pitfall for thought that does not go beyond them. The idea of metaphysical or religious transcendence must indeed make use of the image of spatial elevation, but only in order to transcend it, as the mathematician's eye rests upon the geometric figure while his intellect reasons on the basis of a concept. But the risk must always be accepted since the mind requires such a support. The image of "up" or "heaven" expresses the idea of an unqualified transcendence in the order of being, perfection, and life.

This significance of height also explains why men have always cultivated, and gradually made a reality of, the dream of mastering the peaks of the higest mountains and the aerial regions and heaven itself. The heights of earth and heaven summon human effort more imperiously than do the dark depths of what is "below." Orientated towards the heights, man wants to fly in order to go ever further beyond his earthly limits. From the myth of Icarus down to the exploits of the contemporary cosmonauts, the ambition to rise up into the regions of light, life, and immortality is one motivation for many scientific and technological feats. To the subconscious mind of individuals and peoples and in virtue of the solidarity that radically unites us all, the conquest of upper space represents a kind of apotheosis of man as such: he lays hold of the heavens and claims equality with the supreme powers that rule the universe. The achievement of such a Promethean dream explains the festivities that mark the victories of the space pioneers.

The lower pole or "down" provides material for an analysis which is a point-by-point antithesis of the one we have just finished.

The surface of the earth is man's proper domain: he takes possession of it by setting his feet upon it, and he finds in it his primary and familiar support as well as the field in which to exercise his mastery. In alighting for the first time on the lunar surface on July 21, 1969, man in the persons of Neil Armstrong and Edwin Aldrin trod upon a star located above his head as an "earthly" being; he turned the moon into a "below," and earth. It was an historical act of conquest. The meaning of the underground is entirely different: it is a dark, poorly known, impenetrable region in which man cannot breathe, see the light, act, or even survive. If a space opens up there, for example a deep cave or a well, I am torn between curiosity and repugnance. The depths "disorient" me and make me lose my sense of sure physical balance; I experience vertigo and the morbid and terrifying attraction of the void, of nothingness. Even short of such boundary situations, it is well known that a miner's life is exceptionally difficult and that speleology and underwater fishing attract far fewer participants than surface or high-altitude sports; that it takes a deliberate decision, quite painful for some people, to plunge one's head into the water for the first time; and that exploration of the oceanic depths or life aboard a submarine requires a special courage. Finally, the existence of a central fire, as revealed in volcanic eruptions, cements our conviction that the depths of the earth are the most hostile and inhuman place man can conceive.

In turning from the heights to the depths, the direction takes on a new meaning. A man who falls, hurts or kills himself. For the mountain climber, the aviator, or the sailor, a fall into the depths means death. After hard work I "can't stand up," I "collapse from fatigue." Each evening after my daily toil I throw myself on the ground or on a bed in that admission of weakness which going to bed and sleeping represent; the ultimate form of weariness is to "sleep standing up." With much more reason can it be said that the invalid who has never been able to stand up has not experienced his full humanity. Illness, failure, or discouragement often "prostrate" a person.

In a struggle, sometimes I am "on top," sometimes "on the bottom." My life is acquainted with "ups" and "downs." Perhaps I have even experienced "deep wretchedness," "deep sorrow," or "the depths of suffering." Doctors and friends then apply remedies to restore my physical and psychic strength, to "get me up on my feet again." Sometimes hatred of another person gets out of control, then, to reduce him to powerlessness or to slavery and finally to kill him are ways of "bringing him down" (like putting an axe to an oak) and taking from him the enjoyment of his upright stance which is the sign of his strength and dignity. Thus the fall becomes the symbol of every kind of failure. A moralist or an honorable man will think that a fault is a "fall" and sometimes brings a "downfall"; or that the libertine has "fallen into the depths of vice."

For every man, however "high" he may have risen, the inexorable laws of life follow the same curve and bring him back one day to where he began. Physical growth and mature stature are soon followed by a decline. A settling down from his full height, sometimes a stoop, undermines the priviledged upright stance of man, the vertical animal. At the same time, the limitations of age force the elderly person to yield up his highest responsibilities; often, "having reached the top, he wants to come down." Finally, the last trial of all "fells" a man, casts him down to the earth on which he once supported himself only to separate himself from it in the process of "straightening up"; he takes to his bed in the first posture that was his as a newborn child. He is at the periphery of the world of healthy men, withdrawn from daily activity and more and more absent from others. Soon the acknowledgment of his powerlessness becomes irreversible: death destroys his upright stance. He is now man lying down; he will be "bedded" there forever. Yesterday he was "felled," cast down to the earth; today he is put into it, interred—"earthed"—as death marks the return of the human being to the *humus* that once nourished him. To be "six feet under" is to be dead. Henceforth this man is no longer part of the world "above," the world of light, warmth, life, activity, and social life; he has fallen prey to the world "below," the world of darkness, cold, oblivion, and shadows. Whether it be the Hades of the Greeks, the Sheol of the Semites, the "Lower World" of the Latins,[30] or some other of the many conceptions found in the history of human thought, the inferior pole of our existence and the gods of underearth always have the same fearful meaning.

It is easy to see, then, that being shamed in the eyes of others should be regarded as a descent towards death, a "mortification," or towards the earth (*humus*), a "humiliation"; that a salutation offered to another often consists of an inclination of the head or even a bow, which diminishes my stature and turns my face towards the ground; that the greater my respect for another, the deeper my bow; that the most expressive mark of respect I can give is to prostrate myself face downwards in a gesture by which I renounce the sign of my own dignity (my upright stance) and admit my powerlessness and noth-ingness. If the other is not really superior to me or if I abdicate my basic human dignity even to a real superior out of low motives or flattery or self-interest, I am said to "crawl." If, on the other hand, aware of my superiority, I lean protectively over someone inferior to me, then I am adopting an attitude of "condescension": I consent to lower myself a little to be on his level. Thus the primordial and universal experience of upright stance is the substructure of countless spontaneous ways of acting and speaking.

Upward and downward: the two poles between which the whole cycle of human life runs its course also constitute the two terms of an endless interior debate. It is a psychological, metaphysical, moral, and religious debate: shall I be content with my native condition, or shall I try to rise above it by force or by cunning? Shall I have the wisdom to accept my condition as mortal man, or shall I give in to the temptation of *hubris*: "You will be like gods"?[33] But the even more tormenting debate, the one which involves the whole meaning of my earthly life, is this: after death, shall I be forever the man asleep, relegated to the underworld, in darkness with regard to myself and others? Or, against all the probabilities, shall I be able to return to the realm above, to stand up once more, my feet set firmly on the earth, and raise my eyes again to the light?

Sitting

Between the upright stance in which I stretch out most fully towards the upper pole and the lying-down position in which I surrender to the pull from below, I am often forced to adopt a kind of compromise: an intermediate position which spares me the costly effort of standing straight while not forcing me to the total self-abandonment of lying down. I substitute for the narrow supporting surface which my feet provide the wider surface which a seat offers: *I sit down*. Strictly speaking, the ground can supply what is necessary here. But a seat, however rudimentary (a tree trunk, a crate, or a foot-stool), provides a much higher degree of ease since it enables me to bend my knees at right angles. A chair brings the further addition of a support for my back. The supporting muscles relax; the legs are relieved and can be extended or crossed. The sitting position is one of relative rest, of elementary ease. The first act which politeness towards a visitor requires is therefore to beg him be seated. On the other hand, technology is always busy inventing new ways of travelling around while seated, and of thus combining a restful posture with increasing speed: from the palanquin and sedan-chair to the armchair of a supersonic plane or even a spaceship's cabin.

Unless he is travelling, a seated man has surrendered movement; the pleasure of discovery which moving about brings with it is replaced by the security of being in one place. Here is the sitting person, fixed in one spot of which he is, for a shorter or longer period, the peaceful possessor. In sitting down a man takes root, as it were, and makes his own a part, however small, of the universe. This de facto occupation even confers in many cases a genuine right: if I yield my place on a bus, I renounce my right in favor of someone else. But if sitting is a posture of rest and if I thereby appropriate for myself a spot which becomes the center of my world, sitting can also by that very fact become a claim, the expression of a determination that is being resisted by others. Strikers simply sit down in their workshops in order to occupy them and claim their due. A general stops the kind of fighting which involves moving about and "sits down" in front of (besieges) a city to show his determination to conquer it: the attitude of rest thus becomes, by an odd reversal of meaning, the symbol of military action.

Because of the balance and muscular relaxation it provides, the sitting position frees my energies for various occupations. Many manual tasks, such as shoemaking, sewing, or watchmaking, require this position which makes minute adjustments and careful finishing touches possible. I sit down to eat; the restoration of my strength is better served if I go about it in a restful position, whereas eating "on the run" can be harmful. I sit down to converse with another. If I let him sit down and remain standing myself, I show a certain unwillingness to be at his disposal and I tacitly ask him to shorten his visit, whereas if I sit down I express an openness and a willingness to listen. Do we not say at times when we offer someone a chair and sit down ourselves: "I am at your disposal"? In the semi-repose of a straight chair or an armchair each person can express himself and be receptive.

Bodily ease fosters mental attention and effort. It is possible to reflect while walking, and a little excercise may sometimes stimulate the flow of my ideas; but sitting is usually the position for intense intellectual effort, whether or not it involves writing. From the little boy in school to Rodin's *Thinker*, from the man who intends to erect a tower to the king who is planning a war,[34] a seat is needed for successful reflection. Reading, meditation, public or private debate, the meeting of the President's Cabinet or an administrative council, conference or colloquy are all "sitting" activities. Language bears witness to this by such terms as study session, parliamentary session, sitting of the council or assembly. In such sittings, standing is not at all excluded, for each posture takes on its full meaning only by contrast with its opposite, and alternation between them adds to their expressivity. Thus the speaker stands up and adopts the attitude of leader or prophet when the need to convince his hearers requires extra effort from him. While standing, the speaker dominates his audience from on high; his arms are freed for broader and more effective gestures. If he sits down, he shows that he is sure of himself and is adopting the attitude and tone of the master who is dispensing a knowledge about which he is quite certain. Correlatively, sitting is the posture for calm listening—the posture of disciples and willing, or even eager, hearers. In such a state the listener lets the word enter more deeply into him like a nourishing food.

The stable balance of the sitting position and the calm assurance it supposes both in the sitter and in his surroundings make it the attitude adopted by solidly established power and by authority which is sure of itself and accepted by others. The "president" at a banquet or an assembly is the one who sits in the place of honor (*prae-sedet*—sits ahead of, in front of); the position belongs to him by right and he maintains it, while others may rise to perform one or other necessary service. The president opens the session by sitting, dissolves it by standing up. Sitting is also the posture adopted in all societies by one of the most formidable and feared personages, the *judge*. The serene authority which belongs to justice requires that its authorized agent shall work sitting down. For a tribunal to "sit" is to exercise its judicial function. A Court of Assizes deals with crimes and certain serious misdemeanors. But it is the *monarch* above all who affirms his own sovereign power by sitting on his throne: royal or imperial authority is so firmly established, and its subjects are so fully submissive, that the monarchic power is exercised in a position of rest. The reality of this imperturbable, unique, and supreme power is thus given material expression by the seat itself. While a chair, and especially a folding chair, is a most movable piece of furniture, the throne is characterized by its appearance of weighty solidity; as immovable, it symbolizes the immutability of the power it represents. The meaning is further heightened by the values of the materials in the throne, the richness of the decoration, and the height of the dais and the back of the throne (the monarch would like to have his throne reach the clouds if that were possible). From his lofty throne the absolute monarch exercises all the political powers, legislative, executive, and judicial; he has the power of life and death over his subjects and enjoys a kind of transcendence over them. Inevitably, then, to accede to monarchic power is "to ascend the throne"; the investiture ceremony is called "enthronement"; to be "enthroned" means to rule in the literal or figurative sense; and the throne itself is the symbol of sovereign authority.[35] Thus, "to sit" is never reducible to a posture without any meaning; to sit is an *act* and involves the whole man.

In an organized gathering, then, the places where people are assigned to sit are very important. The position of each seat in relation
to the president corresponds to a definite degree of dignity. Whether
the master of the house sits at the "upper end" of the table or at the
center, the guests receive places according to their respective importance. In official ceremonies the chief of protocol has the difficult task
of acknowledging the dignity of each person by assigning him his
place. Language therefore makes "rank" a synonym for social dignity.

If the sovereign or the president of an assembly calls me to sit beside
him, especially at his right hand, his action is full of meaning. We
shall be inquiring later on the reason for this preeminence of right over
left. In any event it is a constant fact that the place of honor is at the
leaders's right hand and that to be called to sit there is a mark of
conspicuous distinction. Sitting at his right hand means that I acquire
a share in his authority and dignity; he who is first acknowledges in
me a kind of equality of rights, raises me to his own level in genuine
social equality, and singles me out for homage from the group.

To sit is thus a specifically human act, and a seat bears witness to
man. The piece of furniture is built for the sitting body, provides for
its comfort, and, to this end, adopts its shape. Feet, back, arms, and
sides are terms applied both to the sitter and to his support. The piece
of furniture creates a space to receive the user, it calls to him and
invites him; my armchair extends its arms to me; the ever empty
chairs a museum displays strike me as looking rather silly. But, over
and above the general relation to man which all chairs have, I discover
a particular meaning in each kind of chair. The reason is that use
determines the design, the lines, and the functions of the seat. Thus,
folding chairs or the benches in public places are made for
"everyone," and are therefore impersonal and undifferentiated. A
baby's high chair, an old man's easy-chair, the convalescent's
lounge-chair, and the invalid's wheel-chair are each made for a particular age or state of health. An ottoman or a simple mat, a folding
stool for the beach, a saddle for horse or bicycle, a bank of seats on a
bus are all reduced to the minimum form which their use requires.
The easy-chair, the sofa, and the settee are all made with comfort or
conversation in view. Sedan-chairs, palanquins, and the "period
piece" bear witness to an age or a civilization. But the seat can also
become the exclusive symbol of a definite function: the Pythoness's

tripod or three-legged stool, the curule chair of the Roman consul, the Roman Holy See (seat) from which words come *ex cathedra*—from the teacher's chair—the academician's arm-chair, the deputy's seat, the professor's chair, and the dock in which the accused man sits: each signifies a function, a dignity, or a social position. Between seat and sitter there is a *circulation of meaning*.

Front and Back

In addition to up and down, my body also introduces into the world the distinction between anterior and posterior. An invisible plane, passing through head and shoulder blades, separates my front from my back. But while up and down had reference points independent of my movements in the opposition of heaven and earth, front and back are entirely relative to my position in space. I need only turn around for what is in front of me to be now behind me, and vice versa. The distinction is, of course, not entirely subjective or a matter of my whim. The fixed points of the universe continue to be my guide: the north is in front of me if I turn my right hand to the east and my left to the west;[36] I can combine these various givens, but I cannot abolish them. The front, or "facing side," of my body is that part of me which directly presents itself to the gaze of another and whose native action is to move ahead. Later chapters will analyze the "pre-ventive," or anticipatory, character of the word, the hand, and the face. Let us note here simply that I am constantly leaving my "here" in order to go "before" (i.e. to meet) the world. I cross the distance in intention and would abolish it if I could. My locomotor powers obey my wish, but always in a forward direction: to walk is to "pro-gress," i.e. move forward. Directed by my pro-spective gaze, my feet pro-pel me and effect my physical presence at a given distant point in space.[37]

The anterior part of my body is thus the part which manifests the intentionality of my consciousness. This movement is evident even in refusal, immobility, and silence. If I wish to break off a relationship with another, I cannot continue to remain facing him, even in iciest indifference, for my whole being, correlative to his, would continue to make him inevitably my partner. I must therefore turn my back on him or deliberately take the offensive. Consider also a sleeper who has lost all awareness of the world and other people; he still unwittingly affirms that he is correlative to both, by the anatomy of his face, his limbs, and the whole anterior part of his body, made as it is for perception, action, and encounter. When death has taken away all possibility of confronting reality, then the body's pro-spective morphology, and indeed the whole body, collaspes and disappears.

I project my own morphology on the things that are in close contact with me. Thus my clothes match the division of my body into front and rear, and it will always be a blunder to put a garment on backwards. My house has a "façade," with perhaps a flight of steps and surely a reception hallway. Evey store has a forward section where merchandise is displayed and a rear section for utilitarian purposes. Our vehicles, from the most modest wagon to the supersonic plane, are orientated from back to front; according to the law, backward movement is an abnormal operation for which the driver is entirely responsible. Above all, consider a ship: it has a forward part with a "prow," the latter sometimes decorated with a human figure, sometimes armed with a beak or "rostrum." The rear with its "poop," the sides (starboard and larboard), and its slender lines help give the ship a kind of "humanness" like that of the man who sails her.

The forward thrust of my entire being assigns very definite meanings to that part of the world which lies in front of me. That region is defined by the direction of my efforts. It is a field in which I am present, ahead of myself, as it were (*prae-sum*); a field which I already occupy in intention; a field open to my perception, desire, work, domination, and freedom. It is a field which I hardly allow to be shared; if another crosses my path, he interferes in my project and must say, "Pardon me!" It is the place of every encounter, every confrontation, and every shared enterprise; the place of public life and social responsibilities. For an individual as for an army (a kind of gigantic individual), "before" is the realm of adventure, danger, and courage. "Forward!" is a call to action and conflict. It is an area which is at my disposal and which therefore I possess; I want "to have something ahead" of me. It is the area of that mysterious possession which is my future; according to my age, "my future is before me," more or less. It is the area of success: if I succeed in my profession, I will receive "ad-vancement" or be "pro-moted." It is the area of individual or collective prosperity; "pro-gress" is, after all, the forward march of humanity. In short, my native orientation makes "in front" the favorable region of the universe for me and the direction of untrammeled effort, hope, courage, daring, victory, and all good fortune.

The *back* of my body is that half of my being which is less expressive of me: my "reverse" side. It is difficult for me to recognize myself from the rear. I have no sense organ there, except for the sense of touch which is coextensive with my skin itself. Behind me is the region of absence and the unknown—not seeing what is behind me, haven't I sometimes wished I had eyes all around my head? It is also the sphere in which I cannot work, and at the same time the sphere of voluntary and involuntary forgetfulness. Aesop's two sacks, the one suspended in front filled with other men's faults and the one suspended behind filled with our own, is a good illustration of the front-back distinction as a distinction between the real and the nonexistent, the known and the unknown. When people have something to do or say concerning me, frankness demands that they do or say it "to my face," and I am annoyed when they whisper about me "behind my back." And yet I myself cultivate ideas from "the back of my head," on occasion "mental reservations"; since they are most personal to me, they are the ones I cherish most and sometimes the most decisive with regard to my conduct.[38]

If in front of me opens up the horizon of my future, behind me closes off the horizon of the past. My history, like that of mankind as a whole, is behind me, all the way to that mysterious horizon I speak of as the night of time. Do I wish that some trial was not still to be undergone, some task not still to be accomplished? Then I say I wish they were "behind me." As I advance along the line of time, my future comes to meet me, is realized for a furtive moment I call the present, then flees into the unfathomable past behind me. The myth of the god Janus, whose two faces made him equally present to the future and the past, gives vivid expression to my impossible dream of a knowledge which is absolute and a presence which is total.

But behind me is also that part of the universe through which I have already passed and which I have arranged for my own use and subjected to my own needs. For an army the rear is a place of precautions taken, of security and rest, of reserves and provisions, and of possible retreat. There the soldier feels at home, sheltered from accidents and attacks. There he keeps those whose weakness excludes them from the fight—women, old men, children, the sick. Others deliberately remain there because they fear the uncertainties of the front and of the advance.

The dynamic thrust of an individual or an army in action can be countered by the enemy. Moving towards his "front" in strength, he can force his opposite number to retreat. "Backwards" is then defined as the direction of movement under constraint, overriding the initial forward thrust of the vital forces and of the desire for victory, the direction of failure and defeat. If I refuse this backward movement which my adversary is forcing me into, there is often no alternative but death.

Behind me is that part of the world from which I am open to the most unexpected attacks. The warrior's fear and his assailant's trick is the "stab in the back," impossible to parry and only too easy to give. For an army in the field the security of the rear is ambiguous and relative, for it sometimes lessens the will to face dangers that seem still on some distant front. An able foe will then reverse his tactics and attack from the rear. Now there is confusion and distraction, for the front has suddenly moved to the rear; or, rather, the front is everywhere at once: here and there, right and left, above in the shell-filled air and below in the mine-filled earth. Deprived of its natural orientational structure, the army runs to its destruction. In like fashion, once an individual, whether a soldier or not, is attacked from all sides, he can no longer "con-front" or "turn his face to" the danger. A man is lost, once the front is everywhere and there is no rear at all. The leader of an army or an athletic team must then "secure his rear" and arrange a "rear guard." The man of action thus gives a figurative meaning to expressions which reflect an essential anthropological structure.

At other times movement to the rear, whether forced by an enemy or deliberately chosen, takes the form of a complete turnabout. The about-face, the half-turn, the wheeling ("con-version") of a skier or an army then acquires an important meaning. To turn the horse's head, or simply oneself, and to retrace one's steps is to turn front into rear, rear into front. To pivot one hundred and eighty degrees is to turn the universe I had made for myself completely around. I give up my earlier intention and now set before me as the goal of my efforts what I had previously thrust into the realm of forgetfulness and neglect. I break with my original purpose in the same way that I put an end to a relationship with another: by turning my back. Have I been bested in a struggle? Then my turnabout is an admission of impotence, weakness, error, the inordinate character of my initital undertaking. Now I seek only to save the little I have left, with which I identify myself. I deny myself in denying that world-for-me that I had desired and brought into existence. Backwards is then the direction of flight, surrender, shame, and dishonor—*terga vertere*, to turn one's back to the enemy!

But my turnabout, physical or spiritual, can also be rather a renunciation of lesser values in order to devote myself to higher ones. In social relationships I turn away from an egotistical concern with myself in order to turn to others in friendship and devotion. I then arrest the movement that is taking me in the direction of my self-interest and become effectively present to my neighbor: I am at his disposal. A spiritual *conversion*, moral or religious, turns me away from empirical values and towards the ideal, towards God. What I rejected yesterday becomes my project for today, and this new purpose carries me forward into more strenuous efforts and more admirable achievements. In this instance my sudden turnabout is really the choice of a higher good and my apparent surrender is a deeper fidelity. In changing perspective with my own reversal, the universe of values shows me its truer face. My turnabout has effected a change in the world.[39]

Right and Left

The vertical axis which runs through me, linking me with the reaches of heaven and earth, also divides my body into two symmetrical lateral halves. Whichever way I turn, therefore, I divide into right and left the visible hemisphere of which I am the center. But like the corresponding parts of my body and of the world, my two hands are not interchangeable: the right hand is regarded as superior, the left as inferior. Most human beings are not ambidextrous, and left-handedness is treated as abnormal.

Men will doubtless be investigating for a long time yet the basis of this anthropological structure and the prevalence of right-handedness. Are we right-handed because our brains are left-sided, as Broca thought? In other words, is the preeminence of the right hand due to the greater development of the left cerebral hemisphere which,

as we know, controls the opposite side?[40] Or is right-handedness only
the product of education and social custom?[41] Or, finally, has a small
anatomical difference provided the basis for a functional asymmetry?
But whatever the foundation of the anthropological structure, its
significance is more important to us here.

My right hand is stronger and more skillful than the left; it is the
preeminent and more precious hand, the one I take greater care of.
Manual skill makes me "adroit," a man of "dexterity." In figurative
language, my "right arm" is the man who is my closest helper. My left
hand, on the contrary, is less strong and less precise in its movements;
I assign it, therefore, the easier and less noble tasks, while reserving
penmanship and work requiring precision to my right hand. In
figurative language "left-ness" (gaucheness) is a synonym for
awkwardness.[42]

This division and its attached meanings I also project outside
myself into the world. That part of the world which is situated "on the
right hand" is the region of affluence and success. Benjamin, "son of
the right hand," is the preferred son. "On the left hand" everything
bears the mark of weakness, difficulty, and failure. In Roman religion
the soothsayers foretold good fortune or bad fortune according as the
flight of birds which provided the omen came from the right or the left
half of the heavens (divided for the purpose by the sacred rod).
Sometimes the opposition of right and left corresponds to the opposition of the sexes. In central Africa where Sango is spoken the left is the
feminine part and the right the masculine part of human morphology
and of the universe, as the vocabulary shows: the same term is used for
woman and left, and the same for man and right.[43] Similarly, among
the Boulous, a Bantu tribe of South Cameroun, the right hand and the
husband are expressed by one and the same word, as are the left hand
and the wife. In India, the opposition of right and left corresponds to
the opposition of pure and impure, and is an illustration of the
hypothesis that the distinction of right and left is really the distinction
of sacred and profane.[44]

In French political life, ever since the Revolution, the half of the
parliamentary assembly at the president's right represents the conser-
vative party, the party of the established order; the left represents the
party of change—an example of how easily we identify order with
stability and disorder with change. Finally, social custom in large

measure regards the right side as the more honorable and reserves it
for the guest or for.the highest-ranking person present. By placing the
guest on his right, the president of the assembly or of a banquet gives
him, as we remarked earlier, a share in his own dignity and singles
him out to receive respect from everyone present.

Orientational structures are thus *meaning* structures as well, and for
the human subject the divisions of the world have an existential value.
Two consequences of this situation will call for closer examination.
On the one hand, I am present in intention wherever I am transported
by meanings which I originate. On the other hand, my language is
orientated no less than my experience or than the body itself in which
language has its roots.

III. THE MASTERY OF SPACE

I Appropriate Space by Moving About in It

Local motion in a living being aims first of all to satisfy the primordial
need of food. Unlike the plant or certain sedentary animals, an animal
which does not find the necessary food within immediate reach must
move about in order to secure it. The living being thereby traverses
the surrounding space and, to that extent, conquers it. It is well
known that some groups of animals divide up their space in a kind of
tacit contract, whereby each has a territory on which it grazes or
hunts at will. Among men the juridical concepts of territorial waters
and air space have an analogous origin. The underlying reason is that
the struggle for space—whether vital space or not—is absolutely
primeval, the land is always one of the first assets to be coveted. The
problems of immigration are the source of many a dispute and many
an armed conflict. The conquered party sees his frontiers contracted
and his territory divided up. In North America the redskins were
crowded into "reservations," and the Indians of South America into
"reductions" with their revealing name. For the Spaniard, poverty is
the most dire when he doesn't own a spot to fall dead on.

However, man is always giving local movement a fresh and expanded meaning, for if primary needs and desires offer a partial
explanation of our moving about, they are far from being its sole
motivation.

Through local movement I seek to free myself from the narrow limits of my existence. For I suffer at being a prisoner of the ludicrously restricted place my body occupies, and from a sense of the contingency of my position in space: "When I consider. . . the tiny space that I occupy and even that I see, plunged in the infinite immensity of the spaces which I do not know and which do not know me, I am terrified and astonished to find myself here rather than there, for there is no reason why I should be here rather than there."[45] Hence I feel the need of breaking out of my confines, enlarging my existence by expanding my horizon. In moving, I change my perspective on the world and see it from new points of view. I give the world-for-me a focal point and centers of reference which it did not have before. I thus confer upon and discover in the universe a new "aspect" (the Latin *aspectus* means both my looking and the view perceived). In moving from one point to another, I am constantly looking with the fresh gaze of youth at the face which the world and other men present to me and am myself rejuvenated in the spontaneity of these encounters. This is why I feel renewed on my return from a journey: I have discovered a universe and acquired a new mode of existence. The eyes with which I see my familiar surroundings are not the same as before I went away; for by broadening my spatial horizons I have broken out of the confines of my own mind, and, enriched by a new world, I am richer in humanity. Thus journeying is a specifically human privilege: an animal *moves about;* only a man *travels.*[46] The man who has never travelled, or the islandman or internee (another kind of island man) is threatened by mental narrowness, a mind which is closed to every new departure in thought and conduct, and even—perhaps above all—with xenophobia. Fear the man of one place as you do the man of one book.

The extending of horizons is thus an essential human need and the drive behind all the great explorations. In antiquity man's earth—the inhabited earth, the *oikoumene*—was centered in the Mediterranean basin, from the furthermost eastern point reached by Alexander's armies to the Pillars of Hercules in the west. The expansion of the Roman Empire extended the geographical horizon towards northern Europe. But this whole area, so laughably small by our standards, was bounded on all sides by the unknown—*terra incognita*—and was little enlarged during the Middle Ages. It is difficult for us to imagine the intellectual upheaval precipitated by the great discoveries of the late fifteenth and early sixteenth centuries: the world men knew suddenly burst into fragments; the horizon of existence seemed to be extended towards the infinite along with that of the navigators. Thus the decline of medieval civilization, the shaking up and splitting up of Christendom, and the formation of a new humanism were all of a piece with the shocking expansion of the inhabited world. Today the exploration of cosmic space is freeing us from our exclusively terrestrial bonds and opening up limitless horizons for science, technology, and man's dreams. Humanity has conquered a new space. Whether or not it is possible to accept Lemaître's hypothesis that the physical universe is expanding, it is at least certain that human space—the spatial domain inhabited or traversed by man—is constantly growing larger.

The conquest of a part of the universe already known to science requires the movement of man's body for its completion. As long as man's body has not gone "down there" or "up there" to turn these places into a "here," the world is not fully mastered. The various machines launched into aerial or terrestrial space are only forerunners: the child's kite, which his eyes follow so eagerly, the space laboratory with its scientists, the soundings taken by navigators or cave explorers all express a desire for the kind of journey which would enable man to take *bodily* possession of the new domain; then space would really belong to us. Wasn't it the movement of their respective fleets which permitted the Romans of old to call the Mediterranean "our sea" and the English to call the Channel the "British Channel"? Similarly it has taken the efforts of the cave explorer and the miner, the submariner, the alpinist, the aviator, and the cosmonaut to convert the depths of sea and earth and the heights of space into man's possession. On the earth's surface, whether in military conquest and renaming or in the householder's peaceful walk around his garden on a Sunday afternoon, it is by the movement of his body that man asserts his mastery of space. It can of course be objected that movement of itself tends to a state of rest and that a simple passage across a place, especially at the speed of a spaceship, is hardly the same as an occupation. But each moment in my total movement is at least a momentary taking possession of a place and creates the possibility of a future return to it.

We have already glimpsed one meaning of *speed*, or why we develop engines capable of ever greater acceleration. On the one hand, the continuousness of my movement effects a kind of continual metamorphosis in the universe; the latter is being ceaselessly transformed, vanishing and being reborn, and presenting a new face. If I hurry, the rate of change is speeded up; if I slow down, the rate of change does too. I determine at my whim the disappearance and renewal of my world and experience the satisfaction of curiosity and a pride, even an intoxication, in my act of re-creation.

But at a deeper level of significance, the speed of our movements manifests and obeys our desire for ubiquity. Not content with being in one place and one time, I would like to be everywhere at once; I yearn for an all-embracing and simultaneous vision of the world. My struggle against the limitations of space and time has a deep metaphysical meaning: I seek to transcend the limitations of my embodied existence and to lay hold on the world in its totality. My thirst for speed betrays my desire for transcendence. I use the body to escape its own limitations; because of my body I am subject to space and time, and by means of my body I make myself master of space and time. Unlike the swiftest of animals, then, which aims only to seize its prey or escape with greater assurance, man uses speed to make himself present to the "all" and thereby shows himself to be a spirit, open to the universal.

Physical and Intentional Presence in Space

Man's dream of ubiquity will always be unrealizable. If he really broke through the limitations of space, he would go out of himself and get rid of the problem by getting rid of his body and himself. But short of this extreme case and apart even from technological possibilities present and future, I am constantly transcending *intentionally* the narrow confines of my physical presence.

My awareness of being inevitably "here" is an awareness of both limitation and nonlimitation. I understand my "here" to be a sample, a tiny portion of a whole from which it is inseparable. I am at a unique and limited point in the vast totality of space, but in this privileged center the whole circle comes into existence and is gathered up. While being physically present at a single point I am thus intentionally present to the whole universe. To grasp this idea better, let us suppose that on a hike I come to a "lookout" where I see spread before me a vast "panorama" (literally, "total spectacle"). I am in admiration of the new horizon which gravitates around me and of which I am the center and focus. I feel crushed by the immensity which environs me (am I not an insignificant quantity?), yet present to the whole of space. My gaze traverses, masters, and unifies the universe; I take up my place in it and put order into it according to my own primordial orientational structures: up and down, front and back, right and left. My gesture embraces the whole. An existential necessity makes me feel mysteriously present to this nearby village, that distant forest, and indeed all points in the universe. Better still: I identify with them, for "I am the space where I am." The feeling is so intense that I cannot bring myself to let my grandiose perspective vanish with my departure. I therefore take a picture which will immobilize the spectacle,[47] or I heap up some stones and plant a stake to perpetuate the vision I had; such is the origin and meaning of the medieval "montjoy," the cairn, the observatory (the tower or "belvedere"), whether furnished or not with an indicator for various landmarks. I have left a sign that there is a special view from this point and an invitation to other passersby to make this same horizon their own. Above all, I have consecrated this "here" which I occupied for a fleeting moment and have tried to perpetuate my presence in it, to survive henceforth in this point of space.

My presence to the world is thus both bodily and intentional, but it is more intentional than bodily. I am constantly transcending my body,[48] always going beyond it and filling the whole extent of space; the little whole that I am is always bestowing itself upon the immense totality of the world.[49] The field of my intentional presence is, first of all, the field of my perception: I am wherever my ears and eyes take me. Let the noise of the city or the sounds of farmers at work come to my ear and they carry me off, despite myself, to where they originated: street, workshop, distant countryside; I am "distracted," divided between distant places or focuses of interest. If I want to concentrate on my work, I must limit my field of perception and the field of imagination, which is vaster still, and try to make my intentional presence coincide with my physical presence.

My intentional presence is, furthermore, coextensive with the whole field of my activity, my words, and my desire. A child in front of a store window stretches out his hands to a desirable plaything; material distance has been crossed in intention and eliminated by desire: where his treasure is, there his heart is too.[50] In like fashion the political candidate describing with large gestures tomorrow's world (what he will do for you if you vote for him) makes himself and us present across time in this blessed future. The same holds for our interpersonal relations: I am present to this man on whom I gaze, whom I hear and address, and to whom my hand is extended; I am even present to the man on the other side of the earth to whom I am writing.[51] And, finally, the praying man who raises his hands to heaven is opening hmself to God's gifts, pulling himself up to the Most High, grasping him and in a sense being grasped by him; he is, in short, becoming present to the infinite in his lively consciousness of his own extreme littleness. Geographical, temporal, metaphysical, and moral distance does not matter, nor do the laughable limitations of my gesture. The latter is already effective, for I am wherever my gesture and intention direct and carry me rather than where my body keeps me.

A gesture is, in fact, not simply a witness to or translation of a meaning. It is this meaning itself made effective as soon as it is conceived and willed: meaning that is created, grasped, communicated, and objectified in one indivisible moment; a spiritual and a bodily act in one. Even the carefully calculated gesture does not escape this law, for though it is first thought out, it does not exist as a gesture except in the "execution" of the meaning. *A gesture is meaning in the body, just as meaning is a gesture in its nascent state.* My intention, experienced in this member or organ, tends towards the world, reaches it and seeks to master it and fill it. In the same way, the intention embodied in words passes beyond the range of the voice, linking in depth two personal subjects. The whole body is a global gesture, for while indeed an organism, it is also the place in which countless meanings are constantly being born and "taking shape," sometimes abortively, sometimes achieving full expression. As subjective, the human body bears within itself the consciousness of what it is signifying; as intentional, it is movement towards the world. Thus my intentional presence is incommensurable with my physical presence.

If I can make myself present to any point in space whatsoever, I can also in thought embrace space as a whole, apart from any perception of it and any actual gesture. An animal crosses space, but he does not think it. Orientation at a distance, so remarkably developed in some animals, is not knowledge but know-how. Man, on the contrary, is able to think immensity, which supposes an effort to transcend the limits which enclose him and a surpassing of matter and the conditions it imposes. I carry within my mind the whole extent of space, despite my own limited dimensions. "By space the universe embraces me and swallows me up like a speck; by thought I embrace the universe"[52] Pascal's brilliant play on words voices the paradox and grandeur of our metaphysical situation. In thought I embrace, enfold, and dominate the total reality which surrounds me, presses in upon me, and overwhelms me. Unlike the brute animal who has neither geometry nor geography, man is both geometer and geographer. He can conceive the infinitely great and the infinitely small and be present to these opposite extremes. Is this not the mark of a condition which transcends the order of extension and matter, becoming and death, and the sign of spirit itself?[53]

My Possessions Situate Me in Space

The space about me is not empty immensity; countless things fill it and make of it an "environment" for me. But these things which my eyes distinguish and bring into order are not only objects for knowledge, seen in varying perspectives. They are also means which sustain my life, give me pleasure or pain, and make it possible for me to act. The ones that are most useful or necessary I try to retain in the area of which I have exclusive disposal and to appropriate for myself.

Such a collection of things which I attach to myself forms a little universe which is my own and in which I have a sense of ease and familiarity: I prefer my own pen, my own watch, my own room, to any that another might lend me. The reason is that the microcosm of my possessions is highly personalized; it is organized and gravitates around a center which is I myself. If the world I perceive turns on me as a perspectival center, the circle of my possessions forms the nearest portion of that world, the portion which tends to become identified with my very being.

It is not enough to say that my "I" is at the center of my possessions, for the role of the body is essential here. If I buy a loaf of bread or a pair of shoes, I clearly link them with myself for my body's exclusive use. But the same is true if I buy a book or rent an apartment: the book is at the disposal of my hand and the apartment is the habitual shelter for my body. Things present themselves to me as possible prolongations of my body: sometimes as tools, sometimes as objects for consumption, as with food. I am well aware of this connection between my possessions and my body when I make preparations for a trip: I would like to take everything with me—that is, along with my body. There was a time when important people did take a large baggage-train with them.

The act of taking has its prolongation in an effort at increasingly intimate "incorporation." The child hugs its dearest toy; I put my wallet into the inner pocket of my coat; the miser devours his money with his eyes. Moreover, a kind of identification gradually takes place between me and my possessions. They become an increment to my physical and psychic being, endow it with a kind of substantiality which gives me added importance in my own eyes and the eyes of others. And so the French idiom which means to increase my estate —extending my lands or enriching myself even in the purely monetary sense—is literally "to round myself out" (*m'arrondir*), which comes close to our living experience. My possessions become incorporated with my being and tend to become indistinguishable from it. Whereas I am physically present only at one point in space, I am intentionally present to all my possessions. Where my treasure is, there my heart is too.

I can *lend* my possessions—that is, temporarily relax the bonds of possession without breaking them entirely. But if the borrower is slow in returning something to me, I feel the delay as a disorder; I feel a sense of absence, though presence and absence are properly predictable only of persons. What I am experiencing in this removal of my possessions is a kind of absence from myself. To regain the enjoyment which has been interrupted and come into actual possession of my goods once again is to regain a certain plenitude of my own being.

I can also *alienate* a possession by gift or sale. Then I set up a permanent distance between it and me and restore it to its original condition of being foreign to me. It is not clear, however, that the object can fully return to that state. A mysterious bond still links it to me despite all the juridical acts, the interior renunciations, and the lapse of time; something of myself continues to be embodied in that trinket or that family possession. With much more reason do I have this painful feeling when my possession is *lost*. The very word "lost" is revealing: as soon as the object is removed from my use, I regard it as having ceased to exist; its whole reality is measured by its being-for-me; once removed from my hand, it is no more. It takes a great deal of detachment for me to reflect that the pen I have lost may be useful to someone else, and even more to find any consolation in the thought.

With far greater reason am I shaken in my very being by legal confiscation—when I am stripped of the possessions that wrapped me around like clothing, clung to me like a second skin. If I lose my fortune in a disaster, I have again the experience of real ontological alienation. I no longer *am* myself because I no longer *have* my possessions. I am a "ruined" man; that is, I have become a ruin, like a house in decay, with the crumbling of my assets. This is why "it is a horrible sensation to feel that everything we have is slipping away";[54] everything we are seems to be perishing along with it.

Yet the numerous things I attach to myself are not wholly confused with my most personal "I." Their meaning is always ambiguous: they are not pure objects, "things in themselves"; neither are they quite myself. Between the outermost periphery of the "I" and the most intimate of my possessions there remains an unbridged distance which nothing in the world, not even the most prolonged familiarity, can eliminate. This is because my possessions, focused as they are on my body, share in the latter's ambiguity; they constantly swing between the opposing poles of the exterior and the interior, objectivity and subjectivity.

Of its nature, therefore, *having is at the service of being*. The basic function of possessions is to give stability to my existence as an embodied being: "The necessities of life," says the wise man, "are water, bread, and clothes, and a home with its decent privacy."[55] Without such possessions for consumption and use I would be destined to an early death. Take clothes, for example. A newborn child is extremely frail; its life is exposed to countless dangers from without and subject to countless needs from within. The first possession, long held in readiness by the mother, which we offer this endangered being, is a warm layette as shelter against the cold and against the rough assault of elements and things. Clothes are a *second skin*, added to the overfragile one that nature gives us. In fact, it is basically the skin, the fur, the wool of animals that provides for this need. If clothes, like my dwelling place, protect me from the weather, they also protect me, again like my home, from the inquiring eyes and the attacks of other men. While the naked man is stripped of all defenses, clothes provide security and a physical and psychological privacy; in short, shelter for my personal self. It is not surprising, then, that these possessions become identified with my very being and that I should say to a waiter who has spilled food on me, "You have stained me," rather that "You have stained my clothes." Nor is it surprising that I should be pigeonholed and identified by my manner of dress or that various social functions require a particular costume.

Since it is a means of assuring my existential stability, property has its full justification only in relation to my freedom. Not every living thing is capable of possessing, even though it may be subject to the same necessities as I am. The dog's kennel, or his bowl, does not belong to him but to his master. Only one who can impose various finalities on things and deal with them as he wishes can be said to possess them. The use a dog makes of his food or his kennel is, however, determined by the nature of these objects and by his own instinct for self-preservation—he cannot prepare his own food or build a fire out of the wood of his doghouse. In other words, *ownership is an act of freedom:* it brings freedom into play, sustains, fosters, and increases it. Since I am in control of some possessions, however modest they are, I take up a position relative to the empirical or ideal values which invite my free choice; I actuate my being as a moral subject in making decisions about my possessions. In this respect money, which is possession of its essence—that is, the most indeterminate of all possessions—lends itself to all my wishes and whims and gives me the liveliest sense of freedom. By way of contrast, the young man who has not attained his majority, the convict whom justice has condemned to a loss of his rights, and above all the slave who is stripped of his freedom, cannot exercise the legal right of ownership. It is enough to say, then, that possessions have as their function to guarantee my being as a free subject.

Possessions give me *stability* in space and time. Without these living quarters of which I have at least the use, I would be a man without hearth or home, lost in the vast universe. Thanks to my possessions, I make a portion of space my own, take root in it, become capable of orientating myself: the sun rises and sets at a definite point in my accustomed horizon; the unvarying rhythm of my world gives me an existential security. Similarly, were it not for the furniture I have today as I had yesterday, or the patrimony I have perhaps inherited, I should be caught up in a dizzying fashion in the flight of time. The permanence of my possessions in successive situations gives my being and my self-awareness solid points of reference. My possessions have been witness to my troubles, my joys, and my labors over the years, and they are the sign that I myself do not flow away with the lapse of time. They are an accessory—but precious—element in my personal identity. The continuity of my ego is maintained by the stability of my possessions.

Finally, by the very fact that they fix me in space and time, my possessions "locate" me in the eyes of others and give me a set place within the social group. It is noteworthy that people often designate me in terms of what I have: just as a lord once took the name of his manor, so today I am the man who owns that farm house or the house across the street or the litttle grey automobile. There is also, and more importantly, the regrettable fact that public opinion tends to allocate its respect and consideration according to the extent of glamor of a man's possessions. A passerby esteems me if I am driving a high-class automobile; some hotel managers refuse me a room if I have no baggage. We are at the root here of the tragic situation of the impoverished sectors of some countries in relation to their well-off fellow countrymen; these poor people are too poor to count in the eyes of the powerful and are therefore locked into the hellish circle of wretchedness. In the eyes of the more fortunate he who *has* nothing *is* nothing; he who has, and he alone, really exists. In fact, each man's right to possess some goods is based on his right to exist and to be a man and a free man. This shows the universal legitimacy and the equally undeniable limitations of private property.

If having is thus ordered to being, it therefore has the power to delude and deceive. On the one hand, my possessions can give me a false security: false, because even if I managed to acquire the whole world, I would not escape the inherent vulnerability of human existence; the death of other men, however rich they are, is constantly reminding me of this. Furthermore, because they do make for stability, my possessions can attach me to the temporal to the point of alienating me from myself. I am then trapped in the quicksand of my goods, though these are intended of their nature to bear me up. I am prisoner of the empirical and immanent, and scornful of the transcendent and ideal. My person is then reduced to my individual ego, my being to my having, and my body, which is the heart of all my having; when I idolize my possessions, I cease to be a free man. I thus come to see the need of achieving a balance between the centripetal movement which draws things towards me and the centrifugal movement which orientates them towards others. Instead of folding inwards towards the trunk of my body, my hand is extended from it, holding out to others the things which till now had remained within the area defined by my own gestures and my sphere of action and enjoyment. I remove from my body what I formerly brought into its orbit and direct towards my fellow man the possessions which once gravitated around myself; my tight clutch relaxes and my hand opens in the gesture of giving. Hence the being of others becomes the term of my efforts, the goal of my having—of my superfluities and even my necessities. I rejoice to see my fellow man find, in his turn, a stability in existence and the full exercise of his liberty. All the while I am rescuing my own freedom from the dangers of avarice, purifying my being by lightening my load of possessions, and discovering more clearly both the vulnerability of my empirical existence and my dignity as a person open to the ideal.

Let us note, in conclusion, the close connection of my body with my having and with the cosmos. In my human body and its needs I am able to sound the universe and interpret it—all that it offers me today or has in store for me tomorrow. My look, my eyes, witness to the spectacles the world can show, as my lungs to the oxygen in the air and my tissues to the elements. My corporeity is that by which the world manifests itself to me and that by which I project myself on the world. It is thanks to my body that things and possessions exist for me. "The mysterious relation uniting me to my body," says Gabriel Marcel, "is at the foundation of all my powers of having."[56] Because it is inseparably subjective and objective, my body mediates between my "I" and the world of things and is the place of encounter between my consciousness and the universe of objects. Just as one must forget the body, along with Descartes, in order to reject the world, so one need only acknowledge the lived experience of the body in order to transcend the subject-object dualism and the blind alleys of idealism.

Language and Spatiality

Through my body I experience the world, put order into it, and enrich it with countless meanings. This has important consequences for the language in which my experience is uttered. As I am, so I speak: *my language is orientated*, as is the whole being of which *it is a part*. Here "spatial" language finds its critical justification, which is not an abstract legitimation but a justification of the existential order. Man has a strict right to give utterance to the world in the way he lives it bodily throughout his days; he has the right to express himself in the lived language of his relationship to the world, that is, in the language of *empirical phenomenology*. When I am speaking figuratively, it is entirely permissible for me to signify the acquisition of an important role in society by speaking of an "ascent" or an "advancement"; and it is equally legitimate to clothe in spatial metaphors even the purest metaphysical or religious concepts. Today many an abstract statement has recourse to the images of level, stratum, dimension, circle, sphere, line of demarcation, and so forth. Admittedly the practice often results in defects of style, for the appeal to spatial experience is so spontaneous that the writer becomes oblivious to the requirements of metaphor considered in itself. But far from being an absurdity or an indecipherable puzzle to the man of the atomic age, such language has a permanent expressive value, for it is based on universal experience. Of course, it is no less necessary that the scientist working with rationally elaborated concepts should avoid spatial representations. Indeed, the matter is not open to argument, for mathematical space is not space as experienced. We observe, however, that the geometrician draws figures on the blackboard to help his eyes and his imagination and even to support his mind as he reasons with abstract concepts. And once his conceptual undertaking is completed, the philosopher, the theologian, or the mathematician will revert to empirical language to express his lived experience. He too can "rise" or "descend" in the social hierarchy; "fall ill" and then "get onto his feet again." Thus the thinking and the language of the scientist return to the experienced space from which they have been briefly separated.

Apart from these considerations, no thinking man is a slave to language. To know what you want to say is to use language without being its servant, to translate an intended meaning into a system of words, images, symbols, and concepts without allowing this meaning. to become encrusted with words or to dissolve in verbiage; to play on these various linguistic stops with sovereign freedom, using them always as a means of transcending them. If you become the slave of the various tools which language offers, you show that the real nature of words has escaped you. For the word—what is meant—is in fact something that always transcends the vocable, the image, the symbol, and the concept; it is power, movement, life in continual rebirth. The signs are only a springboard for the word. It would be fruitless, then, to oppose the subjective language of experience to the objective language of science with the purpose of reaching a definitive choice between them. The two registers of language are both necessary and irreducible to each other, like the subject-object ambiguity of the body on which they are based.

NOTES

1. If I do not recognize my room when I wake up, I am either wandering in mind or have been removed from the room.

2. The books of Gaston Bachelard, especially *The Poetics of Space*, illustrate the distinction fully. Cf. also Georges Gusdorf, *Mythe et métaphysique*, 2nd ed. (Paris: Flammarion, 1963), pp. 192 ff.

3. Descartes, *The Principles of Philosophy*, II, 10, in *The Philosophical Works of René Descartes*, trans. Elizabeth S. Haldane and G.R.T. Ross (Cambridge: Cambridge University Press, 1911), Volume 1, p. 259.

4. An analysis of eating will be made in Chapter 7.

5. There are more than a few instances of restless, even anxious, "fat men" and of optimistic "thin men." Yet corpulence is often taken as a sign that the person is fully at home in life; it is supposed to have cordiality and easy-going familiarity with others associated with it; the heavy man readily inspires confidence; people like to speak of a fat man as good. Thinness, on the contrary, is often taken as a sign of inferiority and a lesser hold on life; it is less of an invitation to open up and talk to the person; a very thin man often arouses misgivings. There is a great deal of prejudice here: common sense spontaneously identifies physical and psychic health with corpulence, thinness with deficiencies. Of course, between the two extremes there are many

86 THE HUMANITY OF MAN

degrees of slenderness, svelte slimness, and average corpulence. Cures for underweight and overweight have as their purpose precisely to bring the person to his optimum volume and bodily space; the interplay of straight and curved lines begets elegance, or at least the balance of a well-proportioned outline. Fashion also urges in this direction and, if it cannot always master the *reality* of the bodily place which the client occupies, it modifies its *appearance* at least; horizontal stripes on garments make the figure seem larger to the eye, while vertical stripes and materials that hang loosely taper the lines.

6. The meaning of welcome and rejection will be taken up later on, in Chapter 6, in the analysis of "at home" and the visit.

7. Cf. below, Chapter 3, part 2, for the study of bodily attitudes. Cf. also Frederick J.J. Buytendijk, *Attitudes et mouvements: Etude fonctionnelle du mouvement humain*, tr. from Dutch by L. van Haecht (Paris: Desclée de Brouwer, 1957), pp. 79 ff.

8. Cf. Jean Lhermitte, *L'image de notre corps* (Paris: Nouvelle critique, 1939); François Chirpaz, *Le corps* (Paris: Presses Universitaires de France, 1963), pp. 25 ff. (study of the bodily schema); Paul Schilder, *The Image and Appearance of the Human Body: Studies in the Constructive Energies of the Psyche* (New York: International Universities Press, 1950).

9. Cf. Gabriel Marcel, *Metaphysical Journal*, trans. Bernard Wall (Chicago: Regnery, 1952), p. 191; Maurice Merleau-Ponty, *Phenomenology of Perception*, trans. Colin Smith (New York: Humanities Press, 1962), pp 198–199. The subject-object dichotomy does not emerge only in the presence of others. At each moment I also take myself as object, as is shown by reflective verbs where the action has the subject for object: *I* wash *myself*, and *I* also reassure *myself*, etc.

10. *Civil Code* (France), article 102, and ordinance of October 7, 1958.

11. Cf. Mircea Eliade, *Patterns in Comparative Religion*, trans. Rosemary Sheed (New York: Sheed & Ward, 1958), pp. 367–387; *The Sacred and the Profane: The Nature of Religion*, trans. Willard R. Trask (New York: Harcourt, Brace, 1959), pp. 36–47. On symbolism in general, cf. Eliade, *Images and Symbols: Studies in Religious Symbolism*, trans. Philip Mairet (New York: Sheed and Ward, 1961). On Romanesque symbolism, cf. Marie M. Davy, *Initiation à la symbolique romane, XIIe siècle* (Paris: Flammarion, 1964).

Many of the ideas developed hereafter in this book can be illustrated and enriched by consulting Gérard de Champeaux and Sébastien Sterckx, *Introduction au monde des symboles* (St.-Léger-Vauban: La Pierre-qui-vire, 1966. Referred to henceforth as Champeaux-Sterckx, *Symboles*). On the distinction between reductive interpretation, which tends to eliminate the transcendence of what is signified, and restorative interpretation, which uncovers this transcendence, cf. Gilbert Durand, *L'imagination symbolique* (Paris: Presses Universitaires de France, 1964), and Paul Ricoeur, *Freud and Philosophy: An Essay on Interpretation*, trans. Denis Savage (New Haven: Yale University Press, 1970).

12. Cf. Noël Arnaud, *L'état d'ébauche*, quoted by Bachelard, *The Poetics of Space*, p. 137: "I am the space where I am"; and Anatole France, *Le livre de mon*

ami, 229th ed. (Paris: Calmann-Lévy, 1921), p. 36: "My life was a very small thing, but it was nonetheless a life, that is, the center of things, the mid-point of the world. Don't smile at that or, if you do, smile only in friendship and think: Whoever lives, even if it be but a little dog, is at the center of things." We must note, however, that man, being intelligent and free, makes himself the center of the world by a radically new title of which the animal knows nothing; we will have to return to this point. Cf. also Merleau-Ponty, *op. cit.*, p. 82: "My body is the pivot of the world." What is true of individuals is also true of peoples; for the national consciousness the homeland is the center of the universe. China long called itself the "Middle Kingdom."

13. Cf. Merleau-Ponty, *op. cit.*, pp. 243–298.

14. Pascal, *Pensées*, Fr. 72 (in Brunschvicg's numbering), trans. Martin Turnell, *Pascal's Pensées* (New York: Harper, 1962), Fr. 390, p. 215. (Henceforth, Pascal will be cited by the fragment number according to Brunschvicg, with Turnell's number and page in parentheses.) The Turnell translation is quoted except in a very few instances where the context calls for a slightly different wording.

15. For example, the navel or center of the earth at Delphi; cf. Eliade, *The Sacred and the Profane*, pp. 36–47.

16. Cf. David Riesman, *The Lonely Crowd*, abridged ed. with new preface (New Haven: Yale University Press, 1961).

17. Cf. below, Chapter 3, section 1, "Silence and Word."

18. Cf. André Gide, *Nouvelles nourritures terrestres*, 22nd ed. (Paris: Gallimard, 1935), pp. 76–77: "It is in man's brain that the things scattered about the world acquire a name. Sounds, colors, odors exist only in relation to man. The softest dawn, the most tuneful wind-song, the reflection of sky in water, and the trembling of the waves are but meaningless movements of the air, as long as they are not perceived by man, and as long as man's senses have not brought them all into harmony."

19. The whole history of the Desert Fathers (in prolongation of so many biblical episodes) bears witness to this mystery of solitude. The reader can find an anthology of texts in René Draguet, *Les Pères du désert* (Paris: Plon, 1949).

20. Cf. Eliade, *Patterns in Comparative Religion*, pp. 239–264; *The Sacred and the Profane*, pp. 142–143. Cf. Ps. 139:15.

21. Cf. Eliade, *The Sacred and the Profane*, pp. 143–144, and Gen. 3:19.

22. The symbiosis of man and the soil is given striking expression in Alphonse de Chateaubriant's *La Brière* (Paris: Fayard, n.d.), p. 99. Aoustin, the hero, has lost a hand and has cut a wooden hand for himself from the trunk of a dead tree buried for centuries in the earth of Brière, and fitted it to his stump. He then challenges the assembled magistrates: "I defy you to tell me where Brière ends and I begin!" "Such a fusion of the human form with the very substance of their land troubled them deeply."

23. Cf. Aristotle, *Physica IV*, 1, 208b8f.; *De caelo IV*, 3, 310a33. According to the theory, earth and water would naturally move downward, air and fire upward.

88   THE HUMANITY OF MAN

24. André Ombredane, *L'équilibre et l'orientation* in Georges Dumas, ed., *Nouveau traité de psychologie* III: 1 (Paris: Presses Universitaires de France, 1937); Edouard Claparède, *L'orientation lointaine*, *ibid.*, VII: 3 (1943).

25. [The author here and frequently throughout this whole section on orientation is playing on the double sense of the French word *sens*, which means both *direction* and *meaning*. Translator's note.]

26. Cf. Aristotle, *Historia animalium*, I, 15 494a26f., trans. D'Arcy Wentworth Thompson, in W.D. Ross, ed., *The Works of Aristotle* 2 (Oxford: Oxford University Press, 1930): "In man, above all other animals, the terms 'upper' and 'lower' are used in harmony with their natural positions; for in him, upper and lower have the same meaning as when they are applied to the universe as a whole." Cf. *De partibus animalium* II, 10, 656a10-13. On the symbolism of ascent and fall, cf. Champeaux-Sterckx, *Symboles*, pp. 332–333

27. Cf. Eliade, *The Sacred and the Profane*, pp. 141–144. On the standing position, cf. Buytendijk, *Attitudes et mouvements*, pp. 125 ff.

28. Mark 8:24. Unless otherwise noted, translations of the Bible are from *The New American Bible* (New York: Kenedy, 1970).

29. Biblical literature often makes use of this parallelism. Thus, the just man (Ps. 1:3 f; 52:10; 91:13–15), the wicked man (Ps. 37:35), young people (Ps. 128:3; 144:12), and Wisdom (Eccles. 24:12–19 are all described as sturdy trees; cf. also the splendid passages in Ezek. 17:1–10 and 22–24; 31:1–18. The parallelism of human body and temple column also deserves attention. The Jewish psalmist is appreciative of the tall slender shape of the female form sculpted on the corner column (Ps. 144:12). The reader will recall the artistry with which the architect expressed and immortalized the same conception in the Caryatids of the Erechtheum at Athens. On the symbolism of man, cf. Champeau-Sterckx, *Symboles*, pp. 239 ff.; of the tree, pp. 297 ff., 329 ff.

30. To be able to observe animals without frightening them off and to arrange some rather startling "face to face" encounters with them, I must kneel or squat. Cf. Plato, *Timaeus*, 90 a-b: if man enjoys an upright stance, it is because the superior part of the soul, which God has localized in the head and which has an affinity with the heavens, makes man a plant of a heavenly, not an earthly variety. Cf. Basil the Great, *Homilia in illud: "attende tibi ipsi,"* 8 (PG 31:216); Gregory of Nyssa, *De hominis opificio*, 8 (PG 44:144).

31. We could readily quote here numerous significant expressions. Let us mention only the distinctions between upper and lower courts of justice and higher and lower kinds of work; the titles: high and mighty lord, high commissioner; the phrases: summit conference, high society, high authority, higher studies; the raising and lowering of prices, etc. On the symbolism of the ascent, cf. Champeaux-Sterckx, *Symboles*, pp. 161 ff.

32. *Inferni* or *inferna*, usually translated as "hell," are related to *inferus* and *infra* and, strictly speaking, mean "the lower regions."

33. Gen. 3:5. The moral fault beyond all others for the Greeks was *hubris*, or lack of moderation, and consisted for man in trying to be the equal of the immortal gods; the idea is at least partially coextensive with the biblical idea of sin.

34. Cf. Luke 14:28–31.

35. The meanings of high and low and of sitting on a throne are admirably illustrated by Isaiah 14:12–15: "How have you fallen from the heavens, O morning star, son of the dawn! How are you cut down to the ground, you who mowed down the nations! You said in your heart: 'I will scale the heavens; above the stars of God I will set up my throne; I will take my seat on the Mount of Assembly, in the recesses of the North. I will ascend above the tops of the clouds; I will be like the Most High!' Yet down to the nether world you go to the recesses of the pit!"

36. The phenomenon of orientation is as old as man himself, for we are under the evident necessity of determining our position in the universe. But the term itself shows that man takes the east as his basic reference point. The fact raises an anthropological question: Why should man choose the east as primordial reference point? Without claiming to give a definitive answer we may suggest one approach. If man uses the east as a reference point, it is because this cardinal point marks the place where the sun rises and where light, and with it the whole world, is born (*orient* and *origin* are connected, both expressing the idea of "rise out of, be born"). In "orienting" himself a man returns to his origins, to the first morning of the world, in order to renew himself. Orientation amounts to a rejuvenating bath. When I turn to the east I seek to relive symbolically the mystery of the world's origin. Thus I determine my position in space by returning to the beginning, just as I situate myself in time by reference to the beginning of the Christian era or of the hegira, and so forth. (On the return to the world's beginning, which is a widespread cultural constant, cf. Eliade, *Aspects du mythe* [Paris: Gallimard, 1963], p. 110.) The other cardinal points of the compass also draw their meaning from their relation to the sun. The south marks the apogee of a star; consequently, in Chinese culture, to turn to the south is to reign. The west is the place of decline; we speak of the "waning of life." The north, as the only cardinal point through which the sun does not pass, has a neutral or negative anthropological meaning: it is the region of cold and is hostile to man; for a Chinese to turn to the north is, figuratively, to submit. It was the use of the compass, which was widespread in Europe by 1400, that gave the north its primordial importance as a scientific reference point. The resultant rivalry between north and east as reference points illustrates nicely, once again, the difference between the space of lived experience and the space of science.

37. Animals which can move about show the same structure: the bird, the fish, and the land animals have a front and a rear. It is difficult to teach a horse to back up.

38. Cf. Pascal, *Pensées*, Fr. 310 (Turnell, Fr. 918, p. 405): "I, too, shall have my hindsight"; Fr. 336 (Turnell, Fr. 181, p. 153): "We must possess hindsight and judge everything by it, though using the same language as the people."

39. In applying his myth of the cave, Plato assigns education the goal of effecting a complete conversion in which the whole soul of the learner turns away from the world and towards the good (*Republic*, VII, 518c).

40. The hypothesis of a physiological foundation finds some support in the

fact that if persons left-handed from birth are forced to become right-handed, they often develop psychological or motor disturbances such as stuttering.

41. Plato (*Laws*, VII, 794d–795d) objects strongly to social custom, which he regards as sole cause of the inequality of the two hands: "It is due to the folly of nurses and mothers that we have all become limping, so to say, in our hands" (trans. R.G. Bury, 2 vols., Loeb Classical Library [Cambridge: Harvard University Press, 1961–62], Vol. 2, p. 25).

42. The adjective *left-handed* also has two meanings, literal and figurative.

43. The right arm is "the male arm," and the left "the female arm." As a result a man must call his left arm his "female arm" and a woman her right arm her "male arm."

44. Cf. Robert Hertz, "La prééminence de la main droite: Etude sur la polarité religieuse," *Revue philosophique de la France et de l'étranger* 34 (1909) 553–580. On the whole question, cf. Jean Brun, *La main et l'esprit* (Paris: Presses Universitaires de France, 1963), pp. 65–67. The influence of the right-left distinction on language has been studied by M. Jousse, "Le bilateralisme humain et l'anthropologie du langage," *Revue anthropologique* 50 (1940) nn. 4–6 and 7–9; reprinted in his *L'anthropologie du geste* (Paris: Resma, 1969), pp. 193 ff. This latter publication contains studies of great interest on the corporeal bases of language.

45. Pascal, *Pensées*, Fr. 205 (Turnell, Fr. 116, p. 142).

46. Man too, of course, is said to "move from place to place" when his local motion involves no genuine discovery; we also speak, quite accurately, of "moving a business from one location to another."

47. Cf. below, Chapter 5, section 1, "Appropriation."

48. Cf. Jean-Paul Sartre, *Being and Nothingness: An Essay on Phenomenological Ontology*, trans. Hazel E. Barnes (New York: Philosophical Library, 1956), pp. 303–359; cf. p. 326: "the body is perpetually the *surpassed*. The body . . . i.e., that *beyond which* I am in so far as I am immediately present to the glass or the table or the distant tree which I perceive."

49. In suggesting the idea of "primitive space," Eugène Minkowski, in *Vers une cosmologie* (Paris: Aubier, 1936), pp. 69–78, was indicating that lived space is filled with my presence.

50. Matt. 6:21.

51. Cf. Pierre Gallet, *El padre* (Paris: Edition Ouvrières, 1967), p. 80; the author writes from Brazil to his parents who have stayed in France: "I stretch my arms across the ocean and feel that I touch you."

52. Pascal, *Pensées*, Fr. 348.

53. From the immensity of cosmic space man claims a portion that is cut to his measure, reserves it for himself, fashions a shelter in it, and fits it out as he pleases: his dwelling, his "at home." The subject is developed below in Chapter 6.

54. Pascal, *Pensées*, Fr. 212 (Turnell, Fr. 152, p. 148).

55. Sirach 29:21

56. Gabriel Marcel, *Being and Having*, trans. Katharine Farrer (Boston: Beacon, 1951), p. 84.

CHAPTER 2

HUMAN TIME

To be born is to enter time and history. It is, of course, possible to measure even embryonic development in terms of time; and in the embryo we have that primordial genesis which involves man in duration. But in the eyes of society a new human being begins to exist only at birth. Only then is he presented to the world, to others, and to himself; birth is, then, a kind of absolute beginning for the subject and the transition from a time which was not his own to a time which he inaugurates.

I. EXISTENCE AND TEMPORALITY

My Body Places Me in Time

The same body that puts me into space introduces me also into time: "Our soul is tossed into the body where it finds number, time, dimensions."[1] But, though the same word is used for it, my time is not the mathematician's time. The mathematician deals with an abstract time as with an abstract space; human time, however, is concrete. The former is an object of thought alone; the latter is lived. The former is homogeneous; the latter is heterogeneous, and its quality is constantly changing. The one is impersonal, the other highly personalized. What we are concerned with here, then, is not the indeterminate medium of mathematical science but human time or lived duration.

This measure of time which is proper to me, namely, the duration of my life, has an element of uncertainty in it which distinguishes it sharply from my body's place in space. The latter is bounded by my skin, and any variations I may experience in size and weight are, after all, rather limited. The temporal measure of my life is, on the contrary, very uncertain: its anterior end is determined by my birth, but its posterior end, the date of my death, is unknown to me and others. The length of life has, in fact, no limit common to all men and no personal limit which the individual knows in advance. The indefiniteness of my future helps create the illusion that there is no limit.

The measure of my duration is essentially biological, that is, it is my body which determines the limits of my history. I live, act, and exist in the world as long as my organism continues its vital exchanges with the outside world. This unstable balance which, despite hygiene and medicine, is hardly within man's control, is my true measure. My life and my "time" thus have the character of something given, a gift received whose origin and terminus are both wrapped in obscurity.

I also experience my personal duration as a kind of interior, a "within" where I am and which is quite distinct from the time in which I did not yet exist and which unfolded "apart" from me. We will have to inquire into the significance of humanity's past and of the mysterious portion of time which anteceded my existence. Here we can at least note that the measure of time which I occupy and take for myself out of the world's whole history is a kind of dwelling or a field which, like my bodily place, receives its limits from me. I am necessarily in "my time" as I am in "my place"; this particular "temporal space" is mine. I live it from inside; it is, in a certain sense, myself.

If my duration is thus identified with its subject, namely, myself, it also involves a degree of change which I find disconcerting. My time is not a mathematical line along which I advance with an unvarying and undifferentiated motion. My duration, on the contrary, follows a kind of parabolic curve. The years of childhood and youth are marked by incompleteness but also by growth and progress; we speak of youth being "on the way up," a phrase which shows how intermingled the spatial and the temporal are. At the other end of my life is decline and old age; it is the "downward slope of life," and like all my fellow men I avoid looking too closely at its end. Between the two extremes the time of maturity unfolds: my prime—or, more accurately, my flowering; it is in this period that my being and powers are at their fullest. It is important, finally, to note the extent to which my duration is spontaneously identified with my inmost being as a person. My age, along with my name and sex, is one of the major components of my identity. Spatial and temporal measures thus make up my "I" through the mediation of the body and are "incorporated" into my person.

I can equally well say that my duration is the measure of my being or that my duration is itself measured. It may be evaluated in two quite different ways. On the one hand, I live and "am" this duration; I appraise it from within because it is one with my very being. On the other hand, I express my age in impersonal figures determined by the inexorable laws of arithmetic. Lived duration and numbered duration: one and the same life furnishes the basis for both evaluations, and yet I do not straight off regard the two as equivalent. My lived duration seems shorter to me than my numbered duration. I have the same experience when I look at human history and the temporal distance which separates me from a given event; the Emperor Augustus, for example, seems very distant if I think of him as ruling two thousand years ago, but near if I translate that period of time into some ninety generations. For the same reason I have an odd inability to recognize my age, a way of feeling younger than arithmetical calculation would make me. I feel like protesting when faced with the age assigned me in official documents and I ask, at least jokingly, whether a mistake has not been made. All this is a sign that my duration, like the space I occupy or my home or my body itself, has a twofold aspect, subjective and objective. I live my time, but it is the rational faculties of others and my own which measure and think it, and I will always have difficulty in recognizing that my body as I live, experience, and feel it is identical with the body that has such a height, such an age, such a weight, and so forth. Subjectivity and objectivity, both real and inescapable, both coextensive with my whole being, will always search for and flee each other in a game of hide-and-seek which is part of my human condition.

The duration at my disposal often seems more threatened than the space I have. Doubtless there are times when I must inconvenience myself in giving my seat to another on the bus; doubtless, too—and even more—the housing shortage gives rise to a great deal of suffering and numerous protests focusing on living space. But in much more unforeseeable ways, especially in the highly organized life of the cities, my time is at the whim of events and other people. Because time is almost infinitely divisible, my fellow men seem to me always to be preempting a part of mine for their own use. The government takes the years of military service from me. The length of the working day is the subject of endless discussion between employer and employees. One man asks me to lend him "a hand," another knocks at my door, still another calls me to the telephone or writes for a favor. They all want me to give them a part of my time—that is, in the last analysis, a part of my life. The annoying, the importunate, person encroaches on my time, letting his time eat into mine, as it were, just as the intruder on the bus lets his bulk overlap into the place of my body. I say in such cases that someone is making me "lose my time." What does that mean? A third person looking on and evaluating my doings might say that I lose time sometimes by not doing anything, sometimes by doing nothing—that is, doing things he judges worthless. But in my own view I lose time when I have to engage in occupations which I did not choose as worthwhile for me. My time thus derives its whole significance and value from the purposes which I determine or could determine for its use. It is in relation to these goals and to my program of work and leisure, that every unforeseen diversion of my energies seems to me to be inopportune (a "contretemps," "against my time"), and the approach of the other to be untimely. Time is a precious good of which I am so jealous only because we are not dealing here with one possession among others; my time goes beyond the order of having and is deeply involved in the order of my being. What the other asks of me and what I rebel against giving him is a part of my existence. I am torn between the temptation to refuse and the call to be generous.

Temporality and Reality

Insertion into time gives each thing its coefficient of reality. Only that to which objective temporal coordinates can be assigned is real for me.

Imagine a man who says he witnessed a murder or a rescue but confesses that he cannot give even a remote approximation of the date of this event—his deposition will very probably be regarded as worthless and rejected. So it is that what characterizes a mythical narrative is that it refers to a time quite alien to human duration, one from which measurement has vanished and wherein our human points of reference have no bearing. Whether it is conceived as primordial and antecedent to history or, on the contrary, as post-historical, the mythic time in which gods and heroes live out their existence is perfect, immutable, and indestructible; its indefiniteness makes it congenial to all the fantasies of dreamers. Don't the tales which nourish the imagination of children usually begin with the formula "Once upon a time"? These words, by their vagueness, suffice to produce a clean break between the imaginary and the historical, mythic time and real time.[2] Indeed the truth of a myth does not belong to the historical or scientific order but to the existential order: it resides in the imaged and symbolic description of an exemplar, or model, situation, or aspect of the human condition. The myth is the vehicle of a wisdom without temporal or spatial frontiers: a work of art, it suggests a truth by making reality speak, without concerning itself with objective dimensions. Intended to stimulate endless reflection, conceived to make men ponder their own existence indefinitely, the myth is situated in an indefinite space and time. For objectifying science, an event is not real unless it can be localized and dated.

For the human subject this objectification is an inescapable necessity. No doubt to interiorize time is something which belongs to my consciousness: I appropriate time and personalize it exclusively in terms of the movement of my own duration. Nevertheless my own reality is not reducible to that of a transcendental Ego: on the contrary, it includes the basic and inexhaustible ambiguity of conjoined subjectivity and objectivity. It is through its spatial and temporal measurements that my existence becomes a fact, something which is given and gives itself to others. My identification papers carry the date of my birth, when I entered the universal history of mankind and, beyond that, the immensity of cosmic duration. My *curriculum vitae* shows a series of exact dates which give an objectivity to the major moments in my life as a member of society. As my days pass, my gestures, words, actions, and a multiplicity of projects accomplished manifest and detail my historicity. My existence as a man can unfold only in the form of an historical series of major and minor events which all add up to a "time body" analogous to my organic body extended in space.[3] If someone ventures to question the historical factuality of one or other of my actions or words, I feel that my very being is under attack, that I have been maimed; an element of my living reality has been cut away. As an extreme case, suppose that the facts, achievements, and utterances in the life of some personage were one by one called into doubt and denied existence in human time: it would be the person himself who would gradually lose his historical reality, be reduced to a phantom or a name, and finally disappear. Paradoxically time, which is the sign of my existential fragility, is also the measure of my ontological stability.

We must realize, then, that position in time is inseparable from situation in space; every historical fact is localized and dated in a concrete space-time continuum. However, the "where" and the "when" do not lend themselves equally to analysis and expression. As Bergson pointed out, language is forced to express time in terms of space.[4] We speak, for example, of a "point" of time, a "length" of time, and temporal "distance," and the terms "ancestry" and "descendants" transpose the temporal order of generations into the spatial order of "up" and "down." The reason is that extended reality is visible, tangible, and traversable at will; it presents itself to our external senses and motor experience. Time, on the contrary, is accessible only to consciousness or thought as a measure of becoming. By translating time into space I go beyond my subjective experience of time and express its objectivity. We thus come back to our initial observation: fleeting and deceitful though it is, time is the measure of reality.

My Embodied "I," Center of Time for Me and Perspectival Focus

However brief my earthly existence must be, I am situated at a point in time, and this point is necessarily the center of history for me and the gravitational center of all events—past, present, and future. I date events of world importance, like the declaration of a war, as occurring in the year when, for example, I graduated from school! I situate great

HUMAN TIME 97

men of the past like Mohammed and Napoleon in relation to my "today." With an inevitable naïveté I even regard my appearance on the temporal scene as the blessed term towards which all previous history was moving. That I was "born in my own due time" is a richly meaningful statement for me, and not the truism which it seems to be when taken literally. The history of humanity before me was lost in the night of time, but with me a clear day dawned, the day of my consciousness which gives past, present, and future a new meaning. My entrance into time was both a goal and a kind of absolute beginning, like dawn at the end of night.[5]

The subjective need to center history on ourselves can never be totally set aside, even in our spontaneous consciousness and the language which expresses it. Self-love prevents us from struggling too hard against it and rather makes us see in such a need, which in fact shows up our limitations, a factor in our own greatness. Those who tend to be more blinded than others by this illusion are precisely those who play, or think they play, a role in history. A political leader tends to regard his active years as the center of national and international history, as the memoirs he sooner or later publishes demonstrate. Many a writer, especially if he is the leader of a literary school, transposes and applies to himself in his own mind Boileau's famous words, "Finally Malherbes appeared . . . . " It is likewise self-evident that Hegel presents his own system as the fruit and ultimate goal of the whole history of thought.[6] This same conviction finds expression in the work of an Auguste Comte or a Léon Brunschvicg: their systems embodied an immense advance in the history of philosophical thought.[7]

Reason intervenes, however, to modify somewhat the egocentricity of my outlook on time and the allurements of self-love. Important dates and outstanding men furnish mankind and individuals with reference points to control the flow of time and give the present time part of its meaning; here we have "epoch" in its original sense of "fixed point." The Old Testament chronicles situate events in relation to the Exodus or to the current royal reign.[8] Romans went back to the foundation of Rome: *post Urbem conditam, ab Urbe condita* (after the foundation of the City, since the foundation of the City.) The Christian era and the Hegira relate to key events which a whole civilization regards as a kind of absolute beginning. If I adopt the Christian or the Muslim perspective and do it not from social necessity but from a commitment of faith, I give up the idea that I am the center of history and link the insignificant event which I am to an exemplar-event from which my existence receives the best part of its meaning. As I grow in faith, I renounce even more fully my pretensions to historical importance, in order to deepen my sense of dependence on Christ or the Prophet.

In my lived experience, however, I continue to be the center of a temporal horizon within which things, other people, and events take their place. I am necessarily *one of the possible centers of time*, if we may adapt Pascal's image of the sphere of which the center is everywhere and the circumference nowhere. My temporal horizon is, in addition, more or less vast, depending on the extent of my knowledge of history. But I sometimes give in to the illusion of thinking of myself as a fixed point of reference. Thus, after a long absence, I am surprised and saddened to find that things have deteriorated and faces grown old. What is happening is that, to my own advantage, I am transposing to my temporal duration the spatial illusion of geocentrism: I am judging the becoming of beings and things from the vantage point of my own supposed immobility. But in fact the same movement which sweeps others along carries me with them, and I need only to look at myself impartially to realize this. On the other hand, it is admittedly more difficult for me to see that duration surreptitiously modifies my perspective on events and that my viewpoint is constantly shifting. I even deny, without realizing it, my earlier judgments on historical personages, because I am further away not only from them but especially from a past "I." The twofold movement of events in relation to me and of myself in relation to events accounts for the change-ableness of my judgments. On the other hand, this same fact is what accounts for the inexhaustibility of history: the viewpoint of the historian is perpetually changing and constantly discovering new meanings in the events.

"Now" and "Then"

Being involved in time through my body, my "I" is correlative with a unique and personal perspective on contemporary events as well as on history as a whole. Each passing moment is a new view-point on duration and what fills it. Just as I distinguish "here" and "there" in space, so too I must distinguish "now" and "then" in time.

The etymology of the French word for "now" is full of experiential meaning, for my "hand holds" (*main-tenant*) a given object only in the passing moment and is the organ of the actually given, the present, the immediate. Only what happens "as my hand holds it" is fully real and able to be grasped, and nothing seems truer to me than what is happening now. "Now" is therefore my "here" in time, the point of duration in which I exist, which I occupy, and in which I lay hold of and possess my own being in the most real way. Existence is given to me only in the instant, that sharp point of time, that mobile summit, on which life "main-tains" me (holds me in its hand). But the real paradox of the "now" is that it is both inalienable and yet always alienated. It is inalienable because the instant is always mine and I cannot leave it without ceasing to be. It is always alienated because that same instant (from the Latin *in-stare*, to stand in, to urge) contains the sense of both imminence and instability, of unsteadiness, of movement—"moment" (from the Latin *momentum*, movement), a fleeting reality which can be grasped only to slip away at once. The "now" is the portion of time which is nearest to me, even to the point of being identified with my very being, yet which is constantly moving away; its nature is simultaneously not yet to be, to be, and to be no longer.

Thus the instant is not reducible for me to some kind of ideal boundary, of the mathematical type, between past and future. The lived instant is not the instant as thought, and my "now" has breadth and fullness. Bergson has shown that the immediate past survives and the future is anticipated in the present of consciousness, just as, we might add, my environment and the distant spatial horizon are present in my consciousness of my "here."

Beyond the present moment extends the rest of temporal immensity. Apart from the "now" everything is "then," just as apart from the "here" everything is "there." "Then" can be applied both to the past ("formerly") and to the future ("soon," "later on"), and its meaning thus shifts from one pole to the other. But the two opposite poles have in common their contrast to the "now": "then" is the point in time which eludes me, in which I am no longer or not yet; it is time alienated or not yet seized, time foreign and inaccessible, the time of a vanished or a still unborn self. "Now" is near, "then" is distant; "now" is uttermost smallness, "then" is limitless immensity. Yet any point in this great immensity has been or will be "now," owing to the irreversible movement of duration. A particular "then" was or will be the "right moment," the "opportune moment," and in fact there are confluences of circumstances which seem to supply the elements most propitious to the carrying out of my projects. The animist tendency which is unconsciously alive in every man makes me see a providential intention in such conjunctures as fit my desires; I have the impression that things have divined my mind and are holding out a hand to me as they come to meet me. "My hour" is, above all, the moment I have wanted, expected, hoped for, and prepared for when my most cherished plan can finally be brought to fulfillment, whether it is for personal promotion, dedication to a noble cause, or revenge plotted over the years. Everything depends on knowing how to recognize and grasp this unique moment when the future becomes "now."

Just as "here" is narrow and staled by habit, so too "now" imprisons me and often bores me. The rest of time attracts me by its extent and mystery. It sometimes seems to me that in another time or another age I would be more myself and would show what is really in me. But any real journey in time, except the one I am now making towards my still unmastered future, is radically impossible, and I can do nothing to make it a reality. In addition, I always carry with me my "now" and all its narrowness and banality. On the other hand, a real journey creates the illusion that I am going not only away from here but into the future ahead of time; I flee from the inescapable daily "now" and rush towards the "not yet" in order to summon it into being. At a deeper level, my thoughts, desires, and actions of all sorts are plans rather than existent realities; I live ahead of myself, beyond the "here and now," and my "project" is identified with my very being.[9]

Temporal Distance

"Now" and "then" are thus separated by temporal distance, and I am able to transcend that distance.

We noted earlier that I have the power to divide myself mentally into two selves and to transfer myself intentionally into the space where another person is and from which I can look at myself "coming." In like fashion, I "go" and "come" in time. We have an instance of this in the epistolary past tense used by the Romans. The letter writer put himself, in his mind, at the moment when his correspondent would receive his letter, and therefore he expressed as past the actions and states of mind which were his as he wrote the letter. *"Nihil habebam quod scriberem*: I had nothing to write about." The writer abandoned the "now" of his actual writing and put himself into the more or less distant moment when the other would be reading his letter. This "then," which will be the other person's "now," becomes his own "now," and from this new vantage point he looks back at himself writing. Such crossing back and forth shows the transcendence of the mind over time.

I have the same experience with regard to historical distance. From today an infinity of lines radiate out to the unassignable boundaries of the universe's duration, and on these lines events, persons, and things have their place—that is, their date. This temporal distance, like spatial distance, separates me from a given historical fact but also links me to it. Time "elapses" in the etymological sense of the word (it slips away), for duration seems to me to have "slid" off into a bottomless abyss. But there is also a connection, a continuous line, especially if, as we mentioned earlier, we express this duration in terms of generations; for the lives of men, all proceeding as they do from other men, overlap and intermingle to form a living tissue of which my own life is a part. Through my ancestors, known and unknown, I am connected without any break to the reality of history.

Subjective Duration and Measurement of Time

As Alexis Carrel has shown, our chronological age, which is measured by the calendar and ultimately by the course of the stars, must be distinguished from our real age. The latter is determined by our body, the condition of our tissues, and the rate of aging, and is perhaps calculable by the time it takes each person to form scar tissue.[10]

The average duration of a human life furnishes me with one current unit of measurement. I apply this criterion to others and claim to reach an evaluation which has some objectivity. But subjectivity is in fact never entirely eliminated. If I look more closely, I find that I am estimating the longevity of others in terms of my own "life expectancy." The same holds for the value I put on the age of my fellow men. I take stock of a child not only from the height of my adult stature but also from the higher altitude of my greater age. Children take the same attitude to one another, and the five-year-old thinks of himself as "bigger" (in age as well as size) than younger children.[11] Parents, whatever their age, are regarded as elderly, and if I were ninety myself, I would think myself young as compared with a centenarian. Someone "older than I" will always be around to make me feel young and to give me assurance. Consciousness of my age thus gives me a feeling sometimes of superiority, sometimes of inferiority, in regard to others. In strength I am inferior to my younger brother but superior to my elder; but in terms of respectablility and the rights it brings, the relations are precisely reversed. I try, therefore, to make myself older or younger depending on the situation, just as I try to acquire a portlier or a slenderer figure. The categories of "young" and "old" which I am constantly using are relative to my awareness, at the moment, of my personal age.

The empirical measurements which traditional societies apply to time and age are especially rich in significance. A man is, for example, as old as that tree over there. In one Madagascan tribe a child's age is measured by the periodic fairs held in the area: a child is "two fairs," "three fairs," and so on. But even I myself often abandon the scientific reference points supplied by calendar or clock and adopt an- thropocentric measurements. I measure duration by reference, for example, to familiar actions or physiological functions: the time it takes me to dress or to smoke a cigarette; for a very short period of time, I may say "in the twinkling of an eye."

When science proposes time units which are outside my experi- ence, I can doubtless make intellectual use of these notions with ease and accuracy, but I cannot fill them with any concrete content. Thus the solar year has meaning and real significance for me, because it is on the human scale. Geological eras, on the contrary—or, at the opposite extreme, the micro-second—awaken no vital echo in me at all, and, in fact, I find such huge or minuscule measurements rather dizzying. The abyss of the infinitely small and the abyss of the infinitely large both have power to swallow me up.

Within my own personal duration, as Marcel Proust has brought home to us, the passage of time is disconcertingly flexible. An hour or a day can pass in a flash, and a minute can seem like a hundred years. Some temperaments are much influenced, in this respect, by changes in the weather. Persistent rain or snow will make the hours drag, but so will a blazing sun and an overwhelming apathy. Time (*temps*) thus passes more or less quickly according to the weather (*temps*). Yet it is not strange that time and weather should be homonyms (in French), for the weather lends a certain appearance and meaning to the time that is passing with the weather and is indeed identified with it.

When I must reach an important decision by a given date, the day sometimes seems infinitely distant, and sometimes the distance vanishes and the day seems on top of me: "soon," "the time is coming," "here we are," "now"! In daily life such variations in the feeling for time depend in part on my coenesthetic state. Excitants accelerate subjective time by stimulating the nervous tonus and the digestive and circulatory systems. Euphoria lightens the burden of duration because it arouses a sense of ease and productive activity. Fatigue, on the contrary, and the use of certain narcotics relax the tonus and slow the speed of life. The same observations may be made of psychological factors: interest hastens the flow of time or even suspends the awareness of its flight; anxiety, expectation, boredom, stretch the hours out, empty and drain them. A wearying occupation always seems long whatever its objective duration. The idle prisoner or the sick man kept to his bed lives out a time that is beyond all measurement.

The case of *duration in a sick person* is very significant in this context and deserves special attention. When I am ill, my duration is wholly determined by the physiological processes involved in the development of the sickness. My will is powerless to speed up the course of events. Other people try to make me hold out by telling me: "It takes time." Every personal project is excluded from this very special, gloomy kind of temporality. When pain does not torment me, my weakness and physical apathy empty this duration of all content and character and rob it of any assignable limits; the time of former, and eventual future, health is forgotten or seems implausible; there are times when I seem to have been living forever in this wearying, shapeless, and empty duration.

Time as experienced by the ill person is completely broken off from the time of "other people," that is, the healthy. This sense of not fitting in is surely the factor that most radically separates the world of healthy men from the world of the sick. "They" come and go, play and work, have their leisure, their interests, and their business. But I exist in a tasteless, monotonous, empty "now." If neighbors and friends visit me, I see them filled with their plans, their present or future obligations, and the countless purposes which lend meaning to their duration. If they try to get inside time as I experience it, they are unsuccessful, as I am when I try to get inside their time. Standing near my bed or lounge-chair, they set their full duration alongside my obstinately empty duration. However great our friendship or love for one another, there is an irreducible lack of understanding owing to the change in our respective sense of time.

My break with objective time is no less marked. The unchanging temporal reference points provided by meals, the striking clock, or morning and evening, seem desperately far apart and lose their ability to orientate me. The sick man's time is a kind of desert in which landmarks sometimes vanish, sometimes loom up illusorily like cruel mirages. Duration in this case tends to resemble the undifferentiated, isotropic, homogeneous, and inhuman time of mathematics. In addition, diurnal duration must be distinguished from nocturnal. My suffering during the day comes from having nothing to look forward to; duration is then completely slack, and I can assign no meaning to it; it has no goal worthy of interest. There is only one goal in sight, and I reject that with a sense of horror: the night. But the night inescapably comes; I sense its approach and would like to avoid it; but I could do so only by immobilizing myself in the emptiness, grown greater by that very fact, of an endless day. My suffering during the night comes from waiting with anguished impotence for the coming of the day; from having no longer even the landmarks provided by the actions of the healthy, estranged though I have become from them; from counting and anticipating the striking of the hours as they translate not so much the lapse of time as its refusal to elapse; from feeling the extreme weakness of my vital powers under their shroud of darkness and doubting the possibility of their victory. Then at last day returns, only to restore me to the apathy of a duration without substance or shape.

Thus, whether ill or well, I journey in a time which is subject to two incommensurable gauges, and their interplay now amuses me, now fills me with bewilderment. The constant use of a timepiece illustrates the point. I keep it in my vest pocket or wear it on my wrist, but in either case I fasten the mechanism, with its capacity for accurate measurement, to my body: it is there to bear witness to objective time, so that I may confront my subjective experience of duration with its relentless rhythm. At death this personal duration ends and time escapes from me; my watch continues to run, an impassive witness to time and cosmic indifference. But we do not put the dead man's watch back on his wrist, for the life it once measured has stolen away. Instead, we remove the instrument—keep it as a memento or appropriate it to serve as the measure of some other existence. Thereupon a new temporal relation begins between the survivors and the deceased. The man who has died is outside the time common to mankind: he "endures" no longer, and the rhythms of day and night are as indifferent to him as are those of work and eating and leisure. In relation to him, temporality has only an objective value now: time only measures the slow disappearance of the body which has now become an object, erases the material support of a presence. Henceforth the deceased is the absent one par excellence, denied any encounter with others in the moments of time. Yet the bond of personal relationships is so strong that the survivors persist, despite all appearances, to attribute to the dead man a subjective duration whose mystery at once fascinates and terrifies them.[12]

The contrast between subjective and objective duration could provide endless material for analysis. When, for example, I am eager to carry out a plan, I grow impatient at the restraint imposed by the clock and by the many factors which condition my activity. Here we find the explanation of the odd expression to "gain" or to "lose" time. I lose time if the march of objective time is allowed to overtake the execution of my plans; I gain time if my undertaking is accomplished sooner than the nature of things would have let me expect. We find the same fundamental distinction at work in the difference of meaning between "the day" and "my day." The day is an objective measurement, my day is a lived duration. The former is an impersonal container, the latter a content which is peculiarly mine. The former is unchanging, the latter has a variable fullness.[13]

Above all, however, my day has a very important symbolic value, for it condenses and sums up my whole life. Dawn is the daily renewed birth of the world for me and of myself for the world. The morning is youth, midday maturity. Soon comes the decline, and evening is my old age and the world's; night is our common death. Our language can speak, then, of the morning and evening of life. My day thus permits me to live symbolically, in a concentrated way, what I live out empirically over the course of many decades. Other measures of time such as the week, the month, and the year render me an analogous service, each in its own way. I contract my whole duration therefore into the vitally experienced present, and today makes me "present," even if I am not very explicitly aware of the fact, to the sum of my days. Each day contains all the others; each day reenacts for me the mystery of my birth, which I once experienced in unconsciousness, and the mystery of my end which may also, in its empirical moment, escape my awareness. It is up to me freely to impose a meaning on this unique life, which is both long and short, and which each morning is put wholly into my hands.

Here we see why men allot time each day for the values they think most necessary: work, rest, sleep, leisure, family life, charitable activity, prayer, and so forth. If I decide to learn Russian or acquire a better physique, I make room in my daily time-table for fifteen minutes of study or of exercise. Tell me your daily schedule and I'll tell you what is important to you. Some occupations, of course, take place in relation to larger temporal units: the week, the month, or the year. But here again, periodic repetition of activities gives symbolic expression to a hierarchy of values.

My Embodied "I" Modifies Time

My bodily duration, we noted above, involves me in the history of mankind and the world. It does more than that, however, for it also enables me to discover the reality of this vast history. The child, as we know, regards the past as nonexistent. The history lessons he has to do in school are to him a kind of abstract mythology which does not touch him and which he cannot make real. The reason is that, being without a personal past, the child cannot conceive of humanity's past. He cannot yet practice temporal retrospection. The child's world, after all, began with himself, and inevitably so. Consequently, until adolescence the human subject thinks of himself as having marked an absolute beginning; he inevitably thinks "With me creation began," just as the old man is tempted to say, "After me the deluge." But as the years slip away and he builds up a personal past, the adolescent comes to see the possibility and reality of a time in which he did not exist. In other words, the experience of a personal past opens up the historical retrospective. My bodily duration, indeed my body itself, is the unperceived prism through which the world's duration manifests itself to me.

If I look back to the past of the universe (five thousand million years, some say), I distinguish two sections whose length is uncertain but whose quality is very different. The dividing line is the appearance of man. Before that point the world's duration seems to me to be "dead" time, undifferentiated and devoid of meaning. In that prehuman cosmos our solar system and our planet were formed and the lower kinds of life began to appear. At times the elements released violent energies, at times they were calm. But these were all raw facts, not yet events, for there was no human eye, no human consciousness to observe, suffer, or enjoy; there was no human destiny to be decided by the avalanche or the lightning, no life to be sustained by the sun's warmth or the murmuring brook. A world of unconscious things is the theater for facts that have no lived meaning. Thus such purely cosmic and elemental duration adds up to an empty time, a kind of *temporal desert* analogous to the spatial deserts of the Sahara or the polar caps. And I feel the same difficulty in conceiving this kind of solitude as I do the spatial deserts—the same difficulty in answering the question "What was the world like *when* there was no human being?" As in saying what this same world is like *where* man is absent, or what my home is like when I am not there. I know the prehuman duration of the world only as something unknown; I project myself in thought into that *tempus incognitum* as I do into *terra incognita*, only to exclude myself from it at once. The meaning of that time is that *then* it had no meaning for anyone.

By way of contrast, once consciousness has awakened by imperceptible degrees until finally the phenomenon of man has appeared, the duration of the world is immediately transformed and illumined. The dawn of consciousness puts an end to the night of time. The clash of blind natural elements ceases to constitute a series of raw facts. As we shall later on insist, as soon as the fate of man becomes involved, the play of the multiplicity of determinisms becomes a tissue of events, auspicious or inauspicious. Far more, then, are the numerous encounters of personal subjects fraught with meaning. Each event, great or small, is both an end and a beginning: it terminates an earlier system of relations with the world and other men and initiates a new balance; it brings a situation to a head or resolves it and marks the preceding duration with the sign of the past, the completed, the "no longer," and subsequent duration with the sign of the new, the future, the "henceforth." The destinies of free persons, whether they are supported or threatened by determinisms, nevertheless decide their own course and issue from within themselves. In short, prehistory, protohistory, and history together make up what might be called the *time of events* or *meaning, lived-in time*, the time of man.

The indissoluble union, or marriage, of man and time has experienced constant ups-and-downs in the course of history. The great ages are those rich in humanism, the ones in which man, as man, has reached some peak. Inversely, the steps backward in the march of human progress mark the ages of "transition" or "low" periods (here, as always, spatial language lends its support to the expression of temporality), when time, as it were, remains in a state of expectancy, waiting upon man, to rise with him to some new summit. In my own unimportant personal destiny it is possible to recognize the same law: the great dates of my life are those on which I was decisively involved. My "best years" are marked primarily by the intensity of my personal life. The days, months, and years which the calendar lists as equal and identical are not at all interchangeable for me. My days follow upon one another, but they are not alike; I give each a special quality and meaning.

The quality and meaning I give to time are so essential that a simple "pastime" often strikes me as anomalous, a kind of parenthesis, a lacuna, a gap between two periods of plenitude. Because of physical or psychic fatigue or adverse external circumstances I may be unable to confer a personal meaning on some particular portion of my time. Then I try to "kill time," to take up some trivial occupation, pleasant if possible but always rather "meaningless," a sort of makeshift to avoid total boredom. But if even this trivial pastime does not arouse my interest, then I get *bored*. The specific element in boredom is disgust with a duration on which I can impose no meaning.

The new meaning which time receives from man is to be understood, when all is said and done, as orientated movement. It is from its distant terminus, its mouth, that a river mysteriously derives its direction as soon as it springs out of the ground. It is also from its end that every human activity derives its meaning. We cannot reflect too much on this determination of the present by the future, of what exists here and now by what is yet to come, of the actual by the eventual. Are we really speaking here of the causality of nothingness and a nonexistent causality, as the opponents of finality claim? Or are we not rather dealing, despite appearances, with something that is invisibly and impalpably but very effectively present: my thought and volition and the plans which give anticipated reality to the end-result I seek? We must stress the fact that the goal I aim to reach really exists in my mind, which conquers temporal distance. Thanks to the reality which it has in my mind and will, the goal effectively determines my action and gives it its meaning. Though it is the last thing to appear in the order of execution, the goal is first in the order of intention and causality.[14] Far from being pure nothingness, then, the end is the most determinative and active element in my present consciousness.

If I inquire, then, into the ultimate origins of this meaning of "my times," I must place them in the purposes which I freely adopt and, deeper still, in my very being itself. Is freedom anything but the power to be the man I want to be by setting up the ultimate goal which gives direction to my whole existence? "Such as a man is, such does the end seem to him."[15]

The passage of human time is thus not simply the flow of a psychic duration; it is also movement towards a mysterious term, ceaselessly sought, specified, and debated by our successive choices. My history and mankind's seem to me to be an irreversible journey, set in motion and directed by a nameless magnetic pole. This is what gives time and history their inexhaustible character as we reflect on them. It is, of course, not evident that human time is moving towards a fullness of transcendent meaning. But the hypothesis that the human adventure is purposeless (whether its movement be linear or cyclical) is just as ungrounded and, in addition, dizzies the mind until it is tempted to absurdism. Moreover, the philosophy of history will never succeed in resolving the problem of time, for reflection is carried on within the context of the problem itself, and thought cannot totally rise above the primordial conditions of its own activity. To use the favorite distinction of Gabriel Marcel: we are not dealing here with a "problem" which can be fully objectivized and conceptually expressed; man is the being who lifts time to the level of "mystery."

If man thus gives duration an exhaustible meaning, he in turn unwittingly receives from it a good measure of his own meaning. The characteristics of my own age largely make me the man I am. The state of civilization, of culture, of the contemporary mind, colors my judgments, decisions, and ways of feeling, reacting and, ultimately, of existing. Had I been born at another moment in history, I would not be the man I now am in every respect—or rather, though it is easy enough to formulate the hypothesis, it is impossible to work it out. Consequently my insertion in time is no less deep nor less significant than my rootedness in space. "My time" is a kind of soil whose vital energies nourish me: when it is harsh, it makes me rugged; when it is readily yielding, I am in danger of becoming soft. It would be hard to recognize the Roman of the ancient empire in the Roman of the Byzantine Empire.

Representative men, therefore, are those in whom an age sees its own most specific traits brought together and magnified; those who have made their own the desires, needs, aspirations, judgments, and ideals of their contemporaries, fused them in the crucible of a powerful personality, and given them a highly personal expression. How mysterious this interaction of fidelity to one's time and fidelity to oneself! The conformist disappears into the impersonality of "they" and the nonconformist is alienated from himself in pretending to a pseudo-originality, but the representative man fulfills his own personality by embodying his age. This is why history gives a century or an era the name of the man who has dominated it. We must note, however, that some of these men, through major undertakings, have redrawn the face of their times, while others have been only signs or symbols of their age. Men of the former type gave their name to the Age of Pericles, of Augustus, or of Louis XIV; a person of the latter type gave her name to the Age of Victoria. Among historians the discussion is admittedly not closed: Saint-Simon was bent on playing down the influence of the Sun-King on his age while Gaxotte feels justified in writing of "the century of Louis XV."[16]

The Event

The preceding observations make it possible for us to get a bit closer to the complex reality we call an *event*. We have already made the point that an event exists only through and for a consciousness and a personal destiny. It is reserved to man to elevate a "raw occurrence" to the new dignity of meaning. Alone among all the beings in nature, I am the one whose coming brings events and history into existence.

An event is the basic unit whose constant multiplication constitutes history. It is the essence of the event that it multiplies and forms a series in which each term develops out of the preceding and is pregnant with the following. The Second World War carried within itself the postwar period, even as it itself emerged from the period between the wars and the agony of 1914–1918 and thus contained, from one event to another, the whole of previous history. In every event the whole of human duration, however far it stretches into past and future, is in some sense concentrated, gathered up, and woven into unity; antecedents and consequents are summed up and, as it were, fused together. In the pregnant moment, past and future join and become one. Duration seems to suppress its own flow in an attempt at "involution" which gives the present an extraordinary fullness of content. But then this great tension is relaxed once more and, in an opposite movement of "evolution," duration is in motion again, deploying the virtualities of the preceding event and manifesting the consequences that yesterday were hidden within it. Then, at another point of time, duration is once again concentrated and gathers, unifies, and gives new depth of meaning to isolated, scattered significances. Through such an uninterrupted concatenation of great and small events, the flow of duration avoids dilution into meaninglessness: it abides and is enriched as mankind itself is continued and renewed in successive generations.

Every event is thus terminus and starting-point, fulfillment and relative creation. It gives meaning to the part of duration that preceded it and to the part that follows it. One face of the event is turned to the future which it obscurely "prefigures," heralds, and promises, and to which it gives even now a kind of inchoative and germinal reality. Whether the men most involved realize it or not, the event determines the direction of the future or at least sketches the main lines of its thrust. At the same time, however, the event which was yesterday predicted or foreboded has come at last, and the present event thus sheds retrospective light on the interim, that portion of duration which links this event with its antecedents. The face of the new event which looks back to the past illumines earlier events, and in a kind of revelation manifests their hidden meaning. Thus events are correlative to one another all along the course of history; the knowledge of their interactions, their harmonies, and their respective and interrelated meanings constitutes the intelligibility of history.

This specific kind of intelligibility is often baffling to the mind. The reason is that an event is a tight and tangled knot of the most diverse determinisms, on the one hand, and men's free initiatives, on the other. Physical phenomena, spontaneous biological, psychic, and social activities, and highly deliberate intentions all converge, mingle, and are locked in an inextricably confused struggle. Think, for example, of an outsized event like the Second World War: the mind reels before the infinite complexity of all the factors to be considered and must admit itself incapable of measuring their various causalities accurately. The intervention of freedom is what gives an event its depth and history its obscurity. We will never have a final answer to the question of how far man is subjected to history and how far he shapes history. The reason is that human freedom is not the free will described by some seventeenth-century thinkers: a disincarnate power detached from the body, the world, and the countless determinisms that operate in both. On the contrary, human freedom is "situated," that is, it is rooted in the physical world, and bound up with a body and a psyche which are ruled by constant laws. Were it not so rooted and supported, freedom would have no grip on reality and would be condemned to radical impotence.[17]

Composed as it is of a collection of external factors and a complex of subjective intentions, an event has a body and a soul, a matter and a form; it has constituent factors and a meaning. An event thus reflects man's own image; the ontological structure of one corresponds to the ontological structure of the other. Bultmann tends to reduce historical objectivity for the sake of subjective meaning; structuralism, on the contrary, makes structure primary, to the detriment of intention (as though a structure could derive its internal shape from anything but its meaning); we maintain that an event is both body and soul, structure and meaning, constituent factors and intention. Misunderstanding of the event always proceeds from a misunderstanding of man. If man gives rise to events, he does so, in the last analysis, in order to come to grips with himself, to confront himself through the many determinisms which work upon him from within no less than from without. The subject is thus manifested to himself in events; he recognizes himself in them, discovers himself, and takes his own measure. It is in this sense that man is called to fulfill himself through history.[18]

II. ORIENTATIONAL STRUCTURES

My Embodied "I" Is Orientated in Time

The universe about me gives evidence of a considerable age which scientists attempt to evaluate. I see things crumble away, living beings come into the world and die. The unfailing alternation of days and nights, months, seasons, and years gives my body its own rhythm and awakens my awareness of living in an ordered world. I feel that I am journeying from a starting-point, my birth, towards a terminus, my death. My personal duration thus has a definite orientation; it even involves several directions which it is important for us to determine.

As soon as I enter life, I establish a perspective on time; I am the center of "time for me." Thereby I introduce into time, as I do into space, several divisions or dimensions and give each of them a meaning. If the mathematician's time and space are empty and homogenous, my human duration is concrete and filled with meanings which I am constantly living out. Because I am present within it, time is divided, broken up into several zones, and ordered around several pairs of opposite poles. I exist in the moving instant, but I conceive of eternity and, in a sense, take my place within it. Behind my present moment, the past stretches out and flows away. In front of me, what is to come opens out as a limitless field into which day by day I advance. In the present moment, finally, there are several reference points by which I can define my position. These, then, are the cardinal points of my temporal sphere. It is in relation to me that this threefold division exists and from me that it receives its meaning; for I project upon the universe structures of which my being is the source. My embodied existence is the privileged point at which time is divided and becomes lived duration. But if I divide the universe, I am also constantly restoring it to unity. Through my being passes the vertical axis linking the instant to eternity; in me past and future meet; and the events which are the reference points of the present moment look towards me, as it were, and converge upon me. I am thus the point which both divides duration and guarantees its continuity; in me time is constantly being divided and gathered up again, differentiated and recombined. I effect, in my very being, the analysis and synthesis of the temporal universe as I do of the spatial universe.

The divisions I introduce into duration have a well-grounded objectivity. Past, present, and future cannot be confused; common sense shows it is well aware of this when it says: "You cannot be and no longer be." Each of the divisions, moreover, has its own specific internal homogeneity. The grammatical rule of the agreement of tenses illustrates this fact in the area of language: if the verb of the main clause is in the past tense, the verb of the subordinate clause should also be. Furthermore, my duration, though it is my own, is not without objective, external reference points; that is to say, the events by which I orientate myself in the context of reality have their own historical density.

In another respect, however, my subjective duration tends to set up a kind of osmosis between the sectors of time. The continuity of my "I" means that I retain in my present the immediate past and attract to it, in a constant movement of anticipation, the proximate future. Here again we find the twofold aspect, objective and subjective, of my relation to the world.

Instant and Eternity

In whatever point of the universe I happen to be, the vertical axis which passes through me connects the center of the earth with the zenith. My position in time involves an analogous structure: the one that separates and reunites within me the temporal and the eternal.

Existence is given to me only in time, time only in the present, and the present only in the instant. It is almost a tautology to speak of the "present instant," for my present is so vivid only because it is instantaneous. In this present, however, unsteady though it is, I find my steadfastness in being and living. My present is the "place" of existence and the real, of "holding in my hand" (*maintenant*—now), of what is effectively given and received, of the "distance-less" and immediate. Consequently I give the name "presence" to the act by which I encounter another, for only in the "present" can we give ourselves to each other without any intervening distance. In short, it is in the instant that time is given to me, and there that my existence has its foundation; the "now," like the "here," is the point upon which I stand, and stand tall, as a human being. My position in time is not totally defined, however, by the inferior pole of the instant. I know that my balance in time is precarious and my present fleeting. I know that the instant is constantly undermining, restoring, and undermining again my threatened stability within the moving duration of the world. Such an awareness of the passing moment and of the moving as moving implies a reference to a fixed point that is not subject to becoming. I must take my place in an invisible observation tower if I am to be able to pass judgment on the flow of things. Anxiety at the inevitable flight of time, an anxiety which is specific to me as a man, is possible only because I situate myself at the other pole, at a nameless height from which I can become aware of the flow of time. Still more simply put, the very fact that "I" can conjugate a verb in the past, present, and future tenses shows clearly that while I am rooted in the temporal I no less certainly rise above it. A fine point of my being culminates in a supreme and immovable pole. My awareness of time is also an awareness of eternity. I am situated within the instant but not a prisoner of its movement; I am involved in the unstable present but not swallowed up by it. At each point in duration which advances me along the horizontal line, I continue to stand vertically, by virtue of my upright posture, and to keep my head raised to the zenith. I am drawn towards two poles whose opposition causes tension and even suffering, but I am also ceaselessly reconciling them in my own person and uniting them to one another in the undivided act of my own consciousness. The instant thus manifests itself to me as the mobile point through which the eternal enters, is inscribed, actualized, on the moving register of duration.[19]

It seems, furthermore, that at certain privileged moments the instant stops and is absorbed in the eternal. Consider, to begin with, the case of *mystical ecstasy*. According to the great spiritual masters, there are certain states of soul in which an absolute truth, beauty, and love manifests and gives itself to man. What had been until then only intermittently glimpsed now shows itself and gives itself to be tasted in a motionless present which, in itself, could last forever. Augustine's account of his vision at Ostia[20] or the revelations of Teresa of Avila and so many others, all tell us that in ecstasy time seems suspended or, rather, absorbed into eternity. The reason is that the absolute is immutable and communicates its changeless stability to the gaze which apprehends it and to the act of contemplation. Only the needs of the flesh soon force the spirit to descend again to the lower pole of its existence: to the temporal, in which the instant ceaselessly comes into being and disappears.

Consider, too, the *tragic instant*, which is something quite different from the drama in its ordinary course of critical moments of crisis and denouement. Drama is (in the Greek derivation of the word) "something done." In an action filled with special complexity, the balance of relations established between the persons of the play is compromised and breaks down; the denouement occurs in the establishment of a new set of relations. Thus, like every event, drama is enacted on the horizontal plane of duration; the arc it describes is wholly within history. But the tragic instant, by contrast, breaks through the limits of time and involves the intervention of the transcendent—whether blind fate, a man-made divinity, or the personal God of theism. Thus Oedipus's destiny, viewed from without, would be only a sequence of "various facts" of a particularly painful sort; but seen from within, for what it really is, it is contingent upon the hostile will of the immortal gods. Precisely because of this, duration seems to freeze. Perceiving the intervention of the gods, the tragic hero in a sense breaks through the limits of space and time. His heart seems to stand still, while his look is fixed on a debate which transcends the world of becoming and engages the absolute. The mobile instant is arrested and absorbed into eternity. This is the tragic ecstasy. For the instant is the only unit of temporality in which the tragic can manifest itself; outside the instant, the tragic would be diluted into duration. The real purpose of the classical law of the three unities (of place, action, and time) was to allow the instant to receive its maximal existential density.[21]

In two opposite experiences—the tragic and the beatifying—it suffices that the tension between eternity and time should reach the breaking-point for the indissoluble bond between the two extremes to be manifested.[22]

Future and Past

The division between future and past which I introduce into objective time corresponds to the spatial distinction between before and behind and manifests the same ambiguity.

However old I am, the future is in front of me, as the portion of time towards which my existential project is directed. I look towards the future as I look towards the spatial horizon. Just as every visible object is outlined against the horizon where heaven and earth meet, so every activity, every achievement, however modest, emerges out of the future.

The future (French *avenir*, to come) is the portion of time which seems to come towards me; I spontaneously attribute movement to it. But in fact is it really the horizon of time that moves? Is it not rather I who move? Despite the frequent imprecision of our language here, it is not the retirement age that reaches me and causes my professional death; it is rather I who reach it willy nilly. The movement is in me and carries me inexorably towards the future which it devours in each dying and reborn instant.

The future is thus also the field of my freedom. Hemmed in by the narrow limits of the present, my free will turns to the future and defines the future by that very movement: the future is the portion of time which I still have at my disposal—"The future, the future, the future is mine."[23] Everything that I can and want to do, experience, and discover, I spontaneously project "in front" of the instant. If I have a good chance of succeeding, people will say I have a future. It is in the future that I shape a happiness to my own liking, build my "castles in Spain," imagine a success proportioned to my ambition, and engage in all the activities which would finally bring me total fulfillment. There, too, is where I locate the opportunities for revenge: "He who laughs last laughs best." Welcoming, available, and stretching out endlessly, the future accepts all that I entrust to it and gives possibility, probability, even certainty to my least desire and most outrageous dream. In short, the future and my freedom are coextensive; their limitlessness is reciprocal, and they call for, answer to, and measure each other. More precisely, the limitless immensity of my free will creates a future that suits it, tends to forget the uncertain limit which death establishes, and pushes back its own horizons so far that the temporal and the eternal fuse in a kind of twilight zone.

But this future, however intoxicating in its limitlessness, is also fraught with uncertainty. My future is the most exposed part of my life, like the front of my body, whereas the past is no more and the present is known to me. However far ahead I look, however carefully I search the recesses of the time to come, countless unforeseeable risks are hidden from me in this silent darkness. A multiplicity of determinisms are weaving an unbreakable network which poses a challenge to my thinking and my freedom. Thus I am left undecided in face of the future's ambiguity, torn between the intoxicating idea of so many possible victories and the anxiety of threatening misfortune. The future attracts and repels me, summons me and rejects me; for it shows me two faces, and my freedom constantly hesitates between them. Is the truth of the future a promise or a threat to me?

It is far from true, of course, that these two faces of the future are always seen with equal clarity. But it is I, often unknown to myself, who determine which face the future will turn towards me. Temperament, character, and the mood of the moment are surely some factors behind the variation. But age is the greatest determining factor, not chronological age but psychological age, for this is the true measure of my harmony with existence.

Youth has no past; it is nothing but a project and lives wholly ahead of itself; its present is hardly more than an anticipation of a future sometimes dreamt of, sometimes prepared for. Since the adolescent has usually not been tested by experience (since he has little or none of it), he extends unlimited credit to life, that is, to the future; his imprudences arise from ignorance and a kind of wild trust. The proof of this is youth's thirst for *adventure*, that particular form of the future (of what is coming: *ad-venire*) in which the unforeseeable prevails over all carefully laid plans. Confronted with such an undertaking, a man hardly knows in which direction to set out; the greater part of the risk to be run is still unknown. This ambiguity is precisely what entrances the young in heart; darkness fascinates him and he trusts the obscure.

Or rather, the future returns to one who trusts in it his own look, with its freshness, certainty, and limitless hope.

In the measure that age weighs a man down with a past in which failure has tempered success, a sort of contamination sets in between the two parts of his duration.[24] The future thus begins to look different in the light of past experience; it appears less promising and shows itself capable of treachery; it becomes a partner who is not wholly to be trusted. Finally, to a man tormented in body and spirit by trials and weakened by age, the future often inspires only distrust or apprehension for himself and others. Yet we find elderly people who are astonishingly open to the future and able to look forward to it without fear. And isn't a man's real age the age of his spirit, not of his body? The children and grandchildren clustered around the grandparents are really the future in promise or even the future already here, already given. Doesn't each of them imprint his fresh young face on a future which without them would be only a disturbing shadow? And beyond our shrunken temporal future, do not certain immutable values, at least as a possibility, open to the gaze of the soul a future which is mysterious and limitless? Thus the future, like a mirror, reflects the face which our energy, courage, and faith have first imaged in it.

Whatever position he adopts with regard to the question of survival after death, a man always seeks to master his future. Assuredly the most obvious means, indeed the primordial organ, of this conquest is the hand. Along with my words, my manual gestures demonstrate my purpose—prefigure, prophesy, the work which is to come into being. Especially by its labor my hand prepares for tomorrow, begins it in today; for it is in the effort of the passing moment—the moment now in hand—that the world still to come receives its shape and direction. The future is thus a field always open to the prevenient efforts embodied in my actions. Such an outlook presupposes, of course, that human time is conceived as fruitful and large with a future still to be born. Admittedly "time is money" can become the maxim of a faith in progress pushed to the extreme consequences of gross materialism. But at the other extreme, every faith, every mentality, which regards time—whether cyclical or linear—as sterile and without value leaves the material forces to their chaos, the hand to its inertia, and man to his primitive destitution. It would be interesting, from this point of view, to study the influence of the main concepts of time—Hindu, Hellenic, Judeo-Christian—on economic and social development and underdevelopment.

There is another way of overcoming apprehension about the future: by trying to wrest its secrets from it. This is what all forms of *divination* attempt to do, from spiritualism, card-reading, and horoscope-casting to the most obvious form, palmistry—which, interestingly enough, in its attempt to read the future in the lines of the palm and the shape of the fingers, puts man's future in his own hands. The man who is conscious of what a limited influence he has on the shape of the future plays countless silly or dangerous games in attempting to obtain at least some insight into the enigma.[25] Do not certain kinds of futurism, too, show the kind of giddiness and morbid fascination produced in the mind by the shadows of the future?

Magic rites, often connected with divination, give man the initiative in his wrestling with the future; in magic I try to bend to my will the hidden forces which supposedly control events. The practice of magic expresses at once a belief in the effectiveness of human intervention and a sense of the heterogeneity and the radical newness of the realities thus encountered. Likewise, man often attempts to master the future through the *word* and shape it according to some plan, evil or noble, mean or grandiose. The word then becomes imperative and prophetic; its power compels the unforeseeable. Such verbal action varies with circumstances and with the genius and intention of the speaker; its modalities will be subjected to analysis later on.[26]

In between efforts to make conscious preparation for the future and abandonment to baneful illusions, there is a third type of action which has become a business in the modern world: the *insurance contract*. Here the individual does not try to build the future world through his own activity; he does not try to penetrate or domesticate the mystery of his own destiny; he does not deny the dangerous uncertainties of the future. On the contrary, he admits these risks and calculates their statistical probabilities, but he does so in order to defend himself against the consequences, for an insurance policy is a defense or, better, a stationing of guards. In the extreme case, an individual prepares as many counterthrusts as the future has discernible dangers. Illness, accidents of all kinds (even to the loss of an umbrella), theft, fire, and flood give rise to as many kinds of contracts. Men seek to limit the damage done by the supreme and inescapable danger of death. Life insurance (what a euphemism! "Death insurance" would be the logical name, but not good for business) brings material help to a family when its breadwinner is taken away. Such a cruel blow seems to be softened a bit by the insurance.

Modern man is not content, however, with purely passive means of defense. He also develops rational techniques for actively mastering the future: *planning* and *preparation*. [27] The empirical foresight of the experienced man is replaced by a strict calculation of chances or probabilities; in this way an effort is made to introduce necessity into the contingent, at least insofar as the complexity of the determinisms at work allow. Knowledge of probabilities seeks to develop certainty, without ever fully succeeding, in order to guide the hand's efforts, which will always be primary.

Despite all such activities and techniques, I remain in a state of waiting, so far as the future is concerned. My life is a vigil. Sometimes I am drowsy when my concern abates; sometimes I am watchful or impatient; in either case, the guard I mount keeps me on my feet and defines my existence as a "project." If confidence wins out over anxiety, I look at the future with expectancy and hope. *Expectancy* is a serene waiting and relies on rational calculation: the means I use are proportioned to the end I seek, and the outcome will be the due result of my efforts. *Hope*, on the contrary, is not grounded in reason or the rational; stripped of self-reliance, the man of hope awaits an initiative from elsewhere, from a source superior to the world, which will satisfy his needs and minister to his native wretchedness. Without settling back into passivity, the man of hope feels that the fulfillment of his labors can come only from a limitless generosity and a transcendent love; for him, lying concealed in the future is the promise of an event which will be a gracious gift.

As the years move on, my future is more and more balanced off by my *past*. Maturity is the age when an equilibrium is established between these two portions of my life, the age when I look back to the past as well as forward to the future. The future is ahead of me; the past extends back from the present moment; the former I try to fore-see, the latter to re-see; the former is manifested to my creative imagination, the latter to my memory. Little by little the balance proper to maturity is disrupted in favor of the past; my perspective changes, and my being seems constituted more and more by what I have already experienced. At the term, death marks the complete conversion of yesterday's future into an irreversible past and puts an end to both.

The past may seem at first sight reducible to nonbeing or a "no longer," but in fact it involves a permanence which too often escapes our notice. The past is permanent because it is incorporated into my present self and constitutes part of my identity. My body's age and relative strength, its carriage and appearance, bear witness to the trials and labors and efforts it has had to endure or to the easy conditions in which I have lived until now. At a deeper level, thanks to memory, the consciousness of my past becomes part of the consciousness of my personal identity.[28] My *curriculum vitae* helps define me as a social being. An amnesiac, on the contrary, has lost his past: his familial, social, national, and professional history, even his name; it is a radical alienation which, in the extreme case, can look like madness. As Jean Anouilh has shown, such a man is a traveller without baggage, who must choose a family, a past, and an identity for himself. For a less extreme case, take the man who wholly lacks historical knowledge, and especially the "rootless" man. He has an individual identity but is totally ignorant of his family's, his country's, and humanity's past; "formerly" is total darkness to him. Here he is, thrown into time with no stars to take his bearings by, no cardinal points to help him orientate himself; a stranger to his own roots, he is also largely a stranger to himself, absent from himself and the human community. This is the wretched situation of some modern sub-proletariats.

My past is then, in large measure, the area of my possessions; it is the life capital which I have amassed. What is "behind me" constitutes, as it were, an existential storehouse; my experience is my past as decanted and condensed. I live out of this interior store, and I incorporate it, consciously or unconsciously, into the present moment and into my desires, judgments, behavior, and projects. I find support, security, and reserves of all kinds in this "back" part of my life. My today is nourished by my yesterday. Even the moral wounds received in the present moment sometimes heal by passing to the "rear," where forgetfulness gradually forms scars over them and finally obliterates them altogether.

My past is also the area of what is beyond my reach, the field in which I am totally powerless: the past is closed off, determined forever, and I can change nothing in it. With time, therefore, I myself also pass; I cannot relive my own history, rewrite my life, or change the person I have become. Each new instant is a point of no return and puts the seal of irrevocability on what has preceded. I am filled with regret and may even come to be afraid of this past which, like the spatial area of the world which is in back of me, is withdrawn from my intervention. For I can have reason to fear that from that obscure region others may summon forth my blunders, failures, or faults like baleful and accusing shades.

Like my future, my past, too, therefore, has a double meaning: it is the region of what has flowed away, fled, and become lost, but also the region of what I have acquired, amassed, and definitively made my own; it is that portion of my life in which I am both torn down and built up, annulled and fulfilled. Consequently I will always experience some disturbance when I confront this ambiguous reality.

Yet my moral consciousness has the strange power of liberating me from my past by *disavowal*. I can freely reject my own past, alienate it, and refuse to recognize myself in it henceforth. I can indeed change nothing in the material facts of the past, but I attribute my past actions to an inauthentic self from which I now claim to be emancipating myself. I turn away from what I have been, renounce every complacent backward glance, and locate my true being from now on in the future and the new purposes to which I dedicate it. My freedom has this wonderful power of deciding not only what I do but even what I am; of changing the meaning of my own duration and existence and causing a new man to rise up at every moment from the ashes of my past. Then my life is remade by a deliberate *conversion*. [29] But such a way of acting, which signifies a break with the past, also supposes a continuity with the past. If there were no permanent subject, there would not be a conversion but the annihilation of one person and the creation of another. The astonishing thing is that I can say: I was, I have been, I am, I will be. Conversion thus throws into sharp relief the continuity of the "I" which is felt in every experience. In this fashion, the "I" affirms that it transcends the moving multiplicity of acts and states which are scattered along its duration, and situates itself in eternity.

Auspicious and Inauspicious Actuality

My personal present is immersed in the present of mankind and participates in the events which fill it. My individual duration thus exists within an immense and rich present which we call actuality.

This milieu in which I must orientate myself is the "now" of the world and of men; its structure is simultaneity, synchronism, the "at the same time." The breadth of this present varies in part with my openness of mind, my desire to be present to today's world and to share its anxieties and joys. If I am not content to look only to my selfish interests and to local problems, if instead the needs of men in Japan or Chile awaken my concern, then my present enlarges until it becomes coextensive with the world.

The field of actuality also depends, in part, on my access to information. In our age the enormous development in the technology of social communication (press, radio, television, film) can liberate me from neighborhood gossip and parochial squabbles. Even if I cannot really journey into the past and future, as men do in science–fiction, I can travel about the present without ever leaving home. If an important event is happening somewhere in the world, I can follow its unfolding moment by moment and listen to the echoes it awakens in all the capitals of the world. My present becomes coextensive with mankind's.

In the midst of this multiform actuality, I instinctively try to orientate myself. From among all the events of the moment I pick out some to serve as reference points by which to take my bearings. The little details of daily tasks, incidents in family life, local, national, and international occurrences all form a circle around me; I sort them out through the spontaneous operation of my own interests. I pass over one event, highlight another, am afflicted by one and rejoiced by another. I introduce order into the temporal field of the *now* no less than into the spatial field of the *here*. Determining my own perspective, I distinguish in events what is auspicious and inauspicious, just as I divide space into right and left; I describe events according to my own anatomy, calling at least certain kinds of misfortune "sinister." Those facts which serve as reference points, cardinal points as it were, allow me to get my bearings in the world's present.

However, I also have more valuable reference points: my *contem-*

poraries. I live "at the same time as they," in a common today, and they people and enliven my present, unwittingly structuring it and providing me with firm supports. I situate myself, for example, by relation to people who are well-known: officials, celebrities, even film.stars. They are there in the field of my present and silhouetted against my horizon; they contribute some small bit to my making because I unconsciously orientate myself by them. Later on I will be proud of having been a great man's contemporary, for the fact of having shared the same present associates me in a small way with his glory.

The people of my generation who are closest to me—parents, friends, acquaintances—provide me with more everyday reference points. A common duration and a common mentality unite us, and the same events have shaped our lives. I recognize myself in them to some degree and I receive from them a secret assurance about my own reality. Each of them is a reliable reference point for me: I compare the dates of our birth, schooling, and professional life. Respective joys and sorrows are judged, weighed, and shared. In this way, the people of my generation supply me with a *structured milieu* which supports me and allows me to get my bearings in time. If one of these people dies, one support is taken away and my balance in my present existence is disturbed; I must redistribute my weight, so to speak, over the living companions I still have. The ultimate limit in this regard is reached by the last survivor of his generation; he is a man lost among men, a stranger to his fellows, with no bearings amid the ongoing world; too many eyes have closed in death which used to give him assurance, too many faces are gone which sustained his will to live.

III. THE MASTERY OF TIME

I Appropriate Time by the Movement of My Own Duration

I am master of my own movement in space and I move according to my needs, desires, and wishes. But I do not have the initiative when it comes to moving in time. Between my birth and death the pace of my journey is regulated by a determinism beyond my control. My desire to stop the flow of time at some especially happy moment ("O time, stop flying") or the opposite wish that in anxiety or expectation the days would run more speedily is frustrated by their inexorable rhythm.

Whatever the apparent speed or slowness of time, I appropriate for myself by the movement of my own duration that portion of time which is my lot. I like to speak of "my" time, "my" days, and "my" year, for the inevitable and necessary movement which I accomplish by "en-during" is a progressively victorious appropriation of time, even if it is balanced off by a constant and equal loss. Similarly, historical time is that portion of cosmic time which mankind gradually masters by the movement of forward-looking existence.

This journey in time, like movement in space, allows me ceaselessly to shift my temporal perspective. Between the retrospective horizon of my past and the prospective horizon of my future, my present—that is, my point of view—is constantly changing. I can never again look upon the world and man with the same eyes, for from one moment to the next my sight is enriched with new spectacles. Much more, then, does each stage of life have its unique perspective: the naive and wondering gaze of childhood, the clear-eyed gaze of maturity, the peaceful and detached gaze of the old man. One by one the years pass which effect this ongoing transformation. But we must note that the transformation does not take place uniformly. Though equal in objective duration, one year is not as enriching as another. Under the weight of trial, a man can age ten years in a few weeks, and a short period that is rich in discovery matures us as much as whole years might do. Finally, over the last two centuries, mankind and man's vision of himself have been transformed more radically than in long ages before; we speak of "history speeding up." We have the impression that the pace of our journey in time has quickened and that our life is, or will be, shorter than we had thought. The reason for this is that our days, for all their mathematical equality, have variable existential fullness. The number and seriousness of the events we have lived through conflict with the uniform movement of the clock's hands, contributing their weight to our duration. We live such moments more intensely and rapidly. The world's face changes quickly and its successive appearances give greater maturity to our outlook. More accurately: these events are now part of our outlook on man and the world.

Technology offers man, especially today, some amazing means of resisting the inexorable passage of time. *Speed* is a challenging of our temporal limitations no less than our spatial, a challenging of space-time as we concretely experience it. From the speed of the galloping horse, which for millennia was the fastest transport men knew, to the speed of spaceships, we use speed to overcome time, to "recapture" it by traversing a maximum space in a minimal time. We "run against the clock" and try to "gain time" in order to escape the limitations of objective duration and reach the point, if possible, of experiencing a total perspective in an instant. However extraordinary his technological accomplishments, man could doubtless not free himself totally from subjection to time without thereby ceasing to exist. But the very effort to overcome spatio-temporal limitation is, as we said earlier,[30] the mark of a being which in some hidden apex of itself—the spirit —transcends the order of material becoming. In trying to reach ever greater speeds, man is trying to make himself eternal.

Time becomes mine through the movement of my own duration. But in the expression "my time" the possessive can have very different meanings. We apply this ambiguous phrase to our past. If then my time is in the past, is the present therefore not mine? Are we exiled in the present moment and in the actuality of history? The accumulated past may doubtless seem in some respects a more solid reality than the moving moment, for we have thrust longer and deeper roots there. Yet are not the harvests of the past stored up in my being itself? How could I continue to enjoy them except in the present? We must be on our guard: nostalgia for "my time" or for "the good old times" may well be a sign of psychological aging.

Such aging is what is happening to the "reactionary," the man who likes to praise the way the world was in his youth; living in the present, he sets up some past time as a golden age, an ideally perfect period, and longs to return to it. He is a man of regret and inverted desire; he reverses the natural direction of his existential project and wants to put "ahead" what is forever "behind him" and to convert mankind's past into its future. Such an about-face is possible in space but not in time. You can deny your past, but you cannot rewrite history. It is wise, then, to prize the contributions of the past, but the return of mankind to a past age will be forever an idle dream.

Another kind of person will do the opposite: he will put both his own time and the golden age into the future and try to wipe out the past. Like a child or adolescent, he has no historical sense and regards himself as an absolute beginning, for he idolizes what is modern or what will be tomorrow and wants not only to be "in the mainstream" but ahead of it. He is in great danger then of dreaming instead of acting, and of deceiving himself and leading others astray. Furthermore, the idea of continual progress with no retrogressions or delays is a hypothesis that has never been proved. As the future becomes the present, we find that it too has its deep shadows and ugly cruelties. Finally, our most recent present emerges out of the distant past, and the man of yesterday survives in the futurist of today.

If I am thus tempted to locate my own time or the golden age in the past or the future, the reason is that, straitjacketed by the narrow limits of the moment, I try to escape from myself and to find in past or future what the present denies me. Just as "elsewhere" often seems more attractive than "here," so too "formerly" and "later" seem richer than "now." In fact, however, the time that is most my own is and must be today, the present of my own and mankind's existence. Behind me I no longer am; ahead of me I am not yet. It is only now that I exist and can exercise my freedom. In short, I am "at home" in the "now," for that is the portion of duration which I can tailor to fit me, and I live in it as I do in my house. I take up my abode in it by adapting to my use all that the historical, social, cultural, and economic conjuncture is willing to give me. I adapt to it, in turn, by summoning up my courage against ill fortune and accepting what I cannot bend to my will. Even if conscience forces me to disavowals and I refuse to idolize the slogans or the violence of the day, I do not therefore take refuge in an idealized past or future. Instead I make my own the events of my time, the resources which reality provides, the sufferings and hopes of mankind. I remember and draw profit from the contributions of the past and work to prepare a better future for tomorrow. My time is mankind's today.

Physical and Intentional Presence in Time

What we have been saying makes it clear enough that if I am physically present only to my present (language, mirroring experience, forces us to this truism), I can on the other hand be intentionally present to all the moments of duration. My privilege as a man is to journey across the modest landscape of my own life and the immense panorama of world history. While continuing to be "here and now," I transport myself in mind to the "there and then."

We noted earlier the disconcerting effort I must make if I am to conjure up in my mind the time before history, the time when there were no men. That period, we said, is a temporal desert, an indistinct duration which lacks the living landmarks of men and events.[31] But it also true that the scientist's knowledge of successive geological eras and the appearance of the lower life-forms changes these hitherto unknown raw facts into significant events in retrospect, for they were the prelude to mankind's appearance and thus have a meaning for us and in relation to us, the men who finally came. Once we reach prehistory and protohistory, our intentional presence to the past finds firm ground to stand on. Thanks to the traces he has left behind as mute yet eloquent witnesses, I can move back to a time when man was already there, a "lived-in" time, and thus enter into relation with my most remote ancestors. The Lascaux frescoes may doubtless interest me for their sober and refined artistic qualities and their sense of movement. But I am still more fascinated by that human presence, so far and yet so near, which has at least been restored to us. Men passed here; their eyes and hands traced, caressed these figures. Now, for a brief moment, I become their contemporary from seventeen thousand years away; the mist enveloping time past thins, is almost dispersed.

Once we reach *history* in the proper sense of the word, I am able to walk as I please in the vast extent of human duration, in surroundings marked out by all sorts of great and small events. Growth in my historical knowledge multiplies my reference points in times when I did not yet exist. I move about and travel, then, in that time before my birth, in the "before me" age of the world. I bring back to life, in a sense, the men who went before me; I establish a relationship with them and enter their inner lives. The relationship is admittedly onesided, for within the time which others experienced who cannot know me I preserve my incognito and go and come as an invisible spectator. Nonetheless I do become a contemporary of past generations as I make myself intentionally present in the limitless field opened to me by historical retrospection. As I follow along the course of time, I see the early history of mankind gradually preparing for our own age and finally bringing into existence the reality in which my personal present is immersed.[32] In this way I claim my privilege as a man: just as no other animal is a geographer, so no other is an historian. The intentional mastery of time reveals the transcendence of the mind.

The world's "before me" ends with my birth. The latter marks the anterior boundary between my time and time to which I was unknown. But my birth did not coincide with the awakening of my clear consciousness or, much less, of reflective consciousness. I was not aware of being born.[33] From the fact that I exist today I conclude that I was born on a day which was my first. I can also find out about it from the birth records kept by the state and have my parents tell me of the events which accompanied this primordial event in my life. But the event itself I will never know directly. I can only reach back to it intentionally through discursive knowledge, as I can to any other historical fact. Yet my birth does mark my entrance into life and begins a new time, even—I might be tempted to say—a new age of the world; the age in which I appeared, came to know men, things, and events, and was known in turn.

The limit of my personal future is death. Ignorance of its date allows me to continue projecting myself always further ahead. Until the last second of life I will be hoping for a future. I cannot become genuinely present to that boundary-moment, for though I know myself to be mortal, no experience puts me in the immediate presence of my death. I experience death only in others (which is really to say that I do not experience it), and my own death will not be an experience, because it will do away with all possiblity of reflecting on the event. Thus I grasp my death, as I do my birth, only through mediated knowledge. These two boundaries of my personal duration inevitably escape me.

A time will come, then, when I shall no longer be: this will be the "after me" age of the world. But just as I can place myself through thought in the time between the beginning of the world and my own coming, so I can put myself intentionally in the time between my end and history's end. Here I have a temporal field which is symmetrical with the former, a "future after" my death which corresponds to the "past before" my birth. Thus I cross the frontier established by my death as I do, by historical awareness, the frontier of my birth. Now I am in the "not yet," the "after me," and I observe it as an invisible spectator. The men of that coming time will doubtless have forgotten me, and I shall no longer exist for them. But I can now make them exist for me as my imagination wills them to be or as prevision based on present data allows me to glimpse them.

There is something more. If I can shape my personal future before death through work, foresight, and insurance, my will to live also provides me with various means of surviving my death itself. These means are so obvious that we hardly attend to their depth of meaning. *Offspring* is the first: a man begets children in order to acquire extended existence and a prolongation into the world's future for his personal self.[34] Just as my contemporaries provide structure for my present, so my descendants are already shaping the distant future for me; they make it possible for my anticipative thought to take its bearings in an area that would otherwise be indistinct, and through them I live in the "after me." In all those born of him, the patriarch is intentionally present in mankind's tomorrows.

Work plays an analogous role. The ambition of the artisan, as of the artist, is to produce a lasting work and thus to overcome time and perpetuate his creative ideas and desire. Whether my talent is inspired, moderate, or quite without pretensions, I want to survive in the creations that issue from my hands.[35] Thus I project myself beyond my own death. My consciousness as a worker envisions and relishes this extended existence or temporal "sur-vival" (extra life) which my body refuses me and my creative energies are willing to give me. Doubtless there is a great deal of illusion in all this; few works are immortal. But what is important for our purpose here is the attitude of the creative consciousness, its transcendence of the limitations of time, and its intentional presence to history. Life insurance has an analogous meaning, for by making it possible for me to provide for the future of those close to me, it makes me effectively present to a time which I shall not share with them. By a *testament*, especially, I dispose of my goods in the time "after me" and give myself a hold on it. The political or spiritual testament is intended to exercise influence on the distant tomorrows of mankind and to order them according to the ideals and values which I honor. In short, when I write "This is my testament," I am aware of giving myself a kind of earthly survival.

Social man is no less desirous than the individual of guaranteeing himself the benefit of such a presence in the distant future. Take, for instance, the monument which perpetuates the memory of the 1918 victory: it is intended to play in time the same role which a landmark plays at some noteworthy point in space. Having reached a peak of its existence in an event in which immense suffering and glory were united, the nation came to see its own history in a wholly new perspective. Whichever way it turned, past or future, the horizon was filled with fresh significance. Seen from this vantage point, the series of great and small events which had preceded the crisis took on a new meaning which was revealed precisely by the term to which they had, all unsuspected, been leading. The present and the proximate or distant future were in turn dominated by the consequences of the terrible testing of that war. Similarly, every major event is a "point of view," providing a unique perspective on the history of the fatherland and the world. The unrepeatable instant the social group has lived through must therefore be perpetuated and consecrated forever by establishing a fixed point, the *memorial*. Religious or profane, triumphal arch or tombstone, the monument will be raised, set up as a signal and a rallying point for the gaze of all. Its role will be to remain there as a challenge to the centuries, like a lighthouse on a rock in the midst of the turbulent sea. It will survive the last survivors of the age, perpetuating in the future a vision and a perspective upon human duration. In erecting the memorial, the men of today make themselves intentionally present to the national future. In their ritual gatherings around the monument, tomorrow's generations will make their own this focal point of a privileged perspective on which, to some extent at least, their history centers, falls into order, and takes on meaning. Thus men of the present and men of the future place themselves at a unique point in human duration in order to comprehend a part, or even the totality, of their common destiny above and beyond all temporal frontiers.

The establishment of an *institution* likewise projects an intentional presence to the future. A people adopts a new constitution, a legislator promulgates a law: such acts of institution are directed towards the future, which they claim to structure, for at issue is the system of relationships which will provide organization for the social group and enable it to survive. The legislator thus makes himself present to the extended future, embraces it, and imposes order upon it. Those in turn who accept the institutional form and freely allow themselves to be regulated by it enter into his purposes. The basic ambition of any institution is to endure forever, and through it the consciousness of its originators is present to the immense time-field of the future of society.

We must here recall, therefore, the observation made in connection with space: my intentional presence is out of all proportion to my physical presence. The puniest of men can become present to all duration and overcome the fears arising from his own littleness.[36] From each moment of my life, as from a point-sized observatory, I can traverse in thought the limitless immensity of the time which preceded and follows me. I project myself into this infinite reality, gather it up and enfold it in my mind, just as my wide-stretched arms intentionally embrace the whole universe. In both cases I grasp a totality as such. No temporal boundary—neither that of my birth nor that of my death—hinders this outward thrust of my being. If I must live in time along with the animals, I also have the prerogative of mastering time by my thought. If my tiny empirical ego is swept along with the flow of time, my free and thinking "I" takes its stand on the vertex of the instant, at a summit from which I dominate the universal flux. We can express this privilege in Pascalian terms: by means of time the universe embraces me and swallows me up like a speck; by means of thought I embrace the universe.

NOTES

1. Pascal, *Pensées*, Fr. 233 (Turnell, Fr. 343, p. 200).

2. Cf. Eliade, *The Sacred and the Profane*, pp. 68–113.

3. Cf. Camille Mayran, *Larmes et lumières à Oradour* (Paris: Plon, 1952, p. 36, and Gabriel Marcel's observation in the Preface, p. 17.

4. Henri Bergson, *Time and Free Will: An Essay on the Immediate Data of Consciousness*, trans. F.L. Pogson (New York: Macmillan, 1910), pp. 98–99. Recall, for example, the successive positions of the hands of a clock or the displacement of the shadow on a sundial, etc.

5. The "world-for-me" exists only through me. Pascal brings this out by putting himself at the other end of earthly existence, death: "Each of us is a whole to himself; once he is dead, the world is dead for him. That is why everyone believes that he is everything to everybody. We must not judge

134 THE HUMANITY OF MAN

nature according to ourself but according to itself" (*Pensées*, Fr. 457 [Turnell, Fr. 164, p. 149]).

6. Hegel, *Lectures on the History of Philosophy*, trans. Elizabeth S. Haldane and Frances H. Simson, 3 vols. (London: Kegan Paul, Trench, and Trübner, 1892), vol. 3, pp. 545–54.

7. Cf. Léon Brunschvicg, *Les progrès de la conscience dans la philosophie occidentale* (Paris: Alcan, 1927).

8. Cf. e.g., 1 Kings 6:1; 15:1, 9, 25, 33, etc., where reigns in Israel and Juda are dated in relation to each other; elsewhere the current reign provides the reference point, e.g. Isa. 6:1, Jer. 1:2–3, etc.

9. Pascal. *Pensées*, Fr. 172 (Turnell, Fr. 84, p. 131): "We never live in the present. We anticipate the future . . . or we recall the past . . . we wander through ages which are not ours."

10. Alexis Carrel, *Man the Unknown* (New York: Harper, 1935), pp. 159–190. Cf. Pierre Lecomte Du Noüy, *Biological Time* (London: Methuen, 1936). Cf. also Eliade, *Images and Symbols*, pp. 85–91: the Yogis are able to slow down the flow of psycho-physiological time by breath control.

11. In these cases the child's age is being measured empirically by its size. This exemplifies a remark already made: to measure time we translate it into quantitative terms.

12. Cf. Plato, *Phaedo*, 115c-e, where Socrates corrects Crito on this point. Cf. also John 11:39: at Lazarus's tomb Martha says of her brother that "he is in his fourth day." The personal turn of phrase and the masculine gender (in Greek and Latin) of the adjective and the unexpressed subject betray the irresistible tendency to attribute to the body not only a latent life but a subjectivity. The funeral rites of various cultures show the same tendency, as, for example, the custom of putting food near the dead person; this represents an effort to keep the person in the duration proper to living men (cf. below, Chapter 7, section 3, "Sharing and Covenant").

13. Originally, the French words *an* and *année* expressed a distinction analogous to that between *jour* (day) and *journée* (my day).

14. Cf. Thomas Aquinas, *Summa theologiae*, I-II, 1, q. 1 ad 1; q. 3 ad 2; and especially a. 4.

15. Thomas Aquinas, *op. cit.*, I-II, q. 58, a. 5, who is quoting Aristotle, *Nichomachean Ethics*, III, 8, 114a32–b1.

16. Pierre Gaxotte, *Louis the Fifteenth and His Times*, trans. J. Lewis May (Philadelphia: Lippincott, 1934).

17. There can be no question here of going into the difficult problem of the relations between determinism and freedom. But we must at least call attention to the current mistake of confronting these two terms as though they were antagonistic realities of the same order, so that the discovery, for example, of some new psychological law would automatically diminish the scope and even the reality of our free effectiveness. As a matter of fact, since our freedom is situated in a world, in a body, and in a psyche which is subject to laws, it constantly grounds itself in all these in order to carry out its own

initiatives. Freedom obeys nature only in order to command it. A psychiatrist, for example, tries to bring into play in his patient the biological and *mental mechanisms* which will restore to the man the use of his *freedom!* Thanks to this rediscovered freedom, the man who was formerly alienated from himself will once again take charge of the world's blind forces. This is not to deny that our freedom concretely is limited and even crushed by certain determinisms. It is simply to say that man is *by nature* endowed with freedom, as he is with reason, sight, and hearing. The *exercise* and actuation of this freedom are always a victory to be won.

18. We take up this point in our book *Le témoignage spirituel* (Paris: Editions de l'Epi, 1964), pp. 182 ff.

19. Thomas Aquinas, *Summa contra gentiles*, II, q. 81: "the human soul . . . is . . . as though it existed on the horizon of eternity and time" (trans. James F. Anderson: Saint Thomas Aquinas, *On the Truth of the Catholic faith* [*Summa contra gentiles*], Book two: *Creation* [Garden City: Doubleday, Image Books, 1956], p. 265).

20. Augustine, *Confessions*, IX, 10, 24–25.

21. Some modern writers feel this and limit the temporal and spatial dimensions of the action they portray; the result is at times a masterpiece. Cf., e.g., Ernest Hemingway's *The Old Man and the Sea* (New York: Scribner's, 1952) and Sidney Lumet's film, *Twelve Angry Men.*

22. We will show later on that every creative effort in the service of the true, the beautiful, and the good effectively mediates between time and eternity; cf., below, Chapter 4, section 2, "The Artist's Hand."

23. Victor Hugo, "Napoleon II," v. 36, in *Les chants du crépuscule*, in Francis Bouvet ed., *Oeuvres poétiques complètes*, (Paris: Pauvert, 1961), p. 178.

24. Cf. Jean Guitton, *Man in Time*, trans. Adrienne Foulke (Notre Dame, Ind.: University of Notre Dame Press, 1966), pp. 27–45.

25. Necromancy is a very odd kind of thing; I ask a dead person, a man from the past, to reveal the future to me. Such behavior supposes a belief in some sort of survival and also that the dead person enjoys a superior kind of duration to which my orientational structures with their sharp lines of demarcation do not apply.

26. Cf. below, Chapter 3, section 2, "Word and Action."

27. Cf. Gaston Berger, *Phénoménologie du temps et prospective* (Paris: Presses Universitaires de France, 1964). In 1957 Berger set up the Centre international de prospective.

28. Cf. Georges Gusdorf, *Mémoire et personne*, 2 vols. (Paris: Presses Universitaires de France, 1951). Augustine's disquisition in *Confessions*, X, 8, 12–26,37 deals rather with the function of memory. In the positive sciences explanation involves attention both to the beginning or "archeology" and to the end or "eschatology."

29. Cf., above, Chapter 1, section 2, "Front and Back" (towards the end).

30. Cf., above Chapter 1, section 3, "I Appropriate Space by Moving About in It."

31. Cf. above, this Chapter, section 1, "My Embodied 'I' Modifies Time."

32. But we must note the necessity of some temporal distance if the past is to emerge with clarity and show its real shape and meaning. A reporter's account can be a testimony but not history; the idea of an "immediate history" is a delusion.

33. Cf. Harriet Beecher Stowe, *Uncle Tom's Cabin*: when Topsy, the black child without a family, is asked about her birth, she keeps repeating, "Never was born!" and "I 'spect I grow'd."

34. Cf. Plato, *The Symposium*, trans. W. Hamilton (Baltimore: Penguin Books, 1951), p. 88: "Mortal nature seeks, as far as may be, to perpetuate itself and become immortal. The only way in which it can achieve this is by procreation." Cf. Aristotle, *De anima*, II, 4, 415a16–415b1. trans. J. A. Smith, in W. D. Ross, ed., *The Works of Aristotle* 3 (Oxford: Oxford University Press, 1931): "For any living thing that has reached its normal development . . . the most natural act is the production of another like itself . . . in order that, as far as its nature allows, it may partake in the eternal and divine." Cf. Sirach 30.4: "At the father's death, he will seem not dead, since he leaves after him one like himself."

35. Cf. below, Chapter 4, section 2, "The Artist's Hand."

36. Cf. Pascal, *Pensées*, Fr. 205 (Turnell, Fr. 116, p. 142): "When I consider the brief span of my life, absorbed in the eternity of time which went before and will come after it . . . I am terrified and astonished."

PART II

THE MEDIA OF
EXPRESSION
AND COMMUNICATION

I humanize the world by giving it a meaning, and it is in the major forms of expression and communication that I get a glimpse of meanings in their nascent state.

Word, manual gesture, face, and gaze are not simply juxtaposed but complement each other organically. Meaning is given only by the whole human presence and is constantly circulating through it. Such interplay is complex and subtle to the point of resisting any attempt at an exhaustive analysis. Sometimes word, gesture, face, and gaze confirm one another because they agree in the intentions they express. Sometimes there is contradiction due to imperfect self-mastery. Sometimes one corrects another, as when the glance softens a rough word or gesture. Sometimes one operation complements and makes up for the deficiency in another (the gaze of the paralyzed person, the gesture of the blind or the mute). In short, without the hand, the word cannot manifest man's whole will to be effective, and the hand is not fully expressive without the word. Each of these in turn receives its fullness of meaning from the face I gaze upon and from the exchange of glances, for here is manifested the personal identity which makes its own, unites, and animates the whole.

CHAPTER 3

THE WORD

Man is the animal who speaks. The word is the act of a person, ceaselessly takes its origin from the person, and cannot be separated from him, any more than running water can be cut off from its source. Furthermore, the basic intention of words is self-expression and communication with others. That relation to a hearer largely determines the very nature of words and grounds the possibility of dialogue.

I. SILENCE AND WORD

Paradox it may be, but we must say that the word would not exist without silence; and, inversely, there is no genuine silence except in relation to a possible word. Each contributes to a primordial, vital, and indestructible rhythm; far from simply strengthening each other by contrast, they engender and define each other in a kind of reciprocal genesis.

This does not hold true for the silence of things, which results from inertia, apathy, and total lack of consciousness. A thing, considered in itself, is that for which I do not exist. It exists for me, of course; I apply my senses and intelligence to it, transform it or use it, but I am not the term of any communication originating in the thing. It is simply there before me, without a voice or a gaze; there is no reciprocity between us except that of our common location in space and our respective "objectivity." The muteness of things is due to ignorance and absence. If I question it with my senses or my mind, the answer will never come from it but only from myself, as I unconsciously play a double role in this odd dialogue. If a thing seems hostile or scornful of me, it is once again I who in spontaneous animism project such supposed sentiments upon it. The paradox is that the thing is both there and eludes me; such a strange absence from me is due to the relative absence of a nonconscious reality from itself.[1]

If I stand outside an empty room and look at things in it through a window, the soundless space and furniture may give me the impression of being in a state of suspended meaning, a stultified world which is the debris, as it were, of a world once filled with meaning and now mysteriously emptied. If I look at things on a macrocosmic scale, their silence may seem like a universal absence of meaning. My mind becomes aware of the force of Pascal's temptation to vertigo and terror, I see myself "plunged in the infinite immensity of the spaces which I do not know and which do not know me";[2] "when we look at the whole dumb universe . . . I am overcome by fear";[3] "the eternal silence of these infinite spaces terrifies me."[4] But we must ask whether this silence may contain a hidden word and whether some wholly interior sixth sense may enable me to hear its message.

Silence manifests itself first of all as the field of the human world. A voice that suddenly speaks to me in the depths of the forest immediately fills the surrounding space and perhaps awakens an echo; it immediately takes control of the silent world of things, setting it in motion, transforming it, and giving it a new meaning. In an abrupt change, a voiceless universe becomes the universe in which man speaks. The words therefore lay hold of me in my deepest self. I tremble as though someone had seized me, and I feel the power of the words enter into me. But such power arises less from the vocal capacity of the speaker than from the silence which was simultaneously broken and filled by the word as though it were a medium ready to receive it. Conceived in the womb of silence, the word is born by breaking out of it. In this respect, a loud voice must cry out in a desert if it is to have its full power to stir the hearer, for then it fills the whole silent space available to it; it spreads out and reverberates to the boundaries of the desert solitude; there noise begins to resist it and eventually swallows it up.

If exterior silence is the space required for the spoken word to find a place for itself, there is another space, the silent heart, in which the word which is heard must reverberate. The sudden words that surprised me in the forest entered not one but two universes: the silent world of things and that other silent world, born perhaps in the favorable atmosphere of the first, which I carry within me. I can receive the word, welcome it in a profound way, "hear" it in the full sense, only if I admit it into this inner desert. The most solitary of hermits will be deaf to the Spirit's voice if he has not silenced within himself the countless soliticiting voices of things. The true desert is within us. The word has two faces, and there is a twofold desert: the sound of the voice without is only the other side of the word I hear within. The heart's space and the heart's silence are incommensurable with those of the universe.

Interior silence is an inner fullness, a spring rising from the depths, a life-giving matrix. The heard word gives birth to another word, which is hidden and perhaps will always be hidden, a daughter-word that is the same as, yet different from, its mother-word. Born both of another and of myself, this new word draws its greatest strength from the silence which, in each of us, nourished it. He alone, then, knows how to speak who also knows how to be silent, and the wise man's words are valued according to their rarity; such words are still wrapped in their originating silence as in a mantle of truth. A man's "last words" derive their value both from contrast and from a mysterious continuity with the eternal silence that follows them and continues to give them life.

Silence can, paradoxically, be a means of expression and communication. There is, of course, the silence of inertia and meaninglessness; this is eminently the case, as we saw, with the silence of things. But silence between persons is something quite different, for it is bound up with the ties which nature establishes between them. By the very fact that he exists, each person has a "meaning he wants to communicate" (*veut dire*), and does in fact communicate, to others, sometimes in words, sometimes by silence. Or rather, the silence always contains the word in one way or other, whether it is the silence before speaking, the silence within speech, or the silence beyond speech.

Before speech: the mere sight of another person silently working or praying touches me and invites me to imitate him. His concentration concentrates me and calls me back to my own inner depths. In other circumstances, my silence may be a word held back, delayed in its birth yet expressing me, as when I hesitate to approach the stranger sitting near me in the railroad train. Uncertain of what reception it will meet, my word remains in suspense. My silence is then an imperfect presence. But I can also be silent from indifference or contempt. Then I act as though the other did not exist; attempt to deny him, to thrust him back into nothingness, and to break any ties between us. At times heavy with menace, at times protesting an offended dignity, at times expressing approval or connivance or passivity or helplessness or need for reflection, silence can have greater meaning than the word the other waits for.

If the word is in fact spoken, there is silence *within the speech.* Speech retains the silence within it as its own inner depth and as the matrix out of which it continues to be born. In the course of speech the pauses, long or short, play an important role in communicating meaning; at such moments, words are returning to their originating source and acquiring new depth and fullness of content.

Silence can, finally, lie *beyond speech* as the latter's limitless prolongation. Between real friends or long-time spouses, after a life of shared work, sufferings, and joys, words are not needed for communion, any more than the clasping of hands or the exchange of glances; silent presence is enough. Better than words whose sound might disturb the deep peace of two hearts, silence nourishes union and becomes itself a mediating word. The same holds for a group of people gathered in shared attention or sorrow or prayer. What a mistake it is to think that an unceasing flow of words from someone presiding or leading is necessary for participation! Rather, there is a necessary *rhythm* of word and silence, and in it the absence of sound itself becomes word and communion. Such silence is an action, and not mere passivity; a shared fullness, sometimes in a very high degree, and not a void. The sign in word or gesture that is suppressed is then more eloquent than any sign that might be used.

Even in the silence of absence, as we pointed out, the other person is still given to me in a way; I know that, like myself, my partner exists and is a human being. Letters and modern means of communication make it possible for me to actualize that mutuality; a letter is both presence and word. But, paradoxically, voluntary or involuntary silence can be filled with greater meaning than a written message; for though such silence may, of course, be a sign of estrangement, it can also express a fidelity beyond the power of signs to communicate. In this latter case, it is enough for me to think of my friend and to know he thinks of me.

The opposite, or the enemy, of the word is therefore not silence but *noise*. Noise is neither word (articulated and meaningful sound) nor music (the highest form of sounded language). Word and music must be heard by the mind no less than by the ear, but noise is a chaos of sounds without meaning; it strikes the ear and often torments it with its violence, but it afflicts the mind still more with its lack of meaning, for it is only debris, waste. The dividing line between sound and noise is doubtless a shifting one according to circumstances, but noise seems to make its appearance when a certain material and human order is disturbed. The blows of the village blacksmith on his anvil, the creaking of wagon wheels on the road, and the herdsman's call to his animals all express the calm activity of men and supply a framework for my world. The mind recognizes in all these noises a familiar order and a peace-giving meaning which sustains the mind's own inner balance. But the sudden explosion of sound from a supersonic airplane upsets and destroys all harmony; it tumbles me into chaos, as its violent, meaningless roar invades my consciousness and threatens both my organic well-being and my inner order as a personal being.

The word too can, without our realizing it, become mere noise and destroy itself. The noise of quarreling voices or voices in a crowd brings me many words, but their meaning is gone. Again, the individual, as the moralists of every period have pointed out, can destroy his own words. The chatterbox with his idle gossip turns his own words into vocables, and the vocables into mere noise. Verbosity kills the word, hypertrophy of the sign swallows up the meaning, and logorrhea is the death of the logos. Today, with our means of social communication, we are in danger not only of eliminating all silence from modern life but, worse still, of inspiring in men a disgust, even a kind of terror, of silence. The uninterrupted flow of words that comes from the radio and television becomes devalued like an inflated currency; it no longer has *meaning*, for it fatigues the senses and lulls the

mind into a vague passivity, so that silence in the house seems like a
void or an abyss to be filled up at any price. To escape such silence and
oneself, one deliberately opens oneself to the trashiest kind of verbiage. Yet if exterior silence disconcerts a person interiorly, it is
because noise has already emptied the mind. A silence cure through
contact with nature or in a place of retreat becomes a necessary means
for securing psychic and moral balance.

II. EFFECTIVENESS OF THE WORD

The Word as Beginning and Act

Of itself the word has initiative and creative power. I can find myself
sometimes addressing myself interiorly as I face a task: "Let's not put
it off! Courage!" Similarly, an *order* given to a subordinate tends to
upset the existing balance of an established pattern of rest or routine
and to inaugurate a new *order* of things. The *Acts* of a sovereign are his
creative words. At the start of every enterprise, a word is spoken
which overcomes inertia, sets an activity in motion, and gives birth to
what did not exist before. The word is thus the mediator between
thought and volition, on the one hand, and action, on the other.

Every initiating word, therefore, however hidden, is already an
act, for it bears the future work within itself or, better, constitutes, in
a strict sense, its "coming to birth." As fruitful matrix, the word
continues to contain the result being sought, nourishing it with its
own substance and directing it as its basic pattern; as it is articulated,
the word forms the offspring it bears within itself, shapes it, and
brings it to maturity. At critical moments in its slow development, the
work will journey back, as it were, to its sources, returning to the
generating word where it finds its meaning and pattern. Because of its
origin in the word, the work becomes a word in its turn and overcomes in certain respects the muteness native to things so that it
becomes "eloquent," revealing the intentions and even the person of
its maker. To interpret a work, I must continually move back and
forth between the word embodied in a material thing or an undertaking and the word which originally conceived and expressed the thing
or undertaking. A biography sheds light on a masterpiece, just as the
latter does on its creator. The man expresses himself in his work.

We must go even further here. If the work reveals its author, it also involves him and, in a way, re-creates him. The initiating word which is the spur of the undertaking remakes its speaker in turn, giving him a new mode of existing, and acting as an effective *mediation* between what he is and what he can be. I will be a man of a particular trade, a particular undertaking, a particular book; my social existence and my inmost truth are both defined by this fact. Corneille is forever the author of the *Cid* and Dvorák the composer of *The New World* symphony. Thus I am reborn over and over again out of the words which decide what my action will be and commit me to it. Better than any fountain of youth, each of these words is an act by which I am regenerated or, inversely, destroyed. The word comes from the man as he is and decides to be; if he is to remain faithful to himself, he must constantly return, especially in moments when he is uncertain of himself, to those initiating words out of which he once decided to be born to his own truth.[5]

At a deeper level, the word is an act insofar as it commits me to another person and to the ideal values which judge us both. Even an ordinary agreement or an everyday appointment puts me under an obligation. Much more, then, does a promise in a serious matter or an oath or a word of honor involve my whole right to the other's respect. A man "of his word" is aware that a promise made or an agreement reached makes him accountable before the supreme tribunal of the True and the Good and that to go back on his word amounts to denying himself as a free and rational being. This power of the word given, involving the person as such, poses the many problems connected with fidelity.[6]

The Anticipatory Word

The interior word which the master artist speaks anticipates the work itself, as we have indicated, and creates it within the mind before the hand makes it a reality in the material world; the creative word precedes the work in its finished reality. But the word is also a means of communication with others, and by means of it one person takes the initiative in approaching another. This prevenient power of the word comes clearly to light when one person addresses another.

If the silent forest in which I am walking suddenly echoes with a voice that calls me, I am startled, and I stop and turn. The peaceful quiet of my solitude has been abruptly shattered. Another overtakes and joins me at a particular point in my journey and reflections. His word confronts me before I can speak or act. While still a stranger and unknown to me, he anticipates me, taking the first step towards me and dispelling my illusion of being for a short while the only person in the world. The bonds linking me with the society of countless others are reestablished. The anticipatory power of the word makes me exist once again for others.

This same power was strikingly expressed in the person of the herald in antiquity, as it is today, to a lesser extent, by every spokesman. The herald of old was a sacred and inviolable person, the protegé of the gods and of Zeus himself,[7] as well as confidant and spokesman for the sovereign. It was the inherent power and essential dynamism of the word with which he was entrusted that urged him forward, obliging him to run on and on, even at the risk of falling dead.[8] Such an anticipatory movement was twofold. On the one hand, the herald went before his lord and on the other—more precisely—the lord went ahead of himself in the word and in the bearer of the word. The herald's function was to translate into visible form, in his own movement, the movement proper to the word. For the word is vital, active, quick: it seeks to be "spoken ahead" (pronounced), "shouted ahead" (pro-claimed), hurled into the distance as it were; it runs and spreads, reaching places before the speaker does. It has no material mass to weigh it down: what, then, can hinder it? On the other hand, if the word moves out from the lord in order to *go on ahead* of him, it does so in order to *come before* the people, seeking attention, a hearing, an encounter. It knows a thousand artifices to force their interest, to overcome any estrangement, and to encounter the hearer at the heart of his existence and inner searching. The word, whose articulations give form and meaning to the matter represented by the voice, is born of the struggle to conquer the barrier of distance.

Technology has always sought to increase the range of the speech organs. In antiquity the theatrical mask made it possible to reach a large audience.[9] But in our day this innate ambition of the word has found fulfillment through the extraordinary media of the telephone, radio, television, records, and tapes. By means of them, another's word can reach me in every possible place and time and vanquish my solitude; it is even in danger of profaning my privacy, and I have to make an effort to escape from its grasp. Prevenance has lost its delicacy, but at least it is simply a question of the native movement of the word being carried to excess. For the word is essentially "intentional," that is, it expresses the movement of one consciousness towards another and stubbornly seeks to effect the communication of which it is the privileged instrument.

The Word as Act of Presence

While a silence that is indifferent to others is the mark of an imperfect presence, my address to another "breaks the ice" and tears down the wall of coldness that separates us, making us now exist for one another. Words set us on the road leading from a purely passive presence, which is simply juxtaposition in space, to a presence which is reciprocal commitment and an *act*.[10] The quality of such presence can doubtless vary greatly according to the quality of the words exchanged. The "commonplaces" of conversation (a significant image!) are always open, like "public places," to me and the passerby I meet, but they offer the possibility of only an impersonal mutual presence. They are the area inhabited by Heidegger's "people" and can even serve as an excuse for refusing any intimacy; but they can also, on the contrary, pave the way to intimacy. With words of sympathy, friendship, and love, presence passes through all the degrees of nearness and becomes a communion. Then, as we said earlier, words often cease, for silence itself has become a word and a presence.

The word is doubtless the major factor in mutual presence and the privileged place for exchange; a blind man is much more present to others than the mute or the deaf. Even though he must do without the precious exchange of glances, the blind man is linked to a limitless multitude of partners by the invisible threads of dialogue; his word enters into others, and the words of others enter into him. The deaf and the mute, on the contrary, while grasping others as visible and tangible beings, must remain exterior to them, somewhat after the fashion of material things juxtaposed to other things and isolated in their own materiality. If presence is the privilege of the person, it is because man is the animal who speaks.

It is in virtue of such presence that the word exercises its prevenance. To be present is to be ahead of oneself (*prae-esse*), and prevenance expresses the fact of coming ahead of another (*prae-venire*). I am present to another to the extent that I am outside of myself in a movement of self-giving to the other. The word, in turn, is an act of giving; through and beyond the exchange of ideas and sentiments, it tends to an exchange of the two subjects themselves; in prayer my words surrender me to God, cast me upon him. If words refuse such giving and receiving, they degrade themselves to the level of empty vocables, of impersonal verbal machinery which communicates no specific personal meaning. Words are no longer their authentic selves when they refuse to mediate a presence. Inversely, the "verbal space" or "verbal field" of an orator is measured by the number of hearers he can come before and make his own.

We can today have an experience which shows this essential connection between word and presence. A record or tape brings back to us, when we wish, an event as it occurred and the words of those who were actors in it. It does the same for the voices of the dead; I am always deeply moved when Claudel's words issue from beyond the tomb. It is the man himself who, in a strict sense, "comes back" like a ghost in the power of his voice restored to us. I do not see his face, but the word spoken in my ear brings me, far better than the written word, an urgent sense of the man himself given in the instant. Recordings of voices we love would greatly modify our relations, across the gulf of death, with those who have gone before us. To speak is to be there.

We must, then, reaffirm the basic anthropological distinction between physical and intentional presence. Just as my body is an insignificant quantity in the whole of nature, so my words, carried on a breath or even fixed in writing, are no more than a quickly fading sound or a fragile script. But the extremely precarious existence of my words as a phenomenon bears no comparison with their ambition with respect to intentionality and prevenance. Fixed though I am by my body at a particular point in space and time, I am subjectively present to the correspondent, however far off he may be, whose letter I read and to whom I reply. In all discourse, whether oral or written, I am present to all the things of which I speak, whether they are past, present, or future, nearby or distant, as I am to all who hear me or eventually read me. I am "there," where my words carry me, even more than I am "here," where I speak them. Am I aware of myself as the bearer of a universal message? Then my words aspire to leap across all distances, to fill the whole universe, to carry me to the ends of the world and of history. In itself the word has the power to fill a limitless field of hearers. In my personal word, I affirm a presence which seeks to become "total."

The Word, Medium of Revelation in Dialogue

Whether the person who addresses me is dead or alive, his words are always in some degree a revelation: they draw back, or at least lift, the veil which hides his inner self from me (thus *re-velare*, to draw back the veil). In a particularly frank conversation, I have the feeling that the other person is manifesting himself to me, disclosing his intentions, delivering them to me in these words that spring from his intimate self. In varying degrees, according to circumstances, I become an associate in the life and the plans of my partner in dialogue.

But however deep are the thoughts revealed to me by the other person, they do not exhaust his existential wealth. In all speaking, there is an element of intimacy held in reserve, one which neither will nor can find full expression: a personal mystery is now and always wrapped in silence. Even if a total self-manifestation were possible, words could not effect it without profaning the person—treating the person like a thing, a surrender which would amount to a betrayal. The limitations on communication, whether in word or in gesture, safeguard an essential interiority.

Thus the word presents the ambiguity inherent in all revelation, that of a mystery which is communicated without being exhausted. An exchange of words communicates one person to another, awakening and preserving a mutual openness: but at the same time it leaves ungiven something which is inexpressible. It is not that there is any duplicity here but that the person, in his intentions and his liberty, is ineffable: words let some light filter through but necessarily veil the source from which the light comes. Always inadequate to what they manifest, words are necessarily multiple (if the word were perfect, one word would be enough) and raise endless questions in the mind of the person addressed. They answer the mind's questions, yet leave it still unsatisfied; respond to its desire without ever fulfilling it. In this respect the word is the *privileged instrument of all revelation*. For the proper object of revelation is mystery; reality made known yet remaining ineffable. The quasi-immateriality of the word—light, subtle, volatile—destines it for the murmured confidence, the veiled communication, the secret whispered so softly as almost to remain unsaid.

The reason for all this is that the word is more than the dress of thought: like the gaze, it has its origin in the meeting of matter and spirit. A perceptible phenomenon and a sounding phoneme, the word is related to the body and has a physical reality whose properties are the subject of scientific examination. Is it not the breath of life which bears it, the air which carries it to another person's ear? And yet the word is not reducible to the body in which it originates; rather, it is breath only in the restricted sense that soul (*anima*) or spirit (*animus, pneuma*) is. It springs from two sources, body and soul; or rather, from a single and indivisible source: incarnated spirit, embodied soul; and it has power to touch the emotions in their most instinctive depths as well as the highest reaches of the spirit. With greater precision, we can say that the intelligence of the speaker shapes this living matter —the voice—from within and articulates it into distinct words. The spirit—intelligence and freedom—gives rise to the word, creating it, regulating it, using it as its own privileged instrument. We have a sense of this when the child's intelligence awakens and tries to express itself: intended meanings are there, alive and struggling in consciousness, trying to force their way out through the barrier of the as yet unmastered verbal sign. When words are finally subdued to the will's desire, the latter tastes its victory over the body and rejoices in expression and communication; intended meanings then emerge in the verbal signs, using them without being subject to them. When the sounding voices are still, the unique meaning still endures in the minds of the speakers as a bond created by their fleeting but deeply experienced encounter.

We must not make the mistake of thinking that the person reveals himself only in discourse in which he speaks directly of himself: verbal confidences, autobiography, "confession," lyric poetry. Discourse about an object or a third person also manifests the speaker, often without his realizing it. Even what is seemingly the most impersonal exposition—a scientific or technical report, for example—tells the alert listener something about the speaker. The choice of words, rhythm of phrasing, intonation, gestures, and gaze express the *subject* no less than the *object*. The word arises out of the man himself and never communicates things as such in their raw and opaque objectivity, as though the word were a material "double" of the thing or an identical copy of it. For the words presuppose knowledge: in the word a man knows things; that is, he interprets them, takes hold of them for his own use, and re-creates them, expressing the world indeed as he sees it and wants it to be, but also manifesting himself as symbiotically at one with his world.

This twofold relation to the speaker and to the object spoken of gives the word an unusual complexity. An analyst can never make up his mind definitively which of these is here and now more fully manifested. Yet, to add to the complexity, a third factor also plays an essential part in the origination of the word: the person of the one addressed. To speak is to speak to someone. Even the inner word which sustains solitary reflection is not exempt from this law and creates a fictitious partner for dialogue. According to the identity, character, and real or supposed intentions of my hearer, whether present or at a distance, I make my statements more nuanced or stronger; I develop my exposition or concentrate it; I multiply images or use them sparingly, quicken or slow down my delivery, and make my gestures more sweeping or more reserved. Even before any approval or opposition from my interlocutor and simply because of his presence, my words tend to be inflected and my vision of the world transformed, sometimes to correct itself, sometimes to conform to the deeper truth of the other person's perception. A man of character is one who is constant in his word and who does not sacrifice this fidelity in an opportunist spirit. In the extreme case, the faithful witness will not change his account, no matter what tribunal he stands before and whatever the cost, even if it means his life.

But we must also admit that our thinking would not really be master of itself if it were not challenged, measured, and refined by that of others. My word (cf. the German *Wort*) evokes from my interlocutor another word (*Ant-wort*), which may be a simple reply, a retort, or a genuine response, sometimes opposing my position, sometimes confirming it. In speaking his word in turn, the other reflects my own thought back to me as it has germinated and borne fruit in him or, on the contrary, has remained uncomprehended and sterile. Dialogue reveals to me what my own thought is: its motivations—laudable or not, generous or egotistic—its narrowness or breadth, its haziness or precision, its proximate and remote, witting or unwitting implications, its impotence or practical effectiveness. My word is thus an extraordinarily complex reality, arising as it does from me, from you, and from the rest of reality! But for the same reason words exchanged effect a *communication of revelation* in several different directions, for they present to each interlocutor the world, others, and himself.

The Word as Mediator in Solitary Thought.

That dialogue reveals each participant to himself and to the other in the act of exchange is an obvious fact and has often been studied. Less notice has been taken of the fact that even the solitary and silent word exercises a mediating function at the heart of thinking itself. Spontaneous, unordered and unexpressed, thought in its nascent state —the kind of thinking which occupies the greater part of our inner duration—is only a highly confused rough draft, as it were: a kind of mental chaos in which countless intended meanings, images, and odd ideas intermingle with affective states, desires, and impulses of every kind, without succeeding in taking shape. No judgment emerges, no chain of reasoning is constructed, no critical view develops—simply because no word is fully formulated at this stage. But as soon as I try to express my thoughts, my thinking becomes calmer, ordered, and articulated; now I am able to criticize it, adapt it, complete it. Then my thinking really becomes my own and really becomes thinking.

Sometimes phrases will get written down to achieve greater clarity, objectivity, and correctness.. The word, therefore, is thought trying to say itself to itself, just as thought is the word struggling to articulate itself; word and thought come to birth together. The word is thus the mediator between thought in its germinal state and thought come to maturity; it is the instrument of thought as it thinks itself out, a kind of living mirror in which thought gradually discovers its own face, orders its features by accentuating one and shading another, and introduces harmony into the whole in order to reach its own full truth. The reason is that language is not simply a container into which thought can be poured and from which it can issue at will without ceasing to be itself. Born at the point at which body and spirit are joined, word and thought are, like them, inseparable. One sign of well-articulated thought is that the discourse in which it is expressed cannot be broken up without destroying the thought itself; another is that it cannot, strictly speaking, be fully translated into a foreign language: the first text is original in its newness; original because its birth coïncides with the coming into being of what is meant; and finally, and above all, because it in part engenders this thought itself.

In enabling thought to reach the stage of reflection, the word reveals the thinking subject to himself, gives him the means of taking hold of himself in an image. The plight of the deaf-mute is that he is alienated from himself as long as some language, however rudimentary, has not opened to him the way to self-reflection. By way of contrast, the self-mastery of the normal man is in large part measured by his command of the means of expression. The various genres of subjective literature (the personal journal, the "confession," lyric poetry, for example) are so many attempts by the writer to, so to speak, "tame" his ego by means of the word.

I am not, then, limited to speaking for the sake of speaking. When the literary critics suppose that the written word has no end outside itself, this can only be a working hypothesis. All the evidence points to the intentionality of the word. To be a man is to belong to oneself, to the world, and to others through the word.

Spokesman, Presence, and Revelation

If the word comes to me through a borrowed humanity, so to speak (a herald, a messenger, a spokesman), it manifests in a new way its twofold value as presence and revelation. The man who stands before me has renounced any discourse of his own; he has freely surrendered the right to speak of and for himself. He is now wholly dedicated to the thoughts and intention of another, which become the law and judge of his own action and to the service of which he intends to dedicate all the power he may possess of eliciting a response from others. In the person of such an envoy I am confronted not by a lifeless letter entrusted to paper and ink, but by the very person of the *other*, the one who sent the envoy. The sender's thoughts, sentiments, and wishes reach me, not as abstract lifeless bits and pieces but as vital, urgent intentions, because of the envoy's existential reality. In the envoy the word being transmitted has the same kind of human wholeness that it has in its original source: it is a living word with power to address me or even to summon me. The characteristic quality of presence is that it is evident, immediate, and inescapable; it calls upon me and bids me acknowledge it and affirm myself in the face of it; I cannot evade the reciprocity which it urges upon me. Thus I experience myself as being in mutual relation with the envoy: the identity of our bodily structure orientates us to one another, since our gazes are made to meet, our hands to reach out and clasp, and our words to be exchanged. Even the mutual efforts we may make to avoid each other are themselves proof that neither can reckon without the other. The envoy thus imposes his presence on me; but in addition, and however I may feel about it, the reciprocity which binds the two of us also involves me in the reciprocity which connects him with his principal. As a *re-present-ative* he confronts me with another *presence*, which is embodied in, and as it were identified with, his own. The distance—spatial, temporal, or social—which separates the man facing me from that other so far away and therefore separates me too from him, is eliminated. Then the word being communicated really takes on its full vital power: it is indeed that *other* who speaks to me through a borrowed mouth, and it is to him that I must respond and show honor or scorn.

In this mediated presence the envoy is a sign, a total human sign which gives the verbal sign its full value as a *revelation*. I am addressed by a word that is simultaneously near and far, by means of a voice that is as it were stripped of itself. I encounter a second "other" in the act of dialoguing with the first.

Yet I cannot but feel somewhat disturbed in the presence of this man who pushes the ambiguity of signs to the extreme limit. I am tempted to restrict my attention simply to the person before me and to regard him as being my only partner in the exchange. But that would be to eliminate the envoy and the meaning he has as such and to take his words simply as his own; thus he would cease to be for me the representative and manifester of someone else. In thus moving totally into the sphere of the immediately given, I would choose to regard the distant person who addresses me as nonexistent. If then I am to come to grips with the revelation being offered to me, I must go beyond the immediate person of the envoy to the extent that he himself has chosen to look beyond himself; that is, I must accept his word as what it wishes to be, the sign and intermediary of another presence and another word, and I must use it to vault beyond it. Then the voice of the spokesman, expressing the meaning intended by his principal, will involve me in a genuine dialogue with the latter.

The Word's Power of Enhancement

If someone refuses to speak to me, to meet my eye or shake my hand, he shows the contempt he has for me; he tries to reduce me to a mere nothing by acting as if I were not there. He rejects the reciprocity that exists between us, and his silence is equivalent to an excommunication. Every prevenient word, on the contrary, binds me to the other and renews the bonds that unite us. I am then recognized as real, acknowledged as a man, accepted as "you," and made a partner in the common action of dialogue.

We are familiar with the important part played by the opening of talks between warring groups. Military action seeks only to destroy the enemy and to annihilate him in defeat and death, but the request for and beginning of parleys is an admission that the other party exists and has a right to exist. The word about to be spoken already indicates a turning away from aggressivity, a quest of coexistence, and an admission of some equality. Often, of course, the opening of talks is effected through the intervention of a third party (a neutral power or some respected and impartial person), so that the belligerents may be spared the difficulty of having to deal directly with one another. In any case, such talks always begin in the third person; that is, each party continues for a while to be "they" to the other and only gradually becomes "you." We thus find ourselves listening (especially with modern communication media) to successive monologues which glance off each other, pass each other by, and even cover the same ground, without ever *meeting*. But the decisive moment when the other becomes "you" cannot be put off indefinitely. Dialogue begins at last when the parties agree to turn from the third person to the second person, from an attitude of hostility which regards the other only as an object to be destroyed, to an attitude of acceptance which recognizes him as a subject and a partner. As .the first words are exchanged, each is established as an interlocutor, for each has been enhanced by the other.

In our daily exchanges a man of higher rank honors me by speaking to me; he distinguishes me out of the crowd, raises me to his level, and establishes a certain equality between us. I am proud to be able to say that I exchanged a few remarks, however banal, with a great person. If the dialogue is prolonged or, better still, becomes a recurring thing, I am involved in an exchange in which I acquire a new and nobler role: as confidant or counselor. Then I am not only recognized for my inherent dignity but am promoted to a new status and re-created socially and perhaps even in my innermost self.

This is even more true when the content of our conversation concerns the recognition of my merits. The word then exercises its enhancing power not simply because a superior person addresses me at all but because of the testimonial he gives me. The avowal magnifies me; it is an ontological command, as it were, which confers a higher degree of being on me in my own eyes and in the eyes of the group.

The Penetrating Power of the Word

Moving beyond the mutual recognition of partners, the word also concerns the interiority of each; despite the limits inherent in all communication, it seeks to penetrate into each. In point of fact, verbal expression, like the human gaze, has unusual penetrating power. Our gestures and bodies remain external to each other because of their materiality: the hand-clasp, however expressive it may be, is situated at the periphery of our being. But when a word—light, subtle, almost immaterial—is addressed to me, it enters inside me, into that center which I had thought inaccessible; in some cases it even touches my most secret and personal life; and my answer, in its turn, will link my interior self with the interior self of the other. Doubtless we often exchange superficial words, and the meeting then takes place on the ground of "commonplaces." But such exchanges, as we pointed out, are always gauged in relation to a genuine communication, since they are sometimes pathways to a deeper exchange, sometimes sophisticated ways of avoiding such an exchange.

This penetrating power of the word can be used for good or for ill.

"Death and life are in the power of the tongue," says the wise man, (Prov. 8:21), and Aesop's fable about the boy who cried wolf too often is saying the same thing. At times the words of another may be deliberately or accidentally cruel; then they enter into me like a knife and cause me deep pain. Sometime another's words show me that I am an open book or that my inner weaknesses are evident, all unknown to me; then the words undermine my modest self-confidence. Sometimes, again, another's words show me that a friendship or love or respect which I thought was mutual is really not or that people I thought faithful are suddenly betraying me. Sometimes, finally, another's words express a hate and contempt that overwhelm me and crush me like a death-blow. The moralists of every age have preached against the harm done by indiscretion, slander, and calumny. The wicked man's tongue is a sharpened razor, a sharp sword, or a serpent and a venomous asp, says the Psalmist (Ps. 52:4;57:5;104:4); it is a murderous arrow, according to Jeremiah (Jer. 9:17).[11] Beaumarchais's Basil personifies the treacherous and immensely destructive power of the calumniator.

But the word can also bring most precious blessings to my innermost self: "Deep waters, such are the words of man: a swelling torrent, a fountain of life" (Prov. 18:4; Jerusalem Bible). A few words are enough at times to unveil for me an evil in myself which I had been unwilling to see. Then I am revealed to myself and urged to make the necessary changes. The word may heal my wounds and restore me to peace above and beyond the pain which has rent me interiorly; it may unite me once again to another person, reconcile me to the world, and restore my existential security; it may strengthen, console, and refresh me. In short, because the word penetrates to the deepest wellsprings of my being, I can be reborn through a word accepted as I can die because of a word. My freedom to be the man I want to be consists in large measure in my power to choose what words I want to hear.

The Nourishing Word

Whether beneficial or harmful, the word I hear is a food. Do I not sometimes "devour" or "drink in" someone's words? Even if they are simply thrust upon me, the words of others remain in me like a nourishing substance, and I never wholly rid myself of words received. Socrates made the point long ago to his young disciples who were listening uncritically to the self-interested sophists: the food you buy in the market you can carry home in a basket, and ask a more experienced person about its quality and its use; the soul's food is not carried in a basket but must be received into your soul itself, so that when you take yourself off from that place, the good or evil is already done.[12]

The word I hear is subtle in its movement and persistent in its action; the subsconscious and the unconscious mind register it and store it up; then it stimulates interior words in me in the form of silent meditation or unconscious rumination which can become obsessive and go on even in my dreams. My innermost life is a closed field in which the countless words I have taken in are locked in struggle with one another; it is a kind of culture in which they grow and proliferate like bacteria. Sometimes healthy, sometimes poisonous, they transform me interiorly. I have the feeling that certain words strengthen what is worst in me, while others stimulate, strengthen, and develop the best in me. The word is a food, but, while I assimilate it, I cannot boast that I am always its master; for it also quite irresistibly assimilates me to itself, whether I like it or not.[13] I sometimes find myself, to my surprise, adopting words, gestures, and attitudes in which the I of another day would not recognize itself. Self-examination then enables me to find at the origin of such new behavior the influence of a certain book, advice, suggestion, or even advertisement. Moreover, education itself uses words as its special instrument. The mother's words to the child are what awakens his mind in his earliest days. Education is nothing but the process of introducing into the consciousness of another the noble motivations which will enable him freely to move towards authentic values; and words, along with the witness given by the lives of men, are the only thing that can enter into a man at such a depth. In a similar way, when the chairman of a session turns the meeting over to the appointed speaker, he is entrusting the audience to him for better or for worse. Words knead men like dough. The Greeks were well aware of this when they decided that the art of persuading is the secret of power; so are modern politicians and rebels, when they take control of the mass communications media. Thus I am daily born or reborn through the words of others, and fed by them to the point where the words become indistinguishable from my existence itself. I am willy nilly the man the countless words I have received have made me, whether I listened to them eagerly or simply heard them. In feeding me, the words of others have the awesome power to lead me towards my most personal truth or towards my least authentic self.

Word and Action

The *verb* is the part of speech which, beyond all others, expresses action. Capable as it is of advancing me to a new existential status in the course of dialogue, of penetrating into my innermost being, and of transforming me as food does, the word obviously seeks to be effective; it is active and produces what it signifies. To speak, to give an "order" is, as we pointed out earlier,[14] to inaugurate a new "order" of things. "In the beginning was the word" (John 1:1)—"In the beginning was the deed."[15] The two statements are less alien to one another than may at first sight appear; in fact, they may even be stating the identical truth. The word is an *act*, in the sense that it determines what work is to be accomplished and thereby commits a man to become this or that kind of person. But the word is also an *action* because it has an inherent effectiveness, an innate power over things, inasmuch as it shapes and fashions them, in a certain degree, according to the project of the speaker.

Consider the vital continuity between word and hand: a man deliberates with himself or others before he puts his hand to things. The word in this form is an action, but it seeks to flow over into another sphere of reality in order to achieve its own realization in a surer way. Once the decisive word which defines the work to be done is determined upon, the leader's order passes it on to his subordinates and moves them to action, for the imperative mode of speech has effective power. Work in turn is a word brought to bear on reality. From the leader's word to the worker's hands there is a mysterious connection which bears fruit in the work they all do together. The word mediates between the mind which conceives the work and the hand which carries it out.

I may even myself join gesture to word in the moment of execution. The two elements then interpret each other. The verb proclaims the meaning of the gesture, and the gesture obeys the effective wish that is expressed in the word; the creative initiative of the mind sets in motion, animates, and guides both word and gesture. *Though distinct in themselves, the three movements are fused into a single vital act.* The work is, then, thought and word as embodied, brought to maturity, and perpetuated in the reality which fulfills them.

But even apart from such translation into manual activity, the verb seeks to transform man and the world. Whereas gossip, disputes over words, empty rhetoric, fruitless deliberations, and all the behavior in which words are an end in themselves, are condemned to impotence, genuinely to speak is to act and master reality. We have already noted the primordial role of speech in education as well as in suggestion and all forms of moral action upon others. But the observation can be universalized: I speak in order to take hold of the world.[16] The word has *interpretive power*: it interprets men and things and gives them a new meaning. I speak the world in order to master it.

Even in my most personal life, my own discourse helps me overcome countless recurring difficulties. A simple admission to a friend of my various concerns or trials enables me to get them into better perspective, to define them more accurately, and to master them or at least face up to them. If the most obvious as well as the most ancient therapy for anxiety or discouragement is to confide in others about them, the reason is that speaking of them puts them in my power to some degree. To utter the world is already to be overcoming it. The word is action in its nascent state. In *singing*, the transformative power of speech is added to that of music; their joint effect is to make life appear renewed to me. If man sings the world, it is in order to re-create it.

This power of the *logos*, as being both *acting* and *making*, comes out most strikingly when it confronts events. We know what infallible effectiveness some civilizations (notably, the Semitic) have attributed to the blessing and the curse. The idea is that the word by its nature brings to pass what it signifies.[17] The magician thinks the same when he claims to bend supernatural forces to his will through charms. In an analogous way, the mythic or epic narrative and the historical testimony have as their purpose to summon up past events and make their hearers or readers relive them. The modern West has largely lost this feeling for the word and has preserved hardly anything

more in this area, than the conventional usage of wishes expressed in
certain fixed social circumstances. The lifeless residue of what was
once a rite, such wishes are considered to be all the less efficacious the
more "pious" they are, and they do not really touch either party. Yet
our modern mentality does still contain some superstitious traces of
the belief in the power of the word. If someone speaks to me of some
past or still possible misfortune, I may beg him, "Don't even mention
it!," for I secretly fear that speaking of it may bring it to pass. The
same belief is expressed more humorously in saying of someone:
"Talk about a symptom and he starts thinking he has it!" For such a
way of looking at things, to e-voke is to pro-voke, to make present the
thing or event.

There are times when the control speech exercises over reality
comes to light—for example, in serious crises of social, national, or
international life. The feared or desired event is then fended off or
brought about, shaped, molded, and mastered by the power of some
decisive word. Man has power to master events as he tames the savage
beast. To the extent that he dominates his fellows or a situation, the
person with clear ideas and a strong will defines the future as he sees it
and wants it to be. He does more than prognosticate; he prescribes
and issues decrees which influence history. The word evokes and
summons the future into existence by imposing a meaning on it. Then
the word is the source of the event. The event is a word brought to
fulfillment but also, in its own turn, itself a word since it is what it is
only by reason of its meaning. In the second stage, the word goes back
to the event in order to comment on it, to "draw lessons from it"; the
word helps us to think about the action we performed yesterday and
to discern its prolongations into tomorrow.

In everyday life, the efficacy of the word is clearly shown in
"oratorical action"; here, again, the language used is revealing. Here is
a candidate for public office: facing his hearers, he remains standing,
in the attitude of a man throwing himself body and soul into what he is
doing. The inflections of his voice, his stance, his facial expressions,
and above all his gestures with arms and hands all show clearly
enough the will to change the world and his hearers by means of his
words. As his words are uttered, they take hold of the present
moment of history and reshape it; call into existence the better world
which could come to be, giving it even now an inner coherence and a

seductive reality; summon others to want that world and to build it. In a similar way, a rumor which becomes widespread, a campaign to influence public opinion, manages to make the imaginery real and the most absurd myths coherent. If an ingenuous child fully believes in the reality of the bogeyman or of Santa Claus, we must remember that the myths of the superman and of a golden age, whatever the form they take, have never ceased to seduce vast numbers of adults. The word has creative power.

And so with good news: here the efficacity of the word is carried to its extreme. A joyous announcement effects a break with an old world in which my aspirations went unfulfilled; it touches me in those hidden depths where I harbor both frustation and hope; it comes as a response which sometimes makes me aware for the first time of the depth from which my appeal came. When the good news comes, my existence is transformed. My body experiences the euphoria of sudden joy. It is not uncommon to have good news bring about a recovery from illness. A man's face relaxes, his expression has a new vivacity, he begins to smile, and even his limbs share in his joy and exultation as he dances and claps his hands. Beyond my bodily experience, it seems to me that the world has been remade; humanity, the whole of life, wear a new face. Endowed with a power of interpretation which goes to the roots of reality, good news makes all things new, confers on them a wonderful meaning which keeps me dazzled.

The relation between word and action can also be seen in the work of the legislator. The laws of the state, and indeed every program of action—social, economic, political, or educational—are so many words which provide an authentic image of tomorrow's world and bear that world within themselves as in matrixes, or molds. The same thing holds for every institution. The solemn initial juridical act which defines a new system of relations among men (the constitution of a state, for example) is nothing other than a word which is active and creative, which lays a foundation (*institutio*, act of establishing). The structure which issues from that act incarnates that efficacious intention concretely in the conditions stipulated and the rights granted; the structure is a word brought to fulfillment and established (*institutum*, that which is established). The legislative act and its product are distinct realities, related to each other as "establishing word" and "established word." Thus the intention which becomes a word and the word which becomes a structure can rule the world and transcend time. The word is inherently anticipatory; it has prophetic *power*.

Word and Culture

The word thus has the power to achieve its own embodiment in the many kinds of work produced by human genius. This fact indicates the source of each civilization's unity and of the inner connections between its manifold expressions. There is, it seems, some basic word in which each great cultural epoch tries to express man and the world. The theme, of course, has an unlimited number of converging variations; each variation is a work, that is, an embodied word, and each gives voice to the message of the age. The many productions are also linked with each other by secret or open affinities. We are familiar, for example, with the frequent correlation between writing and architecture: the semicircular arch corresponds to the uncial script; the pointed arch makes its appearance under the mason's hammer and the copyist's pen. The possibility and the interest of the study of comparitive literature are based on the differentiated unity of cultures. In the rich and diverse products of a given "age"—classical, romantic, or other—the same endlessly repeated word is incarnated, pervading the whole with the subtlety of a living soul.

If the human word seeks to transform the world according to the design of the speaker, its efficacy is not limited to the production of an external result. In a marvelous return which is too little perceived, the word I speak comes back to me like an echo reverberating from the walls of the world. Each statement I utter contributes to the definition of myself, expressing and determining my being. In one indivisible instant it proceeds from me and returns to me, a reflex upon the speaker which leads to the shaping, correction, or defining of his characteristics. Thus, having attempted to act upon things, I am myself transformed. By virtue of the interpretive power of the word, I unknowingly interpret myself when I speak.

We must insist here that we are speaking of the effectiveness of language properly used. It is clear enough that if we use unrefined or incorrect language, we slip into mediocrity of manners or mind; that affected language confirms me in my affectedness; and that careful language fosters a healthy self-mastery. A person whose language is undeveloped, impoverished, or corrupted, and much more the person who is illiterate, are condemned to cultural stagnation. Tell me how you speak, and I will tell you what kind of person you are. If the style reflects the man, the man also reflects the style, and in choosing how he will express himself, he is choosing himself.

The Name

Among all the possible types of word, there is one which strikingly shows the conquering power of the verb, and that is the word *name*. Naming is a prelude to taking possession of something. I learn this to my cost in a foreign country where I do not know the language. I then have no way of getting hold of things. They elude my grasp because I can take no verbal hold on them; I must learn to name them if I am to grasp them. In this respect, to learn a new language is to conquer the world once again.

Yet it is an even more marvelous thing that an animal, which has no conceptual language and is unable to grasp the meaning of speech, should recognize himself in a word spoken by his master, acknowledge his submission when he hears it, and check the spontaneity of his instinctive behavior at the call. The name is the privileged word which gives me power over the animal and subordinates him to my will, for the animal grasps the name within his very being. The Semites were well aware of this when they represented Adam giving a name to each newly created animal in order to exercise his mastery over them (Gen. 2:19-20).

The same kind of behavior occurs, but in a deeper way, in human relationships; here too the word is active and gives me power over others. But once again the power in all my words takes second place to the power of the name, the primordial word. In the child, as in the animal, the name acts as a *stimulus* which elicits a conditional reflex. Soon thereafter the little child is speaking of himself in the third person: "Johnny wants to play, Johnny wants to go out." But as the personality develops, the name becomes internalized and inseparable from the secret "I" and the social self. To the question, "Who are you?" I answer by giving my name. This is the word which manifests me, expresses me to others, and gives them access to my being. I truly exist only for those who know my name; anonymity and the incognito are like alibis, combining the advantages of physical presence in a place with those of a kind of "social absence."

This essential connection of the name with identity and the mystery of the person entails diametrically opposed forms of behavior in different civilizations. In some cultures the name is incommunicable, and to know it or make it known amounts to profaning the person. In one Madagascan tribe a brother does not know his own sister's name; when he comes to Europe, he feels deeply pained every time he must give his own name. In the West, on the contrary, the personal significance of the name is such that its use is a sign of respect; consequently the practice of regimental numbers in the army and certain forms of identification in hospitals, and even in some schools is felt to be an expression of contempt for individual persons, since the latter are thrust down into the mass and, as it were, annihilated.

If my name expresses me to another, it also hands me over to him and puts me in his power. By declaring my name, I surrender part of my autonomy; from now on, the other exercises possession and mastery over me. Isn't a primary concern of the teachers in a boarding school to learn the students' names so as to be able to control their actions and maintain discipline? And are the police not very careful to know the names and the many surnames, or aliases, of suspects, so as to control their movements?

The name expresses not only the person but his social position and function. Every new commission brings with it a new name and the birth of a new personality. This fact is well known for the Semitic world through the cases of Abraham (Gen. 17:5) and Simon Peter (Matt. 16:18). In contemporary France some names have persisted which were first conferred during the Resistance. It is at least a universal fact among civilized peoples that a man's advancement is expressed through naming: a leader "names" his subordinate to a higher office. Social position is expressed on many occasions by a series of titles attached to the personal name so as to indicate a person's merits. Inversely, social regression is expressed at times in the withdrawal of these supplementary proud titles. Even the use of insults shows how effective a hold a name has on the being of the person. To "call a man every name in the book" (meaning, obviously, the most unflattering names) is to attempt to substitute for his real identity an identity one can heap scorn on. In a similar fashion, the vernacular of the streets debases things and makes them ugly, whereas a new name renews them. The name thus always embodies a kind of *ontological decree*.

Every man's spontaneous ambition, therefore, is "to make a name for himself" for his own aggrandizement. Numerous offspring, wealth, professional or political success, military exploits, heroic acts, scientific, artistic, or literary achievement, and even (by a telling aberration) a monstrous crime—all these are among the means man uses to transcend his own limitations through a word or name that expresses him. The reason behind this phenomenon is that a name is a basis of presence. Wherever my name is known and spoken, I am intentionally present to others; notoriety would satisfy my desire for ubiquity. Such a presence of a person's name can, moreover, be singularly active: for example, to act or speak in the king's name is to act or speak with his sovereign power and to demand for oneself the respect due him. Finally, not content with transcending the limitations of space through his name, man also breaks through those of time: if he brings glory upon his name, he will survive himself in it.

Unitive Power of the Word

Man is a "political animal" (that is: called to live in civil society) because he is endowed with speech.[18] Every word which aims to be creative is, in effect, a principle of union. Burgeoning multiplicity tends towards nothingness, while unity is a criterion of being. It is a well-known fact that men who are separated by language barriers are likely to be hostile and even seek to destroy one another; but in any event, they cannot "hear each other" in the full sense, that is, understand each other and combine their energies in seeking their welfare or common good. Even today the almost unlimited linguistic divisions paralyze the men of whole continents by isolating each group in its native impotence and poverty. When, on the contrary, a single language is adopted, minds can unite to plan a work and wills join together in a combined effort.

We find evidence of this in our city streets: let a man with initiative, be he merchant or mountebank, harangue the passersby and soon a crowd forms. People listen together, and the germ of a human group is already there; for to listen together is wittingly or unwittingly to involve oneself in a society in its embryonic stage. If the man is an orator and bent on public action, if he knows how to capitalize on his hearers' deeper needs and explicit or implicit questions, he awakens hopes and focuses the wills of men on himself. The listening community is stirred by the power of the word to communal response and action. Thus, in moments of crisis, when courage declines and the group is in danger of falling apart, it must return to the words that gave it birth; from these as from a fountain of youth the threatened society will seek a new birth and a source of new unity.

All along the ladder of the large human groupings, the same law holds. Whether it is a matter of founding a state, concluding a peace, making cultural or commercial agreements, or whatever, special words are exchanged and ratified and become the source and bond of the unity sought. A constitution, a treaty, an alliance, a convention all initiate new relationships between men, that is, a new and different kind of cohesion. If the unity should someday be undermined, the original words remind the parties that by their own free acceptance *they are now one in that declaration* and must either settle their differences or else revise—or reject by common accord—the words that have till now bound them together.

In an exchange of words the unitive power is even more evident, as, for example, the matrimonial consent. The consent is an impalpable and fragile thing: a simple "yes," breathed between the partners, unites two lives; the two are now one in the word they offer each other, for each is identified with his word and gives himself in saying it, while he also receives the other's word and thereby gives it its full validity. Upon these two words become one is based the most primordial and universal, the most fragile and persistent, of social unities: the family.

The word can also, as we indicated, ravage and treacherously undermine the strongest social groups. But even the unitive power of the word can be misused as an instrument of collective uniformity. If the newspaper, radio, and television daily immerse every home in the same trivial slogans and shabby evaluations of things, the passive recipient is threatened with slow depersonalization. A vibrant people may decay into a shapeless mass in which the priceless originality of the individual is lost forever.

Spoken and Written Word

The volatile subtlety of the word, which gives it its penetrating power, is also the source of its fragility, for it flees on the invisible wings of the wind: *Verba volant*, "words fly away." Thus the effective and creative thrust of the word is threatened and even frustrated by its immateriality. What good are the most splendid conceptions of genius or the most solemn commitments of the heart if the least breath dissipates them? A word which would defy time must have the means of carrying out its intention. It is undoubtedly true that oral tradition makes possible, with a sometimes amazing fidelity, the transmission of cultural treasures. From one mouth to another, down long series of generations, immensely long literary masterpieces or short formulas of popular wisdom have survived simply with the help of rhythm or rhyme.[19] But to be secured against the deadly effects of forgetfulness the word must acquire firmer supports than those. Men have therefore applied themselves to developing a system of material signs corresponding to the spoken signs, and spoken language has been duplicated in a written language committed to stone or papyrus or wax, or parchment or paper. The written word has thus, like every sign, a soul and a body; the limitlessly variable material for writing carries a meaning which transforms it and gives it its value. The value of the material used, the beauty of the lettering, are incommensurable with the value and beauty of the meaning recorded there, for the latter puts me in lasting contact with another mind, near or distant, average man or genius.

The stability of the written word inevitably makes it the *instrument of all institutions*. The written word and the institution alike seek to rise superior to the passage of time. Therefore the living word, after being solemnly exchanged in the establishing of new relations between men, is immediately consigned to writing on durable material (stone has been the durable material par excellence). Henceforth, between the words once exchanged and the existing social structure the written document will always intervene (charter, constitution, statutes, etc.), preserving the original dialogue and serving therefore as a norm for the institution. All disputes about the nature of the institution will have to be settled by recourse to the written word which serves as the standard. This explains why the name "act" is given to such a document, for it fixes forever the words which will always be a new beginning and a creative gesture. In the lives of individuals the practice of making testaments, and especially the holograph testament, relies on the definitive power of writing. The document perpetuates the will of the dead person and takes effect immediately after his death.

Every literary work is, in a sense, a testament. Thanks to writing, I can be in contact today with the thought of a Plato or an Augustine. Their voices have been silent for long centuries, but they still carry on a dialogue with mankind. This is partly due to their genius, no doubt, for great words are words which will never cease to awaken echoes as long as there are men. But it is also due to the miracle of that fragile thing we call a written text. Our great libraries of manuscripts and printed matter thus have a strange kind of value: meaningless to the animal, the child, and the illiterate adult, they are for me places of recollection, almost sanctuaries. Setting at naught the measureless abyss of death, countless men come to a meeting with me there: their thought lies sleeping, as it were, needing only my wakeful, practiced eye to awaken it. The written word is doubtless definitive; it cannot now be revised, developed, made more accurate. But that very immutability enables me to pursue the dialogue at my own pace, to break it off and renew it interminably, as long as the other's thought is fruitful for me. Unlike the images of a film which rush in on me like a tide, reading enables me to reflect, slowly absorbing or deliberately rejecting.

Word and Vocable

The weakness of the written word consists in this distance which forever separates it from its author. A manuscript in the author's own handwriting in some sense restores to me the presence of the man himself. The intervention of a copyist makes the distance greater but does not affect the proper human quality of the written sign. But printing completes the depersonalization of the material sign, preserving only its conceptual value. Finally, as the temporal distance created by the movement of history increases, the written word becomes more and more detached from the time, place, and cultural context in which it was born.

A piece of writing always comes into existence within a tradition and tends to perpetuate it. The reader must then make an effort —sometimes a long-sustained effort—if he is to recapture the atmosphere which gives the word part of its meaning. Nevertheless it would be a great error to reduce the word to a simple resultant of the original historical factors and to dissolve the unity of the work into the numerous details of the materials that went into its making. Taine succumbed to this temptation: "The productions of the human mind, like those of living nature, can be explained only by their milieu."[20] Race, environment, and epoch produce the work in a strictly deterministic way: "Here as elsewhere, we have only a mechanical problem."[21] This is, in practice, to deny to genius, and to the mind itself, the power to initiate; it is to explain the plant's growth by soil, moisture, air, and sun, while saying nothing about the seed. It is also to fall lamentably short of the requirements of intelligent historical criticism. For it is obvious that the same cultural elements (literary themes, ideas, sentiments) can enter into very diverse constructions whose meanings are, in the last analysis, wholly different. Can't the same stars in the firmament organize themselves into many distinct constellations? So too, for every genuine word, and more especially for the words of genius, it will not be enough to reflect the environment in a servile way; rather, the word gathers up these cultural elements but makes fresh use of them in original creations. Without such bold initiatives, which introduce a fruitful discontinuity into a cultural community, the progress of thought and the very possibility of a history of literature, philosophy, or religion—in short, the possibility of culture itself—would be gone forever.

In other words, the error here would be to confuse the *vocable* with the *word* and the letter with the spirit. In itself the vocable is a stereotyped sign, common to all who use the language, and acquiring a value only in relation to the thing it designates. It is an isolated element which can be used in countless different ways, and it has no intrinsic reference to the indefinitely large number of speakers who will someday use it. In fact, the very perfection of the sign requires that the vocable not be related to any particular hearer or reader, for it must be intelligible to all, fixed in its meaning, and stripped of any subjective overtones. The word, on the other hand (whether it employs one or many verbal signs), is a discourse of someone to someone. If it describes the objective world, it simultaneously involves a twofold subjective relationship and unites this subject to that other subject; the reference of the word to some third term (a thing or the world generally) is incorporated into an interpersonal communication. For illustration of the distinction here being made between word and vocable, think of a long-awaited speech in which the personal relation of speaker to audience is to be the major focus of interest. But then the hearers are disappointed: the speech went on and on, but the speaker "said nothing" to his hearers. He talked a lot, but genuine "words" were few and far between. Here the verbal machinery was interposed like a screen between speaker and hearers. There was no genuinely personal meaning to take hold of the stereotyped signs and give them vital significance.

The lexicographer, for his part, is constantly struggling with this dualism of word and vocable, for when he endeavors to determine how the signs which make up the language are used, he is trying to decide on their general acceptations. But he is then not satisfied with the latter and tries to give "the feel" of their use; he therefore cites an utterance from a good writer, in which the living use of the vocable shows its fuller value. Immediately, however, a new difficulty arises: "In imperious hands the vocable bears now one meaning, now another."[22] The use of citations—of the living word—runs the risk therefore of indefinitely extending the list of various meanings. The reason for this state of affairs is that, contrary to what structuralism maintains, words are prior to any language system, literatures precede all the dictionaries, lexicons, or vocabularies,[23] and the vocable is, in relation to the word, a residue or, as it were, a degraded form. This is why "a dictionary without examples is a skeleton." The vocable is a product of analysis and must constantly be resituated in the context of the living word which is the source of all meaning.

We see, therefore, the limitations of any philological, historical, or literary analysis which would pretend to be the exclusive method for textual study. Dissect a phrase word by word and syllable by syllable; you've done a worthwhile, but also a thoroughly inadequate, piece of work. The thought of the writer is even more likely to escape you as the greater minuteness of the analysis makes you lose sight of the discourse as a totality. Similarly, a study of the elements of a musical phrase does not give you the melody. An analysis of the motives and contributing factors to a free decision does not give you the final word on why the decision was taken. Or, since man expresses himself through gesture, gaze, and bodily appearance as well as by word, a surgical examination also provides an analogy. However exploratory the operation, the surgeon's scalpel will never bring to light the original and unique meaning of the person whose body lies under the knife. If he operates on a man's eye, the surgeon distinguishes the various histological elements but does not lay hold of the human gaze. A dissected hand reveals nothing of the many meanings it derives from the person. The reason is that in every instance an analysis grasps only elements, each of which, taken separately, is distinct from the meaning. The signifying act is simple and indivisible, however numerous may be the elements of which it makes use. *The meaning expressed is therefore also simple and indivisible, and is given only through the sign as a whole*; the latter makes use of all the "parts" which can be distinguished in it, but it is sovereignly free in respect to them. Neither a detailed list of the elements nor the material sum-total of the vocables yields the meaning. A meaning is never given except in the sign taken as a totality.[24]

The interpretation of a discourse is thus something quite different from a process of juxtaposing the meanings of the various elements that make it up; it requires, rather, an act of re-creation in which the interpreter enters the author's mind and tries to experience the original meaning-giving act. I must place myself within the stream itself, at the exact point where it springs up, if I am to see the meaning flow out, as a living, temperamental thing, into the river-bed which the signs provide for its free movement. The literary themes, too, however well known and fixed by usage they may be, are used by genius in new and unforeseeable syntheses or with a brilliantly new significance. But the interpreter needs great discernment if he is to discover the new reality under the ancient garb, the mark of genius hidden in the seemingly ordinary.[25] Only a synthesis which is based indeed on analysis but also goes to the heart of things will be able to do justice to the creative uniqueness of the ideas. Where devotion to the elements (the vocables or the literary themes) replaces respect for the word, the real meanings remain uncomprehended.[26] In short, "when you read too quickly," (a lack of analysis) "or too passively" (a lack of synthesis), "you understand nothing."[27]

In this perspective, Bergson's critique of the conceptual intelligence seems to be largely grounded in a confusion between word and vocable. Bergson believes that since the vocable is an image of the material thing and the concept an image of the vocable, conceptual intelligence is incapable of grasping vital phenomena. But is this not a confusion of the tools of thought and verbal expression with the thought and expression themselves? Vocables and concepts form two systems of signs, verbal and mental, which refer to things in a stable way. But intelligence uses these signs only in order to go beyond them; it plays over the entire keyboard of language without limiting itself to any one register; no vocable or concept and no collection of vocables or concepts imprison it. The intended meaning makes use of these elements, but it moves from one to another, masters them, goes beyond them, and suggests in the end what they cannot express. To speak or to think is not to pronounce vocables or simply to produce concepts; it is not a process of putting together the dead pieces of a puzzle. To think is to judge, to re-create the real in its simple and always vital act of existence; to speak is to say *how* the world *exists*.

The same observations must be made in connection with the debate on structuralism. Language is indeed a system of signs, and each vocable is what it is by relation to all the others. The need, if one is to be master of a language, of knowing synonyms and perceiving the finer nuances is a prime proof of the fact. But we cannot stress too much the fact that language is secondary in relation to words and that man speaks both himself and the world before he ever composes dictionaries. A discourse is structured, but the structure is not the whole of the discourse, nor does a sum of words make a phrase. The wonderful thing about language as a vital function is the possibility of making a finite collection (the materials of a given tongue) produce a limitless number of utterances. The possibility is there because within a very narrow linguistic matrix meaning is constantly flowering, sometimes seen or felt in advance, sometimes rising up unexpectedly and surprisingly or even with the mark of genius on it. As soon as a meaning presents itself to my mind, it immediately searches out from among all the vocables at my command the one most suitable for expressing it; it pushes this one aside, mulls over a second, passes a third one by, until the right term, well known but just not in the foreground at the moment, finally appears for my choosing. Then my thought recognizes it: this is the correct term, predestined for my use here and now. The meaning takes possession of the sign, enlivens it, and, in this mysterious marriage, also fully discovers its own self. The word has refashioned the vocable.[28] The development of a language is also explained by this constant initiative of the mind as it gradually emerges victorious over the inflexibility of its instruments and bends them to its will, acting sometimes as an artisan, sometimes as an artist. The great minds are the real renewers of the language, and their feat is to make the instrument more supple without breaking it and to enrich it by their use (the only case where usage does not entail wear and tear). Finally, since it is both the means and the result of a continuous rebirth, language does not imprison man within a closed system; instead, it gives him access to the world and to himself, as our earlier discussion has made sufficiently clear.

Word and vocable, spirit and letter: living language is born of these encounters and brings them to fulfillment in writing. The deeper reason for writing can at last be recognized. It is because man is soul and body that he invents graphic signs in his own image, for they too are matter and spirit. The structure of writing corresponds symmetrically to the metaphysical structure of man.

Word and Truth

Language at every point, even in its most elementary use, supposes that words are essentially related to truth. The infant very early distinguishes between truth and lies. In this respect, "when . . . that is in the word which is in the knowledge, then it is a true word."[29] Only a true word is genuinely a word. If the truth cannot be spoken, then words must yield to silence. But, since I cannot say everything I think, I must think everything I say.

Truth is doubtless found primarily in thought, in that mysterious act of knowing in which the mind utters the world to itself. Such a true thought is not a material replica nor an arbitrary construction but a laying hold of the world for my own sake and at my own risk.

However, it is through words, as the privileged means of communication, that the possibility of truth and error is introduced into interpersonal relations. As the channel in which thought flows, the word must of its nature remain in living continuity with the latter. To speak things as one knows them constitutes the truth of words, or veracity. Even when my statement is erroneous because my knowledge is deficient, it retains an inalienable truthfulness: sincerity, which will always deserve the respect of others. On the other hand, it may happen that though I want to lie, I say what is in fact the truth; I err in thought and my lying words unwittingly communicate the truth. But, even if it is materially accurate, my words are at fault in betraying the natural relationship they ought to have to thought.

Words therefore have considerable power, since they enable me to lay hold of the truth and treat it as I wish. Apart from the temptation to lie, two equally harmful ways are open which would lead me, if I enter on them, to reject the absolute character of truth. On the one hand, I can come, consciously or not, to consider the truth as a possession and a personal conquest which is at my disposal. In scientific matters, it is doubtless true that service to mankind through the results of research must be combined with the legitimate rights of the scientist who is an inventor. In philosophical, moral, and religious matters, however, the danger is greater. If I treat the truth in these areas as my personal possession, I am confusing my own small person with the absolute truth and making use of the latter to domineer over, or even to condemn and crush, others. I turn the truth which I ought to serve into my servant; I make it a means of oppression when it is by nature a liberating force, and I give it such a false and repelling face that I prevent others from recognizing it.

The other temptation is to treat the truth in an offhand way and to trim it to fit my whims or the taste of the day for selfish purposes —those of advertising or demagogy, for example. In an attempt to outdo other people, each person arrogates to himself the right to say anything to anyone at any time or in any place. People think that the truth matters little and that the important thing is to catch the public ear, to "shock" others, even if it means misleading them. A noisy rhetoric of negations, brilliant paradoxes that are filled with ambiguity, formulas resounding in their very emptiness, and catchy slogans all pervert the essential relation between word and truth. Despite appearances, the second temptation really grows out of the same conviction as the first: that truth is my personal possession and that I can "manipulate" it as I wish. The word is then caught in a crisis, but so is respect for other people and for myself, since we are all, as free persons, the subjects of rights and duties before the supreme tribunal of truth.

There is another kind of truth which embraces not only my words but my whole conduct and binds me closely to others: *fidelity*. Since I am able to transcend duration by thought, I can also challenge the future with a freely given word: sometimes an everyday agreement (such as a simple business deal), sometimes a more solemn engagement (a promise, a vow, any form of commitment). Here the word finds its supremely daring form, for it claims to determine the shape of my future, simply through the decision it embodies. Whatever may be the unforeseen blows fate deals me, I determine my conduct in advance in words which I make the standard of my action, which judge me today, and which I call upon to judge me tomorrow. My truthfulness is not here limited to a declaration about the present, but embraces my whole existence, present and future, intelligence and free will, today's word and future deeds. The word, as beginning and act, anticipates the hand's work: I will be faithful if I "keep my word" and if my hand also "keeps" it, that is, fulfills the promises which the word contains.

It is clear that my relation to others is itself involved in this requirement of truth. I do not commit myself towards things but only towards persons, for they alone are capable of "hearing" the word and gauging its seriousness. Fidelity is nothing but the truth of my relations to others; it supposes, in them and in me, a knowledge of the risks which duration brings and of the efforts required if contingency is to be mastered. My word of honor turns my commitment into a point of no return, for I agree that if I violate my word, I am no longer to receive from others the basic esteem due to every human being.[30]

A commitment highlights and activates the inherent connection between word and freedom. Fidelity can only link together two wills. Being responsible for the word which creates an obligation, and being capable of taking the initiative—of going back on his word or moving on to an even better fidelity—each person admits that he is himself called to choose what kind of person he will be. Furthermore, every word, whatever its content, is an act of freedom. Veracity and sincerity or falseness and duplicity are possible only for an autonomous being. If the exercise of my autonomy is sometimes hindered by extreme pressures, this does not prove that it is an illusion; illness and mutilation even attest in a negative way the natural integrity of the body. Men rightly claim for themselves, therefore, freedom of speech and freedom to use the other means of communication which allow them to express themselves. Freedom is the basis for speech, even as speech is the sign and act of freedom.

Contrary to current opinion, then, we must not limit ourselves by saying that the intellect is *the* power that deals with truth. Truth is not wholly correlative to an act of pure knowledge, nor is it reflected in the mind like an object in a mirror. Freedom, too, is closely related to truth. It is for me to acquiesce to the truth, freely to will it, to accept it, and to ratify it for what it is. I am free to the extent that the truth is a reality for me and I am ready to submit my whole existence to it. I am called to be free because I am committed to speak the truth.

Word and Belief

My word is the expression of my personal thought and it is also ordered to the expression of truth: on both grounds, my word claims a "hearing." In one sense of the term, "to hear" is less than to listen, since "to hear" may simply mean to perceive a sound, however passively I do it. But in another sense, "to hear" is more than to listen, for it also means to understand or to seek to understand. *Ex-audire*, the Latin verb from which the French *exaucer* ("hear and heed") is derived, means to hear to the end, to hear and accept the consequences of the hearing, that is, to give graciously in return.

But can I "come to an agreement" with my interlocutor if mutual trust does not prepare the way? Can we really hold dialogue if each does not believe in the other's sincerity and the reliability of his words? Every word claims the right to be believed; by its nature it calls for belief or at least a presumption of truthfulness. Even the most limited kind of social relations presupposes such a positive outlook if it is to be at all possible. The stranger who approaches me in the street to ask directions immediately puts his trust in me, and I in turn do not doubt that he wants to get to a certain place. Sometimes in dealing with others I stress my claim to be believed: "I'm not lying," "Believe me," "I assure you." Ordinarily, however, my claim is implicit, for it is inseparable from words themselves, and to express the claim is an admission that it is a weak claim.

If the other refuses me the presumption of truthfulness and suspects that my words do not correspond to my thoughts, then the bond between us is weakened and perhaps broken. The gap which he supposes exists between my words and my thoughts creates a gap between me and him. The suspicion of duplicity is the most penetrating and the most painful of disruptions of human community. Once it takes root within a group, words are no longer believed, mutual suspicions undermine every dialogue, and the social relationship and the group itself are close to dissolution. The effort may then be made to palliate the harm done by mutual suspicion with the help of oaths. In an oath, a man recalls his basic relationship to the truth, puts off all self-interest, and stands at the interior center of himself where the True and the Good summon him and pass judgment on him. But an oath can only be an exceptional means; if used frequently, it would itself be devalued. Furthermore, since the consciousness of the oath-taker is impenetrable to me, I cannot believe him unless I presume his truthfulness. To believe in the word will always involve, therefore, trusting the speaker.

The various statements I make are quite unequal in importance, and I do not expect from others the same kind of acceptance of them all. In ordinary conversation no one doubts my sincerity, and others show that they are accepting my words by the interest they show in a bit of news or by the way they take a bit of advice. Where the other disagrees with me he can make a retort, which is, as it were, a verbal reflex whose roughness or sharpness amounts to a rejection. The reply may also be a polite one, but the other nonetheless clings to his own views and refuses mine. Contemptuous silence and ironic or violent contradiction are other forms of rejection.

In some circumstances, however, my deeper relationships with my fellows are at issue, whether it is a matter of important business, or convictions, or an ideal to be shared. In this last case especially, my words seek to touch that inner center of the other person where his most personal decisions are made, his freedom or his "heart" in the biblical and Pascalian sense of the term. When it penetrates into this inner sanctuary, my word is an invitation and an urgent call; it seeks to move him, not in a purely affective way but at a deeper level where respectful of his freedom, it will enable him to make an authentic commitment. I am not looking for an extorted avowal, a forced "Yes," for these are only a caricature of true agreement, and perhaps even a betrayal of it. What my words seek to awaken is a freely given belief, the trust that is the beginning of communion.

The human word which beyond all others calls for the other person's belief is the *word of love*. If I tell another sincerely that I love him, I want him to believe me and I call for his "faith" in me. I am aware that my love, however passionate, is a wholly interior thing. It is a disposition of my free will to seek the happiness of the other, a desire for communion with him and for sharing his existence; these are not evident, visible, or tangible facts that can be exteriorly controlled. Assurances, protestations, gifts from me, themselves call for a response of belief. There is nothing, therefore, to force a response of mutual love from the other person. That response is uncertain, contingent, absolutely free, and improbable; if given, it will be a kind of grace. Nonetheless, and contradictorily, I tend to claim a kind of right to the other's trust. I do not force him to love me, for a forced love is not love; the most desirable of gifts is the willing homage of a free being. But I demand at least that the other believe me when I say I love him; I want him to believe my words of love and thereby to believe *me*, for my words here are my very self.

The other recognizes the situation and is well aware that my word can be for him an object of belief and no more. Words of love are doubtless what he most ardently desires, for love is the supreme wish cherished by the person, and every man hopes that sooner or later, in one way or another, love will come to him and acknowledge at last the unique and irreplaceable value which he embodies. But even though it is the most desired, the word of love is also the most improbable, unpredictable, and uncertain of words. Anything that is certain and predictable in social relations belongs to the order of give-and-take, of commutative justice and mutual interest. In this sphere everything is foreseen, calculated, rational, and expected; it is for that reason also irremediably "old" and hostile to all creative initiative. The whole principle involved in barter—"you give me, and I'll give you"—is radically false: for since reciprocity has been agreed upon, neither party really gives; each is governed by the law of profit and self-interest. Hope itself is no more than a reasoned anticipation based on the normal connection between human effort and its consequences. By way of contrast, the law of love is the order of generosity, of pure altruism and genuine giving. Look down at the street where everyone is busy earning his livelihood; spurred on by the profit motive, everyone is absorbed in his own affairs. All is regulated and determined by self-interest, however legitimate. But see: someone has stopped and offered to help a blind man cross the street; this is the manifestation of something radically new. On the bleak horizon of profit, a word and a gesture inspired by love have appeared: the old order is challenged and even, to some extent, broken and rejected. A breakthrough has been made which discloses a wholly new horizon—fragile, improbable, but vast and filled with light. It is the vista disclosed by that disinterested love which alone is creative. The blind man hesitates a moment before letting the other man take his arm: the word of love addressed to him does not have the obviousness of a geometric axiom or a plain fact: it cannot be for him other than an object of belief; he can receive it only in faith. Thus, more than any other word, the word of love asks to be—can only be—*believed*. In conjugal love, the offering of one's love and the acceptance of being loved are expressed in a wonderfully meaningful formula: to pledge one's *troth*, or trust.

Among all the words of love there is one which, above all others, can only be received by way of belief: the word which is an offer of *salvation*. Salvation is directed only to someone who is lost; that is, someone who can no longer do anything for himself. Until now, this man has been proud of being self-sufficient, or at least of trying not to be a burden on anyone; the work he did enabled him to earn his living. An admirable formula, this: his daily labor was worth his daily bread; in a sense he owed his existence, his continuance in being, to his initiative and courage. Now, abruptly, this legitimate assurance has crumbled; his apparent autonomy in existence was only an illusion. If through some misadventure he should fall into deep waters, a man suddenly discovers the fragility of his life, his powerlessness and his absolute need. He is lost, a wreck which the deeps will swallow up: his existence—that unique and irreplaceable "all" which he is—will slip away from him forever. Unless . . . unless some other sees his distress and cries out to him from the shore to hang on: he is coming to save him. Save: the one word the drowning man longs to hear—longs not only with the full force of desire but with the tensed energy of a bodily being aware of the value of his life and of the extreme peril it is in. Moreover, it is a word in itself improbable, for it is the expression of total disinterestedness, willing to take the ultimate risk. To the unfortunate man such an unforeseeable initiative on the part of another can only be the object of hope, not of reasoned expectation; and then, if it is offered, of *belief.* The refusal to believe in it would be the greatest insult to the savior. Yet the word of love of such extraordinary generosity, the promise of salvation, cannot be accepted otherwise than through an unparalleled act of faith.

There is more to be said. Suppose the savior is willing not only to risk his life for the lost man but deliberately to lose it. Suppose he takes my place, wretch that I am, in the abyss which is about to engulf me.[31] Then the law of exchange, of give-and-take, reappears, but with a total reversal of its meaning. The savior loses his whole self to assure me of my whole existence: "I give you my life," he says in substance; "take mine." Here love reaches the ultimate limits of gratuitous self-giving, but also the limits of contingency and improbability. No word of love is more to be desired nor more difficult to accept than this. Surely no such renunciation of rational calculation, of the facts of experience, and of the dictates of common sense can be demanded of me. One must oneself be capable of great love in order to accept from another the proof of a still greater love.

To reject the good news that salvation is at hand is at once to exclude oneself from all help and to show distrust of the savior, the most insulting of attitudes. After all, if a person communicates a little of himself in every sincere word, then a savior gives his whole self in the words which express his willingness to sacrifice his life; to reject his words is to reject and deny him, to wish him nonexistent, to try to annul his sovereign act of love. ·

The offense may seem less if the savior reaches me through an intermediary. The spokesman, we may say, is essentially an ambiguous person; he presents himself as only a representative of another who remains unseen; his look, gestures, and voice express intentions which are not his own; the mandate he claims can always be questioned, even if only because of the limitations, weaknesses, or faults from which no man is exempt. The messenger is indeed always, from some point of view, unworthy of the credibility he claims; and this is all the more true when the message is improbable. Yet, even in these circumstances, a refusal of the proposed salvation will gravely offend its offerer; the spokesman was accredited and the words were those of his principal. To reject the message and the messenger is to reject the savior himself, responding to his supremely generous offer with scorn and deliberately excluding oneself from the proffered communion.

But to believe the news of salvation is to accept the savior's renunciation of his own life even as one also renounces one's own supposed certitudes. It is to allow the other's word its absolute effectiveness; it is to believe him capable of supreme love; it is to abandon all calculable expectations and lay oneself open to a sovereignly free act of love. Between the one who is going to survive and the one who is going to die, a wholly unheard of regime of relationships is beginning. The one who is saved will, of course, contract an unpayable debt to his savior. But, above all, there is a sense in which he will henceforth live out of the sacrificed life of the other, for he accepts the offer of a death and a life; he receives the savior into himself, into the heart of that *act which makes him to be*, in a mystery of coexistence at whose core will be the ever living word that has been offered and accepted. Putting everything at stake, to believe is to trust in nothing but unqualified love.

Word, Witness, Tradition

Received in faith, the word that is the bearer of a truth decisive for human existence cannot be simply preserved for its own sake. This is the case with a moral or religious message of universal scope. With an irresistible impetus, such a word tends to give itself, diffuse itself; it advances constantly, flying from mouth to mouth; it penetrates into the conscience of the individual and the whole household—not to be hidden there, but only to rest a moment before setting out again with new élan. No one has the right to treat it as his own possession; to hoard it would be to destroy it. For a message of great import is the bearer of a truth to which every man has a right; it gives itself without being diminished, is communicated without being divided, is spread far and wide without being profaned. It tends to shape every existence it touches, to bring to every mind which receives it light, consolation, and perhaps salvation. If one individual keeps it as though it were his own, some other who was waiting to hear it may die in despair.

But not every truth is self-evident, and least of all those truths which transmit the call of an ideal. The messenger therefore must compensate by the ardor of his personal conviction for the lack of evidence which characterizes his message. Since what is involved is a living truth, his whole life must be a proclamation, a word, a witness. The witness is a man who is a sign. Whether the witness is borne before the tribunal of justice or that of history, it testifies here and now, above and beyond temporal distance, that the crime, or the event, occurred as he says it did. The witness to a moral or religious value attests that all mankind is called to accept the same meaning for life as that which has illumined his own person. Across the incommensurable distance which separates the visible from the invisible and the empirical from the ideal, the spiritual man is a sign: within the concrete circumstances of history he signifies the imperishable presence of the value to which he is witness; he embodies it and may some day sign his deposition with the supreme act of martyrdom.

Since each witness raises up one or more further witnesses, witnessing gives birth to tradition. Or rather the witnessing is tradition in the active sense of transmitting or communicating in a living way. The transmitted belief or faith is, in turn, tradition in the passive sense of a deposit that is preserved and shared without being divided. This continuous transmission of a truth gives rise to a line of believers. Across the living and unbreakable network of the generations of men who appear on earth and then sleep in death, a hidden life of faith persists and grows, tenuous but stubborn.

The active handing on of the words of life is never reducible to a material transfer from one point to another. The messenger who carries them must not only be faithful to the letter but interiorly faithful to the spirit as well. Full adherence to the message thus requires perpetual interior renewal, a continual effort of assimilation. In the man who carries it, the word produces its full fruits once the rhythm of interiorization and attestation permeates the whole of his life. In this way the message itself, while remaining unaffected in its original tenor, is enriched by the countless spiritual experiences to which it gives rise in the course of history. Tradition becomes a life-giving milieu in which the word is constantly engendered anew.

If the message seeks a firmer support, writing then defines the message and guards it against the dangers of distortion and forgetfulness. The tradition within which the writing is done contains it, and constantly renewed experience guarantees the vitality and fruitfulness of both the writing and the tradition.[32]

NOTES

1. It is by misusing words that Sartre opposes the "in itself" or unconscious being to the "for itself" or conscious being, as authentic being to degraded being. For the perfect coincidence with itself that is defined as the privilege of things really expresses the fundamental law of every being: every being is all that it is and nothing but what it is. But this necessary kind of presence to self is the most rudimentary kind of presence. Though present to itself because it perfectly coincides with itself, the "in itself" is, from another point of view, absent from itself, because it does not know itself. It is opaque to and blind towards itself. The conscious being, on the contrary, is present to itself not only by coincidence but also by self-knowledge; to the extent that it is transparent to itself, it has an apperception of itself and "grasps" itself, enjoying thus a kind of "duplicative" presence to itself and existing on an incomparably higher level of being. To define consciousness as a "distance" which the being creates in relation to itself and to conclude then that in man being denies and "annihilates" itself even while contorting itself in a vain attempt to coincide with itself, is to build an ontology and anthropology on a spatial image and to sacrifice metaphysics to dialectical games. On the moral plane, on the contrary, man is, in a sense, always searching for himself and working to become what he is meant to be.

2. Pascal, *Pensées*, Fr. 205 (Turnell, Fr. 116, p. 142).

3. *Ibid.*, Fr. 693 (Turnell, Fr. 389, p. 220).

4. *Ibid.*, Fr. 206 (Turnell, Fr. 392, p.221).

5. Cf. Edmond Barbotin, "La signification de l'oeuvre," in *Actes du IXe Congrès des sociétés de philosphie de langue française* (Aix-en-Provence, 1957), pp. 144–148.

6. Cf. below, this chapter, "Word and Truth."

7. Cf. Aeschylus, *The Suppliants*, v. 248: the herald carries a sacred staff which protects his person and those who accompany him (cf. also *Odyssey*, II, 37). The reason is that as "messenger of Zeus and men" (*Iliad*, I, 334; VII, 274–278), the herald is "divine' (IV, 192) and "dear to Zeus" (VIII, 517).

8. Cf. the well-known incident of the messenger from Marathon who fell dead as he brought the Athenians news of their victory. Cf. also 2 Samuel 18: 19–23.

9. In the ancient theater the actor's mask amplified his voice, enabling it to ring out (*personare*). Some scholars derive the word "person" from this *personare*; others reject this hypothesis on metrical grounds, the *o* of *persona* being long and the *o* of *personare* short.

10. By a quirk of language, "to put in an appearance" (French: literally, "make an act of presence") implies mainly a passive presence. "Act" (or the element of activity implied in the English expression) then has a purely formal sense; I satisfy a conventional obligation without involving myself in any very personal way.

11. Cf. Sir. 51:2, 6; on indiscretion, Sir. 28:16–21.

12. Plato, *Protagoras*, 314 a-b.

13. Cf. Pascal, *Pensées*, Fr. 536 (Turnell, Fr. 189, p. 155): "Man is so made that if we are continually telling him that he is a fool, he comes to believe it; and by repeating it to himself he makes himself believe it."

14. Cf. above, this chapter, section 2, "The Word as Beginning and Act."

15. Goethe, *Faust*, Part I, verse 1237.

16. Cf. Plato, *The Sophist*, 219c: "the [arts] which master [lit.: handle] by word and deed."

17. Cf. Matt. 10:12–44 Cf. Xavier Léon-Dufour (ed.), *Dictionary of Biblical Theology*, trans. P. Joseph Cahill *et al.* (New York: Desclee, 1967), articles on "Blessing" and "Curse."—Linguistic taboos and euphemisms are to be explained in this way. In Greek, for example, the word for "left" or "on the left" is *aristeros*, a comparative formed from *aristos*, which means "best." The unfavorable or ill-omened side is thus designated in an outlandishly laudatory way in order to avert possible bad luck.

18. Cf. Aristotle, *Politics*, I. 2, 1253a2-10.

19. Cf. M. Jousse, *Etudes de psychologie linguistique: Le style oral, rythmique et mnémotechnique chez les verbo-moteurs*; *Archives de philosophie*, vol. 2 (Paris: Beauchesne, 1925).

20. Hippolyte Taine, *Lectures on Art*, trans. John Durand (New York: Holt, 1896), p. 34.

21. Taine, *History of English Literature*, trans. H. van Laun (New York: Grosset and Dunlap, 1908), p. 23; definitions of race, surroundings, and epoch, pp. 17–25.

22. Emile Lettré, *Dictionnaire de la langue française* (1863), p. xvi.

23. *Ibid.*

24. Cf. Pascal, *Pensées*, Fr. 115 (Turnell, Fr. 113, p. 141): "A man is a whole, but if we dissect him, will he be the head, the heart, the veins, each vein, each fragment of a vein, the blood, each of the blood's humours?"

25. It has been pointed out that Maine de Biran's philosophy was passed over for a long time because de Biran expressed very original ideas in simple everyday language; cf. Michel Henry, *Philosophie et phénoménologie du corps* (Paris: Presses Universitaires de France, 1965), p. 16.

26. French distinguishes between *parole* (word or discourse) and *mot* (word in the sense of individual word or vocable); German does the same in the plural with *Worte* (=*parole*) and *Wörter* (=*mots*; a *Wörterbuch* is a dictionary). The Italian *parola*, the Spanish *palabra*, and the English *word* neglect the distinction.

27. Pascal, *Pensées*, Fr. (Turnell, Fr. 78, p. 126).

28. Noam Chomsky brings out this creative role of language in his "De

quelques constantes de la théorie linguistique," *Diogène*, no. 51 (1965), p. 14.

29. Saint Augustine, *The Trinity*, trans. A.W. Hadden, rev. W.G.T. Shedd, in Whitney J. Oates (ed.), *Basic Writings of Saint Augustine* (New York: Random House, 1948), p. 848.

30. Cf. Maurice Nédoncelle, *De la fidélité* (Paris: Aubier, 1953).

31. This actually happened during the Second World War, when deported men at times freely offered to take the place of comrades condemned to death.

32. The different aspects of the problem of witnessing are developed in Barbotin, *Le témoignage spirituel* (Paris: Editions de l'Epi, 1964).

CHAPTER 4

THE HAND

If I compare my human hand with the hand of an ape in the zoo, I cannot but feel initially a certain repugnance. The ape's hand is like my own but at the same time unlike it; its morphology is analogous but coarser; though it, like mine, can take hold of things, it also serves for walking, so that it is simultaneously hand and foot. The ape's foot, in turn, has some manual functions, so that the animal is, as it were, undecided whether to be four-footed or four-handed. Finally all these organs are quite hirsute, as though struggling to emerge from the bestial state. In short, like a caricature of a face, the ape's hand attracts my own but also repels it; it reproduces and conterfeits it, bears witness to it and protests against it, reflects it and betrays it, imitates it and "apes" it. Between the animal's hand which comes out to meet mine and my own which hesitates to return the touch, there is a reciprocity, but the reciprocity is equivocal, ambiguous, and highly suspect. More than in any other instance, I cannot decide whether that hand is frankly welcoming me or laying a trap for me, whether it wishes to fraternize with mine or seeks to mangle it, whether the being which expresses itself in this gesture is friendly or hostile, even homicidal. I must make an effort to accept the handclasp, and the contact, however innocuous, with this skin, these bristles, and these claws will surely leave me uneasy.

The disturbance I experience here is a psychological attitude which is correlative to the indecision of the biologist in the order of experimental science. Aristotle,[1] Cuvier, and Broca[2] are not in agreement on defining the hand in such a way that the definition is equally valid for animal and man. Is this not a sign that, despite the similar anatomical structure, the ideal hand is the human hand and that it is a wasted effort to try to identify with it the corresponding organ in lower species? In any event, it would be a serious mistake to regard either the simian organ or the human organ as autonomous and detachable entities. What really troubles me about the simian hand is not its rough appearance so much as the fact that it is the organ of this kind of animal, connected with this hairy body and this grimacing and bestial head. My hand is more perfect, but this is considerably due to the upright stance which has emancipated the hand from the ground and from the function of supporting the body. My organ manifests itself to me and is "lived" by me only as part of my whole personality. Each of the two hands derives its meaning from the whole being of which it is a part and which uses it and expresses itself through it, just as the human word and the human face are inseparable from the person. If I do not recognize my hand as wholly corresponding to the ape's, it is because the ape is not a faithful replica of my own being; I do not feel myself to be, nor am I, his congener. The hand belongs to the ape or to the man: that fact introduces a radical difference into their respective meanings.[3]

I. THE POSTURE

Closed Posture and Open Posture

Since the hand is inseparable from the whole body, the manual gesture cannot be understood except in terms of the whole man. The posture expresses the person, his intentions and sentiments, both in their deeper constants and in their variation; it is a global gesture which is the setting for each particular gesture as the context is the setting for the text.

We cannot here examine in detail the many postures which express us, and shall therefore reduce them to two essential types: the closed posture and the open posture.[4]

The *closed posture* is characterized by the forward inclination of the head, the bending of the extremities towards the limbs and the limbs towards the trunk, and a more or less complete immobility. The person turns away from the world and other people and tends to curl up into himself or to bend back into himself. Such is eminently the posture of a human being before birth. During its fetal life the child lives only in and for itself, totally given up to biological concentration as it prepares to enter the world; it is ignorant of others and even of the mother whose nourishing blood it receives; it is ignorant of itself, for it exists in the darkness of unconsciousness.

Birth marks the cessation of this bending back upon self and inaugurates the *open posture*, which symmetrically reverses the earlier position. Until now sealed in the maternal womb, the child abruptly breaks out into the world of men. The trunk relaxes; the limbs find their place and their movement in space; the lungs expand and breathing begins. The silence of the womb is broken, and the first cry is the necessary sign of a will to live. Gradually the eyes and other senses will begin to react, receiving impressions from outside and mastering their respective fields of action. Birth is the point at which the living being opens up to things, to others, and to life itself; it is the radical beginning of his being-in-the-world. The closed posture is not, however, permanently abandoned; far from it. It alternates with the open posture to form the basic vital rhythm of systole and diastole. This rhythm rules the most fundamental bodily functions, namely, the heartbeat and breathing. Throughout his life, the rhythm of daily rest takes man back to the concentration of the embryonic state; the hands cease to labor, the eyes close, the limbs sometimes adopt the fetal position. Many of the higher animals sleep with their bodies forming a semi-circle, and some birds with their head beneath their wing. The closed posture is often also that of physical suffering. The sick person assumes it to help bear the shock of pain and to gather up his energies. It is well known that in some cultures the dead are buried with knees drawn up to chin; in the great concentration of death, a man once again adopts the fetal position and returns to his beginnings.

Bodily postures have spiritual meaning. The bending inward of the body conditions the bending inward of the spirit; no attention or meditation is possible when the limbs and senses are dispersed. Rodin's *Thinker* has withdrawn his hands from their work; he is seated, concentrated, hand to chin, wholly absorbed in the struggle against the obstacles met by his distracted mind or simply unable to reach the truth. A certain tension of the whole body and an imperceptible movement forward are signs of the interior effort and indicate that the "closedness" of the posture means neither surrender nor impotence. The man is thinking with his concentrated members as with his recollected mind, and thus with his entire unified being. The same cut-off from the surrounding world which is part of the closed posture is found in sadness and mourning; things have lost their interest for the man who is hurt or confronted with the mystery of evil or the absurdity of death. He himself is dead, as it were—beaten down, prostrated, overwhelmed by the total lack of interest in worldly things which is characteristic of the dead.

In our relationships with others the closed posture is one of rejection and even of hatred. While love lights up the face, parts the lips for words and a smile, opens the hand for giving, and makes the whole man radiant, hatred closes him up: the head is lowered, the eyes turn away from the other, and the mouth is closed in a refusal to speak. In anger the fists clench, the face is distorted, and the body coils up to spring and attack.

In less intense situations, the closed face is the attitude of discontent, ill humor, and sulkiness. The same withdrawn attitude goes with conscious guilt. The child who knows himself at fault bows his head, turns his back, and withdraws into solitude; sometimes he hides his face in his arm and leans against the wall; sometimes he sits in a corner, alone in silent dejection; sometimes, finally, he runs away from home, where everything conspires to increase his self-accusation. In closing himself up in himself the guilty person passes sentence of excommunication on himself.

The open posture breaks out of this closed circle of the self. It is characterized physically by the straightening up of the body, especially when standing, by the extension and readiness of the members, especially the hand, by the openness of the eyes and receptivity of all the senses, by perceptiveness and mental attention, and by a sureness and grace of gesture. But we must distinguish two qualitative kinds of "openness." There is a passive openness which is nothing but a relaxing of the discipline required by action and social convention. The games-prefect in Alphonse Daudet's story illustrates this kind of letting oneself go. Such "decontraction," when methodically exercised, becomes "relaxation." But there is an active openness in which the intentional character of consciousness becomes manifest, as the man deliberately directs himself to things and to other people in action, inquiry, and greeting.

In my relation to things, the open posture is the sign of a balanced attitude to the world. It expresses physical and psychic health, youth or a youthful maturity, and an adaptation to life; and it is characterized by fullness and regularity in the relational functions of breathing, moving, and eating (the purpose of the "aperitif" is to "open" [Latin, *aperire*] the organism to nourishment). In work and action, the open posture is the posture of energetic effort and confidence in oneself as one faces a world to be mastered.

Balance in interpersonal relations, too, is manifested by openness to others; the extended hand, the frank gaze, and the word of welcome express receptiveness, sympathy, and love. While the timid or the awkward person hesitates between the closed posture and the open posture and remains finally "half open," the man who is sure of himself and others gives himself readily. The latter has an "open face" and welcomes the other with open arms and open heart; being "well-born," he retains the native attitude which has enabled him to come happily to the world and to other people. Now he remains standing, responsible for himself and at the disposal of others, ready for the public function of chief, leader of men, or prophet; free for action, and alert either for moving out or for watchful waiting. Now he is sitting in an attitude of receptivity for teaching to be given or received, for listening to others and for friendly conversation. A person may also cultivate more balanced relations to the world through movements, exercise, physical culture, and sports. The techniques of yoga (which may be abstracted from any doctrinal contest) are based on the simple truth that each bodily posture can educate the consciousness to a corresponding attitude, and that physical balance tends to effect a spiritual balance.

Understanding of Posture and Gesture

We cannot here study in depth the problem involved in understanding the gestures of others; we refer the reader to what we have written on the subject elsewhere.[5] It is enough to note that the language of the human members, apart from rare cases of ambiguity, does not require a discursive analysis or interpretation; nor do I have recourse to an analogy of earlier personal experience of gestures. Instead, I immediately and intuitively understand the farewell expressed by another's hand or read the discontent written on his face. One reason for this is that the meaning is "embodied" in the gesture, in virtue of the essential soul-body union; the meaning is immanent in the bodily signifying, whereas it is not immanent in a material sign that is distant, either in time and space or simply for the mind, from the phenomenon it makes known. A second reason is that the bodily reciprocity which exists between men makes the language of gestures and postures both possible and immediately comprehensible. In the presence of another person, my own humanity instinctively recognizes itself in his; beyond the individual differences between us there is a kind of specific communion as men which projects me into his body as it projects him into mine. The meanings dormant in me are awakened when I see his gestures, and they find in these latter their own expression. Our "complicity" as human beings becomes a kind of empathic grasp of the language of gesture and posture, even when these express hostility or rejection. At once the current of meaning flows, the spark of understanding is struck, not at the level of abstract knowledge but at the level of lived experience and immediate presence.

II. THE HAND, ORGAN OF RELATIONS WITH THE WORLD

The Hand as Organ of Anticipation

In two well-known passages of the *Timaeus*, Plato contrasts the world which is complete in itself, spherical, and endowed with a circular movement which makes hands and feet unnecessary,[6] and man who is forced to move about through all sorts of places with the grasp and support of his limbs.[7] We are two-footed and two-handed by reason of the need we have of exploring, conquering, and mastering the world. The outstretched hand goes on ahead to encounter the desired object and, in intention, takes hold of it. As I walk, my hand anticipates obstacles I may run into and overcomes them in advance. The perceptive hand which I extend before me into the dark—or, if I am blind, into my night—and which I prolong on land with a cane and at sea with a sounding-line, expresses my whole relationship to the world: an ambivalent relationship of ignorance and anticipatory knowledge, fear and desire, apprehensiveness and eventual prehension, defense and conquest. My hand sees and guides me; as I walk, it defends me from onslaught and prepares me for attacking; it is wholly at my disposal and thus ready for the countless possible situations experience has in store for me. My hand is the organ of my plans in regard to the world or, better, it is these plans in the first stage of realization. The hand itself has an intentional thrust, even as the consciousness which sustains, directs, and gives meaning to the hand.

The Hand as Organ of Contact

The hand is thus the organ for measuring and passing over distance. In cases where direct contact is impossible or useless, my hand extends in the gesture of "indicating"; the index finger points to the object, the eye focuses on it, and the word names it. Through the collaboration of hand, eye, and mental or spoken word, I become really but intentionally present to what is distant. Without leaving this spot, I am already yonder: at the house across the street, a snowy peak, an inaccessible constellation. Pointing is touching from a distance.

Is physical encounter possible? Then, while the feet traverse the distance blindly and carry me from place to place like a simple machine, the outstretched hand is ready for contact; whether helped or not by the eyes, it recognizes the distance, accepts it, explores it, and measures it, all at once. It registers the distance between me and my surroundings, my desire and its object, my present possessions and a possible possession, what I am doing and what I wish to accomplish. But even as it admits my indigence, poverty, and constantly recurring need, the groping hand is also exploring the world, discovering it like a searchlight, interpreting it, and marking out within it reference points, grips, and supports. Stretched out as it works, my hand turns obstacles into landmarks or instruments until it finally reaches its goal. Then it touches this portion of the world which I have finally conquered, feels the objects which fill it, and takes possession of this new "here."

In so doing, an essential need of the hand is satisfied: to touch. It is in the hand that this sense is most actively exercised. Whereas the remainder of the skin surface exercises only a passive touch (at contact with the clothing, for example), the hand feels things, explores and probes them. Its suppleness and vital sensitivity; its full and complex structure of nerves; the differentiation of the papillae of touch in fingers and palm; the many possible articulations of fingers, wrist, elbow, and shoulder: all this makes the hand a genuine instrument of knowledge and recognition, an organ of vision without intervening distance. The hand of a blind man compensates for the now impossible touching at a distance which sight is, while the hand of a man who sees controls the sight.[8] But the knowledge here is not abstract or notional. Manual contact is an experience, an encounter, a meeting of myself and the world. I touch things to assay them, to test them, to explore their obvious or hidden virtues; my fingers travel flexibly over their shapes and contours and judge their strength, weight, and value. If I am a weaver, I judge the quality of cloth by touch; if I am a doctor, I diagnose illnesses with my hand. Contact even has a transformative power. By the mere fact that I lay my hand on a thing, I submit it to my nascent action. (Carrying this to its extreme consequences, King Midas turned everything to gold simply by touching it.) The hand is the first organ of experience, the *organ of reality*. Psychiatrists are aware of this and have their mental patients exercise their hands—in modeling, for example—in order, through direct contact with material things, to restore a sense of the real and of their relation to a "given."

But even as it tests things, my hand is tested in turn by them: experience is a mutual assaying of myself and the world. In investigating things my hand is the first organ to be hurt: it gets frozen, pricked, burned, and mangled (accidents at work are often accidents to the hand). In working, my hand always experiences fatigue, revealing to me the limits of my strength and forcing me to be honest with myself as I confront reality.

The Hand as Organ of Work

What we have been saying shows that the hand is the organ for working, acting, and struggling with things. Through it, as already through the word, our relation to the world is not only one of knowledge but also one of transformation. Some everyday expressions, like "fold one's arms" or "twiddle one's thumbs," express deliberate idleness,[9] while others, like "put one's hand to the plough" or "take in hand," signify the commitment of a man to action. In magical rituals the hand endeavors to master the hidden forces of nature. By great effort our arms struggle with the elements, master them, and bend them to our service. I tame an animal by a skillful alternation of blows and caresses. Human work is not an absolute creation but a manipulation of what is given. The hand is applied to the primordial matter which the universe represents for me, and introduced into an order of things which I regard as disorderly in relation to my needs. The hand conquers the world by humanizing it, masters it by projecting my intentions into it, and awakens in it countless responses to my present or future needs. Everything that separates the jungle or the desert from the most advanced of cities is the hand's work; for the hand clears the ground, cultivates, builds, manages, and embellishes. We can say equally that the hand has technical skill or that technology is man's "handhold" on the universe.

The hand thus brings a certain fulfillment to a world hitherto disordered, sterile, or threatening. Hence we cannot subscribe to a purely "negative" conception of human effort.[10] Work doubtless does initially suppose a refusal of the world as it exists in its raw state, hostile to man and yielding no fruit. I reject the jungle which has first rejected me. I protest against the unhealthiness of the swamp, the aggressiveness of the wild animal, and the sterility of the land that lies fallow. Then I start to work; I set my hand to the world in order to subject it, fertilize it, arrange it, and humanize it—in other words, to perform the basic actions by which the earth becomes the soil. I even give things a new, hitherto unknown, and ideal meaning, for, thanks to art, brute matter can express aesthetic, moral, and religious values. But if my effort is thus conditioned by an initial negation and protestation, it is in itself essentially constructive and creative, giving what is undetermined a determination and imposing *meaning* on the world by assigning it a human *finality*. It is doubtless possible—and sometimes happens—that a transformative activity which is itself disordered and uninformed by true values leads to a degradation of things. "Progress" often involves lamentable abuses. But these are the troublesome results of action that is unfaithful to its own nature. If any negation is involved antecedent to or posterior to authentic work, this fact does not turn work into an annihilation or destruction of the world. It would be a serious mistake to consider negation as the essence of work or progress, for one would then be applying to work the accusation of "annihilation" which Sartre levels at consciousness as such.[11] In reality, any work worthy of the name is positive and affirmation of being and value; it confers on things a human and higher value.

Things also act upon the hand that masters them; they shape and fashion it, leave their mark upon it, distort or strengthen it, make it flexible or stiff, wound it and painfully furrow it or refine it. When a person adapts to a new kind of work, he "gets his hand in," as the idiom intuitively expresses it. The hand of the artist or artisan, the laborer or the sailor, the machinist, the painter, or the surgeon: each bears the mark of the world to which it belongs—the element of which it is master, the form it aims to impose on the element, and finally the tool it is constantly "handling." All the repeated efforts, all the wounds or blows received, leave their living testimony in the flesh. I can read a trade and a human life in a worker's hand. Tell me what your hand is like, and I will tell you what you are.

Better still: do we not delineate the stages in the ascent of prehistoric man according to the material which his hands mastered and the perfection of his manual skills? To cut or polished stone, iron, copper, and bronze there corresponds a particular kind of men. The hand belongs both to the man and to his work; if it is a living mediator between man and the world that is being shaped, it is also a mediator between man today and man as he will be tomorrow. In this respect, to choose a profession is to choose, via the tasks it involves, the kind of hand you will have and the kind of man you will be. Even when he thinks he is being exhausted by the labor of his hands, a man is also being reborn of it; his being is expended in it but also revitalized, lost and recovered: and the hand is the originating source from which, unawares, his own being must emerge. For every man is the child of his own work. And if we look beyond the individual, many hands applied to a single task bring men together. Like the word, the laboring hand has a unitive power; it gives birth to social man. This explains why painters, sculptors, writers, artists of every kind have, in their effort to express man, taken so much trouble to observe,

study, and describe the hand. We need only recall the splendid
studies of a Michelangelo or a Velasquez, and the two contrasting
poems of Théophile Gautier on the hands—masterful portrayals, one
of delicacy and refinement, the other of earthy realism.[12]

Organ, Tool, Machine

Mediating as it does between man and the world, the hand eminently
deserves the name "organ," for it is a living instrument. Other organs
are beyond the control of my will (the internal organs, for example) or
perform only a stereotyped action (the feet, for example), but the
hand is wholly at the disposal of my freedom as it endeavors to
transform the world. It is also superior to all tools that are distinct
from my body and inert, even when they are most easy to "handle."
My hand is fully mine and in solidarity with my whole corporeal and
spiritual being; it is I myself. My intentions instantaneously reach my
fingertips; and there too, at the same moment, I feel the resistance
offered by things. Every organ of my body and every tool in my
workshop are related to my hand as to the archetype which calculates
their value and is superior to them.

The tool is related to the hand as to its source. The hand in itself is
capable of many techniques: it grasps, enfolds, strikes, divides, holds
fast, pulls, and pushes. But each of these varied powers is restricted.
My human strength is limited, my hand is vulnerable to bruising
contact with matter, my field of action is narrow. My mind ranges in
its aims far beyond what the hand can directly do; the work that is
conceived, willed, proclaimed, or promised is immeasurably greater
than my natural powers to accomplish it. My hand, therefore, reflects
on itself as it were, and evaluates the respective nature of the work it
can do by itself and the results it aims at. This critical self-evaluation
of the manual intelligence leads me to conceive and produce artificial
means by which to extend my efforts, to enlarge their field of application and to attempt to narrow the gap between what I *want* and what I
am *able to do:* these means are *tools.* Each of them in turn is provided
with a kind of hand: a handle or grip, which mediates between my
hand and the tool itself. But it is a hand only by analogy, for it is a
thing—inert, without initiative or movement of its own—wholly
subjected to my own hand and attendant upon my hand's good

pleasure. A tool is something strictly delimited and made for a precise action: the saw does not strike or pull, the hammer does not grasp or push; in each of them the total power resident in my hand is, as it were, broken down, specified, distributed, and magnified.[13] If a list could be compiled of all the tools invented by man over the centuries, it would add up to an extraordinary testimony both to the limitations on our manual powers and to their endless variety. As the hand mediates between man and the world, the tool in turn mediates between the hand and matter. The chisel which my hand directs is made of steel; I feel its coldness and hardness; it fatigues my gripping hand; its stiffness conducts the resistance offered by the marble, so that my hand feels it. But at the same time my hand quickens the instrument and is, as it were, its soul. Through the inert density of the tool my energy passes and, even more than my energy, my intention—that interior word in which I give expression to the work to be produced. Under the point of my chisel, the idea is inscribed in brute matter. Under the agile fingers of the pianist or typist, notes and letters leap out owing to the irresistible pressure of the will.

With the coming of the machine, human tools underwent a decisive change. The articulations of the loom, like those of the piano or typewriter, multiply the joints, nerves, muscles, and tendons of the fingers. The mechanical contrivance is thus "my larger hand." But we must not be deceived: at this stage, we simply have more complicated tools, for the source of motor energy continues to be man's body. The machine in the proper sense appears only with the utilization of an independent source of energy, such that the mechanical system acquires a certain autonomy. Then the tool is equivalent to countless expert, accurate, strictly coordinated, and extraordinarily powerful hands.

This is not the place to go into the many problems which the machine sets for our civilization. The only important thing to note is the essential link which connects, and will always connect, even the most complex and autonomous machine to its maker. The switch which replaces the handle continues to keep the machine in the power of my hand. Yet modern man has not infrequently yielded to the ancient temptation of the "golden calf" and adored the machine produced by his own hands. More accurately, the complexity, prodigious speed, and sureness of the operations performed by electronic machines, or the remote control of interplanetary rockets, lead men sometines to devalue human intelligence as compared with machines and to see in these a master, or even a god to whom a kind of worship is to be offered. Without minimizing the immense progress which machines represent, we cannot protest too strongly against such blindness and its disastrous consequences. Whatever the complexity, power, and autonomy of the machine, it will never cease to be man's work, conceived by his mind, brought into being by his hands, and regulated, directed, and repaired under his constant control. All the knowledge of the scientist and all the skill of the engineer and technician are brought to bear in advance to determine how the machine is to function. Thus, even though the apparatus carries out astounding feats of calculation, translation, or classification, it is man who in one or other fashion has thought these out for the machine, programmed it, ordered its use, and supplied its data. Man, too, regulates the sequence of operations, controlling them according to a plan; man reflects on the blind mechanism and his hand intervenes every time the plan is blocked by the equally blind course of some contrary determinism. The constant perfecting of machines, far from constituting any challenge to the human mind and the human hand, daily pays these an ever greater tribute.

Thus prolonged by the tool and obeyed and freed of countless tasks by the machine, the human hand is constantly extending its field of action, from the infinitely small to the infinitely large; it penetrates the atom and, thanks to various new engines, the interplanetary spaces as well. In this way man becomes present to the immensity of the universe; the tools and machines he has made are often connected to him by nothing more than the impalpable radio waves, but they express and satisfy to some extent his desire for ubiquity. This presence, which is both intentional (a presence through knowledge and volition) and technological (a presence through the machine), breaks through the limitations of space and time. In this process, as Bergson pointed out, the whole body of man is ceaselessly transcended, amplified, and increased.[14] For, in prolonging man's hand, the tool and the machine develop his whole bodily self and even tend to equate it with the dimensions of the universe. This is why there is need of the "bigger soul" for which Bergson called if mechanical progress is not to make monsters of men. We will have to dwell later on this essential need, so closely bound up with the fate and even the survival of modern man.

The foregoing discussion indicates how the hand differs from the animal's claw, hoof, and horn. The latter organs are limited to stereotyped or rudimentary ways of action and are incapable of adapting their operation to the unending variety of circumstance. Even when it uses a stick, an anthropoid's hand does not free itself from its present situation in such a way as to reach the universal and abstract relationships which define the tool and adapt it to the situation as such. The evidence for this is that an ape does not store up any tools; his use of them is accidental, connected with chance encounter and in no way premeditated. Man is *the only animal who saves his tools for future use*; outfits, toolboxes, and equipment are peculiar tò him because he grasps the universal. But before there are tools to be saved, the construction of a hammer, a chisel, or a saw requires the manual intelligence to *reflect* on the conditions of its action and to analyze the laborious process required for achieving certain effects. Such a critique of technological action presupposes that the hand is detached with respect to its own needs and can temporarily disengage itself from the world in order to think out its relation to it. Like the hand's intervention in the play of determinisms, such detachment supposes a self-mastery whose true name is intelligence and freedom. The universality of the hand as a living organ and polyvalent instrument and as the tool which virtually contains all other tools and gives rise to them all[15] is the universality of the spirit itself.

The Artist's Hand

Doubtless it is here that we find the capacity which makes possible the work of art: if the human hand is an artist's hand, it is because it is capable of striving for the universal. The same hand of the primitive which shaped the stone was also capable of decorating the walls of the cave. The reason is that imprisoned by his needs within the limits of the immediate, he yearns for the unconditional; he seeks to free himself from his servitude to space and time. Turning aside from the practical sphere, he commits his hand to the service of freely chosen aesthetic values and transposes the world of his experience, idealizing it and transfiguring it into a reflection of the spiritual. But this does not mean that he throws off his condition as an embodied being. He creates only in his own image: what he does corresponds to what he is. By metaphysical necessity as well as by desire, his hand—a thing of living flesh and intelligence—gives body to aesthetic values, clothes the ideal in sentient flesh, and makes the eternal visible at a point in history. Architecture, sculpture, and painting use the raw material of nature to express new ideas, gross elements to convey subtle thoughts; inscribe grace, freedom, love, and life in opaque and dead matter. By the magic of art, the hand even makes the senseless, hard *stone smile* (cf. the "smiling angels" in the cathedrals); the dull opaqueness of marble, cloth, or wood express pain, anxiety, and intelligence. The artist's hand is here mediating not simply between man and a world to be used but between two orders of reality which seek each other out: the world as given and ideal values, or matter and spirit. The work of art is an attempt at incarnation, for it constrains the beautiful to take on bodily form, find a place for itself in a utilitarian world, and exercise an influence there. Through the mediation of the hand and its work, the beyond is present in the here, heaven on earth, eternity in time.

The artist's hand is constantly challenging the deadly destructive power which is inherent in duration as such; it attacks time, pits itself against it, and claims to rise above it.[16] A work of art, like every cultural product, seeks to endure, not with the duration that ends in death but with a duration that lasts beyond death. The Latin poet was thus expressing the innate desire of every artist and his work when he said: "I have finished a monument more lasting than bronze . . . . I shall not altogether die."[17] By the very fact that it does last, even the artistic work which is not commemorative of any particular event gathers up in itself, as it were, the time that is constantly slipping away. A monument like Notre Dame of Paris is enriched by its many centuries of life, for in it the Middle Ages, the Renaissance, the classical period, and the modern age all meet, and the work of art thus stores up duration. In a kind of "involution," the cathedral has collected the flow of history as it was passing. In the inverse movement of "evolution," that history is later celebrated at the various festivities of Notre Dame; that is, the condensed duration flows out once more. At such festivities men recall "the great moments of Notre Dame" and give symbolic representation to the passing time which history in its flow had condensed and committed to the custody of the work of art.

The artist's intention and his hand's purpose, then, is, in part, to rise victorious over time and its destructive power and to gather up duration even within the horizontal realm of history. This desire for perpetuity is common to the work of art and to every memorial. What distinguishes the former from the latter is that the former also seeks to transcend duration along the vertical line that intersects with the instant by linking such duration with the timeless norm of the beautiful. There is question here not only of transcending duration within duration itself but also of transcending the whole of history in an ever-living, ever-present appeal to ideal values which no change can touch. The hand and work of the artist have a suprahistorical value, for they ceaselessly invoke the eternal in order to make it present amid corruptible reality and to bring time back to its roots in eternity. Today the pioneers of technology seek to conquer space; the artist, whether of yesterday or today, seeks rather to conquer time. In both cases there is the human aspiration for a "total" presence.

In addition to this challenge to becoming, the artist's hand expresses and fulfills the artist himself. Whatever its subject matter, the work of art is eminently personal. The perspective chosen and the style of execution give new life to the most commonplace themes by immersing them in the crucible of an individual's existence. The man can involve himself totally in the whole work he produces. Doubtless the artist often questions the image of himself which his hand has made; it may even happen that he cannot recognize himself at all in the product of his activity and must ask endless questions of this supposed mirror of his own being. But it must at least be said that the artist is always in search of himself even as he strives to embody the ideal value; in the two inseparable quests the person is fulfilled. The hand which lays siege to matter transcends the point of immediate application, and no limits can be assigned to how far it can go; for it is the man himself, the artist, whom his hand unwearyingly seeks and builds and shapes.

The *artifact* is in a different category, for here the hand aims at utility. The wooden shoe carved of beechwood, or the pot made on the wheel, is intended for use and will gradually disappear in the process; these are consumer goods. Yet the artisan too is proud of a work which lasts and gives "good use"; he too challenges time in his own way. Above all, the artifact retains an inherent relation to its maker: he conceives the work, can vary its forms, and brings them into being with his own hands. The artisan is conscious of the meaning and purpose of the object, for he is the source of these. The "manner" and the turn of hand manifest a turn of mind. The danger is that the deliberate style may become an end in itself, become "mannered." Finally, in the fruit of his toil the artisan finds a self-fulfillment; he expresses himself in his work and recognizes himself in it. This human depth is what gives value to every "hand-made" object.

The artisan's hand at times is less totally absorbed in the utilitarian purpose of the artifact and seeks to give aesthetic value to the work by decorating it. The latter is then the work of artisan and artist both, and shows the ambiguity of the term "art" as the search both for the useful and for the beautiful. In a further effort of detachment and of "reflection" (bending back) on his own labor, the artisan's hand may decorate the very tool he uses in executing his plans; thus both work and tool are given a twofold finality: practical and aesthetic. Which takes priority, beauty or utility? Beauty may gain the day, and the object may leave the workshop for the collector's cabinet. But even when the object is not thus withdrawn from use, the artist's hand has challenged destructive time and imposed a new meaning on it.

In the so-called "affluent" or "developed" societies, in which the cycle of production and consumption has pride of place, the role of the human hand is quite different. Man aims constantly to produce more and to consume more. The desire to speed up the rhythm of this cycle leads to a maximum division of productive labor among a great number of workers. None of these workers has decided on the result to be achieved nor the means to be used. The individual worker is hardly aware of the goal pursued in common by all the workers and their specialized and stereotyped activities. Such "fragmented work"[18] has countless individual and social consequences which are harmful to the person. Labor is degraded, for it no longer terminates in a *work* that is marked by some individuality, but in a *product* that is uniform no matter how it is multiplied. Similarly, the laborer no longer "works" but blindly takes part in a process of "production," through the repetition of stereotyped actions in which neither intelligence nor free initiative plays a part. Far from expressing and recognizing himself in his work, man alienates his personality in the heartbreaking monotony of the same motion repeated over and over. For, since he is himself a living totality, a man finds fulfillment only in a total work, not in the endlessly repeated tightening of a single bolt. In fragmenting the hand's task, man himself is fragmented; which is to say that he is destroyed.

Moreover, man's relation to time is changed. For man involved in industrial production, whether as manager or worker, there can be no ambition to produce a lasting piece of work. He no longer works for the future but for and in the present; the fruit of his toil is destined to disappear as quickly as possible. Production is speeded up so that consumption may be speeded up, and vice versa. The deliberate acceleration of these two phases, or moments, brings them ever closer together, and the hand which produces seeks also to destroy. At the limit (which, it is to be hoped, will remain only an ideal), production and consumption would completely coincide. Man's hand then no longer seeks to conquer time by creating a lasting piece of work, as was true of the artisan; on the contrary, it becomes the accomplice of that destructive power which is inherent in duration and the instrument of a crass materialism.

Since it is constantly bent on removing any trace of itself, a consumer society forbids itself to build up a past and a retrospective outlook; it loses the sense of history or never acquires it, for duration is no longer being summed up and concentrated in works which form landmarks along the horizon of time. If concern for the future intervenes, it is in order to organize production today so as to stimulate more rapid consumption tomorrow. Man thus lives in the instant, and in the commercial instant: he makes and unmakes, becomes the slave of time and is in danger of disappearing into it; without a past, without a personal or social future, and without any historical awareness, he experiences the vertigo of the abyss and the temptation to nihilism. The *work* has made way for the *product*. Without yielding to the useless and anachronistic desire for a return to a golden age of work (which, of course, never existed), we may at least hope that it will be possible for the human hand still to *work*; then man will have some chance of escaping nihilism by remaining creative.[19]

The Hand as Organ of Grasping and "Possessing"

The hand is naturally made to grasp, take, and master things. The thumb, being opposable to the other fingers, forms with them a grip of amazing flexibility and strength. This function of grasping is so peculiar to the hand and necessary to man that a surgeon speaks of "saving" an injured hand if he enables it to retain the power to grip things. From childhood on, the hand is the organ for grasping and possessing. If I become aware of a need or desire, my hand immediately moves away from my body and my arm extends. When close to the object, my fingers open up, then close upon the thing and grasp it. Then the hand bends back towards the body: the object has been "taken," captured, and brought into the space controlled by my gestures. It has now become "mine," thanks to my hand as organ of conquest. This same hand is also the organ which is vigilant in preserving what belongs to me. The thief wants to lay hold upon my possessions and to take them from me. But I intend to keep the "upper hand" and to keep things "under my hand" or "within my grasp"; my possessions I "keep in hand" or "main-tain."

The hand is thus the organ of all appropriation. If my body is the central reference point around which my possessions gravitate and if the human gaze has conquering power over things,[20] my hand is the living instrument which can actually constitute things my possessions. In making something mine, my hand changes the thing's meaning for me. The thing is no longer foreign to me but familiar; it adheres to me, is attached to my being, and is introduced into the orbit of my personal existence. By a gesture of my hand I adopt the thing, incorporate it into myself in a sense, assimilating it and, as it were, "digesting" it. The "object" enters into my life as subject and mysteriously shares in it. Inversely, through my hand, my "I" tends to flow out upon my possessions and to recognize itself in them in a process of unconscious animism; it relies on them and finds a secret security in them.

It has been said that between my being and my possessions a kind of unperceived osmosis goes on. Since my possessions remain in contact with my hand, I may find myself asking at times where my being ends and my possessions begin. I and my possessions constitute a living unity, and a constant dialectic goes on between the two terms. This constant back-and-forth which leads me to focus things and the world around me on myself by acquiring them, and then to emancipate myself from egoism by giving them away, is expressed above all in the *alternating movement of my hand*: it bends back on itself and closes in order to take, and it extends and opens in order to give. This manual rhythm of taking and letting go manifests and brings to fulfillment the spiritual rhythm of appropriation and detachment. The hesitations of my hand are the hesitations of my freedom.

The Hand as Universal Symbol of Action

Since it is the organ of work and mastery, the hand thereby becomes the symbol of human intervention in the world. In every language numberless figurative expressions refer to the hand's initiative, power, and creative energy. "To take an enterprise in hand" is to commit oneself to guiding it, whether alone or with others; "to have the upper hand" in some business is to be the master of what goes on.

The hand's gesture often expresses the active will, whether in giving an order to a subordinate or in a discourse in which the speaker manifests his desire to reshape men and the world according to his personal vision. Even the style of my gestures betrays the style of my action: abrupt and confused or poised and self-assured; broad or cramped, flowing or jerky, rounded or peremptory, calm or violent, varied or stereotyped, abundant or sparing. In each of these divergent manners a character, a type of action, a man himself, find expression. For the hand and its gesture are the man in action; through them the subject affirms his will and his power, confronts the world, takes its measure, and fulfills himself in the struggle. In the same expenditure of energy the hand remakes the world and the man whom it expresses. If my hand is the organ for all making (*poiesis*), it is also the symbol of all doing (*praxis*); it brings to pass what it signifies: the progressive conquest of brute nature, both within me and around me, by intelligence and freedom.

For this reason the gesture will always be more decisive than the word, since the gesture is action and execution. We judge others, and rightly so, more by their actions than by their words. The public figure, or the private individual for that matter, who gives his "deeds and actions" an interpretation at variance with, or even contradictory to, their obvious meaning is fooling himself and losing credibility. Others always give actions their natural meaning, however long and eloquent the discourse that accompanies them. The reason is that the word can fail to be sincere; in that case it is, as it were, an enfeebled act, inferior to the gesture or the action by which a man effectively commits himself and carries out his intentions.

Symbolic Action

While everyday action brings subject and object immediately to grips with each other, involving the former and changing the latter, symbolic action separates these two terms. The reason for this is that the desired result is not always realizable in the natural world. Between the agent and the goal he envisions there is sometimes an insurmountable distance: a spatial or temporal distance or a disproportion between the means at hand and the goal desired. A group of men may will the downfall or death of a dictator without, here and now, having the means of causing a rebellion. Moral disavowal of the dictator is then separated from effective overthrow. The men may set up a tribunal and pronounce sentence of condemnation. Better still, they make a material substitute for the man to be slain and then kill him in effigy.[21]

The superficial eye may regard such conduct as laughable and poke fun at its impotence. As a matter of fact, however, symbolic action has its own kind of efficacy: it separates the two aspects of all human action, namely the involvement of persons and the production of a result, just as the "symbol" itself was originally something broken in half, with the joined halves serving as a sign of recognition. In the symbolic gesture an act of the will is manifested and a new relationship to the world or to others is begun. The action that will take place, or is perhaps only desired, is anticipated in behavior which simulates it. When rebels burn someone in effigy, they are choosing to be murderers; they kill the other man in his image and in their own hearts. In some instances the moralist would be justified in regarding the actors as killers in the internal court of conscience. The network of interpersonal relations is being "re-handled" by symbolic action, for to judge or kill a man in symbolic fashion is to break with him in the most effective way. The human group in turn is reordered and interpersonal relations are changed as soon as some approve and others disapprove the symbolic action.

Every symbolic gesture thus gives expression to a spiritual outlook and has the value of an *act*, whether the action be a salute to a flag, the laying of flowers on a grave, Pilate's washing of his hands, or a ritual ablution. [22]

Hand and Intelligence

There was a famous debate between Anaxagoras and Aristotle which is likely to continue as long as man exists: is man intelligent because he has hands, as Anaxagoras maintained, or is he endowed with hands because he is intelligent, as Aristotle said? Which is first in nature, the hand or the intelligence? [23]

Because the organic differentiation of the living being proceeds side by side with its psychic development, the hand becomes the criterion of intelligence and is first in the order of discovery. Because intelligence must provide itself with instruments for its mastery of the world, as musical art provides the flutist with the flute, [24] the organ is therefore subject to thought and must recognize the latter's natural priority. But if we leave aside such abstract distinctions and look at our experience, we must admit here a simultaneity at every moment, like the simultaneity between the whole body and the whole soul. We must recognize that intelligence would not be itself without the hand nor the hand without the intelligence. We must, in the last analysis, relativize any question about priority among the components of man by pointing to that always prior, indivisible, and ever-present act which gives man to himself.

The parallel between mind and hand can be pursued and the sense of continuity deepened. If the hand's proper function is to intervene (*inter-venire*, come between or among) in the world of things and to introduce its own activity into that of nature, the intelligence for its part reads, in the heart of reality, the laws which structure the latter (*intus-legere*, to read within). The hand grasps and holds objects, but the intelligence too "grasps," "apprehends," "embraces," and "comprehends" (all of which refer to the same action). There is an intellectual dexterity as well as a manual intelligence. Universality is a privilege in which both share, and the limitless field of reality is their common preserve as they journey together through it. The mind aspires to know all things, the hand to master all things.[25] But the hand, the technician, adventures onto new terrain only if science has to some extent mapped it out. And at the frontier, the sacred, intangible to the hand, is also unfathomable to the mind and ineffable to the spoken word.

We must therefore avoid so linking intelligence with the hand that the latter would absorb it and hold the mastery over it. If intelligence finds expression in the hand, invents tools, and is naturally ordered to working in the world of things, its activity is not limited, as Bergson thought, to technology.[26] In relation to its closest instrument, the hand, and to all of its works, the mind retains a freedom and detachment which give it access also to the realm of disinterested knowledge and contemplation. More precisely, the most "free-floating" speculation is still at work. It may not produce an external tangible result, but it does transform and remake man interiorly. The mission of the thinker or contemplative is to bring man to life and fullness in himself and in others; this is the greatest of works and the art beyond all other arts.

The sign of the spirit's freedom is the hand's repose; for the hand can at any moment cease its work, withdraw, and recollect itself, so to speak, in order to rise above its task and its needs and to measure these against the golden norm of ends and values. Reflect again on Rodin's *Thinker*. He has momentarily stopped his work and sat down so that the body's rest may liberate the spirit's powers. His hand is disengaged from its labor with things; it is freed and is now turned towards his body in a gesture of recollection; at the same time, by supporting the head, it sustains the effort of thinking. The whole man, hand no less than intelligence, is "re-thinking" his action, evaluating his goals, choosing his means. The "bigger soul," therefore, which Bergson saw as necessary for a more and more technically orientated society, can be provided only by the contemplative intelligence. Against all pragmatism, with its subjection of intelligence to the tyranny of need and its reduction of the hand to the status of blind instrument, we must strongly reaffirm the primacy of ideal values and of the intelligence which serves them. The hand could not be the artisan's hand if it were not also the artist's hand; it must think and pray if it is to continue working and producing. Only disinterested knowledge guarantees the freedom and "humanness" of the hand.

The Hand as Organ of My Freedom

When men want to deprive a man of the exercise of his freedom, they put handcuffs on him. They even tie his hands behind his back in order to frustrate the hands' instinctive forward or "pro-tensive" movement and to reduce them to powerlessness. In the extreme case, they nail a man's hands to a cross. Inversely, if I want to preserve full independence in dealing with some business, I ask others to "give me a free hand." In court I raise my hand to take an oath, the supreme commitment of the free subject.

As universal organ of man's intervention in the world of things, the hand is by that very fact the criterion of man's freedom. The claw or the hoof is limited to definite kinds of action, but the human hand has a flexibility which gives it an inexhaustible variety of activity. Any particular action I engage in activates only one of a practically limitless range of possibilities. For every action I carry out, I have countless possible actions in reserve. My working hand draws its priceless value from all that it still conceals and contains within itself; it is involved but also free, it is engaged in a particular task but also available for many others. It is thus the organ of my power, my future, and my initiative, a treasure house of possible actions. For my hand is rooted in the inexhaustible fullness of my being, and therefore embodies choice and freedom.

The hand is thus the constantly moving point, as it were, at which the mind's infinity is inscribed on the registers of matter. From among countless actions recognized as possible, the hand of the laborer, the seamstress, the surgeon, and the artist instantaneously chooses and executes the one that is appropriate. From among the countless words which rise up in the writer's mind and seek to flow from his pen, the hand chooses the only one adequate to the thought. Transposing the Bergsonian image of the inverted cone,[27] we may say that the hand is the privileged point of entry into the totality of my bodily being, the point at which the whole wealth of my active life is brought to focus and concretized in action.

Properly human action looks beyond empirical results to ideal goals, whether aesthetic, moral, or religious. It is in confrontation with these supreme norms that my freedom, in some decisive moment or in everyday life, is most fully actuated. The hand of the artisan or the artist or the man of action orders things to these freely chosen goals; the hand thereby gives meaning to the world, for *meaning* flows from *purpose*. The hand thus shows itself to be an *interpretive organ* and the *organ of my freedom*.

III. THE HAND, ORGAN OF RELATIONS WITH OTHERS

My hand establishes relations between me and other men no less than between me and things. We must note here the specific meanings of the hand's gesture in this unique and endlessly varied relationship which links me to every human partner. The opaqueness and inertia of things precludes any reciprocity with them, but other people are correlative to me; their physical, psychic, moral, and ontological structure makes them the other pole of my existence.

The Hand as Organ of Prevenance and Welcome

With my hand I make signs to another, invite him, call him, and receive him. Anatomical symmetry makes our hands reciprocal; even in rest and sleep each person's hand "bears witness" to the other's hand, while in waking hours these hands are drawn to each other as soon as some possibility of encounter is suggested. Then—at least in the West—each one's hand moves away from his body, stretches and moves forward, anticipating the clasp. The outstretched hand is the active sign of camaraderie, friendship, prevenient love, and freely offered forgiveness. When accepted, each person's hand draws the other within itself and the two tend to incorporate each other. An embrace is even more meaningful: I extend my arms to form a bodily space which is my very self, in order to receive the other within it and to give myself to him. For a fleeting moment we become one in the free encounter of hand and heart. Such gestures can, of course, like every human gesture, degenerate into routine or formality. But the deeper meaning of such gestures remains, and each person must rediscover and accept it. It is also important to note that the handclasp is precisely a clasp of the hand, that is, of the organ of work and action; in clasping hands the other person and I are pooling our energies and our power of acting upon things and men. The handclasp is a covenanting act, a promise of collaboration in common work; it binds us for the present and, more importantly, for the future; we become one strength and one power of initiative. We recognize each other as partners and establish a certain equality between us; if the other is of a higher status than I, his hand, like his word and his gaze, elevates and promotes me.

Inversely, the handclasp refused is an act of rejection; it breaks an existing communion or a communion which I am led to expect in virtue of the good will presumed to exist between all civilized men. Each one then takes "his distance," draws into himself, and maintains that dualism of self and other out of which hostility can at any moment spring. The handclasp refused or accepted thus has an important interpersonal significance; it establishes between subjects a relation of egoistic separateness or of that willed oneness which gives rise to human societies.

Conjugal society being the most fundamental of all, marriage rites (in the West, for example) inevitably give the handclasp a privileged place. "To ask for the hand" of the woman signifies that the man seeks conjugal union. In the ritual itself, the exchange of ring-bearing hands seems to signify in an expressive way the mutual gift of two persons and two lives. The initiative in self-offering is translated into the offering of the hand. The Roman Ritual shows each of the future spouses being asked: "N., *vis accipere* . . . ?," words which are not to be translated "Do you wish to take?" but "Do you wish to receive, as lawful spouse?" In other words, it is a matter of each one accepting the freely offered gift of self which the other person proposes to make. In virtue of the reciprocity between the two persons, acceptance by the one seals the offering by the other and thus is itself self-offering and gift. Each hand receives in the very act by which it gives, and the handclasp unites two lives. The ideal to which every human love and friendship is called, is that in this gesture "taking" should not take precedence over giving.

The Hand as Organ of Contact and Power

If my extended hand seeks to clasp the other's hand or consents to be clasped by it, it is because physical contact is an element in encounter. Mutual touch between persons is admittedly ambiguous. Respect due the other forbids me to lay hands upon him the way I would an object or an instrument. In the age-old civilization of India, mutual touching or handclasp is forbidden by custon. Where manual contact is practiced, it must show a certain reserve. In any event, touching of persons by each other is a way of achieving a communion of the subjects as such, a deeper encounter of their being. If I caress a child's silky hair, it is that I may be penetrated by the child's fragile being; I want it to enter into me and, in turn, I involve myself with the child. The contact thus aims at establishing a vital exchange in which each subject is given to the other, and I am disappointed if the child, with his whims, slips away from me and goes off to play.[28]

In the form of an imposition of hands (often turned into a ritual gesture), manual contact can signify the transmission of some influence or power: magical power, blessing, social function, or authority. In extending my hand over the head of another, I am giving the other a new meaning. In an oath, contact with a sacred object—a Bible, for example—signifies that the individual is now intimately united with the corresponding supernatural power (God who is Truth). In all these various situations, we must note, it is not at all necessary that the material contact should somehow be effective. In virtue of my gesture I am intentionally present to the other, as the child is present, through his outstretched hand, to the thing he wants. For the subject the intentional is already real.

As organ of appropriation, the hand is also the organ of power. The leader's arm, hand, and finger instinctively stretch out to indicate an order, with the gesture embracing both the subordinate and the task to be accomplished and giving a new interpretation to man and the world. The Romans distinguished marriage with and without "hands," according as the husband did or did not take full power over his wife. "To put oneself in the doctor's hands" or "to fall into the hands of one's enemy" mean to be wholly at their mercy. The hand of Justice symbolizes absolute power, even power over life and death. The representation of a hand on the scepter of the French kings or on magical charms[29] likewise signifies effective power. In other instances the commander's baton prolongs the movement of the hand and underlines the intention being conveyed. Every instrument—from sword to shepherd's crook—can become a symbol of authority in society.

The imposition of the hand can also at times suggest a benevolent presence and a protection extended to someone. By this action I cover my fellow human being with the shadow of my power and dedicate my physical and moral strength to keeping him safe. The frightened child is calmed when the mother's hand caresses and guides it: in putting its hand in the mother's, it recognizes its dependence but at the same time receives assurance as it advances towards the world. Manual contact becomes, without need for reflection, the gesture of adoption, protection, and healing. In the last-named case, the gesture expresses not only an exploration of the malady but the will to bring alleviation, remedy, and saving power to bear upon it; the sick person and the doctor both instinctively put their hand upon the spot where pain is felt.

The Hand as Organ of Request and Prayer

When the hand reaches the limits of its own capacity and must admit its powerlessness, it turns away from itself, as it were, and stretches out to others, seeking from some more powerful or better-equipped hand what it cannot provide for itself. The outstreched hand, the upturned palm, the fingers curved to form a cup are all in their openness and emptiness a request and suppliant call. Perhaps the petitioner's two hands come together, make their two concavities one, and expand in the intensity of their prayer; this larger cup, materially so small but infinite in its meaning, signifies the greatness of the desire, the call, and the need.

The gesture of the hand then takes on a universal *prophetic* meaning. In his individual action the petitioner undoubtedly expresses his immediate need: torturing hunger, nakedness, illness, or loneliness, but he is also proclaiming the permanent wretched state of all men, their insatiable desire, their existential insecurity. To me, possessed of what he needs, the beggar recalls or reveals what I am; he reminds me that under my apparent but deceptive self-sufficiency there lurks a poor being whom I would rather forget, an ephemeral creature whose existence is at every moment threatened. The beggar is thus for me an image of my own deeper poverty. We can see, then, why in other social and cultural conditions the mendicant orders were able to institutionalize the prophetic gesture of the beggar. They reminded Christians not only of the undeserved wretchedness of many and the deliberate detachment of a few, but also of the radical poverty of every human being, of that interior emptiness which is part of him and which no inherited or acquired riches, no work however marked by genius, and no social advancement will ever be able to fill. Seven centuries after the appearance of the mendicant orders, in an age when economic development and new customs and mentalities make men suspect, more than ever before, that beggary hides either laziness or an ignoble character,[30] it nonetheless remains necessary for every human being to experience at some point his own poverty and his dependence on others. Unhappy the man who has never felt himself dependent right down to the roots of his being! An essential truth about himself will always escape him.

The tension of the whole being as concentrated in a hand or a face does not simply express a passionate request. Such conduct is essentially intentional and projects the beggar towards the one of whom he begs, rendering him present to that other according to the measure of his desire. The suppliant simultaneously thinks of himself and forgets himself, wills to be himself and renounces himself, identifies himself wholly with his need and loses himself in the other. If he wants an alms, he gauges the inner dispositions of the other towards him and has a sharp eye for the other's awakened feelings, the stirring of his free response, and the signs of his good will and graciousness. The outstretched hand links one existence to another and effects the intentional presence of the suppliant to the possible benefactor. Even before any favorable response, the latter is willy nilly present to the suppliant.

The hand is thus the organ of prayer in the proper sense of this latter word—that is, of petition addressed to God. Man's hand turns aside from the tasks which usually provide him with a living; it recognizes that, whatever it may accomplish by itself, it remains radically empty and poor, frustrated, and scarred by toil rather than fulfilled by it. Sometimes the two hands of the one praying intertwine so as not to be distracted from the one necessary thing and to express, by their united effort, the intensity of the existential appeal.[31] At other times the arms rise up and open out to express the immense abyss which man feels in himself over against God and the total openness of his being to him to whom he prays. The extended hand is prayer in action; it is supplication and appeal. Better still: every hand, by its natural structure, is a praying hand, an avowal of both need and hope, recognition of the self as indigent and of God as the sole good and the sole benefactor.

Here then we have man's hand turned towards another hand that is invisible and inexhaustibly full. In return, God is present to the desire that calls out to him; in fact, is it not God who awakens the prayer, deepens it, and gives it its whole strength and meaning? Even apart from any answer to prayer and any sensible fervor, the encounter of man and God is already effective. The praying hand wills to transcend the basic religious dilemma of immanence and transcendence.[32]

The Hand as Organ of Giving

If the hand can stretch out to demand and beg, it is because there is always another hand that is able to give. The hand is the organ of giving: it extends and opens so that what is mine becomes yours. Whereas I spontaneously tend to make myself the center of things and to draw them to my bodily self as to their inevitable goal, the gesture of giving shifts their center away from myself and redirects them towards others. The hand is the organ of sharing: it breaks bread and distributes it. But the gift of a thing, however necessary to the other or precious in itself, would be deceitful ("he has only made a gesture") if it were not the vehicle for the gift of myself. It is a little thing to give what I have; I must give, above all else, what I am. The manner of giving is more important than what I give, because through the surrender of what is perhaps a very minor possession, my hand must express and effect the sacrifice of my being itself.

Here again the hand is really the man himself. Every hand is necessarily selfish or generous, stingy or liberal, or even alternately the one and the other.[33] It translates into material form a deeper disposition of the "heart" (in the biblical sense of the word), that is, a freely adopted attitude. Every man chooses at each moment to be open or closed, given or withdrawn. The basic spiritual choice is made here: between egoistic self-centeredness, the self-sufficiency of pleasure, and openness to a transcendent ideal, to an absolute value which invites me to surrender myself. Thomas Aquinas makes the awakening of reason coincide with the first deliberate refusal or acceptance of the Good.[34] It is through the goal he decides for himself that a person determines what meaning his existence is to have; and it is often when confronted with the open hand of another that he concretizes and carries out his fundamental choice.

The Hand as Organ of Hoped-for Salvation

The extended hand sometimes looks for more than a coin or a piece of bread, more than a "helping hand" or a passing "hand up"; it looks rather for the ultimate help, the supreme gesture which would snatch a lost man from the jaws of death. In this extreme situation, the hand no longer seeks to work or produce; it is no longer the industrious and agile organ which sought daily bread out of daily toil; it no longer relies on itself but renounces all effort of its own and is reduced to a signal, an appeal for help. The hand of artist or artisan worked yesterday for *progress* as intellectually conceived, rationally planned, and technologically implemented; today this hand which cries "help!" is seeking *salvation*. Once it lived in expectation, now it survives only by hope. It was once a source of initiative, now it is forced only to wait. It used to obey logic and the simple rules of exchange, now it passes beyond the regulated interplay of rights and duties and enters the order of favors freely bestowed. It is nothing now but one freedom appealing to another freedom. The lost man then discovers, far more deeply than in any previous kind of distress, the extreme fragility and the equally extreme value of his own existence. But he also proclaims to a possible savior, a man like himself, his precarious condition. Here the reciprocity of the partners in encounter is concentrated in the interplay of two hands, one of them lost, the other able to save; one calling, the other deliberating, hesitating, then choosing to be indifferent or to give aid. Extreme peril summons forth unconditioned love.

The Hand as Organ of Salvation Offered

The call for help which the hand of a lost person addresses to me forces me to make once again the most radical of choices. I am safe and in health; I have a hold on life. In one moment I grasp the inner reciprocity that binds me to the other man in his misfortune, and the necessity and freedom of the saving gesture which I feel taking shape within me. If generosity carries the day, my hand stretches out to meet the other's hand and seeks to become one with it, taking in order to be taken; it strives to draw the imperilled man into the security which is mine. He now need only grasp the hand I extend to him and he is saved.

But it can happen that the other unexpectedly withdraws his earlier appeal and refuses my help because he feels it a humiliation to owe his life to another and attempts instead the contradictory undertaking of saving himself. The refusal is offensive to the man prepared to rescue him, to the extent that he has incurred risks and generously offered himself; it is fatal for the endangered man since he can in fact do nothing for himself. If, on the contrary, the other agrees to accept the saving assistance I offer and takes the hand I hold out to him, then at last my hand grasps his. The two are now one in a common danger which may overwhelm me along with him. Our destinies are united, for better or for worse. The hand I have offered has now indeed achieved a turnabout, a "conversion." Once an organ for taking, it has now become exclusively an organ of total self-giving. It has understood the truth that the only way to see its own emptiness filled is to give itself without reserve and that the greatest act possible to freedom and to the human hand is to give. Furthermore, in a boundary situation of the type we are discussing, the hand carries out its revelatory mission, for it manifests to each individual his own and the other's innermost being, that is, the deepest thrust of each one's freedom.

The Revelatory Hand

As organ of action, taking, welcoming, and giving, the hand is also a medium of revelation. The expressivity of my hand, like that of my face, is partially reducible to the expressivity of my physical presence or bodily visibility, which we shall discuss at a later point. We shall limit ourselves here to the specific role of the hand in communication.

The hand, we have noted, carries the mark of its usual tasks. But even before it becomes shaped by its labor, every hand manifests a sex, an age, a temperament, a character, and a freedom. And the fingerprints, which are a kind of innate signature, are a criterion of individuality; they must therefore be placed on some legal documents and are a method of identification in police work. In the course of a conversation, a trained person is able to observe and interpret the hand of his partner, even if it is fully at rest.[35]

Much more then do my manual gestures reveal me, whether or not I am aware of it: in the very young child they must substitute for words; in the speaker they make up for the inadequacies of language. We cannot but admire, in this respect, the great flexibility of the hand with its mobility and the articulations that so greatly increase its possibilities. There are the suggestive hands of the stroyteller and orator; the gestures of the mime, where imitation gives reality to the invisible by drawing its shape; the imperious hands of the foreman or the schoolmaster or the orchestra conductor. Hands extended in appeal, desire, and petition; hands agitated by fear, contorted by suffering, joined in prayer, clenched in refusal, open in welcome and almsgiving: all speak a language that is mute but also flexible, living, immediately intelligible, universal in its basic vocabulary, and limitless in its ethnic and individual variations, and this language is spoken and communicates with us whether we like it or not. Look at the deaf-mute who manages genuinely to converse with others through a staggeringly inventive set of gesticulations. After the face, the hand is the most expressive part of our body; the hand is discourse and dialogue.[36]

Painters and sculptors, therefore (think, for example, of El Greco and Rodin), study the model's hand with special care. This most expressive of organs, second only to the face, must be read and reread to achieve access to the mystery of the person. But even while he scrutinizes the hand of another, the artist may continue to be haunted by the mystery of his own hand, which mediates between the work as conceived and the work as executed, between the man and his self-knowledge. This concern of the artist with himself is admirably illustrated by the study of his own hand provided by Velasquez in his *Ladies-in-Waiting* or Michelangelo in the *Prophet Ezechiel* on the Sistine ceiling. We can see, therefore, that a psychology of the hand is not an impossibility[37] and that the hand's natural expressivity supplies a seeming basis for chiromancy.

Examination of the hand is naturally extended by examination of the works which the hand produces. I seek to know, appreciate, and evaluate the man by interrogating the works of his hand; I may even come to designate him in terms of them, as when I identify Myron as sculptor of *The Discus Thrower*, Houdon of *Voltaire*, and Rude of *The*

Woman of Marseilles. The reason behind this is that among the various purposes of any work there is always one, conscious or unconscious, which directs and sustains our effort: the maker wants to find an answer to his questions about himself. He asks the work to tell him who he is; he looks at it as though it were a mirror, searches out the meaning in relation to himself of this or that element, major or minor, in his work, and tries to discover a continuity between the image the work reflects back to him and his spontaneous image of himself. Whether the revelation brings assurance or anxiety, he constantly projects new works or undertakings which will someday draw the final veil aside. The creator is equally concerned to know other men, and relies on the mediating power of his work to find out what is in man. Psychoanalysis claims to investigate even the unconscious psyche of creative men, though the results are often of doubtful value.

Among all of man's gestures and all the works of his hand, *writing* has a special revelatory power. The pen is the lightest of instruments, the most flexible, the most responsive to the slightest movements of thought, feeling, and volition. There is no resistance from matter —that is, from the paper. Everything thus conspires towards a faithful recording of the movement of the mind. Writing is, consequently, the most meaningful of the graphic arts. To the trained eye, everything reveals the writer's personality: the pace of writing, its slow or rapid rhythm, the carefulness or negligence, the precision or capricious irregularity of the letter-formation, and the play of punctuation. This is especially true of the signature. In one bit of writing (single, though its elements be many) with a unique and fixed meaning, the person identifies himself, claims to be incommunicably himself, and accepts and authenticates as his own a text, an act, or a word, in a free gesture which involves his whole self. The signature is a written word of honor, a sign by which the subject adopts a norm for thinking, behaving, or acting, and asks to be judged accordingly. It is no wonder then that the signature should express or betray both the constants and the variables of a personality. Compare the firm, upward-slanting signature of the victorious Napoleon with the downward-slanting, defeated signature of Napoleon after Waterloo. Despite possible errors and frauds, graphology is obviously a solidly based science: writing belongs to the hand, and the hand to the man.[38]

Every *action*, finally, expresses and takes the measure of the man, and the hand is the universal symbol of action. Each person shows himself small or big in the way he faces events and in his personal manner of engaging in action, "handling" men, and shaping history. My undertakings and everyday actions no less than the decisions of the statesman which help to direct mankind's present and future are acts in which the person identifies himself. It was the military or political action chosen in meeting certain situations that manifested the true stature of a Foch and a Clemenceau. Every man, wittingly or unwittingly, communicates himself and reveals his intentions and motivations (primary and secondary, noble and ignoble) in the actions to which he puts his hand, in the setbacks in which his hand must fall idle, and in all the events of which his history is made.

If the gesture reveals the person, it does not follow that it has no objective value in itself. Were this true, gestures could not be a language and serve for communication. Gestures have, in fact, a usual and spontaneously recognized meaning, just as the word has a definable signification. Of itself the kisss expresses affection or love. The gesture doubtless receives strength, life, and renewal from the person, just as the vocable becomes word and discourse in the living subject. But the very fact that the gesture can be falsified by a subjective intention which is contrary to the patent meaning confirms the objectivity. There is a sincerity and insincerity of gesture no less than of word. If Judas's kiss is a betrayal, it is because the objective meaning of love and friendship is contradicted by the homicidal intention.

Here we also have the legitimation of the claim of history to be an objective science. All behavior, of itself, has a meaning, even if the secret motives of the actors introduce some ambiguity into it: a rescue is a rescue, whether it is a purely selfless act or is dictated by vainglory or even by profit. A meaningful process always bears within itself the vital tension between the word and the vocable.

NOTES

1. Cf. Aristotle, *Historia animalium*, II, 8, 502b1-20.
2. P. Broca, "L'ordre des primates: Parallèle anatomique de l'homme et des singes," *Bulletin de la la société d'anthropologie* (second series), vol. 4, p. 228; reprinted in Broca, *Mémoires d'anthropologie* (Paris, 1877), pp. 43–44. On these texts, cf. Brun, *La main et l'esprit*, (Paris: Presses Universitaires de France, 1963), pp. 1–2.

3. Cf. André Leroi-Gourhan, *Le geste et la parole* (Paris: Albin Michel, 1964),p. 312: "The hand of man is not basically different from the hand of other primates; its ability to grasp arises from the opposition of thumb to other fingers. Man's foot, on the other hand, cannot be paralleled to the foot of the other primates." On the other hand, the author points out that "contrary to what used to be thought, man is not simply an improved ape; once understood, he is seen to be quite different from the apes" (p. 166).

4. The following analyses should be linked up with what was said above on spatial orientation.

5. Cf. Barbotin, *Le témoignage spirituel*, pp. 20–28.

6. Plato, *Timaeus*, 33d, trans. H.D.P.Lee (Baltimore: Penguin Books, 1965), p. 45: "Its creator thought that it was better for it to be self-sufficient than dependent on anything else. He did not think there was any purpose in providing it with hands, as it had no need to grasp anything or defend itself, nor with feet or any other means of support."

7. Plato, *Timaeus*, 44d-e, trans Lee, pp. 60–61: "And to prevent the head from rolling about on the earth, unable to get over or out of its many heights and hollows, they [the gods] provided that the body should act as a convenient vehicle. It was therefore given height and grew four limbs which could bend and stretch, and with which it could take hold of things and support itself, and so by God's contrivance move in all directions carrying on top of it the seat of our divinest and holiest part. That is the reason why we all have arms and legs."

8. Recall the gesture of Thomas the Apostle, who was reluctant to believe; touch and sight cooperated in providing a strict control over perception (John 20:24).

9. Cf. the phrases: "to keep one's hand out of something" and its opposite, "to have a hand in something."

10. Cf. Hegel, *Aphorismen*, 32, in J. Hoffmeister, *Dokumente zu Hegels Entwicklung* (Stuttgart: Frommansverlag, 1936), p. 360: "To work is to annihilate or curse the world."

11. We have already indicated that this disastrous ontology is based on a spatial illusion; cf. above, Chapter 3, note 1.

12. Théophile Gautier, *Etudes de mains: Impéria, Lacenaire*, in his *Emaux et camées*, edited by Jean Pommier (Paris: Droz, 1945), pp. 11–14.

13. Cf. Aristotle, *De anima*, III, 8, 432a 1–3, quoted below in note 25.

14. Cf. Henri Bergson, *The Two Sources of Morality and Religion*, trans. R. Ashley Audra and Cloudesley Brereton (New York: Holt, 1935; reprinted by Doubleday Anchor Books [Garden City: Doubleday, n.d.]), pp. 309–310.

15. Cf. Aristotle, *De partibus animalium*, IV, 10, 687a 20–21, trans. William Ogle, in W.D.Ross (ed.), *The Works of Aristotle* 5 (Oxford: Oxford University Press, 1912): "The hand is not to be looked on as one organ but as many; for it is, as it were, an instrument for further instruments." Cf. 687a 31–687b5: "But to man numerous modes of defence are open, and these, moreover, he may change at will; as also he may adopt such weapon as he pleases, and at such times as suit him. For the hand is talon, hoof, and horn, at will. So too it is spear, and sword, and whatsoever other weapon or instrument you please;

for all these can it be from its power of grasping and holding them all." Cf. Amédée Ponceau, *Initiation philosophique*, new ed.; (Paris: Rivière, 1964), I, 51.

16. Cf. above, Chapter 2, section 3, "Physical and Intentional Presence in Time" on *work*.

17. Horace, *Odes*, III, 30. 1, 6.

18. Cf. Georges Friedmann, *The Anatomy of Work: Labor, Leisure, and the Implications of Automation*, trans. Wyatt Rawson (New York: Free Press of Glencoe, 1961).

19. The dialectic of work and product seems to be reflected in the conception of the "new novel." Cf. Alain Robbe-Grillet, *For a New Novel: Essays on Fiction*, trans. Richard Howard (New York: Grove, 1965). According to Robbe-Grillet, description in novels ought to put aside concern with meaning: "it [description] no longer mentions anything except insignificant objects, or objects which it is concerned to make so" (p. 147); it destroys its own objects as it goes: "it has left nothing standing behind it: it has instituted a double movement of creation and destruction" (p. 148). Time, which is "the essential character" (p. 152) in novels of the Balzacian type, "no longer passes. It no longer completes anything . . . . Moment denies continutiy" (p. 155); "an *elsewhere* is no more possible than a *formerly*" (p. 153). Whence "the *disappointment* inherent in many works today" (p. 148). The investigation ought to be further pursued; but it is evident that every society creates a literature which reflects its sense of the meaning of work.

20. Cf. below, Chapter 5, section 10, "Appropriation."

21. Somewhat different in character is the sympathetic magic maliciously practiced on a figurine of wax or wood with the intention of really harming the person represented: here the action attempts to have a material effect at a distance. But we may ask whether a symbolic action like murder in effigy has not, for some agents at least, a magical meaning.

22. For Pilate, cf. Matt. 27:24. See also Deut. 21:6–8; Ps. 26:6; 73:13. The will to spiritual purification inspires the washing of hands in many religious rituals, as, for example, in the Eastern Christian tradition; cf. Cyril of Jerusalem, *Catechesis* 23 (=Mystagogical Catechesis V, 2). The *Lavabo* of the Roman Mass probably had a purely utilitarian function originally.

23. Aristotle, *De partibus animalium*, IV, 10, 687a 6–7.

24. Aristotle, *op. cit.*, 687a 12–13.

25. Aristotle, *De anima*, III, 8, 432a 1–3, trans. Smith, in Ross (ed.), *Works* 3: "It follows that the soul is analogous to the hand; for as the hand is a tool of tools, so the mind is the form of forms and sense the form of sensible things."

26. Cf. Henri Bergson, *Creative Evolution*, trans. Arthur Mitchell (New York: Holt, 1911; Random House, 1944), pp. 167–182.

27. Cf. Henri Bergson, *Matter and Memory*, trans. Nancy Margaret Paul and W. Scott Palmer (London: Allen and Unwin, 1911), p. 197.

28. Since contact plays such a large part in our relations with other people, the vocabulary of interpersonal relations borrows heavily from the language of tactile perception; cf., for example, to be in touch with; to be tactful; to be in touch by letter or telephone; to be thin-skinned; etc.

29. Cf. Brun, *La main et l'esprit*, pp. 78–79.

30. But cf. as early as Sirach (40:28–30).

31. Cf. Rodin, *The Cathedral*.

32. Cf. Maurice Nédoncelle, *The Nature and Use of Prayer*, trans. A. Manson (London: Burns and Oates, 1962); American edition: *God's Encounter with Man: A Contemporary Approach to Prayer* (New York: Sheed & Ward, 1964).

33. Cf. Sir. 4:31: "Let not your hand be open to receive and clenched when it is time to give."

34. Cf. Thomas Aquinas, *Summa theologiae*, I-II, q.89, a.6.

35. It is doubtless the revelatory power of the hand that underlies the secular use of gloves; gloves express a concern for reserve, psychological modesty. "To handle someone with kid gloves" means, figuratively, to be careful about how one expresses one's sentiments to him and to avoid direct confrontations.

36. Cf. Gregory of Nyssa, *De hominis opificio*, 8 (PG 49:144 and 148), notes that the hand, freed (from the need of acting as a support) by man's upright stance, adds its expressivity to that of the word. Cf. Montaigne, *Essays*, Book 1, Chapter 12 ("The Apology for Raimond Sebond"), in *The Essays of Michel de Montaigne*, trans. George B. Ives (Cambridge: Harvard University Press, 1925; reprinted: New York: Heritage Press, 1946, cited here), Vol. 1, p. 601: "What with the hands? We require, we promise, summon, dismiss, threaten, beg, entreat, deny, refuse, question, wonder, count, confess; we show repentance, fear, shame, doubt; we inform, demand, incite, encourage, swear, testify, accuse, condemn, absolve, insult, contemn, defy, affront, flatter, applaud, bless, humiliate, deride, conciliate, command, extol, congratulate, rejoice, complain; we express sadness, discouragement, despair, astonishment; we explain, keep silent—and what not?—with a variety and multiplicity that rivals the tongue." Montaigne continues, going beyond our immediate purview here: "With the head: we invite, send away, avow, disavow, contradict, welcome, honour, venerate, disdain, question, reject, make merry, lament, caress, taunt, submit, brag, exhort, threaten, affirm, enquire. What with the eyebrows? What with the shoulders? There is no motion that does not speak, and in a language that is intelligible without instruction, and in one that is common to all; whence it follows that, seeing the variety and distinctive use of other languages, this one should rather be judged the one best adapted to the nature of man. I pass over what special necessity teaches, on the instant, to those who have need of it; and the alphabets of the fingers, and the grammars expressed by gestures, and the matters of learning which are practiced and expressed only by them; and the nations which Pliny says have no other language."

37. Cf. Nicolas Vaschide, *Essai sur la psychologie de la main* (Paris: Rivière, 1909).

38. Cf. Jules Crépieux-Jamin, *L'écriture et le caractère*, 16th ed. (Paris: Presses Universitaires de France, 1963).

CHAPTER 5

THE FACE AND THE GAZE

My hand communicates but little of me to touch, and it is primarily with his eyes that a partner in conversation or a psychologist or a painter questions me. The word which my lips speak is likewise sustained and confirmed in its meaning by my gaze, my gestures, and my whole attitude. Others read the words on my lips at the same time as they hear them; Victor Hugo noticed this in children; "Everything in them, even their gaze, listens to me."[1] The reason for this is that my body is primarily a visible thing and other people are primarily seers. My personal being finds its primordial manifestation in an "epiphany" which takes place under the gaze of others. Therefore, before studying the face, which is the seat of vision but also the privileged locus of my own visibility for others, we will do well to examine this property of my body as a whole.

I. TO BE VISIBLE AND SEEN

To Be a Man Is to Be Visible

To appear is to make myself seen. But, paradoxically, I am less visible to myself than to others. Another person can see me from the rear, from the front, and in profile, simply by changing his observation point a bit. But because my eyes are set in the most elevated part of my body—the head—and at the front of this, I can see at most only the forward part of myself; even then, my angle of vision, from above downwards, is rather limited. I can see my limbs readily only because they can extend outwards away from my body, so that hands and feet become fully visible. I do not, however, see that by which I see and to which the eyes of others are primarily drawn. My face eludes itself even while it presents itself to the vast multitude of real or potential viewers. It is, of course, true that from my earliest years coenesthesia, touch, and, later on, the analogy of other people's bodies combine to give me an impression of my own body. But the image I form of it never coincides with the image which others have of me through sight. My appearance in the eyes of others will always raise insoluble questions for me.[2]

A human being is communicated first of all through his visibility. An embryo is hardly regarded as properly human because it is invisible to everyone, even the mother. The unborn child counts for little and has no social existence because he is unseen; this invisibility doubtless explains in part the strange leniency of public opinion towards abortion.

The child who is already "in the world" is "put into the world" at birth. Birth is the point of the first "epiphany," the initial manifestation of the self to others. From now on, the child is "in the world through a body," as Merleau-Ponty puts it—that is, through a visible body. It is by appearing before the gaze of another that I begin to count for him. My parents "declared" me as soon as I was corporeally manifested to the world; they provided me with a birth certificate as a sign of my social reality, and the whole familial circle underwent a reorganization because I was now on the scene. To be born is thus not a purely passive occurrence; it is rather an originating act which I repeat throughout my life, each time that I present myself anew to others. To appear is to be reborn.

Awareness of my own visibility has become for me inseparable from my awareness of existing. Let us note a fact to be developed later on: if I grasp myself as visible and existent by looking at my own body, this grasp is refined and deepened under the gaze of others. I am aware that the other sees me and that he sees me better than I see myself. In even the loneliest solitude, the thought of a possible observer is present in the clear or obscure consciousness I have of myself. In this sense I am born and reborn in all the instants through which my bodily appearance persists; "when I say 'I exist,' " Gabriel Marcel writes, "I have confusedly in mind the fact that I do not exist only for myself but also manifest myself . . . that I am manifest."[3]

Inversely, another person first exists for me to the extent that he is visible and presents himself to my gaze. "To see someone" often means, in everyday usage, to meet him, to make his acquaintance, and, consequently, to take him into account now as an existing reality. On the contrary, someone whom I have never seen and will never be able to see hardly has full existence for me. If I "lose sight of someone," I come to wonder whether he is still alive. The shrewd leader is aware of this and shows himself to me, appearing in public at opportune moments simply to strengthen his authority. It is by "appearing" that a person affirms his own existence. The best proof that a given man *exists* will always be that he has been *seen*.

On the other hand, if a *ghost* frightens me, it is because his semivisibility is equivalent to a semireality; there is a disturbing ontological ambiguity about a ghost, because he is equidistant from being and from nothingness. Those who have ceased to exist I spontaneously speak of as "those who are missing, have passed away." To die is to withdraw from the visible world, to fade away; and this, once again, is not a purely passive occurrence but the *act* of a man who takes radical hold of his own existence and renounces it, an act corresponding to its opposite, the original appearance made at birth.

Thus to kill someone, is, like knocking him down, equivalent to "making him disappear." After he has struck the fatal blow, the murderer realizes that killing a man does not entirely get rid of him. The corpse remains, tangible and visible, as a mute yet eloquent witness. Therefore the murderer cannot rest until he has eliminated the witness by burial, immersion, cremation, or some other means. Even then, once this has been accomplished, there are countless traces which give a minimal visibility to the man who has disappeared: his clothes, his dwelling, and so forth. At the end there is at least the trace in the minds of others: his "memory" and the name which evokes it.

Even if to die is to disappear, legal language nonetheless distinguishes one who is "dead" from one who has "disappeared": the former was seen lifeless and his death was duly verified; the latter has only been removed from the sight of his fellow men and from the grasp of their perception. In this second case, the hope may always be maintained that though his "appearance" has ceased, his "being" continues. But this distinction, however well-grounded it may be, and however consoling (though also heartrending) for those close to him who continue to hope against hope, cannot really affect the behavior of others. In practice, the man who has disappeared is treated as dead; since he has been snatched from our sight, he has ceased to exist. After wars or other catastrophes this kind of presumption can lead to tragic situations which form the subject of songs, novels, and plays. The one who has "disappeared" now "reappears," but his place in society and even in his own home has been taken by another. He is now an embarrassment, and the unhappy man feels as if he were being thrust back into the world of nonappearance; suicide often seems the only way to "regularize" his social situation and to make him really be what he is for others.

Incarnate subjects as we are, we will always tend to gauge being by appearance, "to be" by "to be perceived." Consequently, in my protest against the absence of one who is dead or has disappeared or against the distance that separates me from a loved one, I have recourse to the portrait or to the photograph which preserves his bodily image for me; he is not entirely lost to me if he still has some visibility for me, even of an artificial kind. On the contrary, the lack of sensible manifestation will always be a stumbling block when it comes to what is wholly invisible: ideal values, the spirit, or God. Nonappearance is in danger of being taken as nonexistence.

The Face as Freedom and Prevenance

As primordial self-affirmation, the face shows itself in an original *act* in which the subject takes and keeps the initiative: I "make my appearance," I "show myself." In this last phrase the reflexive verb brings out the jealously preserved, free self-disposition which is involved in my appearance: my face is mine, it belongs to me. Every manifestation to the eyes of another, however much the other may desire it, should remain free and master of itself; in a word, it ought to be a kind of free gift. I am not obligated to appear to anyone, but grant my appearance when I wish and to whom I wish; it is freely given, an act of benevolent prevenance. We feel this when we ask a great personage to receive us; we ask him to "deign" to appear or to "grant an interview"; in other words, it is a favor on his part if he shows himself, as it is if he enters into conversation or extends his hand. The appearance of a face is, in short, a beginning, something radically new (however well-known the person may be), a freely chosen movement towards the other.

The reason this is so is that in showing myself to a stranger's gaze I renounce and surrender myself. To see is equivalent to taking, and to be seen is equivalent to being possessed. In the children's game of hide-and-seek, he who is seen is "captured." A person who is particularly aware of this fact is the actor who passes from the wings to the stage. In the wings he belonged to himself, existed only for himself. and a few people nearby; his self-image was within his control, he could rectify it if he wished. But on the stage he is suddenly handed over to the gaze of the crowd; he is studied, judged, and evaluated. Others have now made this human image their own, have torn the man away from himself. Similarly, each time I appear in public, I give others a kind of right to my person; my being is handed over in my appearing, as it is when I reveal my name and occupation or accept an encounter with others. From this point of view, the distinction between private and public life is largely reducible to a distinction between a life that is at times secret, "unseen," and a life that is at times handed over to the gaze of all. It is natural, too, that I should at times seek the advantage of seeing without being seen, of having power over another without falling into the power of his gaze. The old legend of Gyges' ring, which made its wearer invisible, illustrates this desire to be present to others without their realizing it. So too various techniques of building and decoration, such as spy-holes and Venetian blinds, effectively annul the natural reciprocity of our gazes and our visibility.

If my "epiphany" is an act of free and unforced choice, every forced manifestation of myself is an attack upon my freedom. Prisoners of war were exhibited in the Roman general's "triumph" or are exposed today to the jeers of the mob; the crucified man was condemned to die "displayed to view" before the eyes of all;[4] at times men are pilloried: in taking from them the free disposition of their own appearance, part of their liberty has been taken away. No one is autonomous unless he is master of his own appearing, of that instinctive alternating movement of manifesting his own image and keeping it to himself.

There is a problem today of the "right to a personal image" which would guarantee to each person the inviolable ownership of his image. Techniques for capturing and transmitting a man's image have in fact become so numerous and refined that the individual is in danger of being robbed of himself. I no longer belong to myself, I am no longer my own, if my image can at any moment be exploited for commercial or legal purposes. Granted that in certain cases society has the right to force me to "appear" in court for the common good; the manifestation of myself to others continues, nonetheless, to be of its nature a free and unforced act.

The native movement which carries my whole being towards the world is, in virtue of the preeminent significance of my face and of my tendency to personify things, a movement of *facing* reality. If my anticipating hand moves away from my body and stretches out, this movement is nevertheless secondary, and its meaning is to be read in my face. I approach the universe, in the first place, through the outreach of my gaze and the movement of my face, whether lowered in fear or raised in serenity or courage. I thus affirm my own existence when I challenge, question, or simply experience the universe.

But facing and confronting take on their full meaning, whether literal or figurative, only when another person is involved; then the flat planes of the frontal area permit a contact of symmetrical faces. The face of the man coming to meet me seeks out my face, calls to it, and summons it forth in virtue of our inherent reciprocity; our gazes intermingle almost inevitably. Even were I to turn aside my eyes, this would in an indirect and negative way attest to our mutual and original relationship. Thus it is face to face and, as it were, forehead to forehead, that two subjects affirm their presence to each other, take each other's measure, and give themselves to each other in benevolence or love, or challenge and oppose each other in conflict.

Language is filled with expressions inspired by these basic experiences: a man "faces" adversity, "faces it well or poorly"; in his relations with others he "preserves face" or "loses face," "keeps his head," and shows "effrontery" ("front"—forehead or whole face). The sculptor likes to make two faces "confront" one another. The figurehead of a ship expresses determination to "confront" the elements, the enemy, or any adventure.

The Face as Manifestation of the Person

The etymology of "visage," one synonym for face, is significant: it is derived from Latin *videre*, "to see," and is thus essentially correlative to vision and is defined by the latter. As bearer of the eyes, my visage or face is that by which I see others and by which others see me. But the face is also what first catches my eye in others and what first catches the eye of others in me. The face is thus simultaneously seeing, seeable, and seen; it is turned outwards to manifest me and to grasp the manifestation of others and of the world. The five senses are gathered together in the face—except for touch, which is actively exercised by the hand. It is from my face that my words issue forth. Finally, the face is morphologically the most differentiated part of my body, the most finely modelled part, and the part in which the life of consciousness finds expression and is observable to others, even if only by a quivering of the features or a fleeting shadow in the eyes. The face is the primal manifestation of the "I." It would be difficult, therefore, to agree with Marcel Jouhandeau when he says: "Nothing is more revealing of people than the sight of their bare feet."[5] The hand is more significant than the foot, and the face more than either; do we not see gradations of growing intimacy in the kissing of the foot, of the hand, and of the face? "To see someone" is, essentially, to see his face, and if death and burial are so painful to us, it is because they take a face forever from our sight.

The facial epiphany is a primordial, original, irreducible datum, a free affirmation. You cannot deduce a face; it will never be the conclusion of a syllogism; you cannot demonstrate that it is or is not what it ought to be. Aesthetic norms aside, a face cannot be discussed or justified; you either accept it or reject it along with all that it reveals today and conceals unforeseeably for tomorrow. You must either show it sympathy, friendship, or love, or else turn your gaze from it. Everyday language has numerous expressions to express this choice which another person always forces us to make: a face "comes back" to me or "doesn't come back" to me, and so forth. Nothing is more obvious in fact than a face, nothing less obvious in principle.

Like the word or the hand, but in an especially privileged way, the face belongs to the man and gives the most direct access to him; the person is, as it were, situated in his face and a little behind it. To accept a face is thus to welcome another person, to admit him into our private world, to affirm and recognize him, and to stand ready to serve him. To reject a face is to reject the person from communion with us. In the extreme case, we attempt to abolish the person by murdering him. Short of such extreme measures, the blow in the face or the slap is the insult of insults, for I am slaying the person in his most evident self-manifestation. Much more, then, is the "disfiguring" or "defacing" of a person (Latin *figura*, face) through blows one of the actions most injurious to the person. In thus debasing the natural "face" of a man, I torture him in his subjectivity, I simultaneously affirm and deny his dignity as a person. It is not a matter simply of masking him, which would leave the native face intact; it is a matter of degrading the latter and making it ugly. Accident or illness sometimes produces the same insulting and debasing effect; then the person "no longer looks human." Recall the stricken Job and the silent consternation of his three friends. The observer doubts the identity of the victim and imagines that some strange ontological transformation has taken place; he no longer recognizes the person he once knew and esteemed and loved.[6]

The *metamorphoses* we read of in myths should be looked at in this light. In the myth of Proteus, for example, an ever-shifting appearance hides the true reality and leads to the perpetual mystification of others. But there are also metamorphoses effected out of cruelty. Owing to malice or the hostility of the gods (as when the priestess Io was jealously turned into a cow by Hera),[7] a human being loses his natural appearance and is reduced to the rank of a brute animal or other lowly thing. No longer human in face and shape, he feels denatured and depersonalized; the same as he was, yet somehow other. He does not know how to "look upon" himself or treat himself. His existence is now a mysterious intermingling of continuity and discontinuity; his name and his past are present in his memory and the memory of others, but his new appearance ceaselessly belies that identity. He is human in his inner being but dehumanized in appearance, and thus no longer has any "fellow being like himself." The noble and familiar human image which others present to him is no longer reciprocal with his own. Thus, unable to settle upon an attitude towards those near him, he inspires in them a fear and disquiet which reflect his own physical oddity.

Kafka's *The Metamorphosis* seems to be illustrating the existential plight of such an "odd man out." The new appearance which Gregor suddenly puts on during the fatal night is never expressly identified. He has painful and disquieting internal sensations, but it is primarily in the attitudes, faces, and eyes of others that the unfortunate man discerns the progressive and horrifying change in his own appearance. The discovery itself accelerates the process of disfigurement. The image of himself which he sees in the mirror of others' eyes draws Gregor irresistibly, as though it were an exemplar. Thus the transformed man and those around him are mutually involved in the drama created by unanswerable questions: "Who am I?" and "Who are you?," or, rather, "Who is he?" for Gregor ceases to be a "you" and becomes more and more an object. The two questions react upon and deepen each other; they feed upon each other like two cancers. The metamorphosis thus creates a kind of abyss in the midst of interpersonal relations, as each person gradually loses hold upon his own reality. The change of appearance brings about for yesterday's human being, and for those belonging to him, a real ontological "degradation." Those around him are saved only by death, which swallows Gregor up entirely, his reality and his unbearable appearance.

We will have occasion later on to study the role of a uniform or a freely chosen costume in determining how others look upon me.[8] For the moment, let us note that the awareness of my personal image (stature, skin color, complexion, health or sickliness, baldness, spectacled eyes, and so forth) is an integral and large part not only of my ego but also of my "I." *The consciousness of my appearance is inseparably bound up with the consciousness of my identity;* the former is one of the latter's firmest foundations and even guides its development, especially during the years of growth. The eyes of my fellow human, beings are a mirror for me: as I appear to others, so do I see myself and such do I gradually become.

If there can be degrading change and if blows can disfigure, the human appearance can also, through intense joy, great happiness, or exceptional good fortune, achieve an extraordinary development and luminousness. The apotheosis of a hero raises a face and a person to a superhuman condition; the man is said to be "trans-figured." An unsuspected identity is revealed and makes the whole bodily appearance radiant. He is the same person as he was yesterday; there has been no annihilation of the earlier personality and creation of a new one, but a change of appearance. I recognize my fellow man and name him; I recall the past he shared with me in our common human condition. I even discover in his new state the fulfillment of a desire which, deep down, I cherish for myself: the desire for a radical transcendence which would raise me beyond the limits of my empirical ego. In this sense, I find myself fulfilled in the other man in a mysterious process of substitution. But at the same time my fellow's transfiguration puts an unbridgeable distance between us. He is no longer my neighbor, and has been marvelously freed of the fetters of time. Set in the ranks of the gods he is, in a sense, more "another" than ever before, since he has achieved the supreme form of his own being and identity.

The Face as Self-Attestation

The thing that lies before me—an inkwell, a book, a bouquet of flowers—lacks consciousness and self-awareness and is, in this sense, absent from itself. It displays itself without reserve before me and exercises no control over its own surrender and manifestation; or rather, since a thing has no conscious life of its own, I ought to say that it does not manifest or display *itself* but, in a wholly passive way, is manifested, displayed, or surrendered. It is manifested despite itself, as it were, and without any reflection on the matter. Thus the object *undergoes* its own visibility. Of itself it says nothing and does not testify to what it is; instead, I identify it thanks to knowledge I have which is drawn from other sources.

The lower animals are still close to being objects; for us, the butterfly has no gaze. The higher animals more familiar to human beings, such as the cat and the dog, are capable of some mimicry; training gives them a little control of a very rudimentary kind over their impulses and attitudes, so that they are situated halfway between things and man. I can say, using the personal pronoun by way of a distant approximation, that my cat "shows himself" to be a hypocrite or that my dog "gives evidence" of affection for me. In fact, the animal does not freely manifest himself or "appear."

In any event, even if the higher animal has a head provided with sense organs, I do not speak of its "face." A biologist indeed will speak of a dog's "face," but only by analogy. Man is the only animal who really has a face, because he is the only one in which self-manifestation is an *act*. Every human face "means" something and in fact "says" something; and this silent declaration, perceived by my eyes, concerns the very being of the person. Because man is usually master of his own means of expression, all sorts of mimicry, reserve, or hypocrisy are undoubtedly possible, as much as sincere self-expression. Yet, except in cases of mimicry and pretence, the face manifests the person by its very being; as soon as it presents itself, the face is an act, an affirmation, an active epiphany. The human face alone "manifests itself" in the full sense of the words.

If we inquire into the specific manner of this manifestation, we must be satisfied to say that it is exercised by way of *attestation*. Another man's face bears witness; it does not demonstrate or prove. It bears in itself its own guarantees and presents itself to me as a self-affirmation that must either be accepted or rejected, since it is supported by nothing outside itself. It is true, of course, that word, gesture, bodily attitude, and behavior all corroborate and further explicate the facial expression—or, sometimes, contradict it. But the facial expression always has an element of the unqualified and unqualifiable about it. The human face is *affirmation pure and simple*.

We must be careful, however, not to think of this as affirmation without content. On the contrary, the fullness of the individual's existence is discoverable on his face. This affirmation is further related to an act of witnessing by the sincerity we presume it to possess. While the guilty person hides himself or at least covers his face (the child goes into the corner), the man who presents himself openly protests his innocence by that very fact: "Look at me. Here I am as what I am. My reality and my appearance are at one." Even while we admit the many possibilities of dissimulation, we must regard the face as naturally a veracious act.

Even the *sleeper's face*, despite the person's unconsciousness, is an epiphany by way of attestation. A man whom weariness has overcome has turned aside from action, from speaking, from looking upon other persons and things. Without leaving the world, he has withdrawn from all dealings with it. Sleep has suspended his communication activities, and only the vegetative functions which are indispensable for life are still being exercised. The man breathes, and the regularity of his breathing makes me aware how serene and deep his biological concentration inward is. Nonetheless, even though he does not communicate with me, the sleeper continues to express and manifest himself, for his face is there and the observer can examine it at leisure without hoping ever to exhaust its content. The gaze, which is the central factor in facial attestation, is, of course, lacking here. Sleep is able to do what is impossible in waking hours: to make this momentary but immense subtraction from the face; in waking hours, even if the subject deliberately closes his eyes, he continues to be aware that he is showing me his face. But, to make up for this lack, the unconsciousness of sleep effects a relaxation of all the features, so that they can be seen without difficulty. I can measure the proportions of the whole face and examine the curve of the cheek, the contour of the lips and nose, the breadth and height of the forehead. But through all these details of morphology I am in touch with something that cannot be localized or defined: the meaning of the person. This global reality is present in the living totality of the features; it is everywhere and nowhere; it circulates throughout, subtle despite the materiality of the features, indisputable and unprovable. It touches this "surface" of the man which is his facial skin (Latin *facies*, surface), but it has imponderable depths which the concentration of sleep makes more evident than ever. I immediately grasp but never wholly comprehend this irreducible datum which is the *meaning* of a person and a life; it is a free affirmation, a self-attestation, the witness of being to itself. By the very fact that he exists, even a sleeping man affirms his own meaning and presents it to me as a datum, something "given."

When the sleeper wakes and opens his eyes, when his gaze emerges from the fogs of sleep and becomes fully lucid, then his whole face is illumined and acquires its full expressivity. I then modify my earlier judgment, for I realize that even in sleep the gaze was present and active, although latent behind the closed lids, and that all the features were in fact organized about and centered upon the expression of eyes, silently evoking it. The habitual signification of the gaze had shaped the face and continued mysteriously to irradiate it even in sleep.[9] In waking, which is essentially the awakening of the eyes, the face regains its full expressive power. I read in the living pupil why the features are what they are, while they in turn corroborate the meaning expressed by the pupil, which is a mute word and the place par excellence from which meaning flows out. The reason for this is that visibility and gaze are concretely inseparable. In his eyes a man accepts his visibility in its totality, sums it up, and brings it to completion; the timid or ashamed gaze is one which does not freely accept and take charge of the whole personal appearance with which nature has endowed this individual. In summary: while sleep put the man at my disposal in an-avowal of his physical fragility, waking brings home to me the full meaning of the person.

Meaning radiates from the eyes and face over the whole body. The sight of a headless statue is disturbing, and the sight of a decapitated body would horrify me; the reason is not so much the damage or the physical suffering presupposed as it is the metaphysical and human meaninglessness of the trunk continuing to exist without its head; I would rather the trunk had vanished along with the face which was its justification. In every man, stature, bodily structure, hands, gestures, and words receive their final meaning and ultimate reason for existence from the face and the gaze. These are the spring from which the personal meaning, born in the depths of the "I," flows forth visibly. Using the analogy of physical light and the spiritual light radiating from consciousness, Christ could say: "The eye is the lamp of your body. When your eyesight is sound, your whole body is lighted up, but when your eyesight is bad, your body is in darkness. Take care, then, that your light is not darkness" (Luke 11:34-35).

The self-affirmation in the face is constantly transformed with the years, both in its manner and in its content. The eyes of adults as they lean over a cradle are always filled with the same question: "What will this child be?" (Luke 1:66). Adults play the hopeless game of discovering likenesses to the child's parents and relatives. They examine the tiny face with its crumpled features and closed eyes in the hope of reading there its future destiny; in this still confused and obscure text countless unforeseeable events seem already to be written down. As time passes, the face gradually smooths out and its meaning becomes clearer. Now there is indeed a mysterious disclosure of what the person will be later on; the future of a human being is already written there in letters of flesh. A nascent freedom is stirring in the depths of the eyes. The self-attestation here does not concern the past, which the child is unable as yet to evaluate, but the apparently endless future: it is an attestation never before made in human history, despite all continuity with the child's forebears, and it is *prophetic* just as the gaze itself looks outward and forward. Is not the amazing thing about early childhood precisely this prefiguring of the adult to come, this anticipatory proclamation of a new human meaning? On the other hand, if the death of a young person is felt to be such a cruel blow, it is because a prophecy embodied in flesh has not been fulfilled and a promise not kept: life has betrayed him. In short, youth is prophecy in action, as Adam himself was in the morning of the world. Upon the face of the first man, turned towards all the faces still unborn, was written the immense destiny of a mankind still in its infancy. But the prophecy contained in a child's eyes does not concern only an historical future. This candid gaze with its limpid depths bears witness, beyond time itself, to an order of values free of corruption, ugliness, or falsehood. In the mild but inexorable rectitude of these eyes I read an attestation of unqualified demands which transcend the individual and all becoming, yet are inscribed in the depth of conscience.

As the subject moves out of childhood, the prophecy in the face begins to be fulfilled, and the shape of a destiny begins to emerge along with the shape of the face. Adolescence may still be a time of ambiguity when countless promises lend the charm of variety and bring the dangers of uncertainty, but even then decisive choices are already determining certain paths to be followed and lending substance to what the face says; and events, propitious or unpropitious, gradually leave their mark upon it. Thus the meaning of this human face is revealed and realized, sometimes in ways unfaithful to the initial prophetic affirmation, sometimes in harmonious continuity with it. In the mature man the face's attestation is both retrospective and prospective, turned to both past and future; it bears witness to what has been and to what will be, recapitulates them both and integrates them with each other in the living synthesis of a single manifestation.

An old man's face, in its turn, bears witness to a whole past; labors, sufferings, joys, encounters, and numerous events have etched this face and left their mark upon it. The gaze accepts all these imprints which have been the result of both unforeseeable destiny and free will interacting, and unifies them all in its own depths. But even this gaze, which is gradually becoming detached from the world, continues to have a prophetic value: to the extent that the man has surrendered himself to invisible values, his eyes bear witness to an order of ever new realities which no single life, however full, could ever exhaust.

Even in death the face continues its attestation. As long as the features keep their shape, the dead person still expresses himself, manifesting himself now in the serenity and peace of an affirmation that is forever. What he was, he is now for good; his personal meaning is concluded and, as it were, eternalized; it is there in the face, living still and real, active and present, even though communication with others has ceased. The silent testimony of this face is the testimony of a person totally concentrated, turned inward to his own depths, and identified with his innermost and truest self. If we want to see the absence of a "sense of the person" in various societies, look at the practice among some primitive tribes of shrinking heads and making decorative objects of them, or, in supposedly civilized societies, the profitable business of dressing up the dead like dolls. On the contrary, the taking of a death mask, comparable to the casting of the hand and the concern for the person's last words, fixes forever the testimony given by a face and the meaning of a human destiny.

The Face as Revelation

The attestation which a man's face carries upon it is something inherently spontaneous. Any constraint would be an assault, even a murderous attack, upon the person. The free and prevenient manifestation of himself is thus a revelation of the person, a free gift to another in which the subject has all the initiative. In every face turned to me, a person declares himself and, before any word is pronounced or gesture made, says: "Here I am."

Along with the word, the hand, and the whole bodily self, the facial epiphany deserves the name revelation for another reason: its ambiguity. If the face manifests the person, it does not display him; it declares him without dropping all reserve; it affirms him but does not make him an object to be inspected. Through the fleshly appearance, which is made to some extent transparent by the eyes, the "I" unveils and veils itself simultaneously; a light arises like a dawn which will never turn to full noon. The face is a real but limited unveiling, a reserved form of communication. If staring at a person is felt as an aggression, it is because it is an attempt to break down the face's inherent reserve, to make it speak what it wishes to keep hidden: in short, to destroy the face in its role of revelation.

The face, like the hand, ordinarily presents itself uncovered to the observer. Its native tendency is to radiate the light of consciousness outward. The basic form of frank communication is to present oneself to another with uncovered face. All behavior in which the face is hidden thus tends to rouse suspicion of betrayal; the person is hiding his face as if it would "say" too much. Even the simple use of dark glasses which hide the eyes, or of a wig or false beard, is enough to change the appearance and prevent identification. But the hood and the mask have an even more radical effect which shows how interrelated the eyes and the face as a whole are. When the *hood* is the kind that entirely hides the features, with only two slits for the eyes to peer through,[10] it frightens me. Even if I meet the eyes of the other, I cannot interpret his gaze: is it friendly, indifferent, or hostile and ready for some evil attack? I cannot choose among these possibilities because the features are hidden. The latter provide the natural and authentic context within which the gaze is the text; it is thus through the features that the gaze becomes meaningful for me. My distress in this situation arises from the fact that I must oscillate between the various possible interpretations of a piercing look which meets my own but remains impenetrable to me.

The "featured" *mask* is quite different. Here, too, the person's eyes look through while his features are hidden; but instead of disappearing behind a neutral veil, the natural features are replaced by others. Now the facial context is totally corrupted, not just missing. Upon the genuine appearance a false appearance has been superimposed (which brings out the fact that there is such a thing as a true appearance). The meaning of the gaze is now determined by, for example, the cheeks, nose, and grimace of a clown. Even if the mask represents a human type with which I am at home, the true identity of the subject is quite different; he is hidden by a borrowed personality. Thus the natural mystery of the subject is complicated by the addition of an artificial mystery which my eyes cannot penetrate at all. When a mask has been freely selected, I can reflect on the motivations for the choice: Why does this man want to look like this or that person? In what ways do his own features, his "natural mask," seem deficient to him? Of what new meaning does he wish to be the bearer? The mask can tell me what the masked person thinks he really is, or would like to be, or perhaps really is. Paradoxically, the false appearance can bring to light a deeper characteristic of the real being, just as the truth of the person is sometimes conveyed through lying words.

Caricature plays a similar role. It is a sketchy and ridiculous portrait. The original is recognizable, but certain features have been deliberately falsified; the face has lost its natural harmony. The specific note of caricature is that the falsification is a "loaded" one, as the etymology indicates.[13] The caricaturist must first discover or highlight a *real* trait of his subject's character or behavior. The effectiveness of the exaggeration, along with the penetration of the psychological analysis, is what makes the caricature successful and provokes laughter. Here, as in some uses of a mask, the falsification of the face opens the way to a hidden truth.

Of less importance than the mask and the caricature—which, after all, bear a well-defined meaning—is the *extra* in a play or film. The person here no longer has any real role to play, for the natural significance of his face is neutralized. He keeps his own appearance, but this appearance is used in an impersonal way; it is simply there and has no value but to be one of many. The face in these circumstances is no longer the act of a person manifesting himself but is simply a piece of human furniture.

The extra at least retains the appearance which nature has given him, with all its elements and its three-dimensional relief: the *silhouette*, on the contrary, retains only the outline of the face.[12] In the silhouette, a man is stripped of his fleshly fullness and wealth of vitality, and is reduced to a set of lines. Projected onto a plane, he loses his third dimension; concrete appearance tends to become abstract figure. Instead of a full portrait we have a simple outline, a flat structure without depth. Yet the silhouette does still express the person: the shape of the face is always individual and not interchangeable with any other; the lines of forehead, nose, mouth, and chin form a unique whole and retain their original meaning.

The *shadow* is the origin of the silhouette and provides it with its content. But whereas the silhouette is an artistic product, the shadow is a natural thing which accompanies me as a kind of double; it is something of myself, and in it I inevitably affirm the mystery of my presence.[13] Where the silhouette has firm lines, the shadow is often hazy and dim. It is capricious, sometimes preceding me, sometimes following me, sometimes vanishing entirely. It is unpredictable, for it may lengthen and grow slender, offering me an unproportioned image of myself. It is impalpable and obstinately keeps its distance, however far I extend my hand and however swiftly I run after it. Nor can I suppress it any more than I can lay hold of it. It is pitiless in reducing me to an outline that is blind and mute, to a stain on the ground which nonetheless leaves no trace of its presence. Another person's foot can trample on it. It bears witness to my spatiality, the reality of my body, and my body's "pro-jection" and directedness, yet it takes from it all distinctive relief and color, for my shadow is black like everyone else's. It is light, subtle, mobile, and evanescent, and in it I see the insecurity of my existence reflected, and even my nothingness. It proclaims the power to err and be false which my body bears within itself, and it reduces me to a faceless outline. Sometimes I ask myself, "In which appearance is my personal truth reflected: in the image my mirror shows me, or in the insubstantial shadow I cast on the ground?" Torn between my desire for eternity and the challenge death raises to that desire, I may conceive the beyond as a "kingdom of shadows"—halfway between being and nothingness, a place of evacuated images, bloodless apparitions, and expressionless faces. The dilemma of being and appearance is thus complicated by this third and disconcerting term: my shadow, that residue, as it were, of my present appearance, from which every capacity for personal revelation has been removed. I find myself reduced to the condition of an apparition, of an intangible memory, both for myself and for others.

But if such a shadowy afterlife would be a state of nonmanifestation and, in the last analysis, of disappearance, the act by which we vanish away is, paradoxically, revealing. It is a fact that the death of another takes him from our sight but also makes it possible for us to know him better. In withdrawing from the visible world, the dead person leaves a void, the shape of which permits us to gauge his stature better than we did when he was alive. When a man's being is stripped of its empirical limitations and the ignoble contingencies which held him prisoner, his full meaning can be affirmed. At the funeral pyre of Joan of Arc some cried out: "We have burned a saint!" On the death of many an important person, people like to repeat what Henry III said when he saw the corpse of the Duke of Guise: "What a great man he is! Even greater in death than in life!" The memory of close friends and relatives retains this kind of enlarged image, a legacy to them from the dead man's final moments. The dilemma of being and appearance, with which men must wrestle all their lives, is resolved in this final manifestation. The appearance which revealed the other to me also hid him from me. Death is the supreme act of self-manifestation in which the embodied subject both removes himself and reveals himself.[13]

Face and Identity

Since I assert myself primarily by my bodily appearance, it is by it that others judge me and recognize me. My whole exterior, and especially my face, is inseparably bound up with my name and my identity. To know me is to be able "to put a name to the face." As the most expressive part of my person, my face is myself; it is ordinarily enough to distinguish me from all other men, and so my identity card and passport must carry my photograph. Thus, too, our language often designates the whole person by reference to this eminently distinctive part of him, as when we speak of "weak-faced" and "strong-faced" persons to indicate the character of the whole person.

If then I want to pass as someone else, I must take a person's appearance from him: clothing, gestures, words, and—above all —facial features. In so doing I strip him of his identity and arrogate it, in some degree, to myself. This is the talent of the hoaxer who is clever at putting on a borrowed personality. It is also the art of the accomplished actor who gives the spectator the sophisticated pleasure of enjoying an illusion while knowing it to be an illusion. Such usurpation of another's personality takes an extreme form in the *Amphitryon* of Plautus and Molière, where Mercury and Jupiter take on the appearance of the slave Sosia, and his master, Amphitryon, in order to approach Alcmene. In our day, we hear it said that famous personages, such as dictators and the idols of the masses, use doubles to provide themselves with a kind of ubiquity. But this is really the reverse of what the gods do in Plautus and Molière. The god strips away the whole exterior of his victim as a kind of total mask for himself and hides his true identity behind the appearance of another. In the modern instance, the person in question asserts his own real identity with the aid of a borrowed "phenomenality" quite similar to his own; in such cases, it is not the double who is abusively used, but the public. In both instances, however, the appearance presented to the observer simulates a presence which it does not really embody.

Apart even from such exceptional cases, the knowledge of another's name and full legal identity does not give me the inner depths of the person; I want to see him if I am to penetrate into the mystery which he represents. My first judgment bears on that which I first apprehend: the face. In the presence of this silent witness, my gaze always formulates the same questions: "What do you say of yourself? Your face is a 'primordial word of honor,'[15] an attestation of your being, a direct and immediate epiphany which is one with your very act of existing, a privileged place for encountering your personal truth. Are you in fact what your face says you are? You 'have the face' of a fool (or an intelligent man), a coward (or a brave man): are you really such? Must you be considered to be what you seem to be?"

I try to confirm this initial silent statement made by the face through the other functions which manifest a man: words, gestures, attitudes, habitual or exceptional behavior. I ask the views of a third party or parties. But I must always come back to that primordial evidence of the face and compare all testimonies from other sources with it. If I am a good judge of faces, I will be able to exercise critical judgment and coordinate what various sources give me, but they will never add up to a definitive knowledge of the person; I am in the position of a judge who, after proving with documents the *legal* identity of an accused person, returns over and over again to the primordial testimony of the man's face in order to penetrate to his *real* identity.

The reason this is necessary is that man, capable of reflection and mimicry, can look at himself and deliberately "make up a face" for himself, engaging in all kinds of affectation and dissimulation, comedy and tragedy. In the theater such performances are the object of a kind of tacit contract between spectators and actors, and the latter are judged by the perfection of their imitation. In real life, however, harmonious social relations require that faces, no less than words, should be trustworthy. In a given case I may be led to think that another person has two faces; an outward one presented to observers and an inward one turned to himself and expressing his true being. I would like these two faces to become fused into one, the manifested being to coincide with the lived being, and this integrated reality to show itself in the outward appearance. But even in the case of a person of unquestionable integrity, I may, through an excess of subtlety or a lack of experience or sympathy, misapprehend the meaning of a face. I may fail to take enduring traits into account, relying instead on what I observe of a person's mien—his "air"—which sometimes reduces itself to an expression as fleeting as a breath, for which it is impossible to establish any significance. The most unjust evaluations may be reached in this way, bringing dire consequences in their train. Men see only the outward appearance of other men and, unable ever to escape entirely from the dilemma of reality and appearance, remain incapable of judging "the heart."

Moreover—to look at the problem from another angle—man and his face are not objects. As we have already observed, the thing before me is there in its entirety, displayed, surrendered. I examine it "objectively"; I can have a scientific knowledge of it. But another person's body, though possessing the undeniable objectivity of an organism and thus able to become an object of scientific knowledge, also possesses an inalienable subjectivity which permeates every part of it, though not in the same degree. The face takes first place in this respect. From body to face; from face to eyes; from eyes to gaze: we proceed thus to the focal point of personal epiphany, the point at which objectivity seems to disappear, making way for pure subjectivity. The eye is still an organ of which the biologist makes an anatomical and physiological study; but the gaze is not an organ. The oculist who tests a patient's sight "objectifies" it and applies his scientific knowledge to it; but in so doing he is not examining the living gaze, which cannot be the object of scientific study. The surgeon can grasp the eyeball with his fingers or an instrument, but the gaze eludes his grasp far more totally than a drop of quicksilver. Similarly, a painter who makes a close study of the technique of a master in a famous work (of Franz Hals in his *Descartes*, for example) is adopting an "objectifying" attitude: he must set aside the material details if he is to recapture the artist's vision. Like the study of a hand through dissection or of a text through the analysis of its elements, an objectifying study of a living or a painted eye fails to disclose its meaning.

Nor can the gaze be expressed in a definition. It is not an organ but the "act" of an organ; so much so, says Aristotle, that the eye of a corpse or a man-made image has only the name in common with the living eye.[16] At a deeper level, we may ask: Is your gaze still a bodily reality? or is it already something of the spirit? Is it not the privileged point at which the materiality of the organism becomes translucent to let the intentionality of consciousness filter through; the focal point at which the subjectivity of your whole body is concentrated, gathered up, and reaches the height of its intensity in the unseizable look of the pupil; where the soul gives the flesh a marvelous transparency; where the organ's opacity is most fully overcome by the luminous power of your "I" and your spirit; where, finally, the mysterious metaphysical unity of body and soul manifests itself and communicates itself in a quasi-experiential manner?[17]

Resisting all attempts to grasp it objectively, the gaze can only be *encountered* by another gaze: it surrenders itself in the intercommunication of two subjectivities. Only a gaze, then, can preserve the memory of another gaze it once encountered. Long after the death of someone dear to me, his gaze remains a living thing within my own: the exchange of looks proceeds interminably, like the sign and the act of an inviolable communion.

The Face as Interpretation of Man

To have a face gives the human being an original physiognomy. Man, unlike any other being, has the marvelous property of being infinitely variable, with as many variations as there are real or possible individuals. Each face is a new version, an irreducibly original interpretation of a common motif. The mystery of continuity in diversity doubtless strikes us more fully when we compare two faces widely separated by race, age, culture, and profession. But it also comes home to us, powerfully even if in an inverse way, in twins of the same sex, where likeness does not exclude an evident duality; even more, perhaps, in some twins of different sex, for here not only the universal human theme but a unique individual theme as well is given a masculine and a feminine version. The likeness of the faces, so attractive to eye and mind, shows that not only the individual theme but also the universal human type is inexhaustible. To be an individual man is thus to exercise a strange *interpretive power;* it is to interpret, manifest, and differentiate humanity itself and give it a hitherto unknown *meaning*. In this way, every individual is a revelation of man.

We are touching here on the eternal riddle of the universal: one, identical, everywhere present, yet in itself still unreal, it acquires existential reality and a face only from the individual. From Plato to Hegel, and indeed as long as men exist, this problem which belongs to both logic and metaphysics will continue to be raised. Ever since its obscure beginnings, mankind takes shape in each single man, is reborn, recognizes itself, and stands in wonder at its own newness —think only of the admiring exclamations uttered around every human cradle! In this second half of the twentieth century man can interpret himself in more than three billion faces. Accelerated population growth seems to express a feverish and unconscious urgency rising out of the depths of the species: the urgency of a mankind anxious to express itself ever more fully, to assume all possible faces and epiphanies, to bring to the light of day and its own gaze the inexhaustible riches within itself. One of man's most amazing privileges is that he can multiply himself without repetition, say himself over and over without plagiarism, and manifest himself without end.

II. TO SEE

To have a face is to be visible and to be seen. It is also, apart from the accident of blindness, to see, to be capable of gazing. But seeing and gazing are not synonyms. One gazes in order to see well. If it is possible to see without gazing (as one sees objects on the periphery of the visual field, for example), it is also possible that insufficient light, weak sight, or inattention may cause us to gaze without seeing. More important than this distinction, however, is the fact that the object specifies the act of knowledge; consequently, it is one thing to gaze on things, another to gaze on animals or men.

GAZING AT THINGS

Things and Horizon

Every seen object is part of a larger totality. However concentrated my gaze—as when I examine an ant, for example—I am always simultaneously aware of the whole visual field. In this sense, to see is to see a horizon and to situate the immediate object of attention (this book or this flower) in relation to a boundary or a background against which the objects stand out. In fact, a seen object is always related to several horizons, some distant, some close. In front of the vertical plane formed by my body extends my primary visual field, containing the visible objects nearest me. Beyond that there is a second field, defined by the plane in which some more distant but eye-catching object is situated; and so on. Is the beauty of the underbrush not largely due to the series of planes created by the forest as a whole? The horizon recedes ever further and gives the eye a marvelous sense of depth. In open country, the final boundary which sight attains is the horizon in the strict sense: the frontier, for me, between the visible and the invisible.

It is true, of course, that I can imagine other extents of space lying beyond this frontier, so that the horizon of sense knowledge lies far beyond my present field of vision. And if my perceptual experience has been broadened by travel, I have the immensely larger horizon of memory within which to situate objects I shall someday see and to judge them more surely. The same holds for the horizon of the mind. Every new knowledge takes its place within a horizon established by the field of my reading, reflection, and previous knowledge. Is not culture the capacity to take the true measure of things and to interpret them accurately by situating them within the horizon formed by universal values? The opposite of culture is the myopia of the ignorant person or the pedant.

Objectification

In setting things within their horizon I constitute them as objects. I perceive them initially from one limited perspective, from a viewpoint which gives me only a partial grasp of them. It is the nature of a perspective that it causes me to select from among visible objects or that it forces me to one "viewpoint" (one point from which I see) to the exclusion of the others. My "per-spective" thus determines what "a-spect" of the object I shall see; the two words have the same root and point to correlative realities. To escape the exclusivism of the single perspective, I try to adopt as many viewpoints as I can. Sometimes I move the object about in my field of vision, as when I turn a pencil in my fingers; sometimes I move my point of view around the object; as when, after looking at Notre Dame of Paris from the plaza in front, I then move over to the Pont de la Tournelle.

To objectify things is, above all, *to become conscious of their unconsciousness.* We have already taken note of the silence which is proper to them, a silence of emptiness, not of fullness.[18] It is also characteristic of things that they are blind; my gaze carries me within them, into their opaqueness and invincible ignorance of themselves. I see them to be dark, dull, and lifeless, with an "inside" that is wholly material and not an "interior." They exist for me without existing for themselves and without me existing for them. So close to me materially, they are nonetheless at the limitless and impassable distance which separates "someone" from "something." Contrary to what we might expect, scientific knowledge does not lessen that distance but is constantly increasing it. The more science reveals to me the laws of the universe, the more things become "things" for me—that is, lifeless means to be exploited for my own ends; they lie before me as "ob-jects" (things thrown in my path).[19] At the same time, this radical otherness of things turns me back upon my self and sharpens my awareness of myself as subject. The object negates me and stimulates me to affirm myself.

If I gaze out upon the whole world of things around me, I also perceive that they are ignorant of each other. Dullness and indifference characterize their relations, which are relations not of presence or absence but of juxtaposition and nonexistence for each other. Each thing is wrapped up in itself, imprisoned in itself; it neither peceives other things nor speaks to them; it is perhaps coupled with other things, but it does not in any true sense touch them. The distance between it and them is like an abyss of nothingness. My gaze, however, breaks down the confused raw data of things, analyzes it, and then puts it back together in an ordered synthesis; it distinguishes the elements that make it up, perceives their mutual relationships, compares and evaluates them: here is paper ready to receive the writing, a pen to trace the letters, and ink to wet the pen. Thus, out of things which are strangers to one another, my gaze makes a collection, creates an order, and shapes a world; like the luminous ray from a lighthouse it draws this cosmos out of its darkness. But the spectacle has full validity only for me; it is difficult for me at times to bring another to "envisage" it, that is, to train his own sight upon it. Each person is unique, and so is his vision of the world. However old the universe, it is reborn, as in a fountain of youth, in the gaze of every child who opens his eyes to it.

If my gaze directed to objects makes them exist for me, I turn my eyes away from them to reject and negate them and to suppress them back into nothingness. Man likes to deride the behavior of the frightened ostrich which buries its head in the sand to escape danger. But the same reaction arising from the instinct of self-preservation is also found in man, who when confronted with some horrible scene turns his eyes away or buries his face in his hands.[20] Fainting at the sight of blood or a suicide expresses the same meaning in a more forceful way; I make it impossible for myself to see the object, for something no longer seen no longer exists for me; I have, as it were, annihilated it. The gesture of veiling the face as a sign of rejection may have ritual significance, but it also has the basic meaning of which we are speaking.

Appropriation

Even as it introduces order into the cosmos, my gaze is mastering it and appropriating it for myself; it makes things my possession and establishes me as possessor of "my world." I am the point from which things are seen, in relation to which they are situated, and around which they gravitate. The distance at which each one is links it to me rather than separates me from it. For this distance is instantaneously crossed by my gaze. The movement is, however, one-directional, and in this fact my superiority is manifested. My gaze gives the world a kind of face but does not make it a true partner for me: only by an analogy can we speak of man as "face to face" with the world. I see, things are seen; I am a subject, they are objects; they do not know themselves, I know them and know that they do not know themselves; they are tossed down there, I put order among them; they are passive in respect to me, I am active in respect to them; I dispose of them, but they do not dispose of me. They were simply things; even before my hand, as organ of taking and conquest, was extended towards them, my gaze made them *my* things. From now on they are no longer "no one's," but are mine and for me. As my gaze traverses them it makes them my possession, makes them dependent on and related to me.

This function of my gaze as act of mastery is manifested in numerous ways. My desire to master the world is first and spontaneously expressed in the eyes. The intentness of my gaze as it fastens on a desired object is a tension of my whole being; it makes me intentionally present to the object, although with an immediacy that is ambiguous, since it is effective yet unfulfilled. As the child stands in front of a shop window, his gaze crosses the distance separating him from a coveted toy; he "devours it with his eyes" and finds pleasure in it in a kind of ardent, imperfect, even painful, anticipative possession. We can even say he "caresses" the thing with his gaze. The intense movement of the eyes thus anticipates or supplies for holding it in his hands. This greed of the eye[21] manifests the interplay of presence and absence, possession and deprivation, which consitutes desire.[22]

As myself a proprietor and conscious of the threat which another's gaze represents to my mastery of my being and possessions, I take all sorts of precautions to keep that gaze from penetrating into my home. Shutters, curtains, and blinds allow me to see without being seen and to let the air in while keeping the stranger's gaze out; I feel that otherwise I would cease to be master in my own house and lose my sovereignty over my familiar universe.[23] Similarly, if I can be at ease in my walled garden, it is because there are no other eyes to dispute possession of it with me. But if a house is built nearby and its windows overlook my garden, I protest against curious observers. Much more then, if the wall disappears and my garden is open to the gaze of passersby, are my possessions to some extent stolen from me; anyone at all can share in them simply by looking at them. On the other hand, I may invite a friend to see my garden; my gaze guides his along the paths to special spots and flowers. In so doing I honor my visitor, for I share with him, for a few moments, the domain which belongs to my own gaze. (Louis XIV wrote a *Method for Showing the Gardens at Versailles!*)

Language offers numerous expressions which attest to the possesive power of the gaze. "To have an eye" on someone or something is to dominate it and be its master. To "re-vise" or "re-view" a piece of work is to affirm that one is master of it, for it means to judge and emend it. Similarly, the inspection, the military "review," or the "canonical visit," which are actions proper to a legitimate leader, express his authority over things and persons. Subordinates may then hope that the authority will not "look too closely." In juridical language, the "right of inspection" is equivalent to a sharing in authority. Finally, I may "reconnoiter" a place with my eyes; I am then acquiring experimental knowledge which completes or corrects the confused notion I may have had. Such a "re-cognizing" gaze is an act of possession and appropriation.

The use of the verb "take" in "take a photograph" is even more significant. My admiring gaze at a landscape or a face is a passing thing; its object escapes into nonexistence for it as soon as it turns away. Thus the desire is enkindled to fix the scene or to prolong the face-to-face encounter; in short, to take the seen object with me. A sketch or painting answer such a desire and turns my dream into reality; it keeps the spectacle at the disposition of my gaze and makes it fully my own. But not everyone is able to sketch or paint, and, besides, these actions take some time to accomplish. Here photography comes to the aid of my desire to see; it eternalizes my vision through a technique and effort that are within everyone's capability. The mechanical nature of the technique corresponds to the intensity of my gaze which seeks to capture its object: after seeing, I "take" a copy of any spectacle whatsoever. In fact, photography can even turn my mastering gaze into a kind of *robbery*. While painting a picture usually requires the consent of some person (the model, or the owner of a place), photography lets me work without that person's suspecting. The speed of the operation leads me to *steal* from persons and things their visible appearance. When I become a hunter of pictures, I no longer study a model but pursue a prey.

We must insist, however, on the inferiority of the photograph in relation to the painting and especially to the portrait, except for those few photographers from the earliest days of photography to the present day, who have made authentic portraits—and they too are artists. As a mechanical process, taking a photograph often captures only some very accidental facial expression. On seeing a friend's photograph, we are often forced to remark that it's really not "he," because it hasn't caught his habitual expression. A portrait, on the contrary, seeks to capture the more permanent characteristics of a face, the deeper meaning that lies behind superficial variations of expression, and the vision of the world that is created by and reflected in this man's gaze. The painter's work requires psychological penetration and understanding of men. Under the mobile features the painter glimpses the mysterious interplay of freedom and existence. This is to say that the painter's gaze is essentially different from that of the ordinary photographer. The photographer tends to master mechanically the image of a person who inevitably becomes an "object," while the painter makes himself the servant of a "model" who is someone. The meaning of the person is the *raison d'être*, the norm, and the overriding ideal of portraiture. The artist is permeated by this living reality, questions it at length, dialogues and debates with it, dissects and recomposes it, and, finally, is victorious over it to the extent that he has submitted to it. The canvas then captures, if not all the ups-and-downs of this silent face-to-face struggle (as a series of "studies" would), at least its pregnant conclusion. The truth of a portrait, born as it is of the contemplative gaze, is the truth of a living and inexhaustible exchange. It comes into existence at the point where two gazes meet, and it reveals and prolongs both: that of the sitter as received and understood by that of the artist. In opposition to the outlook of the photographer, that of the artist is more oblative than possessive; it is homage rather than appropriation.

The Idolatrous Gaze

Our gaze upon things is deeply ambiguous. As it seeks to master the object, it is in danger of surrendering the subject to the object. A child who is fascinated by a coveted toy, or a spectacle he is contemplating, no longer belongs to himself but has been "captured through his eyes" and taken possession of through his gaze.[24] If I do not know how to protect myself, my own vehement desire may enslave me to what I wanted to master; to some extent, I would be acknowledging to it a right over my person. A dazzling light deprives me only of clear sight, but fascination with things takes away my free mastery of my own behavior. My gaze can subject me to the dictatorship of visible things, as the bird is drawn to its death by the irresistible eye of the snake.

All this holds for the idolatrous gaze. If I am seduced by the attractiveness of a thing, I set this blind reality which is inferior to me in a position above me and give it a kind of transcendence over me; or rather, as I contemplate it, my gaze lends it a kind of mysterious gaze of its own which is correlative to mine and to which I surrender myself, enriching it with every conceivable value and stripping myself of my own dignity. Via my entranced eyes, I surrender my being as a person, and it is lost to me. The idolatrous gaze inverts the natural hierarchy of being and subordinates man to things, thus degrading and debasing him.

Symbiosis of My Gaze and the World

My gaze is a gaze at something, and the something is always situated within my sensible and intellectual horizon. The world which my eyes conquer, interpret, and admire is inseparable from my gaze.

This symbiosis of my gaze and my world is, in summary, the history of my existence; for it begins in the first days of life, proceeds with its intense and profound exchanges during youth and maturity, is stabilized in old age, and ceases with death, which is a break between the world and myself.

The reason for this situation is that if my gaze projects me outward to the world, the world as I see it comes back to me; it gravitates to my gaze, out of which it is constantly reborn; it is reflected on my face and it shapes my features. The face, like the word and the hand, undergoes a far-reaching differentiation in the sailor, the peasant, the mountaineer, and the city dweller. As the sun leaves its scorching mark on the faces of those who are constantly exposed to it, so do vision and contemplation, whether of the senses or the intellect, exercise a transforming power. Plato observes, for example, that one who contemplates the Ideas imitates them and becomes in some small measure like them.[25] Every man is thus transfigured in the image of what he takes to be reality. As I am, so I see the world; but as I see the world, so also do I become. Sometimes that world confirms the meaning which I initially gave it and myself; sometimes it contests this and helps me revise it. To exist is to be oneself through a seeing body and a seen world. Every face is the mirror of a world; it presents an image which is simplistic or complex, tormented or serene, for the keen observer to read. Compare, from this point of view, the portraits of the two Lammenais brothers: that of Jean-Marie, full of a sense of balance and deep resolve, and that of Felicité, in which the face seems consumed by the burning gaze of the enormous eyes with their disclosure of some obscure anguish.

The divers spectacles a man has taken in abide in his inward vision. Have we never found ourselves scrutinizing the face of someone who has witnessed an event, in the hope of discovering in these eyes a living image of the event? I encounter gazes that seem as wide as the universe: that of the child, the strangest of all, presenting me with untouched immensities; that of the old man with its depths of experience. Present there are the reaches of the world of sense and of spirit, of human existence, of culture, and of faith—gathered up, concentrated, incommensurable with that tiny pupil which the gaze animates and transcends. The infinite reality filters through the infinitesimal.

GAZING AT ANIMALS

If my gaze at things can be unreservedly objective and objectifying, my gaze at an animal has a quite different quality. For the animal, and especially the higher animal, is an ambiguous being; its ontological status, to which little study has been devoted, is obscure and disconcerting. It is easy to bring this home to ourselves. If I accept the Cartesian theory that animals are machines and treat my dog as a thing ("It cries out but has no feelings," said the gentle Malebranche), the Society for the Prevention of Cruelty to Animals and even the law will be after me. If I treat the dog as a person, others will laugh at me. Thus I am hemmed in between legal threats and ridicule. In fact, the animal is neither a thing nor a person, but something halfway between. My gaze therefore is a hesitant one as I put questions to this metaphysically equivocal yet irreducibly distinct being: "What are you? What do you have to say about yourself?" but, though it has a head, even the most intelligent and affectionate of dogs has no face and cannot bear witness to itself. Its gaze is not really reciprocal with mine; sometimes the animal is so responsive that it almost seems human, at other times all my efforts to "explain" are frustrated by its unsurmountable opaqueness.[26]

I cannot, therefore, treat an animal like another person. When I turn my eyes towards it, I look down, condescend to a quasi-encounter with a being which is not a real partner for me. On the other hand, an animal does not present me with the inert passivity of an object. My gaze out into the garden I own is not the same as my gaze at my dog or as the gaze of the lion-tamer at one of his indocile beasts. My gaze encounters no initiative at all in things, but a real struggle takes place between man's will and the anarchic instincts of the animal. The lion-tamer's gaze, even more than the sound of his voice or his gestures, has the wonderful power to bend the superior strength of the animal to his will. Therefore the lion-tamer is careful not to take his eyes from the subjugated beast, much less to turn his back on it; for once the eye-to-eye contact is broken, the beast's violence is again unleashed. The whole struggle is thus concentrated, and decided to man's advantage, in the meeting of two gazes: the one asserting the force of a free will, the other a prey to rages over which no reason exerts control. Putting himself by a feat of the imagination in the animal's place, Kipling described man as the being whose gaze is unbearable, always forcing the animal to blink.[27]

The expression of an essential superiority, this power of the human gaze has a metaphysical significance. My human gaze exercises a kind of creative and "specifying" power over its object, assigning each being a particular rank and degree of existence, which, in relation to the reality of the thing, either degrades or elevates it. The expression "to look upon something as if" reflects more than the whim of the imagination; it is a kind of *ontological decree*. If I look upon a thing as a pure object, I am affirming and ratifying it as what it really is, thus keeping it in the precise condition which is native to it; but if I look on it as a living being or as a god, I raise it to a new existential status. If I look upon animals as things, I downgrade them, un-make them; if I treat them as persons, I upgrade them, make them more than they are; if I look upon them as living things which do not have the power of reason, I assign them their true place, "re-creating" and "re-making" them. The gaze of men, like his word and like the name he gives, determines the rank of each being.[28]

Our final point will be the gaze I level upon man himself, and the exchange of gazes with others.

GAZING AT OTHERS

The Appearance of the Other

I am alone in my room, surrounded with familiar objects. I am installed in this little universe which serves my needs, and I am adapted to the conditions of life it imposes on me. I am alone; that is, without a human partner. However numerous and precious the things about me, they have no word or face or gaze for me. The little world is closed and restricted. It doubtless has a window which opens on the outside, but it reveals to me only a wider horizon of things.

Let another person knock on my door and show his face looking in at me, and everything is immediately unsettled and changed around. This is a primary experience, for which no process of thought can ever be a substitute. The reason is that the gaze is a unique thing, and this in several ways. It is unique by its nature: it eludes all efforts at definition, as the embarrassment of dictionary-makers proves. A gaze can be apprehended only by another gaze. It is unique also in its concreteness: two pupils, yet a single gaze, just as a single discourse is uttered through many words. It is unique, finally, in its meaning, as is the person whose gaze it is and who affirms himself in it.

With my visitor's entrance, my everyday horizon acquires a face and a gaze. My universe reorders itself and gravitates around a new center of consciousness which communicates to that universe its own life. In the person and through the eyes of the visitor, the universe looks at me and takes up a position in front of me in a kind of face-to-face posture. Moreover, the limited framework of my life is now shattered. The tiny pupil in this eye has broadened my horizon in ways I cannot pin down; it has opened a window for me onto a new world. My gaze now wings out to an unknown destination.

My partner has opened up a horizon constituted by mankind. For, behind this person and present through his gaze, I sense a limitless number of other men, real or possible. I do not see or hear them, nor can I count them; only a few of them shall I ever meet. But they are revealed to me in the gaze of my fellow man; they form the background or horizon against which he is limned and in relation to which I in turn must situate myself. But the numerical aspect is not the only nor the most important aspect of this revelation. In the other's gaze, the freedom of man is revealed, along with the infinite universe of cultural, moral, and religious values which are inseparably linked to freedom. That invisible, limitless world, still wrapped in mystery, makes its presence felt in the first moment. It is in this sense that the gaze of another person, coming into existence against the background of things, is for me the epiphany of humanity, of freedom, and of values.

The disappearance of the other person furnishes a corroboration of these rather obvious statements. Even the temporary absence of someone close to me enables me to see what an important source of meaning he is for my universe: how much more, then, does the definitive disappearance of death have this effect. The other person is the other pole of my existence. I unconsciously rely on his gaze for support in my living, working, enjoying, and suffering. Although that look had no physical dimensions, residing in the pure and simple depths of the eyes, it filled my world, vivified it, organized it around itself. Like a picture which assimilates to itself, without destroying it, a frame which is really suitable, so the gaze I loved assimilated the universe we had in common by giving it its meaning. Now this world has fallen back into the dreary stupor characteristic of things. Stripped of the human, living, conscious meaning to which my partner's gaze had raised it, it now seems strange and alien to me. More than this: things themselves seem to have become foreign to each other; they no longer make up an ordered universe but have returned to their brute multiplicity. The empty place left by the other person has produced a cleavage in the world, opened up a kind of abyss into which the unity of things is disappearing, flowing away moment by moment.

Here is the room to which my friend will never return. All the things that were part of his daily life are there, but he is not; they constitute a mute and mindless universe which has lost its meaning and is in the process of dissolution. This inanity in itself indirectly bears witness to how necessary the absent person was: the world is like an empty mold which cries out to be filled—a painful source of consolation for me. These things are like the frame of the invisible window through which the one who has died made his escape. I occupy myself in searching for his presence among his belongings.

Or I turn towards the mute witnesses—an armchair, a desk, clothing that still keeps the body's shape, probing them endlessly. I am tempted to keep things as they are in this little universe, resisting the threatened dispersal, with the illusory intention of perpetuating a presence. Perhaps, in order to consummate the illusion, or in response to the call his possessions make for his presence, I place in the midst of these things a photograph or a portrait of the departed. It is no more than a defective sign, of course, but his look is there, giving its meaning to the world and providing my own regard with irreplaceable support. But if I have to break up this universe and scatter its elements, by way of "putting things in order," I have the painful feeling that I am destroying the only true and precious order that is left, completing my loss in a second death by removing the testimony which things still render to my friend.[29] Henceforth the visible world will bear no trace of the gaze which set it in order. I try to look again at the landscapes his gaze once traversed, to recapture the perspective in which he saw them, seeking him through the mediation of the things he saw. But in the world I see, that look is no longer there. I have to shut out the world, close my eyes, turn my look inwards towards its own hidden depths, if I am to come to a new encounter with that look which has left the world. A gaze survives only in another gaze.

The Objectification of the Other

From the moment of his appearance the other person stands out against the background of things; he presents himself as not to be confused with any of them. But my gaze can grant this assumption only to a variable extent, if indeed it must not reject it entirely. Because owing to his corporeity the other has a number of characteristics in common with things: visibility, form, dimensions, weight, and so on. Like any other thing, his body has a number of "aspects" which provide me with corresponding "perspectives." I can look at a man's body, no less than a brute beast's, from in front, from behind, and from a three-quarter angle, and the fact that I use a somewhat different vocabulary with reference to a man—"face," "back," "profile" —does not radically change the situation. I can therefore be tempted to force the other back into the midst of the things from which he spontaneously tends to distinguish himself. The temptation can, of course, change into a necessity, at least in part, if my social function—for example, as a doctor—obliges me to look at another person "scientifically." The person to be known is, by this very fact, objectified; the knowledge I have of him is the kind that turns him into an object to be appropriated; I "reify" him to some extent and reduce him to a "phenomenon" or to one "case" among others.

The "objectifying" gaze is thus the opposite of the animist gaze. The latter attributes a subjectivity and a soul to objects which lack them; the former strips subjects of their consciousness and freedom. The animist outlook creates around me a multitude of "others," a universe of friendly or hostile wills and of mysterious gazes which focus on me without my being able to meet them; I am seen to a far greater extent than I can see in return, and therefore I feel threatened. The objectifying outlook, on the contrary, tends to subdue the world of subjects which surrounds me, to extinguish the gazes that are bent upon me, and to procure for me the advantage of seeing without being seen. The animist outlook is characteristic of the child and the primitive, in both of whom the distinction between the "I" and the "not I" is still imperfectly drawn; but it is also characteristic of the poet, who dialogues with things and wraps them in his own subjectivity. "Inanimate things, have you then a soul, secretly linked with ours and eliciting its love?"[30] Or again: "The house pulsed, like a great stone heart, with all the joyous hearts beating under its roof."[31] And the abandoned house rejects those it once sheltered: "My house looks at me and knows me no more."[32]

Objectification is what happens in *staring*. In forcing the other's face to yield its secrets and attempting to make it say more than it wishes to, I "kill," in some measure, the person himself, for I treat him as a thing which I would like to see emptied out and displayed to my gaze. The fixity of my look here betrays my real attitude, and if both persons gaze thus intently at one another, their looks may become a challenge. But the motives for staring can be many and can differ in degree of injuriousness. The least serious is doubtless simple curiosity: another fascinates me and I want to bring to light what is in him; in so doing, I treat him as an object of scientific knowledge, seeking to absorb his freedom into his phenomenality. The other realizes what is going on and objects that he is not a "strange animal"; that is, he is not an *object* for curiosity, as though his whole being were reducible to his appearance and as though he existed in order to satisfy my itch to see and know. The ontological decree implicit in the gaze emerges clearly here, for the other feels robbed of his human dignity and reduced to the animal level.

But the staring is sometimes motivated by cupidity, the desire to possess another by my senses or my power. Here, as in dealing with things, the gaze is an anticipatory taking of possession; but though I have this foretaste, my possession is still incomplete; irritated by this unfinished project, I feel frustrated by the other person even as I feed my eyes on him. The gaze thus turns the other into a possession, valued for itself or as a means to something else: the lustful gaze of the sensualist, the avaricious gaze of the slave-trader or, more commonly, of anyone who tries to "use" people. The one gazed upon is reduced to the condition of a thing..

The myth of Medusa excellently illustrates this unequal struggle between two subjectivities. If her gaze petrifies anyone who has the misfortune to cross her path, it is because rock expresses unqualified opaqueness, heaviness, inertia, and objectivity. In such circumstances, a baleful gaze (the "evil eye")[33] doubtless seeks to rob man of his power of free initiative. Medusa goes further: she takes away his very awareness of being a subject. She is thus crueller than death itself, for the latter, having reduced the living being to the state of a thing (the corpse), allows him quickly to disappear, while Medusa keeps man in existence in his fallen state of petrification.

Short of these extreme forms of behavior—slave-trade, or social, economic, and sexual exploitation—in which contempt for the other objectifies him as far as possible and the gaze makes him prisoner and delivers him to the hand to use him as it wishes, there are many degrees of scorn for others. In all of them the other is simultaneously affirmed and devalued as a subject: he is considered as in fact "someone" but without being such by any inherent dignity. The scornful gaze means: "You are a 'you' only by usurpation. You are regarded as free, but you are really a thing; you are treated as a person, but it is very unjust that you should be." Scorn thus tends to produce a dichotomy in the other by introducing a kind of ontological contradiction into his nature, an original sin situated at the very roots of existence. This is doubtless the primary meaning of Kafka's *The Metamorphosis*.

Despite appearances to the contrary, this is also the meaning of the deliberately seductive gaze. Like the magical charm whose subtle activity it imitates, the gaze renounces any recourse to physical constraint; it tries to fascinate instead. The seductive approach seeks to alienate the other from himself; to take from him by psychological force his free disposition of himself and put him at the seducer's mercy. There is a will to objectify at work here. But seduction can also be involuntary, accidental, due to temperament or to a passing disposition of the other: two gazes accidentally meet and there is an unforeseeable "lightning flash." Literature, especially the drama and the novel, is filled with such incidents.[34]

The gaze that is simply turned away does not necessarily imply a challenge or struggle of two subjectivities in which each seeks to dominate the other. Yet such a gaze is sometimes more of a repudiation and an insult than any challenge would be. For now I treat the other as unworthy of being faced and fought; I suppress him into nothingness or, rather, leave him in it; I can only be indifferent in the presence of non-being and non-sense. Consequently the first favor the petitioner asks of the king or of God is the favor of being looked upon: may the great man or the Most High deign to look down at this little person and acknowledge that he exists! The gaze leveled at the poor man is the first stage in the restoration of his human dignity.[35]

The "Star"

There is a collective objectification of another by the gaze: the cult of the "star," to which the contemporary development of communications media has given unprecedented scope. The French word for "star," *vedette*, is of interest here. The word, derived from the Latin *videre* (to see), originally meant the little tower which gave shelter to the sentinel stationed on the ramparts; then it also came to be used of the horseman standing watch at a good vantage-point and able to see without being seen. This last advantage was often illusory, and the word came to mean, by an odd semantic inversion, a position upon which all eyes converge and where a person is much more seen than seeing.[36] Today, the "vedette" is the human being who receives maximum exposure, becoming on millions of screens and in numerous illustrated magazines the food of the countless gazes which devour him. The real or supposed talents which were originally the justification for such a display very quickly yield to the person's mere bodily appearance. The image of a person is then reproduced in untold numbers of copies and treated as a theme with endless variations. Moneyed manipulators trade in a human image the way pimps and slave-merchants trade in bodies. We have here a genuine violation of the person, for he is reduced, by force if not willingly, to his outward appearance. For the star, to be is to be perceived. The mystery of the

"I" is dissolved in the bodily epiphany which nature intended as a means of personal affirmation. The unity of the human being is broken down and lost in the artificial multiplication of his appearance. The right of ownership of one's personal image and the distinction between the private and the public, which are basic criteria of individual liberty in every civilized society, are here abolished. The star is enslaved by the gaze of others and even comes to love his chains —which completes his degradation.

With sure instinct, therefore, the public speaks of the stars as its *idols*. For the whole being of an idol consists in a deceptive appearance. The *eidoxon*, which to the Greek meant an insubstantial form, a phantom, an unreal image, became for Jews and Christians the proper name of a false god: the idol is *emptiness*, pure externality deprived of all reality, a lie, and total impotence.[37] Moreover, in virtue of the reciprocity which links all human subjects together, the star-idol subjugates the gazes which have brought it into being; born of the crowd's emptiness, it exerts a reflex action on that vacuity to deepen it. Reduced to a mere image, the star draws each worshipper to the impersonal surface (bodily appearance, worldly advantages) of his own being and holds him there. The emptiness of the false god and that of his followers foster each other. The idol assimilates its followers to itself—makes them hollow, alienated, empty men and communicates its own nothingness to them—in a dialectical process of mutual enslavement. At the extreme, the idolatrous cult of the star would threaten to engender a race human only in appearance: forms without interiority; faces become masks over nothingness. In the star himself or herself we can observe the ravages wrought by such depersonalization. When the human image has faded and the eyes of the mob have wholly devoured it, yesterday's celebrity sinks into the darkness of oblivion. The inner wealth of the person, frittered away in exhibitionism, may be lost forever.

At the other extreme from the cult of the star is the cult of the hero, the wise man, or the saint. These figures doubtless all answer to a need which every man feels to both find and transcend himself in an ideal type taken as a norm for personal existence. But while the star offers only his outward appearance and thereby empties his person of meaning, the hero embodies the call for moral effort, generosity, and self-giving. Provided steps are taken to keep the disciple from the risky path of trying to be a "certified true copy," the genuine hero is a *teacher of interiority;* he calls upon each person to increase his personal meaning and to unify in a radical fashion what he is and what he appears to be.

The situation of the star allows us to understand, still by contrast, the significance of *wearing a veil.* Every face is ambiguous; it is a kind of natural veil which both discloses and conceals the mystery of the person. Un-veiling ("re-velation") must not take an unbalanced form as opposed to reserve, or the subject will be de-faced, reduced to his empirical value, and objectified by the gazes of others. The artificial veil then fosters the reserve proper to the face by concealing the uncontrolled expression of the feelings: shame, vexation, etc. Modesty may in these circumstances be exposed to the opposite risk of prudishness, but it is nonetheless inspired by an awareness of personal dignity.[38]

Care for One's Appearance

In everyday life, concern for our bodily image anticipates and determines the gaze which others direct to us. Our appearance depends primarily on nature and to that extent is beyond our power to change, but it also depends in part on the choice and care of the clothing. Thus civility requires me each morning, if not to beautify myself, at least to put myself in order, before appearing before the eyes of others. In my exterior I translate into facts the idea I have of myself; I manifest publicly how I think of myself and see myself. I invite others to see me in the same way and to share my judgment of myself. *As I show myself, so do I wish to be seen.* As our gazes meet, our appearances are manifested each to the other; in his appearance each expresses himself to himself and to the other. It is clear, then, that the choice of clothing can signify not only a social function but a moral or religious ideal. In donning the yellow saffron robe of the Buddhist monk or the homespun of the Franciscan, a man reveals the moral ideal by which he judges himself and wishes to be judged. The garment is then equivalent to a profession of faith, not proclaimed but "shown," not audible but visible, silent, and inevitable; in short, it bears witness to moral or religious values.

Whatever the costume adopted, the tension between being and

appearing is always alive. Our being-for-others is based on our bodily appearance, our clothing, our lodging, our transportation. Many people today choose their automobile in function of the image of themselves which they wish to project. The subject thus tends to oscillate constantly between the two extremes of affectation and negligence, too much and too little care for his appearance. But it is important to note that besides the affectation of refinement there is also an affectation which takes the form of untidiness, eccentricity, and even slovenliness. The affected person wants to be noticed, to be set off from the rest of men, to compel the attention of others; the most disparate means can lead to the desired success. But excess or defect of care both equally compromise the dignity of the person and turn the subject into an object in the eyes of others. A simple and correct exterior does not rivet an observer's attention, but it does enrich the meaning of the person by its very discretion, like a frame that is well suited to the picture it encloses; singularity of dress attracts the other's gaze to itself. Then I attend only to the dirty or untidy clothes or to the studied care of the dress. My gaze reduces the subject to his externals and wholly objectifies him. The asocial person is nothing more than his disreputable garments and the coquette is identified with her finery or her make-up; the former reduces himself to a piece of wreckage, as it were; the latter, to a plaything without any inner reality (a "doll," as popular slang perceptively puts it). The same danger of objectification threatens the living "mannequins" of fashion; the word itself hints at the painful perception that the human subject is reduced in the crowd's eyes to a simple "clotheshorse" without any meaning of its own.

The Alternative: Objectification–Subjectification

Sartre has engaged in a lengthy analysis of the objectification of the person by the gaze of another.[39] As he gazes about the world, the other dispossesses me of it: "suddenly an object has appeared which has stolen the world from me."[40] Worse still, the gaze of another can only rob me of myself, deny me as a subject, and reduce me to the status of an object: "My original fall is the existence of the Other."[41] Since another is basically one who gazes at me—that is, the subject who, by gazing at me, reduces me to the status of an object[42]—my first reaction will be shame; "not a feeling of being this or that guilty object but in general of being an object; that is, of *recognizing myself* in this degraded, fixed, and dependent being which I am for the Other."[43] But I can react to my shame: my reaction "will consist exactly in apprehending as an object the one who apprehended *my* own object-state."[44] I reply to the objectifying gaze of the other by trying to objectify him in turn: "We have seen . . . that my reaction to my own alienation for the Other was expressed in my grasping the Other as an object";[45] "I am fixing the people whom I *see* into objects."[46]

Thus the exchange of gazes between another and myself is a struggle between two subjects who are bent on destroying each other. Medusa is no longer simply a myth: she illustrates the real condition of human subjects and their deadly conflict in which the issue, in the last analysis, is which will be Medusa and which her victim. But the victor is frustrated in his turn, for his victory destroys his trophy: "My disappointment is complete, since I seek to appropriate the Other's freedom and perceive suddenly that I can act upon the Other only insofar as this freedom has collapsed beneath my look."[47] We recognize here the theme of *No Exit* (*Huis clos*): the impossibility of exchanging gazes and of intersubjective encounter. Thus, according to an expression Sartre often uses, man's gaze can only "degrade" his fellow man. The analyses of seduction, indifference, and sadism develop this basic theme, as expressed in the laconic statement: "Hell is other people." The Sartrean gaze upon man is, beyond all else, a degrading gaze. The humanist aspiration is here compromised or even strangled at birth.

The point at issue is whether the exchange of gazes is really reducible to a process of objectification. As a matter of fact, Sartre's analyses deliberately exclude many experiences in which the gaze, far from reducing the other to the status of an object, brings him to life and gives both subjects in the exchange to themselves. The human gaze has a marvelous power of subjectification and mutual advancement.

From the moment another appears to me, as we have said, my gaze situates him and makes him stand out against the background of things. But the effort at selection does not stop there. There is another background in which I situate and mark the other out: the background of mankind, which is always present in my outlook, even in a tête-à-tête. The man before me is not interchangeable with any other. My gaze sets him apart and highlights him against the immense background of countless real and possible human beings. Against this remote or proximate background, in a face-to-face encounter in a hermitage or in the press of a teeming mob, my gaze "selects" the other and makes him exist for me as I exist for him.

But no aspect of the bodily form of the other can fully satify my gaze. What I seek somehow to reach, what attracts and fascinates me, is the other's gaze. Our gazes sometimes meet, sometimes avoid each other; in both cases they admit they are correlative to one another. Our gazes are reciprocal just as our hands and our words are. We gaze at the other's gaze: I see the other and I see that he sees me. "It was my bliss to see her eyes gazing at me," Victor Hugo wrote of the daughter he had lost.[48] In point of fact, what do I see in an exchange of gazes? Not an object: if I examine the eye, I must lose the gaze. What I try to encounter is not *something* but *someone*. I want to know the other, but as a subject. Such knowledge is of a unique kind, irreducible to any type of scientific knowledge.

To objectify things is to become aware of their lack of consciousness. To meet the gaze of another is to become aware that he is conscious; it is to "subjectify" him. An open box presents to my gaze what is only an inside, but another person's gaze reveals that he is interior to himself, that he is an interiority. The transparence of the gaze is essentially different from the transparence of any object, even a spring of water or the purest diamond, for it reveals that the other can never be delimited, defined, wholly plumbed. Furthermore, in the exchanges of gazes two consciousnesses recognize their reciprocity. The unceasing awareness of my own consciousness seeks to become one with the awareness of his, my "I" with his "I." There can be no science of the other as subject and as freedom; there can only be awareness of him. Even when I seek to play Medusa and to reduce the other to the status of object by a challenging or scornful gaze, I cannot but affirm him as subject and freedom.

Face-to-Face and Intentionality

The mutual anticipation which, as we have already indicated, is involved in a face-to-face encounter can now be better understood. Apart from any movement to draw near and from any word or gesture, faces gravitate to one another in virtue of their very being and the symmetric morphology which channels their intentionality. It is in the gaze, however, that the inherent thrust of consciousness emerges and finds its most powerful expression. The intentionality of the whole being is concentrated there and may be discerned there as it awakens; it radiates to the whole body: the movement of the out-stretched hand or the communicative word follows on and further specifies the initial movement of the gaze. My face is "anticipative"; that is, it seeks a face turned towards me. To be a man is to exist facing others; it is to be able to gaze upon another man and to be seen by him.

Death again furnishes corroboration, for it destroys forever the reciprocity of faces. To die is doubtless to be condemned to see no more the light of day (the thing the Greeks felt most strongly),[50] but it is also to lose the sight of other faces. When King Hezekiah was mortally ill, he felt condemned *no longer to behold his fellow men* dwelling in this world (Isa. 38:11). On the other hand, for the survivor the dead person is one whose gaze is withdrawn or, rather, who no longer has any gaze. This explains the disturbance I feel in the presence of a corpse. The bodily appearance and especially the face still attest a personal meaning with which I was at home, but the living source whence that meaning emerged, the gaze, is dried up forever. Thus I am torn between two contrary attitudes and temptations. One is to treat the other as an object, seeing now in the human shape only an empty form, a residue, an insignificant thing which is wholly a stranger to me; to tell myself, in an attempt to exorcise the horror of the grave, "It is no longer he." The other temptation is to listen still to the mute witness of this marble face; to bring alive in imagination the gaze that has been extinguished, seeking my friend's presence in it; to continue to converse and to prolong an illusory communion. The paradox of a dead person is that he is in the world without being present to the world, near me without being with me or for me, simultaneously subject and object; he is a partner who still seems to give himself, yet withholds himself forever, a human form without its vital intentionality. My word and hand and gaze reach out to him: he avoids the encounter. He does not see that I see him, and his face is visible but does not see. It is probably to avoid having to face this remorseless refusal that we customarily close the eyes of a corpse. A dead person is one whose gaze I can no longer meet.

The face-to-face relation is also broken off in the experience of the *tragic gaze*. When another person confronts tragic horror, I see his face suddenly become expressionless; his features lose the mobility that makes them alive. Above all, his gaze is fixed on a point at some indefinable distance. He is, as it were, blinded by blind necessity, stiffened and rooted by the harsh and inflexible command of fate. His eye dilates to try to comprehend the immense decree. In short, the tragic gaze is a gaze I cannot meet; it ignores me, for it is absorbed in a struggle which transcends history. If I were to approach a mystic in the grip of an ecstatic vision and dead to this world, his gaze, too, would refuse to meet mine.[51]

The Face-to-Face Interrogator

To gaze at another is to ask a silent but constantly renewed question; it is to stimulate that act of self-attestation and revelation which every face instantly makes. This questioning is *mutual*. The most silent face-to-face meeting, whether it is a first encounter or one after fifty years of married life, is filled with countless inextricably intertwined questions and answers, constantly born and reborn, acting and reacting upon each other: "What do you say of yourself, when faced with what I say of myself?" The exchange of gazes is an attempt to sound each other's depths. My gaze plunges me into the other's gaze; I feel captivated by these depths and incapable of exploring them totally; I find myself in them and lose myself in them, I advance and withdraw. Such unresolved instability and constant movement is required for the kind of equilibrium which should be maintained in the exchange of gazes. If I were wholly absorbed in the other's look, I would be fascinated and devoured by it; if I simply stiffened my will in resistance to being held by it, I would end up by denying and objectifying the other. If, then, my gaze continues to oscillate between these two extremes, it is because I refuse alienation not only for myself but for the other person as well. Our ceaseless probing is a recognition of each other as subjects.

Every familiar sight in a sense molds the face of the person who contemplates it; is reflected in this face, transforming it. In the gaze which meets mine I try, therefore, to discover the daily face the world wears for this person. But beyond all visible landscapes, the aspirations of the other person are directed towards a horizon of values which he is constantly discovering afresh. Hence my probing gaze tries to penetrate to this inner, deeper level. In man, *the gaze of the body and the gaze of the spirit, though distinct in themselves, are one in their living manifestation.* I simultaneously perceive in every gaze the eagerness of the sense of sight, the flickering of an intelligence, and the hesitations of a freedom. I therefore ask another's gaze in what landscape of cultural values it is at home, in what aesthetic, moral, and religious sphere it moves, what the nature and requirements of its ideal are, and what answer the other gives to the summons that echoes in the depths of his conscience. "Are you honest, generous, capable of sacrifice? Can I trust you, and how far?" In plumbing the gaze of another, I try to estimate his virtualities ("what he is capable of") and to penetrate into the mystery of his free will. But the effort must always be undertaken anew, for the mobility and depth of the other's gaze make me ever more aware of how limitless and mobile his freedom is.

But the gaze on which I gaze also presents a certain image of me. I try therefore to grasp this representation of me which arises in the secret depths of the other's eyes. The wisdom embodied in language is wonderfully meaningful here: the "pupil" is so named because it reflects a tiny image, like a "little doll," of anyone who observes it or looks at himself in it. I try to see how the other sees and evaluates me: "What kind of person am I to the gaze of your eye and mind? Do you see me as interesting, as worthwhile, as negligible? To what extent do you give me a role to play in your life?" Moreover, I am not satisfied to discern how the other sees me; I also want to detect in his gaze his free attitude towards me. "What do you want of me? Am I, in your eyes, a means to be used or a person to be enriched? Does your gaze see in me a prey to be seized, an instrument to be used, or a value to be cultivated?" At each phase of my questioning I implicitly compare my image as the other sees me with my image of myself. I compare the "ontological decree" by which the other "re-creates" me as he understands me, with the interior judgment I pass on myself. According to the outcome, I shall experience the embarrassment of feeling myself to be overvalued, resentment at seeing myself downgraded, or the confidence born of esteem from others which I know to be justified. But the questioning will not cease, for my gaze and the other's have inexhaustible depths.

The Face-to-Face Encounter as Revelation
of Each Person to Himself

I am a seer who does not see himself but is seen. I am the person most unaware of my appearance. Thus my friends may have occasion to say: "You don't see yourself!" But in offering itself to my gaze, the face of the other, which is symmetrically reciprocal with mine, shows me the specific face of man and thus shows me my own face as well. In this individual face I discover what it means to have a face. Consequently the hypothesis of one man alone in the world plunges the mind into an abyss of questions which it cannot resolve or perhaps even formulate. Undoubtedly such a man would fall prey to a boundary misfortune: he would have no idea of man, and so he would in large part elude his own grasp; his being would in a certain sense drain away through his own eyes because their gaze would encounter no other face. It is in the other that the mystery of the human face is revealed to me. Each person begins his journey of self-discovery by seeing himself in the face of mother, father, and others close to him.[52]

As mirror of that human face I have in common with all men, the face of the other is neither an impersonal archetype nor an impassive mirror. The many expressions on my face evoke limitlessly varied reactions on the face of the other: joy, sadness, uncertainty, revulsion, reserve, anger; sometimes they are fleeting expressions obscuring the permanent set of the features, sometimes they are contortions of the whole face. Moreover, each "other person" reacts in an individual way to the same attitude on my part; this multiplicity of living mirrors and reflected images can be a disturbing thing for me. But the diversity at least contributes to revealing me to myself, for in it I can perceive the varied import and the ambiguity of my own expressions of meaning. Even before any verbal dialogue is begun or manual gesture made, the silent face-to-face meeting is already a dialogue and a gesture, a mutual revelation, a discovery of the self through the mediation of the other.

Even my own fate seems subject to influence from the other's gaze. The "evil eye" wills misfortune for another and can even strike him down on the spot like an arrow.[53] But, more ordinarily, according to the strength of my ties to the other (the submission of the subordinate to his leader, of a friend to a friend, of the lover to the beloved), I can read in his face and gaze the outline of my own fate. *The prophetic power of the gaze I contemplate:* a sick person tries to read in another's eyes how serious his condition is; Anthony, looking into Cleopatra's face beheld[54]

> In those great eyes starry with flecks of gold
> A whole wide sea where routed galleys fled.

The Enriching Gaze

As the experience of nurseries with large numbers of children in them shows, a child deprived of all personal relationships with its mother or some specific substitute figure cannot develop either physically or psychically. A loving, devoted, faithful gaze from another is necessary if a newborn consciousness is to be able to take hold of itself. The first vocation of the human gaze is to awaken another gaze, and it takes little imagination to measure the great trial it is for parents when they will never receive from a severely retarded child the longed-for response of a gaze or a smile.[55]

The meaning of an "educative" and enriching gaze is this: that in becoming aware of another as a person, my gaze says to him, "I see you and I will you to be distinct from me; I accept and confirm you in your otherness. Far from seeing in your otherness a threat to me, I consider it a blessing and a well-spring out of which the best in me can and should be reborn. Become yourself! If you do, I shall think of myself not as somehow diminished but as mysteriously enriched." In thus becoming aware of the other as a psychological, moral, and religious subject, I help him master himself in these three areas. I educate him; that is, I make him come forth; (*educo:* I lead out) from the interior mists which hide him from himself. He is invited to overcome the dangers inherent in his own objectivity; my gaze incites him to become more and more "someone" and to avoid being simply something. We are not speaking here of instruction, although instruction, by helping the person situate himself in the world of things and men, does contribute to the person's enrichment. What we mean primarily, however, is that the gaze of the educator awakens the child to an awareness of his own freedom, and does so in an immediate, intersubjective encounter; the educator's gaze takes advantage of the reciprocity of consciousnesses.[56] The same is true of the leader's gaze: in deigning to rely on a subordinate, the leader marks him out, "recognizes" that he exists, draws him out of the crowd, and sets him apart as a possible partner in dialogue.[57] Is a man not proud to be able to say that the boss or prefect or head of state has honored him with a glance? The gaze speaks, more so than the hand and more so even than some words. No materiality burdens it; without movement, such as the hand requires, or many words, such as speech needs, the gaze speaks to the other and touches him inwardly. Channeled through the pupil, which is sheer depth, the gaze is intentionality pure and simple.

If we ask *how* the gaze of another enriches the subject within me, we must look for the answer once again in the awareness I have of my own visibility. When I meet the other's gaze, I sense that I am "really seen" and that I exist for another consciousness; I shake off my languor, often feeling as if I had been awakened. The other's gaze sometimes draws me out of sleepiness, sometimes prevents my slipping into it. We have all probably noticed that if we are sitting with closed eyes in a train, we cannot go to sleep if we *think* our neighbor's gaze is on us. The simple awareness of being looked at keeps me from dozing; the other's gaze still touches me and meets mine even through my closed eyelids, thus keeping me awake. On the other hand, if I go to sleep facing someone in conversation, I am regarded as impolite: I have not maintained the wakefulness due the other, treating his presence as unimportant.[58] The process of being psychologically awakened by the gaze of another is probably something like this: conscious of being seen, I become more fully aware of myself and see myself with "peripheral vision," somewhat as, when I know any object whatsoever, I know that I know it and simultaneously I am implicitly aware of myself.[59] But in the present instance I know myself as known by another and I come to see myself through the other's eyes. Even my moral consciousness is sometimes awakened by the gaze of another—a child's, for example, when the child's deep and unadulterated rectitude condemns my devious ways. I "return into myself." My consciousness is more transparent to me under the light of another's awareness of me, and receives itself, so to speak, as a gift offered by the other's gaze.

But there is another way in which the other's gaze enriches (or degrades) me. The judgment which every gaze passes on another person has the force of a decree: it assigns this object or this man a definite place in the hierarchy of being and value and tends to put it or him effectively in that place. If the other sees me as contemptible, I feel not only humiliated in my own eyes but diminished in my very being; I feel less estimable than I had thought I was, and I feel that my effort to grow personally, to progress in knowledge or towards some ideal, is doomed from the outset. If, on the contrary, the other's gaze is filled with sympathy and friendship, I feel that I am understood, I have a sense of existential security. And if this gaze shows me consideration and esteem, if I read in it high expectations of what I am called to be, I am stimulated to live up to the ideal image of myself which I glimpse in the other's eyes. Thus the gaze of the successive educators in our life played, and still plays even in our mature years, a determining role in the development of our personality. If we are the children of the many words we have heard, we are also, in a more mysterious way, the children of the many gazes that have met ours. The true educator knows this, and he looks at others as they really are, to be sure, but also and above all as he wants them to be. The juvenile delinquent is often a person who has never encountered a look of esteem that would reveal to him his own ideal image.

If we may trust the etymology (in a number of European languages, at any rate) of the word *respect*, it seems to be essentially connected with the *gaze*. *Re-spectus* in Latin, from which the French *respect*, the Italian *rispetto*, and Spanish *respecto* are derived, means literally a backward gaze. The German *Rücksicht* has the same verbal and conceptual prototype. In English, the words *respect* and *regard* have the same meanings, with the same order among the derived meanings: (1) *relation* or *point of view* (figurative use); (2) *consideration* (for persons); and (3) *esteem* or *honor*. The linguistic facts are rather odd. If the idea of respect is connected with that of a backward look, may not the reason be that while I go forward to my business and my pleasures, I continue to gaze retrospectively on what I esteem, as if I could not turn away from it entirely and forget or neglect it? In brief, the person I respect is one who never ceases to count in my eyes; by this backward gaze I keep him present in my life and continue to acknowledge his dignity. In return, the honor I give him enables me to be present to him and to offer my face to his gaze. "To lose face" is to lose the right to the "regard" or consideration of my fellow man.[60]

The exchange of gazes further manifests its power of mutual enrichment in the *smile*. The smile is a specifically human action. Because there can be no reciprocation, you do not really smile at an animal. A smiling gaze may, of course, indicate a hostile intent: malice, envy, sarcasm, and so forth. But the smile of itself expresses the deep joy of a consciousness that is open to another consciousness, the calm gladness that arises out of two presences, the one offered, the other extending a welcome. The smile is a freely offered gift, and the sign of a benevolent and generous person who is sufficiently detached from himself to find his happiness in others. The egoist does not know how to smile.

If the sympathy, friendship, and love between us reach a certain depth, my searching gaze at the face of the other person tends to conform my vision of the world to his. In the exchange my look silently inquires of his: "How do you see the world? What does man, the universe, existence itself, look like to you?" The question is not a matter of mere curiosity, for love tends to create likeness, and my friend and I tend towards a meeting of minds with regard to the world. More than a simple "rapprochement of viewpoints" in the sense devalued by usage, this is a question of an effort at coincidence: my look seeks to place itself at the precise point where the look of the other comes into being and casts itself upon the universe. In this way I strive to discover the spectacle which my fellow man's gaze creates and reflects. On the face of the other person, which never loses its newness for me, I make out the features of a new world. Depending on whether my friend's features are thus or so, the shape of the world they reveal to me can be totally different: "If the nose of Cleopatra had been a little shorter, the whole face of the world would have been changed."[61] The world would have been different for Anthony, first of all, because he would have discovered on another face and in other eyes another vision of the world. In this respect all lovers, whether little people or great, are of equal status. But because of the extraordinary power commanded by this member of the triumvirate, the course of events and the character of the age would have been altered.

Beyond the enrichment of this or that individual by a look of esteem or love, man himself in his specific universality can receive decisive advancement from a single gaze. The mark of the great moral or religious geniuses is precisely their marvelous ability to see man with new eyes, to disclose new possibilities for him, and to call him to new conquests of himself. The gaze of Socrates, Jesus, Pascal, Gandhi, revealed to humanity a greatness it carried within itself unawares. After encountering these men, man could no longer look upon himself as before. He saw his own face in a new perspective of light and shadow; he felt called to give his life an original meaning. The humanity of today has thus received what is best in itself from the look which the great men of the spirit have cast on it, and the humanity of the future will be enriched by the coming of other such men.

The Face-to-Face Encounter and the Growth of Likeness

What we have been saying doubtless explains the power of the face-to-face encounter to produce likeness. Even a passing encounter with certain faces can affect my mood: I may cheer up or feel depressed after the contact. How much more, then, do daily encounters with a face—open or shuttered, joyous or sullen—shape my state of mind, my character, and even my face itself into a likeness of the other person's. Has it not been observed that a prolonged sojourn in, say, some Far Eastern country—China, for example—tends to transform certain European faces into those of a Far Eastern type? The complexion becomes a little sallow, the cheekbones acquire greater emphasis, the eyes become a little less wide-open. No doubt climate exercises the decisive influence, but surely the encounter with other faces plays some part in this growth in likeness. Even the awareness the subject has of his own facial type can undergo an odd change in the course of this life shared with foreigners. Sometimes a white man living in the midst of associates belonging to another race experiences a fleeting sense of shock when he rediscovers his own fair complexion in the mirror!

In its plastic representations of faces looking at each other, art tends quite spontaneously to illustrate the power of mutual contemplation to produce likeness. No doubt the figures turned towards one another express the inexhaustible reciprocity of the face-to-face gaze. But their symmetry is ordinarily completed by a more or less total resemblance: each face gives itself to the other and receives itself from the other. However immobile it may seem, the confrontation is not an inert juxtaposition but a living encounter involving prevenance and mutual giving. Just as the contemplative grows in likeness to the object of his vision, every face tends to reflect the features of the companion this person has most admired and loved and contemplated the longest.[62]

The danger in such relationships would be that each of the two world-views might be stripped of its originality. In that case the exchange would be effected at the cost of mutual alienation, and the two gazes would soon be extinguished. But in fact the encounter of loving gazes, especially between marriage partners and engaged couples, is inherently creative. The exchange of looks tends towards communion. Thus the face-to-face relation of persons is preserved from the opposite dangers represented by Narcissus and Medusa: the emptiness of the face enthralled by its own image or the total objectification resulting from the gaze of another. From the meeting of two different outlooks a common vision of man and of life in general strives to come into being. This will be the "world for us" whose like no other pair has ever discovered. In this way every home reflects a certain vision of the world that is uniquely its own. And what is yielded by the exchange of gazes between a loving couple is also the product of all relations between individuals and social groups. A shared vision conditions the harmony of wills, words, and hands in a common undertaking.

Gaze, Presence, Encounter

If presence is brought about by word and gesture, it is effected still more by the gaze. To appear before someone's eyes is to put oneself "in his presence." But I also make myself present to him by my gaze. If I am distracted (*distractus:* pulled this way and that), and let my eyes wander from the eyes of someone who is looking at me, people speak of me as "absent": I am offering the other person only a passive visibility. Similarly, a person who is there without seeing (a sleepwalker or a blind man), or someone who hides himself in order to see without being seen, is not fully present. In an encounter it is in the exchange of looks that the mutual gift is given. To "go to see" someone means to meet him. Even the blind man uses this kind of expression (such a cruel reminder for him) and says, when he meets me: "I'm glad to see you." In fact, where better than in the meeting of gazes can the essential thrust of every effort to be present—namely, immediacy —be realized? It is here that the distance which separates two subjects is at once established and eliminated. Is my gaze "distant"? Then my conduct is a living contradiction, for I am simultaneously giving and refusing my presence.

If spatial distance or death separates us, I have recourse to the portrait or photograph. Or again, the sight of a face with a strong resemblance to that of the loved one who is gone revives my awareness of him: "Such was he, in eyes and hands and features," says Andromache to Ascanius, who reminds her of Astyanax.[63] The face is effective presence and effective personal gift. More than gesture or dialogue, my look is not only given, it is a "giving"; it is a manifestation of the subject, a striving for transparency in the encounter. I do not "put in an appearance"—in the existential as opposed to the formalistic sense of the words—unless I am actually seen and actually seeing, in complete reciprocity.

It is also in the face and the gaze that the vicissitudes of the encounter manifest themselves most strongly—interest, sympathy, trust, complicity; or the reverse: indifference, scorn, rejection, defiance. It is here that the emotions appear in their nascent state —sadness, fear, joy, and so forth. It is in the distance which intervenes between the persons in a face-to-face encounter (a distance physically measurable but nonexistent in terms of intentionality) that the basic interpersonal relations of love and hate are established. The malice or kindness of the eye takes its rise from the heart.[64] It is in relation to the face that the opposite forms of behavior represented by the caress and the slap, the kiss which is one of love and that which is one of betrayal, spitting and anointing with scented oil,[65] take on their full meaning. The silent exchange of looks and the mutual presence which it brings about often have the quality of action or drama: something *is done* (the Greek definition of the word). In an encounter in which personal destinies are engaged, the future is determined as the tangle of past events is resolved. Sight can remain passive, but the exchange of looks is an *act*.

Far more than the reverence addressed to things made into idols, the gaze I direct towards another person can have an oblative meaning. By letting my eyes linger on those of another I can choose him and consent to be chosen myself. I can give myself, surrender my whole being. Even in the presence of a third person without his awareness of it, even as they stand motionless and before there has been any communication of word or touch, two lovers offer themselves to each other: the being of each flows out to the other in the exchange of looks. The gaze can also express abandonment to any authentically higher power worthy of admiration, love, and even of worship: the look a child directs towards father or mother; the gaze of a subject upon his sovereign, of a suppliant upon a benefactor, of a man in prayer who is looking at God. There is a prayer of the eyes which is sometimes more eloquent than the prayer phrased in words or expressed in an outstretched hand. The gaze fixed on someone who might become a benefactor expresses respect, anticipatory gratitude, trust, desire for encounter, and immense need. The depth of the imploring gaze indicates the depth of the acknowledged need.

Paradoxically, the refusal to meet the other person's gaze can have the same meanings of respect, abandonment, and supplication. The slave, the guilty man, or the man in prayer may fall face down to the ground before the other person, whether human or divine. In such a refusal to meet the other's gaze there is a practical admission of weakness and a declaration of personal unworthiness. This conduct bears witness to the inherent finality of the gaze: to bring about the mutual presence and encounter of subjects.[66]

The Face of the Mediator

A man conscious of his own unimportance may reject the idea of presenting himself before another person. He then has recourse to a third party who can bear up under the gaze of aristocrat, judge, or head of state without losing countenance—someone to serve as a "re-presentative." The prefix in this word indicates not a repetition but a presence effected through an intermediate person, a presence "at one remove." Through the mediator, the person with no pretensions to importance communicates with the great man in a more discreet way than he could do directly, even if his face were veiled. The representative serves as a veil for the petitioner, shielding him from the effulgence of the redoubtable gaze. But at the same time the envoy—himself open-faced and a living personal sign—enables his principal to avoid the impersonality and lessened effectiveness which inevitably affect a written request, deprived as it is of the support given by a genuine presence. Above all, as someone who is acceptable, the mediator turns the gaze of this man in a position of power to the petitioner, making him view the latter favorably.

In the opposite situation, if I, an ordinary citizen, see an emissary of some very important person arriving, it means that a certain presence is granted to me which I had not dared hope for. There is a face-to-face meeting in which three persons are involved: I am the recipient of the "prevenient" favor of a gaze near at hand but bearing within itself another gaze, more distant and reserved. Yet we must be clear that the envoy, in being an envoy, is not reduced to some half-real status, as though he were an impalable *ghost*, a fleeting *silhouette*, or an insubstantial *shadow*. [67] His living, flesh-and-blood substantiality, far from being diminished, impinges on all my senses. Nor is the delegate cast in the role of a simple *supernumerary*. His presence is neither anonymous nor passive; his identity is known, his role is freely assumed, and his words and gestures actively communicate his message. No physical resemblance to his principal is required of him. The use of a *double*, leading those addressed to think the distant person was himself present, would be only a hoax. The games men play with *masks* are also excluded, since the identity of persons and their relationships are expressly stated. Much less, then is the envoy a *caricature*—that is, a deliberate, derisory betrayal of his principal! Neither envoy nor principal undergoes any *metamorphosis*. [68] Rather, the representative is a *man-sign*. His immediate presence *signifies*—that is, makes known and gives in a mediate way another and inaccessible presence: the intentionality of the one serves as a relay, so to speak, for the intentionality of the other. In carrying out his mission, the envoy relates himself wholly to his principal; as a "lieu-tenant," he takes the place and role of the other, not to strip him of these but, on the contrary, to enable him to fill them.

For my part as the one visited, I am not mistaken. I am not tempted to misinterpret the meaning of the representative. I know that two persons cannot somehow become one. When I wake from sleep, I reject as absurd the phantasmagoric fusion of faces that sometimes occurs in dreams. The respect I show for the envoy present is really addressed to his principal. The representative power which is inherent in every human image, and provides the basis for sympathetic magic and killing in effigy,[69] is exercised here in an essentially higher way since the envoy presents himself in his own living humanness. My gaze is helped by this face, these visible gestures, and this word audible and close to me, in reaching to the man who is far off. Immediately present to the envoy, I am intentionally present to his principal. Having been anticipated by the gaze which mine can meet here and now, I rely on it and trust to its mediation in order to receive the invisible presence. Through the face of his envoy, the principal gazes at me, sees me, and hears me. In short, the mediation of a third face, far from preventing a face-to-face encounter, tends to effect it despite any intervening distance.

NOTES

1. Victor Hugo, "La vie aux champs," v. 58, in *Les contemplations*, I.6, in *Oeuvres poétiques complètes* (ed. Bouvet), p. 381.
2. Cf. above, Chapter 1, "Objectivity and Subjectivity of the Body."
3. Gabriel Marcel, "L'être incarné, repère central de la réflexion métaphysique," *Annales de l'Ecole des Hautes-Etudes de Gand* 3 (1939) 107.
4. Cf. Gal. 3:1.—We will go into the problem of objectification at greater length later in this chapter.
5. Marcel Jouhandeau, *Nouvelles images de Paris*, suivies de *Remarques sur les visages*, 2nd ed. (Paris: Gallimard, 1956), p. 133.
6. Job 2:11–13: "Three of Job's friends . . . met and journeyed together to give him sympathy and comfort. But when, at a distance, they lifted up their eyes and did not recognize him, they began to weep aloud; they tore their cloaks and threw dust upon their heads. Then they sat down upon the ground with him seven days and seven nights, but none of them spoke a word to him; for they saw how great was his suffering."
7. The tragic fate of Io provides the background of Aeschylus' *Suppliants*. See also Ovid's *Metamorphoses*.
8. Cf. below, this chapter, "Care for One's Appearance."
9. If a blind man's face seems wooden to me, is this not because there is no gaze there to bring it alive?
10. With the hood we may compare the black velvet mask—the half-mask—which covers eyes and nose without representing a particular "personage."
11. From the Italian *caricatura*, derived from *carricare* (put on a cart) or "load" (in the literal and figurative senses).

12. The outline of a human form projected onto a plane derives its name from Etienne de Silhouette (1709–1767), a royal inspector of finances. But there are varying explanations of the derivation: one claims that this man decorated the walls of his chateau at Bry-sur-Marne with such profiles (thus Littré, *s.v.*); another says that his tenure of office was so short (eight months) that others had time to catch a glimpse only of his profile (thus Adolphe Hatzfeld and Arsène Darmesteter, *Dictionnaire génèrale de la langue française*, 6th ed. [Paris: Delegrave, 1920], *s.v.*); a third, and more appropriate, explanation is that the inspector's eagerness to squeeze the king's subjects threatened to reduce them to two-dimensional images (Larousse).

13. In India, a Brahman of strict observance will cross the road to avoid being touched by the shadow of a person of lower caste.

14. The completion which death brings is thus needed if we are to take a man's true measure; any monument, literary or other, erected to a living man is provisional and will be outdated.

15. Emmanuel Levinas, *Totality and Infinity: An Essay on Exteriority*, trans. Alphonso Lingis (Pittsburgh: Duquesne University Press, 1969), p. 202.

16. Aristotle, *De anima*, II, 1, 412b18–22.

17. Cf. Anne Philipe, *Le temps d'un soupir* (Paris: Julliard, 1963), p. 48: "Your smile and your gaze, your walk and your voice—were they matter or spirit? Both, and inseparable so."

18. Cf. above, Chapter 3, "Silence and Word."

19. We are here describing, of course, the status of a thing as such, and prescinding from individual or specific differentiations and meanings; a flower, for example, has a quite different meaning from a pencil.

20. Cf. Isa. 53:3: lepers are "those from whom men hide their faces."

21. Cf. Sir. 9:5; 31:13; 1 John 2:16.

22. Cf. Plato, *Symposium*, 203c: love is the child of contrivance and poverty.

23. "Jalousies" (=jealousies), for example, allow the suspicious spouse to keep watch. Note, once again, the circulation of meaning. See below, this chapter, note 38.

24. The Latin phrase, *captus oculis* (captured by the eyes), is especially meaningful; cf. its use in Cicero, *The Second Speech against Gaius Verres*, Book 4, no. 101.

25. Plato, *Republic*, 500c-d, trans. Francis M. Cornford (London: Oxford University Press, 1941), pp. 208–209: "He [the philosopher] contemplates a world of unchanging and harmonious order . . . and like one who imitates an admired companion, he cannot fail to fashion himself in its likeness." The deeper meaning of the contemplative life could not be better expressed. The face and gaze of the great contemplatives reflect, more or less, the world that is familiar to their mind's eye. An acceptable formula would be: "Tell me what you contemplate, and I will tell you what you are."

26. Cf. Jean Gautier, *A Priest and His Dog*, trans. Salvator Attanasio (New York: Kenedy, 1957).

27. Rudyard Kipling, *The Jungle Book* (New York: Scribner's, 1913). Cf. pp. 15, 17, 20, etc.—This observation doubtless provides an explanation for the behavior of the "spitting serpent" (*Naja nigricolis*), which rears up (some-

times to a height of about four and a half feet) and launches a stream of poison into the eyes of man in order, as it were, to eliminate his gaze. There is a real danger of being blinded. We may also note that the dragon (Greek: *drakon*) means, etymologically, "he who stares" (Greek: *derkomai*); but the name is probably a euphemism. In Kabylia, on the contrary, the gaze of the partridge is considered a good omen, and the bird's eye is used as an ornamental motif.

28. Cf. Gen. 2:19–20.

29. Cf. Théophile Gautier, "Les joujoux de la morte," in *Emaux et camées*, ed. Pommier, pp. 122–123.—Gabriel Marcel, *La chapelle ardente* (Paris: Editions de La Table Ronde, 1950).—Anne Philipe, *Le temps d'un soupir. op. cit.*

30. Alphonse de Lamartine, "Milly, ou la terre natale," vv. 15–16, in *Harmonies poétiques et religieuses*, Oeuvres 3 (Paris: Hachette-Pagnerre-Furne, 1876), p. 219.

31. Lamartine, "La vigne et la maison," vv. 165–66, in *Oeuvres choisies*, ed. Maurice Levaillant (Paris: Hatier, 1949), p. 1042.

32. Victor Hugo, "Tristesse d'Olympio," v. 80, in *Les rayons et les ombres*, XXXIV, in *Oeuvres poétiques complètes* (ed. Bouvet), p. 259.—Cf. Job 7:9–10: "he who goes down to the nether world . . . shall not again return to his house; his place shall know him no more"; Ps. 103:16: "The wind sweeps over him and he is gone, and his place knows him no more."

33. Cf. J. A. Jaussen, "Le mauvais oeil," *Revue biblique* 33 (1924) 396–407.

34. Cf., for example, Victor Hugo, *Les misérables*, trans. Charles E. Wilbour (New York: Random House, n.d.), Part III, Book 3, Section 6: "The glances of women are like certain apparently peaceful but really formidable machines. You pass them everyday quietly, with impunity, and without suspicion of danger. There comes a moment when you forget even that they are there. You come and go, you muse, and talk, and laugh. Suddenly you feel that you are seized! It is done. The wheels have caught you, the glance has captured you. It has taken you, no matter how or where, by any portion whatever of your thought which was trailing, through any absence of mind. You are lost. You will be drawn in entirely. A train of mysterious forces has gained possession of you. You struggle in vain. No human succour is possible. You will be drawn down from wheel to wheel, from torture to torture. You, your mind, your fortune, your future, your soul; and you will not escape from the terrible machine, until, according as you are in the power of a malevolent nature, or a noble heart, you shall be disfigured by shame or transfigured by love" (p. 600).

35. Cf. Montesquieu, *Persian Letters*, trans. John Davidson (New York: MacVeagh-Dial, 1929), pp. 199–200, writes in regard to the kings of France: "That he should have been fortunate enough to behold the august countenance of his prince, is sufficient to make a man once more worthy to love. These monarchs are like the sun, which shed everywhere heat and light."

36. The applications of the term *vedette* to various kinds of boats (picketboat, small steamer) are recent.

37. In classical Greek, *eidolon* (image) has no religious meaning, but only profane. The pagan of classical antiquity is the man for whom the distinction between false gods and the true God does not exist; he distinguishes only

between the gods of his native land and foreign gods, without necessarily refusing to welcome the latter into his pantheon.

38. On the significance of the veil, cf. especially Roland de Vaux, "Sur le voile des femmes dans l'Orient ancien," *Revue biblique* 44 (1935) 397–412. Edgar Haulotte, *Symbolique du vêtement selon la Bible* (Paris: Aubier, 1965). René Metz, *La consécration des vierges dans l'Englise romaine: Etude d'histoire de la liturgie* (Paris: Presses Universitaires de France, 1954), pp. 199 ff.; Metz notes on p. 375 that since the veil was in Rome the distinctive sign of married women, the verb *nubere*, "to veil oneself" came to mean "to enter marriage," while the noun *nuptiae* meant "marriage."—In Islam the use of the veil is sanctioned by the *Koran*, Sura 24:31, 59; 33:59 (cf. 55). We must observe, however, that veiling is ambiguous: it may be inspired by respect for the person, but it often signifies quite the opposite, namely, the subjection of women who are turned into objects by their husbands' jealousy.

39. Jean Paul Sartre, *Being and Nothingness: An Essay on Phenomenological Ontology*, trans. Hazel E. Barnes (New York: Philosophical Library, 1956), pp. 252–302.

40. *Ibid.*, p. 255.

41. *Ibid.*, p. 263.

42. Cf. *ibid.*, p. 257.

43. *Ibid.*, p. 288.

44. *Ibid.*, p. 289.

45. *Ibid.*, p. 302.

46. *Ibid.*, p. 266.

47. *Ibid.*, p. 380.

48. Victor Hugo, "Après trois ans." vv. 31–32, in *Les contemplations*, IV, 3 in *Oeuvres Poétiques complètes* (ed. Bouvet), p. 426.

49. Cf. above, this chapter, "The Face as Freedom and Prevenance."

50. Cf., among numerous texts, Sophocles, *Ajax*, vv. 856–857.

51. Cf. above, Chapter 2, "Instant and Eternity."

52. Cf. C. Virgil Gheorghiu, *The Twenty-Fifth Hour*, trans. Rita Eldon (Chicago: Regnery, 1950), Chapter 1.

53. Cf. Jaussen, "Le mauvais oeil," *art. cit.*

54. José-Maria de Heredia, *The Trophies: Fifty Sonnets*, trans. Brian Hill (Philadelphia: Dufour, 1962), p. 41

55. Cf. the well-known verse of Virgil, Eclogues 4, 6, in *Virgil's Works*, trans. J. W. Mackail (New York: Carlton House, n.d.). p. 275: "Begin, O little boy, to know and smile upon thy mother."

56. Cf. Maurice Nédoncelle, *La réciprocité des consciences* (Paris: Aubier, 1942).

57. If the selective gaze is mutual, a pair united in friendship or love is formed. It is in virtue of this law that lovers are always alone in the world. Similarly it is with my eyes that I seek and find someone arriving at a railway station; once the friend is found, everyone else ceases to exist for me.

58. It is also true that a motionless face-to-face meeting can become boring

and put the participants to sleep; but then the two persons have already ceased genuinely to gaze at one another.

59. Cf. Aristotle, *Metaphysics*, XII, 9, 1074b35-36.

60. Cf Littré, *Dictionnaire de la langue française, s.v. Egard*.

61. Pascal, *Pensées*, Fr. 162 (Turnell, Fr. 90, p. 133).

62. Cf. above, this chapter, "Symbiosis of My Gaze and the World."

63. Virgil, *Aeneid*, III. 490, trans. Mackail, p. 56.

64. Cf. Matt. 6:22–23; Luke 11:34–36; Mark 7:21–22: the "evil eye" comes from the heart.

65. Cf. Matt. 26.6: in the East, perfume poured over the head of a guest was a sign of honor and joy.

66. A reason why my eye is so precious to me is that it is the organ of my presence to others and to the world. Cf. the words used of a favorite possession: "It is the apple of my eye."

67. On these ideas, cf. above, this chapter, "The Face as Revelation."

68. Cf. above, this chapter, "The Face as Manifestation of the Person."

69. Cf. above, Chapter 4, "Symbolic Action."

PART III

TWO INTERPERSONAL
MODES OF BEHAVIOR

Mutual presence always forces those involved, whether they are in harmony or at odds, to a rediscovery of meaning. I cannot long remain facing another person without deciding to be kind or hostile, respectful or impolite (the affectation of mutual unawareness of the other's existence is the height of impoliteness). The other obliges me to choose what kind of person I will be to him and to re-create, along with him, the meaning of the world and of myself.

We shall concentrate here on two modes of behavior in which our earlier analyses find an appropriate completion. For in the visit and the meal, the meanings of human time and space, of the categories of expression, and finally of the phenomenon of presence emerge in an exemplary way.

CHAPTER 6

THE VISIT

Visit and meal receive part of their meaning from the place that is privileged to witness the deepening of personal life: the private dwelling. We must therefore examine, first of all, the meaning of "home."

I. THE "HOME"

However closely linked I may be with all of space and with the whole of my own property, there is yet a portion of space which I make my own in a special way, almost to the point of identifying it with myself: my *home*. The French term normally used for home, namely "chez soi" ("at oneself"), adds a special nuance to the idea and yields the rather odd idioms "to return to oneself" and "to live at oneself"; they suggest a kind of doubling and that the self can be, as it were, a place or portion of space into which one enters, in which one stays, and from which one emerges.[1]

The universe is the realm of blind elements which are often hostile to man. To survive, a man must tame nature, protect himself against its attacks, and force it to supply his needs. He requires a certain stability and needs to take root somewhere, for total nomadism would entail an endless struggle with the elements. A man therefore chooses a place which is to be his, from which he can go out each morning to conquer the world, and to which he may return each evening to rest;

he wants a *humanized* shelter, wholly his own and fitted out according to his desires. To this end, he marks off a certain area of ground. Within it the character of the soil and the climate, his personal needs and preferences, and the bearing of the cardinal points all determine how his future dwelling is to be set up. A foundation is laid on the privileged space, and presently the framework is surmounted by a roof, that part of every dwelling so essential that language often uses "roof" as a synonym for the whole house. Walls then complete the isolating of this little part of the world from the rest of cosmic space. From the Eskimo igloo to the tropical hut, from the Bedouin tent to the European house, a dwelling place is a humanized volume of space, an "inside" over against an "outside." To this interior, dangers from the blind elements have no access: security is its reason for being and its norm; ownership is its crowning perfection, for I am more at home in a poor lodging that is *my own* than in a richer one that is only rented.

Within this privileged space my needs must be met, and so I arrange there the basically necessary things: food, clothing, tools. But this little world cannot be a kind of cosmic void from which the natural elements are totally excluded; I must shelter myself from possible dangers from them, but they continue to be strictly indispensable to my life. My dwelling is therefore the place where the forces of nature are "domesticated"; I admit them to the house (Latin, *domus*) and constrain them to obey its laws. Air and light are admitted from outside in varying measure according to the nature of the climate. Fire is needed for transforming things: for cooking food and working metals. In addition, fire as source of warmth and light allows the house to take on a quality of intimacy and to have a hearth or "fireside." Man is the only animal who has mastered and domesticated the "red flower."[2] With the development of modern technology, my home becomes more and more a miniature cosmos into which all the elements are admitted, wherein they are mastered and put into my service.

This arranging of the dwelling (like that of nature as a whole) involves a twofold process which has been noted by Amédée Ponceau: establishment and adaptation.[3] When I establish myself, I submit things to my requirements; put order into them, transform them, and impose my laws upon them. But I soon reach the limit of my power and must, for the rest, accept the resistances which things offer me; I

must submit to their requirements, adapt and transform myself. I
therefore adapt myself to the extent that I cannot simply establish
myself. The two inverse procedures constantly complement one
another and compensate for one another; the result is a certain
equilibrium between my needs or desires and the responses of the
environment. The home becomes the symbol of complete ease: "to
feel at home with."

Equilibrium is always in process of being attained and is variable in
quality: the simpler, poorer, or more lacking in necessities my lodg-
ings are, the greater the effort of adaptation that is required of me.
Ease, comfort, and luxury, on the other hand, attest to my control
over things. Comfort is the perfection of the process of establishment:
then my needs and desires are satisfied and even anticipated; the
understanding, as it were, between myself and objects is complete,
and we are at one in comfortable harmony.[4] Luxury shows the
refinement and wealth of the establishment. Then not only my needs
but even my most foolish whims are anticipated and satisfied even
before being expressed. I may come to think that the world is there to
serve me and that even the needs of other people must yield to any
desires I may have. I can turn man's legitimate control over the
world's resources into an exaggerated claim of omnipotence.

The equilibrium between me and this microcosm is the equilibrium between a living being and its environment. Illness and old age
undermine this harmony and death totally destroys it. Incapable
forever of establishment and adaptation, the dead person has become
a stranger to his dwelling and must be removed from it. The earlier
arrangement disappears with the man, the objects familiar to him are
scattered, and all forms of possession that were his flow away along
with his being-present-to-the-world. Whether he is simply handed
over to the elements he once mastered (earth, fire, water, or wind),[5] or
given a dwelling in a city of dead men, a dead person is one who is no
longer at home in the world. His bodily place is reduced to nothingness, and so is his inhabited place. Burial near the family dwelling or
even within it, such as is often practiced in Central Africa, is doubtless a moving protest against the definitive separation. But such
defiance is vain in face of the inexorable evidence: the dead person has
no longer any home among the living.[6]

Being humanized, my dwelling is also highly *personalized*. Not only the basic needs I share with all my fellow men but also my personal desires and tastes find their lasting satisfaction here. My past, my present, my future (or at least my dreams for it), my cultural and even my moral and religious outlook are projected onto these walls and expressed in the many objects which make up this little world. Thus my home reflects a certain image of myself; it reveals me, perhaps even gives me away. The astute or prying visitor knows this and ferrets me out by running his eye over the books, the recordings, the pictures, and the knick-knacks which surround me. It would doubtless be an exaggeration to regard a person's dwelling as a complete manifestation of his personality. For one thing, the witness of things is ambiguous: a bare interior can signify material poverty; it can also indicate miserliness, detachment, or even a lack of interest in collecting personal things or establishing any kind of life style. On the other hand, an attractive and commodious establishment may have been intended primarily to facilitate the practice of hospitality. Furthermore, many of the deeper traits of personality can find no translation into material form. Nonetheless, by and large my home does express me; the proof of it is the malaise I feel in an impersonal hotel room or in a room whose furnishings have been chosen and arranged by a stranger. In my absence, my home bears witness to me like a mold emptied of its content; my presence still moves among these mute objects in expectation of my return. As soon as I cross the threshold, I find myself again. I feel as though there were two of me, one welcoming and one welcomed, and as though in the same moment the two were made one again. The home belongs to the man. We do not fully know someone until we have seen him at home. The osmosis that goes on between being and having, structure and meaning, is especially close here.

The *home* is a *private* world. The rest of the world is a possession common to all, made up of public places whose use no one can claim the privilege of reserving to himself. My home, on the contrary, is not only private property—the way my garden is, for example—it is also my ordinary and exclusive place of residence. I alone have the right to enter it. To penetrate into it without my permission, especially by violence or housebreaking, is a breach of law and a crime. In this private world I lead a life which no one else has a right to know about; my conduct there concerns only myself, and my freedom within it acknowledges no limitations except the right of my neighbors to be at peace. Consequently, it is there that I satisfy my basic needs: I usually eat there and take my rest and leisure there. Freed from social restraints and the various roles I must play in public, I put off all masks and express myself in an individual way which people outside know nothing about; I present an image of myself which only close friends know well. Whereas in public places people talk little but commonplaces, at home I can "think aloud." In this respect, the home is the *place of truth* where I reveal myself as I really am, with my real defects and virtues; my deeper self manifests itself, sometimes without my realizing it. If at home I am egoistically concerned with my biological needs and never discuss with my family my activities outside the home and what is happening in society, the nation, or the world at large, I am nevertheless manifesting one aspect of my character. If, on the contrary, my conversation opens up the life of the household to wider horizons which enlarge the perspectives of each member, I continue to express myself even in the act of forgetting myself.

For the home is the place of *intimacy*: it is a "within" over against the immense "outside" which is the world, an interior separated off from the exterior, a "here"—in fact, the most privileged of all "heres" and the one in which I most willingly remain. This "inside" is "domestic"; that is, everything here is both under control and familiar—things, occupations, animals, relatives too in a sense, and household staff.

But the interiority of my home is of a special kind, for it is not a matter of geometric "inside" like the internal volume of a box. Everyday language recognizes this fact when it disdainfully gives the name of "box" to a school or professional building whose interiority is wholly material and involves no human intimacy. This is unfortunately also the case with those multifamily dwellings, all too numerous today, in which the arrangement makes any personal life and familial intimacy really impossible. They are no longer houses, but boxes for men. My home, on the contrary, is the place of personal intimacy; that is, I contain this place within myself more than I am contained by it. Physically, indeed, I am "in" my house which surrounds me on all sides. But intentionally I contain this home the way the soul contains the body, for I give it its consistency and meaning.[7] A house has a soul when a human presence is everywhere manifest in it without our being able strictly to localize that presence.

One or more people unobtrusively affirm their existence in every room, in every object, in the general arrangement and the small details, in the decor, the silence, the familiar sounds, in the behavior a visitor adopts almost against his will as soon as he steps in the door. For we are dealing here with a vital environment, and if the presence that is everwhere felt is ordinarily that of the mother, this is because she is the primordial, original environment in which every life unfolds and begins to grow.

Such interiority is, in the final analysis, nothing other than *recollection*. My home is my larger self. As I cross its threshold, I effect an initial return into myself, one which is perhaps a prelude to the more comprehensive return effected in meditation or prayer.[8] At least it is in my home that my strength, spent in toil, is renewed and reborn and here that I experience time which is really my own. Home is a place of silence as opposed to the noisy outside and a place of unity in contrast to the deafening multiplicity of the street; a place of small numbers and not of crowds, of the private self and not of the public or the marketplace, of physical and affective warmth and not of cold impersonality; a place of intimacy and of communion with others in shared conversations, meals, sorrows, and love; a place of the tête-à-tête, the face-to-face and heart-to-heart encounter between husband and wife; a place where new and fresh faces are born of that creative encounter—faces in which the character is increasingly delineated until maturity; a place of children's tears, games, and laughter; a place where the household, daily dispersed, is daily united again; a place of secret suffering which cannot be communicated even there; a place where the old man finds shelter for his solitude and where faces fade and vanish; a place, therefore, of the most decisive moments of human existence: birth, love, and death; a recollected and recollecting place, sanctuary of a mystery out of which the unity of men with each other and with themselves is daily reborn.[9]

It is not surprising, then, that the house should have something of a *sacred character*. "Lodging" is the economist's term, "habitat" the sociologist's, and "residence" the jurist's; only "hearth" and "family home" express a total human value, for they refer to a mystery. The Chinese spontaneously set up the family altar of the ancestors, the Romans that of the household gods, in the innermost part of the dwelling. There, too, the Eastern Christian places the sacred ikons and the Western Christian hangs the crucifix in order to set the mystery of the home within the mystery of salvation. The custom of blessing the house is to be seen in this light. The home which shelters, expresses, and fosters the mystery of the family tends to become a temple. Gathering up in a most intense way the existence of each and all of the members, the house gives man access to the religious sphere—that is, to the maximum fullness of being.[10]

If my home is *gathered up* (recollected), it can then *gather in* (make welcome); having a life of its own, it can offer it and share it according to a vital rhythm: the systole of recollection and the diastole of openness to the world and to other persons. I have provided my house with doors and windows, for we are not, neither I nor my house, Leibnizian monads; our interiority is not narcissism; this little world has no wish to ignore the larger world around it.

The significance of the *window* is initially biological. Thanks to the open window I can remain within the security of my house, yet also enter into communion with the life of the cosmos. The immensities of air, light, life itself, enter my eyes, my lungs, and my whole being. From my window I can traverse the world with a glance, expand to the full breadth of the horizon, make myself present in intention to the whole of space. The narrow confines of my body and my home are broken—whereas a vast hall without windows, and thus without horizons, can look smaller than it is, a tiny room opening onto broad vistas seems larger than it is. Thus my window allows me to glimpse the expanse of my own freedom. Before the immense space which a large bay-window opens up to me, I savor the incalculable possibilities of action and conquest which I sense within myself: the immensity of my "view" reveals the immensity of my will and my capacities. By way of contrast, not only is the room in which a man is held captive narrow and confining, but its window may be hardly more than a slit in the wall, or even nonexistent. A windowless dungeon is the tomb of freedom; transfer the prisoner to a cell with windows and you give him hopes of soon being "at large."

My window keeps me linked to the world of men. A recluse is one who is cut off: the walls with no apertures prevent every effort to communicate with the rest of mankind. By way of contrast, the balcony on which a leader appears to respond to the applause of the crowd makes possible the presence of one man to a whole multitude,

296 THE HUMANITY OF MAN

in a communication that is brief but intense and wide-ranging. Between these two extremes of experience there is the common experience I have daily at my own window. From it I can see passersby in the street and hear them calling to one another: but I could also, in an emergency, cry for help, obtain release—escape, perhaps, from death—and return to the world of living men. In "giving" onto the world, the window gives me to the world and to other men. It is, of course, not a one-way movement, and the gaze of others can tactlessly pursue me inside my home. But such an ambiguity about the window underlines the fact that it is a boundary between the self and the non-self, between the "public" and the "private" sphere, between my "I" on the one hand and the world of men on the other.

The role of frontier belongs even more obviously to my *door*. Here is where the universe common to all beings—where "nature" or the street—comes to an end and my home begins. In closing my door behind me, I set a limit which the elements must not pass. This is evident on stormy nights when wind and freezing rain or snow lash my door, battering, shaking, tearing at it in a remorseless struggle full of wailing and the gnashing of teeth. I am able to defend myself, thanks to my door. But should I cross the threshold and go out, I lose my security, find winter at the door, and make myself prey to the uncontrollable forces of nature.

The door thus presents a basic ambiguity which is reflected in language, for the same word sometimes designates the opening cut in the wall and sometimes the movable instrument used to close the opening. If, as one of Musset's favorite sayings puts it, a door must be opened or closed, it is never definitively the one or the other; if it were, it would cease to be a door and become a vestigial organ. The ambiguity of the door really expresses my free power. In the same way, a city gate fortified with iron locks and bars expresses a proud claim to independence and liberty. Sometimes the door even becomes the symbol of the sovereign power behind it; thus "Exalted Gate" (*Sublime Porte*) once designated the Ottoman Empire.

My threshold is thus much more than a material boundary. It indeed divides "outside" from "inside" for me, but it is also a frontier between me and other men. I can close my door to others in selfish hardness of heart or I can open it in friendship, love, and communion. Our study of the visit will go more deeply into the decisive role of the threshold and the door in interpersonal relations.

The instrument and sign of my authority over my home is my *key*. Its smallness belies its great importance. Whether it is a key to the city or to an apartment, a masterpiece of the metalworker's art or purely functional accessory, the key concentrates in itself the full meaning of the door and the house. Whoever has the key is master of the dwelling: "When he opens, no one shall shut, when he shuts, no one shall open" (Isa. 22:22). The key, then, is the obvious symbol for authority received or delegated. The handing over of the keys is equivalent to the transfer of power or authority. In the figurative sense the key signifies the sole means of overcoming a difficulty or solving a riddle.

My dwelling, my *home*, becomes an element in my identity. People therefore designate me at times by my residence: "Mr. So-and-so? He's the fellow who lives in the big white house." So, too, mention of my residence must figure on all legal documents about me. The house is also an important element in familial identity, to the point where the word can indicate a princely line: "House of Orleans," "House of Austria."

To leave is thus to die a little, to deprive myself of a fixed place and basic spatial reference-point on which my personal awareness relies almost without my knowing it. Much more then is a man disoriented whom some criminal act suddenly deprives of his home, like a ship driven off its course by a storm.[11] At each return, I find *myself* in reaching my home, as well as the image it offers me of my own person, and the faces of relatives who confirm me anew in my existence. I feel my home to be part of my being, to be, as it were, my bodily place expanded: larger than my body but made to my measure and my needs, contained by my consciousness and animated by it as well. Like my body, my home is both objective and subjective. It is objective because it is made of stone, brick, and wood; measurable; with a market value; and transferable to another owner. It is subjective because it is part of me: once a simple object, it has become personalized, assimilated, and integrated into my existence. Too many bonds with life and with other people have been established and dissolved here for me to think of it as capable of being either destroyed or wholly alienated. If I sometimes ask myself, "What is my home like when I am not there?" and am forced to recognize that the question is unanswerable, all the more is it contradictory, painful, unthinkable, that my house should continue to exist and no longer be mine.[12]

In short, my home is my "larger individual self." The group and its institutions constitute my larger social self, but my home shelters my very life and sustains the person in me.

More than this: if I have set up my home according to my needs and tastes and therefore in my own image, it in turn compels me to adapt myself to it, models and shapes me to its likeness. Between me and it there is a constant circulation of *meaning*. Depending on whether it is poor and wretched, comfortable, luxurious, hygienic or unhygienic, happy or unhappy, my home affects my health, character, vision of life, level of existence as a human being. The hovel degrades its occupant. The large dormitory, the barracks, the huge complex accommodating excessively great numbers of tenants—they all tend to give people the character of a crowd, to depersonalize them. In this respect, contemporary architects and urban planners have a great responsibility—one which is insufficiently seen and accepted —towards the mankind of tomorrow. To determine the kind of living accommodations there will be is to determine a certain kind of human being and a cultural style. The rational animal lives in a symbiosis with the domestic microcosm; he belongs to his home as he does to his land.

II. THE VISITOR

As an interpersonal activity, the visit must be studied from the viewpoint of each partner in it. But we must first distinguish the various uses of the word "visit," according to whether things or persons play the predominant role in the inquiry.

Kinds of Visit

In a spontaneously animist frame of mind, I sometimes speak of being visited by illness, misfortune, chance, or events. The Fifth Symphony of Beethoven opens with Fate knocking at the door. But if in such instances a thing plays the role of visitor, it is more often that which is visited; thus I "visit" a country, a city, a museum, an exposition. These are objects whose specific qualities are the basis of my activity.

There are, however, cases in which a visit paid to things indirectly involves men. For example, certain inspections of possessions or places by competent authority are intended to assist in the application of certain legal dispositions. The customs official "visits" the baggage of travelers, the police visit homes, ecclesiastical authority makes canonical visitations. But it is not the intention of the agents of authority in such cases to meet persons for their own sake.

The behavior of a commercial traveler is something else again. He does not come to examine a place, he wants to meet someone; he inquires for me and promises to come again if I am out. But in me what he is looking for is a possible client, not myself as this individual person. It's a matter of "business." The meeting is governed by the far from disinterested law of supply and demand.

A beggar's visit differs profoundly from that of the commercial traveler. The latter offers as his recommendation the quality of his wares and my supposed need. The unfortunate individual who knocks at my door is doubtless seeking alms, and thus also a kind of profit from me. But his letter of credit is not a thing, however useful or however well-known its trademark; it is rather the prophetic meaning of his empty and outstretched hand.[13] This is enough to establish a total difference between the bearing of the businessman and that of the beggar.

However, there is a visit which is a kind of mixture of the two types we have just discussed: the visit of the handicapped person (a blind man or a cripple) who knocks at my door in the hope of selling some small article. His wares relate him to the commercial traveler and spare him the shame of having to beg. I am approached as a possible buyer. However, as with the beggar, the essential point which recommends the visitor is his suffering; this has far more influence than the possible usefulness of the household article he is selling. Often I have no need of the item he offers. Whether or not I buy depends on whether the visitor has effectively touched the person in me or the consumer.

A visit by a doctor has eminently interpersonal meaning. The visit takes place in the home, at the patient's bedside, where the latter is trying to defend his life against the forces of illness. On the doctor's side, the visit has a professional aspect. However, the doctor is called to give help to someone, and is awaited and welcomed as a savior. The medical activity must doubtless be conducted according to objective scientific laws; but it achieves its full perfection only if the impartial gaze of the physcian is allied to the understanding of the humanist. The relàtion of doctor to patient must be one of dedication; that of patient to doctor, one of hope and trust. This combination of factors gives the doctor's visit to the home a strong quality of *encounter*—all the more deeply felt if the physician is the family doctor. A medical examination required by law even of the healthy and undergone outside the home is, despite the language used, not really a "visit" and is far from having the same depth of meaning.

Absence and Visit

I do not visit those whose daily life I share at home, for I see them and they see me. It is only friends at a distance that I want "to go to see" or to receive. A visit thus supposes separation as the usual rule. As silence is the natural environment of the word, so the visit occurs within a context of habitual absence; its basic intent is to conquer distance and to effect a reunion.

We must, however, recall that not all separation is absence.[14] The distance which separates me from things, however much I covet them, does not create an absence in the strict sense. There can be presence or absence only between persons. And among these, only those are absent whom I would like to see or know. The presences I enjoy are few compared with the many absences I regret, a very limited response to my limitless desire.

To feel someone's absence is also to feel absent from myself. Both of us are diminished, robbed of part of our being by the distance that prevents communication in an identical *here* and *now*. I set out, therefore, to overcome the absence, to meet the other, and to establish communication between us once again, however briefly.

The visit belongs to the genus "encounter," but has very clear specific characteristics of its own. A chance meeting in the street is not a visit, for a visit must be intended, sought, willed, at least by one of the parties. Furthermore, the visit does not occur in just any place whatsoever; no public place, such as a street, a town plaza, or a railroad car, provides the proper framework for it. A visit is made to the place where the other person is fully the person I am seeking, whether he is a functionary or simply a private individual. To conduct business with a public man—a mayor or prefect, for example

—with whom I have no bond of friendship, I find him in his office; a meeting at his home would create an equivocal situation, for my attention would oscillate between the public figure and the private individual. If, on the contrary, I am seeking the other person's unadulterated personal truth, then I go where an unconscious *purification* strips him of his pretenses: to his home.

In the strictest sense, therefore, a visit is an intentional meeting, at the other's home, and its basic thrust is to do honor to the person.

Visit and Distance

I may have been planning a visit for a long time. Often what holds me back is not so much the material difficulties of distance and lack of time as the self-denial involved in taking the first step. Finally, by a completely gratuitous decision that could have come sooner or been put off indefinitely, I set out. I tear myself away from the familiar space of my home. I give up my own time: the time spent at work or in leisure. I surrender *myself*, and my departure is as much a going forth from myself as from my house. I deliberately give preference to the other and his interests and needs. The goal of my journey is not some place but someone, not a possession to be acquired but a person to be served.

The visit, as we have pointed out, supposes an intervening distance which I must cross. We think immediately of geographical distance; but there are other distances which sunder subjects who may be close in physical space. Distances of a biological kind: differences of race, of age, of health or illness. A young person may have to overcome interior resistance in going to visit an elderly person; the healthy person has an instinctive repugnance to entering a hospital room. Distance in fortune: the rich man who visits the poor man crosses a much greater distance than the miles on the highway. Affective distances of resentment or hatred. Cultural distances of language, mentality, or knowledge, which make genuine dialogue difficult. Distances of social function—a public figure's visit to a home for the aged or to a disaster area as soon as reported by newspaper and radio. Distance separating free man from prisoner.

Once I reach the other man's door and my finger is on the bell, I hesitate to push it. A mysterious distance, irreducible to localization and measure, still divides me from the other and holds my hand back. Technological progress provides means of crossing sidereal distances and multiplies the media of communication, but cannot suppress the most awesome distances of all: those that separate man from man.

The Visit as Prevenient

Behind every visit there is an initiative taken, often unilaterally, to meet another person. Before I set out, a secret intention links me for days, weeks, or even months, to the other person; it throws a bridge across the distance between us. My plan anticipates the meeting and makes it already real to me. I think of the other person and, even if he is still unaware of my intention, I am in a way already with him.

The visit is thus prevenient or anticipative on several counts. I have forestalled the other person in being the first to form an effective desire to have the meeting. If I inform him of my plan, I have anticipated him in a new way, being the first to "get in touch." Like the desire itself, the announced plan is a mixture of presence and absence: it is at once a giving and a withholding of each person with reference to the other.

The actual visit itself, of course, translates into spatial movement the prevenance inherent in word, hand, and face; I am actually borne to the place whither my organs of expression have already taken me. But the intentionality and communicative power of the latter are in turn intensified. My word will change into a direct address, my gesture will "lay hold" of the other, and my eyes will meet his.

The departure is thus the carrying out of my intention. My journey is the projection of my plan into physical space. At each step I transcend and surpass myself, for I affirm the other as the other pole of my every movement.

Visit and Gratuitousness

What gives meaning and value to all the prevenance on my part is its gratuitousness. The word is not meant here in the derived and negative sense of action that is without justification or is perhaps even irrational. "Gratuitous" in its primary sense means that which is not a payment of any debt; which is not determined by things or rational calculation; and which, in the last analysis, springs from the creative power of love. The gratuitous gives rise to the ever new and fresh reality of the gift. Thus the most authentic visit is the one that is the most good-willed. Any seeking of personal advantage distorts or destroys the deepest meaning of the action. Instead of the presumed benefactor I become a beggar in disguise and continue to be concerned with my own interests in the very movement outward to the other. If I am the one visited, I am painfully disillusioned when I see that a seeming act of generosity is really motivated by self-interest. Visits can, of course, take many forms; business visits or begging visits are legitimate and necessary. But then the intention must be made clear from the beginning, and a visit of sympathy and friendship must exclude any egoistic purposes.

The Visit as Sharing of Existence

To cross another's threshold is to enter his "home," a highly personalized world. I am fully aware of this as I pass through the doorway and even more so as the door closes behind me. The furniture and other objects which now surround me give me access (in varying degrees according to circumstances) to the interiority of another person.

On the other hand, this same movement of mine gives my host certain rights over me. As a visitor, I come to *see* the other, but I also come to *be seen* by him; I surrender myself to his eyes and allow myself to be apprehended by his gaze. The visit is a voluntary epiphany.[15] Moreover, the other is master in his own home; in entering into it, I put myself at his mercy. One of the constant points at issue in a visit is the autonomy which each party spontaneously claims for himself. Which of the two, the welcomer or the welcomed, will prevail over the other by the acknowledged power of his presence or his will? Hospitality becomes even more difficult when two persons share a house but each one claims full autonomy even while offering himself to the other. There is need to insist on the sharing which entry into another's house initiates.

This place which is not familiar to me and hitherto was for me a "yonder" is manifested to me as the "here" of another human being's existence. During my visit, that space becomes my place, or rather our common "here." But this lodging, whether poor, comfortable, or luxurious, is not simply a framework for living: it lives with a personal human life which circulates everywhere among the things in the house and quickens them from within. I discover the other person's larger self; I take the measure of the possessions he has immediately at his disposal and the familiar tools which enable him to take hold of the world. I then hazard a judgment on what he *is*, based on what he *has*. Sharing his place, I share his existence as well.

The recollected space of the home gives a deeper dimension to personal duration. Presence in the same "here" is thus accompanied by a sharing of the same "now." To be together is to live a single temporal duration. My present coincides with my host's; the two in fact tend to become identical according to the degree of our effective closeness. To declare at the door that I have no time to stop or, on the contrary, to delay my departure even though the other is pressed for time are, to say the least, signs of a very imperfect presence. When I, in good health, visit a sick person the difficulty we discussed earlier of harmonizing the rhythms of our interior durations is an obstacle to any deep communion.[16]

Even our respective pasts and futures seek to coincide. If I visit an elderly person, I try to enter into his past, to which so many mementoes bear witness. When I enter the home of someone younger than I, I must prescind from my own past and adopt the future-oriented outlook of my host. In these two opposite cases, the past of the one and the future of the other become our common present.

In order to share another's existence in some degree, I must try to enter into the countless relationships he has with the world. Each home corresponds to a certain outlook on the universe. The other realizes this and is not satisfied simply to show me around his house; he instinctively leads me to a window and shows the portion of the outside world which lies before it. I thus share his "view"—the narrow or broad, sordid, average, or grandiose scene which the world daily offers to him: I stare at the face the world presents to him, see it with his eyes, and share his gaze at it. I appreciate the feeling of oppressive ugliness or dull greyness or serene charm which continued confrontation with such a world arouses in my host.

The other's existential situation is also determined by his relations with the rest of mankind. In the intimacy of the home his professional relations are hardly discernible. But he can confide in me and thus gives me entry into the many-sided world of interpersonal relationships (marked by indifference or coldness, politeness or esteem, warmth or friendship) which contributes to making him what he is. His family situation, too, is revealed in the place which shelters him. I see to what extent he is surrounded by the presence of blood relatives, and I try to grasp the affective tonality of this environment. I attempt to see these familiar faces as my friend sees them, to meet and interpret their gazes as he encounters them. In other cases, it is the absence of such familiar gazes that I must interpret. The solitary is one who has no companions and therefore always sees from a distance. For him the other is always far off, whether in blood-relationship, age, dispositions, or fortune. Adopting this same standpoint, I perceive humanity as a vast, inescapable, and attractive backdrop. But the perspectival point defined by our common outlook has no radii connecting it with that encompassing circumference. I share his fearful isolation and turn to those reference points with which he provides himself in order to maintain his connections, in the absence of men, with the world of living things: the cat, dog, or canary.

In the various kinds of sharing of which we have been speaking, I am always seeking communion with the other in a common existential project. As a visitor I try to empathize with the interior situation of my host, not only in terms of everyday life but also in the face of destiny with its promises, its refusals, its meaning. I put silent questions to this face and gaze in order to grasp the meaning which this man confers upon the world, mankind, and himself. As our gazes meet, I try to welcome his into mine, to understand why it is what it is, to justify it to myself and to him, and possibly to correct some aspects of it at a later point. I make my own the young man's assurance and optimism, the sick man's boredom, the sorrowing man's depression, the old man's serenity or weariness. To visit is to try to put myself in the other's "place," in the physical sense indeed but especially in the existential sense of the word. I would like to substitute for him or, rather, to coexist with my neighbor in that indivisible vantage-point which is his existence.

Perhaps "neighbor" is the revealing word: in joining another across all kinds of distance, in drawing near to him, I recognize him as a neighbor. The term says much more than the kind of thing we find in blood-relations; for relatives, people "close" to one another, can ignore and even hate one another. To say that every man is my neighbor is to affirm that in the moral order I am his debtor and that my debt can never be paid off. I now discover that my recognition of my host's "nearness" began not with the visit itself but on the distant day when I first formed the intention of visiting him. It was because the other, though distant in space, was near me in the human condition—in suffering, joy, or friendship—that I undertook to overcome the obstacle of spatial distance and set out on my journey. The physical approach effects an existential nearness. I signify to the other that despite the risks inherent in every separation, I continue to be his neighbor.

It thereby becomes clear that the relationship of "neighbor" is mutual. The logic of interpersonal relations here parallels the logic of space. Ordinarily, language tends to reserve the name "neighbor" to the other considered as having certain rights over me. In fact, however, "neighbor" applies both to the one who gives, or ought to give, himself and to the one who receives. The Gospel parable of the Good Samaritan brings out this mutuality: "Which of these three, in your opinion, was neighbor to the man who fell in with the robbers?" "The one who treated him with compassion" (Luke 10:36–37).

But the word "neighbor" simultaneously indicates the limits of communion and the impossibility of one person substituting for another. Just as I can never fill the indentical place which another fills, neither can I make his existential position mine in any strict sense. Thus a mother suffers because she cannot take upon herself the suffering of a sick child. When I try to console an afflicted person with such means as true friendship suggests, I may well hear him say: "If you were in my place . . . . You can't know what it's like." Whatever the close links and depth of love that bind us, we remain neighbors; that is, an unmeasurable and indestructible distance will always separate us. To recognize that we are neighbors is to admit that we are still separated. The person is unique and cannot be interchanged with another.

I try to reduce the distance with *gifts*. A gift is something of my own, part of my possessions; its value is the greater, the more fully it carries the mark of myself: a memento dear to me or the product of my activity (flowers from my garden, an artistic creation, something I have made). The gift of such a possession signifies the offering of myself. After I leave, I remain in the other's hands in the form of the little gift I have given him; I continue to be present through the mediation of my "present" and to affirm my desire to give myself.

Thus a visit is an exchange of two visions of the world. For a brief moment, the visit puts us in the same state, lowering or *elevating* the visitor to the same level as his host. The two meet at the level of their common humanness. This is why I feel reluctant to visit the destitute, the prisoner, the sick, and the elderly: I am afraid to share their condition, even momentarily, and possibly to become like them through some unforeseen accident of fate.

Despite the apparently complete lack of connection, my concern as a visitor (to renew my ties with the other and to keep him in the sphere of my vital relationships) throws light on a paradoxical activity: the *visit to the cemetery*, a practice which is, at first glance, absurd. Young people especially shy away from it. The dead man has moved away to an unimaginable distance. On the day of burial, however far I may have walked behind the coffin, I had to stop at the edge of the grave and admit my powerlessness to follow the other into the beyond. At every later visit I am forced to the same admission: the dead person is one whom no pursuit can overtake. The means of communicating with him through the senses—word, gesture, face—are of no avail, and so the departed has become the wholly absent man; he seems therefore to reject my visit. Yet I persist in visiting this other who rejects me. In many civilizations people bring food to the grave. Elsewhere they disinter the dead person and parade him about, in a "return of the dead."

Yet to practice funeral rites and to visit cemeteries (actions unknown in the animal world) is not to indulge in childish fantasies, even where one or other particular practice may be in doubtful taste. Such activities are, rather, full of a rich and profound meaning. In visiting a grave I insist that despite his absence the other continues to exist within the circle of my social relationships; I provide him with a foothold in the world of living things, preserve his existential value by the power of my knowldge and love. However victorious the forces of destruction, our interpersonal bonds are so strong and so independent of sensible support (though the lack of this is deeply felt) that the attrition of change cannot break them. A visit to a cemetery, where a person sees things but not *the other* whom he seeks, is one of the boldest challenges man can level at death. His action has prophetic value, for in it mortal man affirms his intellectual intuition of personal survival.

III. THE VISIT RECEIVED

If I now put myself in the place of the person being visited, the factors in and the meaning of the visit appear in a new light which furthers our understanding of the phenomenon.

The Welcome

Let us consider first of all the welcome given by a friend. There are two cases to be considered: either the visit is unexpected, or it is foreseen, expected, and desired, perhaps for a long time. If expected, the visit gives rise to a state of mind which we can analyze here only in its broad outlines: *vigilance*. How can I let myself be dulled in mind by the monotony of everyday life if I know that the other is on his way or even expected shortly? The visit keeps me on the watch. Such a state effects a real change in my interior duration. My subjective time no longer receives its rhythm and content simply from my daily occupations; rather, it is now in tension towards a coming presence. My desire already makes present the friend who has still not arrived; I possess him, yet he eludes me; I feel him close yet distant. This tension in my interior duration confers an ambivalent value on the various objective measures of time: they are both obstacles to be overcome and stepping stones which bring the happy hour gradually closer. I know the eager joy of ticking off the days and hours. I use the time to prepare the intimacy of my home for the visitor. Above all, I arrange a kind of secret space within myself, according to who the visitor is and the esteem, friendship, and love that I have for him. In the final moments I become impatient, even agitated. The least noise in the street or on the stairway is interpreted by my desire as a footstep, as *his* footstep: "Is it he?" Repeatedly disappointed, I learn again to wait until the joyful encounter. If the other were never to come, I would carry within myself a void and an unanswered prayer.

The unexpected visit of a friend arouses first of all surprise and emotional unheaval. The laws of time and space seem suddenly in abeyance. Here suddenly in my house, within my everyday life with its grey factuality, is someone I perhaps never even thought of, so long as I supposed him to be far away. His unexpected presence is like a kind of blessed violence; it turns all my plans topsy-turvy and shatters the framework of my normal life, while inaugurating a new order of things the outlines of which are as yet indefinable.

If my visitor is an unknown person whom I was not expecting, the welcome takes on quite a different character. At the door upon which he has just knocked, the other waits at my disposal, in need or hope. As he stands in front of the mute, deaf, and blind wood of the door, he is torn between uncertainty and trust as his heart strains towards the possibility of a generous reception from me. Meanwhile I am distrustful and jealous of my security and independence, and I stand behind my closed door and ask: "Who is it?"—or, seeing without being seen, I stare at the visitor through my "judas-window." Thus, concealed or with the door ajar, I seek with my gaze to gain some recognition of the one who asks for welcome. In the visitor, I want to find first of all a fellow man. This elementary and unmediated discovery is made with the help of my own bodily self. Knowing the latter from experience, I try to project the same structure onto the newcomer. His general shape, stature, posture, gestures, face, and gaze all tell me in virtue of our ontological reciprocity that this is a man: "It is someone." Here, much more than in my knowing of things, my body is an interpretive key. The judgment I pass arises out of my connaturality with my species and is pre-reflective; it occurs at the level of perception and shares in the latter's immediacy. In the same moment, I seek to form a judgment of individual identity.

On some occasions I do not recognize the unexpected visitor. Fiction likes to deal in extreme cases and therefore in ludicrous scenes in which I find on my doorstep a fearful animal or a monstrous being supposedly arrived from another planet. Apart from such boundary situations, I may open my door to someone who is alien in race, social rank, and dress; the face, the skin color, the garb, and the appearance disturb me a bit because I do not find there a reflection of my own appearance.[17] I feel challenged and am tempted to close my door. This initial reflex is that of the barbarian. The criterion of a civilized person, on the contrary, is a readiness to receive the other as other. More than this, for many cultures the virtue of hospitality finds in the unknown stranger a messenger from the gods. In recognizing a visitor to be both the same and different from himself, the host elevates him to a superhuman dignity.

At the threshold the other greets me, gives his name, and asks me to listen to him. This procedure is a recognition of my sovereign rights over my home. If I return his greeting, I recognize him as a human partner. But more than this is needed. I must decide either to let him in or to exclude him. To close the door is to cut short the communication begun and to deny the other any share in my security and my words; more than that, it is to deny myself. Perhaps it is also unwittingly to deprive myself of a hidden gift that was being offered to me. If, on the other hand, I step aside and let him enter, the visitor crosses my door*step* in one *step*. The homonymy is significant: the crossing of my threshold is almost effortless, but something decisive has occurred. In my stepping aside and the other's entering, two consciousnesses meet and consent to an exchange.

My welcoming words confirm the meaning of my bodily gesture: "Make yourself at home" (in French, German, and Italian: "you are at home"; Spanish is even stronger: "Take possession of your house"). With these words I offer the other a share of my house, my time, my conversation, perhaps my table; I treat him as an "other self" and make him a center of the little universe of which until now I was sole master. The word of welcome tells the other that even though he was unknown to me, he was awaited in a secret corner of my home and my consciousness; his place was ready; he has finally come to take it.

The test of these analyses is furnished by a very special kind of visit: the *visit of a thief.* Is this really a visit? Or is it not rather the opposite of a visit, since the thief wants neither to see me nor to be seen? On returning home I find my house in disorder. The order I had authoritatively imposed on things has been violated. Things, perhaps precious ones, have disappeared. A stranger has dared cross my threshold, and violence has forced entrance where only my free decision should have given access. Another gaze and hand and presence have been substituted for mine, and my person itself has had violence done through violence to my home. More perhaps than by the loss of some possessions, I feel quite unhinged by the thief's visit as the absolutely unforeseeable, the unthinkable in its pure state.

Distance Overcome: Presence

Between incarnated subjects the body is the support of mutual presence. A visit makes me present to the other in this obvious way.

The entrance of another into the framework within which I live my life introduces something radically new into it: this new gaze transforms the meaning of my home.[18] For the presence of another person is totally different from the presence of a thing. An object is only there where the blind forces of gravity situate it; being opaque, it cannot take the initiative either in giving or refusing itself; it is there for everyone and thus for no one. The "being there" of a thing is not a presence but simply a localization. Doubtless objects do at times escape this complete determinism—as, for example, the flowers put in my room by a friendly hand signify human intention and anticipation. But then, it is precisely the gratuitous decision of "someone" that lifts the flowers out of their state as mere things: their "being there" expresses the reality of a presence. Here we have a confirmation of the truth that only a person has a presence.

The influence exercised by presence can be of very unequal quality. Some visitors think their presence is measured by the amount of noise they make. With no concern for my peace, they assert themselves, invade me. Yet a noisy presence remains very superficial, touching only the ears of the one who is visited. It contributes little, for it attracts attention to itself rather than giving it to the other person; the trouble with it is its hidden egoism. True presence is a gift of self; it is self-renouncing and thereby self-fulfilling. A quiet—even silent—visit fills the whole house; it is everywhere and nowhere; it does not seek to call attention to itself, yet cannot remain unperceived; it can be neither measured nor circumscribed; it upsets nothing, but gives a new meaning to things and to persons. All depth and interiority, it receives into its own mysterious inwardness those who have themselves welcomed it into theirs; for a time it is the subtle, living soul of the home it enters.[19]

Thus true presence overflows the body. My visitor's presence is an aura the body diffuses around and before it. Coextensive with the intentional dynamism of word, gesture, and look, it unites these diverse means of expression into one simple act which wholly resists analysis: it creates meaning and diffuses it like a light. Moreover, since presence is the more communicative the more disinterested it is, a visit received can teach me an important lesson: in the degree that consciousness acquires depth through self-abnegation and the service of ideal values, the thinking subject moves further away from things and closer to persons. Only moral inwardness makes an authentic presence to others possible.

Shared Existence

Dialogue is sharing. Visitor and visited receive each other in the exchange of thoughts. Even more than words, true listening (so rare that we're surprised when we find it) allows one person to share another's existence with its joys and unanswerable questions. Even certain silences have such a quality of communion that we hesitate to break them with a word or a gesture. To be there, before the other, with the other, for the other, is to receive him and to give oneself to him. The most precious fruit of such sharing is that, far from diminishing the store of existence which each possesses, it renews and enriches it.

The space familiar to me in daily life is revitalized by the unaccustomed gaze brought to bear upon it. If I comment to my visitor on the furniture or decoration or on the view of the outside world I enjoy, I rediscover my own home through his eyes. A real presence of this kind gives my domestic space its liveliest reality.

The same holds for my subjective duration: a visit received modifies its tension. If I am involved in some urgent task, the other's presence may strike me initially as an annoyance. But the welcome I force myself to give him forces me to moderate my anxiety and agitation and to realize that in some respects nothing is more pressing or urgent than a presence offered me here and now. If, on the contrary, I'm bored by solitude or illness or bogged down in the stagnation of endless duration, my visitor gives the latter a new content and a meaning. The shared instant has a fullness all its own. My "present" is enriched by the "presence" of the other; once again, the parallelism of words is not accidental. Even after we have separated again, and for as long as the benefits of the visit last, my duration has new value and meaning. I live more intensely for having briefly lived with the other. In the course of our conversation, events large and small—our tasks and projects, sufferings and joys—all put on a new face; the words we exchange profoundly modify the meaning all these things have within the framework of my personal life. My visitor fans in me the hidden flame of being.

All this does not mean that such exchanges are always peaceful or go smoothly. As a matter of fact, every encounter exerts a decisive effect on a field of invisible forces; it creates an interpersonal space in which each person engages in complex action that varies with temperament, character, and circumstance. Mutual presence is a matter of approaches, of inititated or confirmed agreements, of discords, of mutual search and discovery. Such subtle interplay goes on in every dialogue, but in a visit it takes on a special character. Whether I like it or not, my visitor both calls me in question and reassures me.

In the simple intimacy of my own home, especially if I live alone surrounded only by things, I acquire an unconscious assumption that I am a unique person, a man par excellence, in fact almost Man-in-himself! The evidence spontaneously offered by me to myself makes me think of myself as the best, if not the only possible, version of my species. Each person is "self-evident" to himself, and those moments are few and far between when I feel a sense of wonder that I exist and am this particular person. But now another person enters into my intimate life. Here is a new version of humanness; it too is an authentic version and regards itself as self-evident. This unexpected variation on the theme of man undermines my naive self-assurance. So it is possible, then, to be a man yet quite different from me? I may feel a malaise stirring: Isn't this other person a living denial of me, a rival in being a man? Doesn't his presence as a free subject threaten to take away my sovereignty over my own home and impose a wholly other meaning on it? Here is the obscure presentiment which perhaps made me at first inclined to keep my door closed or to close it again quickly.

My visitor seems even more of a rival if the purpose of his visit is to discuss some difference between us. The bonds between us are then put at stake even by the occasion which unites us. Perhaps the visitor has been wrong about me in some way, and in the course of our dialogue he recognizes it. But, in the opposite situation, a visit can be likewise effective in bringing me to repentance. Overtaken in my own intimate retreat by the one who is in the right, I am, beginning on the threshold, interrogated, referred to my own conscience, and summoned to pass judgment on myself. Doubtless it is always legitimate for me to refuse this injunction, fortify myself in the presumed rightness of my position, and break off relations with him. But I can also receive the question into the tribunal of my conscience, just as I welcome the other person into the larger self which is my house; I can do a turnaround interiorly, or be "converted," and then, having recognized my wrongdoing, initiate a new relationship with the other.

In return, as soon as the other person confronts me in his quality of free subject, he offers me reassurance, for we are fellow human beings. When I am alone in the midst of things, however familiar they may be to me, I experience an obscure vertigo at the sense of my rarity. My oneness makes me frail and vulnerable existentially. But the visitor standing before me refers me to the species to which I belong. Our morphologies are similar, symmetrical, reciprocal. I see myself living, recognize myself existentially, in this replica of myself. I am a man like this other and, in certain respects, a man with him, in him, and for him. I feel that my own humanness is confirmed, ratified, and justified by his. The encounter with him, therefore, puts me in an ambiguous situation: my visitor reassures me about our common human meaning but calls my meaning as an individual into question.[20] But this dispute, far from being negative in its effect, can bring me a complement of being, an increase of existential value.

The Visit as Enrichment

We must insist on this last point. However lacking in goodwill towards me my visitor may be, and even if he should end up disagreeing with me or reproaching me, he nevertheless enriches me and helps me to transcend myself. This is especially evident when the other is of higher status than I. I feel wonder and confusion at the prevenient initiative he has taken: Why does he deign to favor me by coming to my house? But it is also the case when my visitor is my equal or my inferior in status or age. A child's visit is a matchless benefit, for it enriches me by bringing a new freshness into my life.

Here in the background of my own home, the outstretched hand, the word, the look, receive all their power to lift the spirits from the anticipative, or prevenient, movement which sustains and unifies them. Sometimes it amounts to a real restoration. When I am cast down by loneliness, captivity, illness, or old age, this gratuitously given presence of the other is like an infusion of life. In the depths of my being I feel joy and hope stir into wakefulness. All unawares, a new light comes into my eyes. This presence coming into view has called me to a kind of resurrection. If I am ill, I now sit up in bed or in an armchair. If I am well, I stand up, recovering in my upright position the full control of my powers. If I am depressed, I feel consoled. If I am lonely or a prisoner, I find myself reunited through my visitor with the whole of humanity, with the free world: a living presence has enabled me to vault over the distance which separated me from other men. A solidarity is resumed which draws me out of my apathy or my despair. I receive myself from the other person in the measure that I have welcomed him. Is this not an obscure intimation of salvation?

All this is especially perceptible when my visitor brings me *good news*. The prevenance and the penetrating power of the word then stand out with the utmost clarity. No sooner has the message, carried by a living man, come to me in the intimacy of my home, than it proceeds to advance even further into my consciousness. Having reached that inner secret place, the wonderful *meaning* of the good news flows back out to the peripheral areas of my existence and my universe: it pervades my body with joy, fills my home and my world with the light of a new day, and transfigures my existence by its radiance.[21]

Gratuitousness and Revelation

The experience of prevenient love has revelatory power. I discover the goodwill of the other and his capacity to give himself. But I also discover myself: the visit forces me to declare myself through welcome or rejection. Above all, I am led to evaluate myself anew. Of course, if I am vain, I will not be surprised at the mark of esteem which the visit represents and will consider it my due. But, provided that I am not a fool, I will understand the other's free act to be a favor and see in it a sign of love. The more unlikely such a favor is, the greater the light it sheds within me. That I should be worthy of being freely sought out in this way signifies that despite my limitations and wretchedness I exist and have value for someone. My inalienable dignity as a person and my meaning as the particular individual I am (concerning which I had, perhaps, been brought close to despair) are thus revealed to me. Human love does not totally create the value in the person loved, but at least it functions as a wonderful revelation of that value. Whoever knows himself to be loved discovers his own dignity and the call of the ideal.

A certain transcendence is thus seen to inhere in every generous visit. Such a visit proves that the sphere of self-interest is not the whole of the real, that there is "something other." Beyond the visible there is a realm of transcendent values where profit has no place. Human subjects, whether or not they realize it, are servants, witnesses, and sharers of that absolute order. The other comes to me as sent by a love that is beyond naming.

The Desire for Repetition

The Latin term for "visit" (*visitare*) highlights the primordial role of sight (to visit someone is to go to see—*videre*—him); the frequentative form of the Latin verb (*-itare*) also brings out the fact that a visit tends of itself to be repeated. What occurs in a visit cannot remain a once-for-all act, for the visit aims to make up for absence; it is an act of temporary presence and fleeting companionship, but embodies the desire for continued nearness and a sharing of existence. As visitor and visited in turn, I have repeated experience of this. Does not this unwritten law often keep me from paying a first visit, because I am well aware that there cannot but be a follow-up? If I go to see the other, I implicitly commit myself to see him again. Thus, once a visit has been paid, I feel urged to travel the same road again some day, in the awareness that I have not been with the other as much as I should have or would like to have been and that I have not found the necessary words and tokens to express this. If I am the one visited, then at the moment of departure, I bid my guest farewell with the words: "I'll see you soon again." Sometimes the other insists, "Come to see me," or, more confidently, "When are you coming to see me?" The visit has given rise to expectations, and the simple words, "He never came back" can express a great disillusionment.

In some cases, custom demands that a visit *paid* be *returned* after a certain interval. This is a question of good manners, but it is not therefore without meaning; it signifies that I want to make myself as present to the other as he has made himself to me. We want our sharing to be equal and our anticipative gestures mutual, as an affirmation of our interrelatedness in existence.

NOTES

1. Cf. Bachelard, *The Poetics of Space*, especially Chapters 1 and 2.
2. This happy expression is found in Kipling's *Jungle Book*. —On the significance of fire, cf. Bachelard, *The Psychoanalysis of Fire*, trans. Alan C. M. Ross (Boston: Beacon, 1964). —As a witness to the mysterious relation between fire and man and even between fire and soul, cf. the following fragment of conversation between an elder and a young man in a village of Central Africa, as they discussed the pygmies of the nearby forest: Young man: "Do the pygmies have a soul as we do?" Elder: "Have you ever seen brute animals making a fire and keeping it going?" Young man: "No." Elder: "Therefore you see the pygmies have souls and are men like us."
3. Amédée Ponceau, *Initiation philosophique*, new ed. (Paris: Rivière, 1964), I, pp. 27–28.
4. We can see a sign of this harmony between things and myself in the way the English languages applies the adjective "comfortable" both to persons and things: "I am comfortable in . . . . " Comfort circulates, as it were, and is exchanged between me and my furniture.
5. The Parsis expose their dead to wind, sun, and birds, on wooden towers built for this express purpose.
6. Cf. the texts cited above, Chapter 5, note 32.
7. Cf. Pascal, *Pensées*, Fr. 348 quoted above, Chapter 1 (note 52).
8. Cf. Matt. 6:6: "Whenever you pray, go to your room, close your door, and pray to your Father in private."
9. It is clear that family intimacy is threatened by the communications media. Radio and television can, of course broaden the family's cultural horizons, but immoderate use of these media threatens to destroy the most precious element of the home: its mystery.
10. Cf. Eliade, *The Sacred and the Profane*, p. 65 and *passim*.
11. The myths of the wandering soul or the wandering Jew show that perpetual instability is a supreme evil for man. The same belief can be found in certain Pygmy tribes: the spirit of a man who has lived an evil life will pass after death from tree to tree, "like the monkey," and never find rest.
12. Cf. the texts cited above, Chapter 5, "The Objectification of the Other."
13. Cf. above, Chapter 4, "The Hand as Organ of Request and Prayer."

14. Cf. above, Chapter 1, "Spatiality and Reality."

15. Cf. above, Chapter 5, "The Face as Freedom and Prevenance."

16. Cf. above, Chapter 2, "Subjective Duration and Measurement of Time."

17. There are many experiences which show the role of our bodily reciprocity in the act of "recognition." We mentioned earlier the disturbance I feel when faced with a monkey with his hand stretched out to meet mine (above, Chapter 4, introduction). On the other hand, if I feel horror at the sight of a wounded or mutilated man, it is because this open wound or cruel amputation touches me as a man: the other is "your own flesh," says the Bible (Isa. 58:7 in RSV). We feel similarly disturbed by a corpse. Confronted with a human skeleton, my body recognizes itself in this infrastructure and recoils from death which will reduce it to the same state. The English language says with grim humor that a family secret, which is carefully hidden and would shock a stranger if he heard it, is "a skeleton in the closet." Finally, the repugnance which many feel at the paintings of a Hieronymus Bosch or some surrealist artists has the same origin. The human form in these paintings is broken and insulted, but in such a way that I can measure the deformity; the paintings exercise a kind of aggression against my own humanity.

18. Cf. above, Chapter 5, "The Appearance of the Other."

19. Cf. Jean Giraudoux, *Aventures de Jérôme Bardini* (Paris: Editions Emile-Paul, 1930), pp. 137–38: "When some people enter a room in which others are talking and laughing, the chill of their mere presence isolates each person there; Jerome had this effect on things. In his presence tables, lamps, and cups ceased to be companions and became only cups, lamps, and tables. He petrified stone, changed wood to wood . . . . Jerome had only to enter and each object became separated from all the others. A terrible wave of egoism or pride swept before him through even the least conductive of bodies, and made even the cork, fallen from the bottle, seem like an enemy." Cf. above, Chapter 5, "Objectification" and "The Objectification of the Other."

20. Cf. Gabriel Marcel, *Being and Having, op. cit.*: "he is really other *qua* freedom; in fact *qua* nature, he appears to me identical with what I am *qua* nature" (p. 107).

21. Cf. above, Chapter 3, "Word and Action."

CHAPTER 7

THE MEAL

The visit brings men together to share their lives for a passing moment, but it is not always enough to satisfy their desire for encounter with each other. Over and above mutual presence and even the deepest understanding of each other, they instinctively seek some act of profound sharing in which they may discover each other in the truth of their common human condition. Thus the visit tends to find its climax in the meal.

The meal is, in fact, the social activity beyond all others, and in it all the interpersonal values we have been analyzing find expression. The meal requires a gathering in one place, at the same time, around one table; it involves dialogue, a face-to-face encounter, and finally a specific communal action which gives all the factors just named their fullest meaning: the sharing of food.

I. THE TABLE AND THE FOOD

The Table

The meal is ordinarily eaten at the family table and derives its full meaning from that piece of furniture.

A brute animal does not use furniture any more than it does tools. Man is the animal who builds furniture and fills the intimate space of his home with it. This need of furniture is connected with the human prerogative of upright stance. The hands that have been freed now want to have familiar objects at their disposal in order to avoid the necessity of constant bending.

The table, more than any other piece of furniture, is at the hand's disposal. Its forms and functions may be numerous: square, rectangular, triangular, oval or round, T-shaped or horseshoe-shaped; tables for eating or draughting, playing or operating, workbench or office desk. There is always, as a minimum, a horizontal, level surface, set on one or more legs at about half the average human height—that is, within the reach of the hand. Ready as it is to receive and hold anything whatsoever, and always there for use, the cleared table (*tabula rasa*) is pure availability; it provides my hands with a field of possible action; its silent invitation makes me aware of my indecision and laziness or, on the contrary, stimulates me to action. The surface, though restricted, is referred beyond itself rather than limited by its edges, and thus manifests to me the unlimited field that lies open to my free action.

The table is, beyond all others, the *social furnishing*. It is, to begin with, the piece of furniture made for reunions; being accessible from all sides, the table is made to be surrounded. People avoid setting it against a wall, so that no side shall be rendered useless. Instead, it is placed in the center of the available space and thus can be approached at any point on its perimeter. Here, then, in the center of a common room, the members of the family have a kind of permanent, though tacit, rendezvous. During the hours when the members are away at work, the unused table in the quiet room embodies an invitation and waits for its own specific "world." It is here that the family, daily scattered, is daily reunited. Each person takes the place which custom, age, or dignity sets aside for him. The head of the family or the president of the gathering used to occupy the upper end; today he often sits at the center. Around this place of honor there is an order of precedence. On the other hand, the Round Table of the Arthurian knights did away with all problems of protocol and remains the symbol of a gathering in which there is no inequality.

As furniture for reunion, the table is also furniture for *dialogue*.

Together with chair or bench, the support given by the table enables people to sit in great comfort. The level surface, the upper limbs resting on it, and the chest and face rising above it, all mark out for each sitter a space for his personal gestures and for countless possible actions. The physical relaxation of the posture gives full freedom for reflection and speaking. The faces turn to one another and the gazes meet. The hands, freed from toil, can lend themselves fully to the effort of self-expression. Each person involves himself with all the others and communicates himself in the process. Thus the table is the place beyond all others for dialogue between members of the family; they sit there to talk "among themselves," to tell of the day just ending and of the morrow, as, with heads close together, they exchange impressions, confidences, and confessions. When the usual, or possible future colleagues are at table together, the conversation is a pooling of suggestions and projects. Future action takes on shape and substance in the twists and turns of the talk. Intentions are clarified in words, and the hands are deployed in sketching out the future task. The bare surface of the table presents those who sit at it with a field into which they may project the limitless possibilities latent in the group. Since it allows multiple face-to-face encounters, the table gives this interpersonal space an unequalled *density of presence*.

We can grasp, then, what it means for two warring groups to decide to sit down at the conference table. The shape of the table now becomes very important. If it is narrow and long, the table isolates those who sit at the ends; if it is square, it may create two separate confrontations and two sets of sides, instead of the general conference intended; if it is round, it makes all parties equal by putting an end to pride of place. After sometimes hard and bitter preliminaries, the sides finally approach the table of reconciliation. Each must renounce the standing position and the constant movement which are needed for violent action: all sit down. The table now unites those whom hate has been dividing, and makes each the other's neighbor. Murderous confrontation yields to the face-to-face meeting of a common quest. Even the calming influence of a green tablecloth contributes to the spirit of disarmament. These men have now left military action and the field of war for peaceful action and the field of dialogue.

But the table is also *furniture for the meal*, and it is in this realm that it achieves its full significance. The conversationalists now engage in an action which, more than any words, deeply involves them one with another. The meaning of the food to be put on the table and to be taken in the hands must first be defined.

The Food

Hunger is man's prime enemy, the basic biological need, and the sign of the radical poverty of our existence. As it becomes aware of the worldwide existence of hunger, contemporary public opinion is discovering it to be one of death's most hideous masks. Man is a being who must beg of things the support for his very life.

It is in relation to hunger, then, that things acquire a value as eatables; it is by reason of need that food, actual or possible, exists. If a famine occurs, men turn into food things or animals which till now they would have been horrified to think of eating. From the plague in Athens to the raft from the ship *Medusa* or even to more recent times, stories about famines abound in such details. Eating is life itself in its perpetual effort to "restore" itself.

Thus the will to live is a will to eat. This primary need is the first stimulus to action; man eats by the sweat of his brow. Working in order to eat, eating in order to work: the circle would seem infernal if it were not, to begin with, the vital cycle which is the condition for human existence and for all human activity, even the most disinterested—science, art, morality, or religion. To eat is an act of faith in life and in man's future. Ascetical fasting or a hunger strike, on the contrary, is a loud proclamation that life is of little value, or no longer of value, in comparison with transcendent moral or religious values that have been flouted through injustice.

In countries where *bread* is the basic food, it concentrates in itself the whole meaning of food, and its inexhaustible symbolism elevates it to the rank of a concrete category. Bread is daily, like the life it supports and the labor it stimulates. To earn one's bread and to earn one's life are the same thing. To beg for one's bread is to admit one is unable to be self-sufficient, or it is to live as a parasite. Bread earned is labor condensed, crystallized, and justified in its fruits; it is also the right to life and the justification of one's own existence. Anyone who has never toiled in order to eat has missed a basic human experience.

In another respect, the number of operations required to produce bread makes it the symbol of human solidarity in work and in the will to live. The same meaning emerges from the fact that bread is intended to be shared; we must come back to this point. Finally, bread as produced from the earth concentrates within itself all the cosmic forces that were required for its production; through the bread he makes, man is rooted in the soil that yielded the wheat and, in turn incorporates that soil into himself. Thus bread is not only something to be highly regarded, it is *sacred:* to throw it away, to waste it, is to make light of all the values of which it is the bearer, the human work it has entailed, and the human life it can save. History attests the religious veneration given to bread in many civilizations.[1] Between the "sacred thing" which man himself is (*res sacra homo*) and the bread which nourishes him there is a fundamental and, as it were, ontological relationship.

The Choice of Food

There may often be no choice about the food to be eaten. A man who tills an unproductive soil must bow to necessity. In the cities, the boarding house and the canteen often offer only stereotyped menus, and those who eat there feel a painful lack. Not only does the perpetual recurrence of the same dishes give rise to disgust, but the impossibility of choosing their food takes away a right which men regard as basic. Restaurateurs therefore use their ingenuity to give the patrons a choice of several menus and particular dishes.

My freedom is much greater if I buy my own food, and especially if I buy it at the *farmer's market*; for here I, the consumer, come into direct contact with the producer. The soil comes to me, as it were, in the persons of the farmers and truck-gardeners and in the piles of vegetables and fruits. I go to and fro, making a preliminary tour of the market, a kind of survey which gives a general idea of the merchandise being offered. Then I compare quality and price and finally make my choice. The goods I carry away in my bag are mine in a special way, because I have chosen them out of countless others; they bear the invisible imprint of my preference and were chosen for definite uses and for sharing on definite occasions. Choice is a process of appropriation: I have done "my marketing."

But even though I have chosen my own provisions and the money I pay makes them legally mine, it remains true that they were produced, transported, and set out for display by countless other hands. The most desirable freedom of all in this matter would be the ever rarer one of growing the produce in one's own garden or field. Then a person would have chosen a particular product from its inception in seed or plant. The fruit or vegetable he eats today he would have planned long ago, cultivated with care, and paid for with his sweat; he would have often ratified his decision by a great deal of effort over the months. His food then is really his own; after God, he is its master and he enjoys produce that bears his personal mark.

Preparation

Once the food has been grown or bought, it must be prepared. Victuals must be turned into dishes.

Why the art of cooking? First of all, because food is not always immediately edible; some vegetables and fruits are, of course, and many dietetic theories urge the eating of raw vegetables whose vitamins, thus kept intact, are especially necessary. But man, unlike the brute animal, cannot digest in their natural state all the different foods he needs. Cooking humanizes the food and acts as a kind of predigestion. In preparing my food, I appropriate it by a new title. The man who bakes his own bread is a rarity now, but how proud he is of it!

The appropriative aspect of preparation manifests itself in the distaste I have for food prepared in ways that differ from what I am used to: I do not recognize myself in the recipe that has been used. Since I cannot prepare the food to my liking, I must try to adapt my liking to the food.

We may note, finally, with Lévi-Strauss, that the art of cooking proper to each society is a cultural phenomenon. Between the raw and the cooked is the gulf between nature and culture. Every book of recipes is a partial reflection of the image man has of himself and the world.[2]

Consumption as Complete Appropriation

The diverse activities we have thus far analyzed have progressively turned the food more fully into my possession, my thing. This process reaches its climax in eating.

Nourishment is the only thing that enters my body in order to lose itself totally in it: it is consumed; that is, it ceases to exist and finds its fulfillment in the use I make of it. In this respect, every meal has a sacrificial character.

The relation of externality in which my possessions are linked to me is done away with in this instance. Food becomes interior to me; I receive it within my "home" (in the strictest sense of this word), I ingest it, digest it, assimilate it, and incorporate it; it ceases to be what I have and becomes what I am, it passes from the order of my having to the order of my being. Nowhere else does having so clearly manifest its essential relation to the being of persons.

Food has a decisive effect on my manner of acting. This is obvious in terms of health: some dishes disagree with me; in the extreme case, a poison enters to destroy my physical life. But the influence of diet extends to temperament and character, too. Without claiming, with Rousseau, that "great meat-eaters are usually fiercer and more cruel than other men,"[3] we must recognize that the kind of nourishment a man habitually takes helps make him the kind of man he is. Through the medium of bread and that of wine, which is the sap and blood and spirit of the earth, the soil permeates man and leaves its mark upon him. The food I have assimilated assimilates me in turn. Tell me what you eat and I will tell you what you are. The British phrase "That's not my cup of tea" means that I am not a man of a certain kind and that there are certain things I will not do.

II. THE CIRCUMSTANCES OF SHARING

A meal taken with other people is an entirely different thing from a meal taken alone. The latter is reduced to a biological function, while the former becomes an eminently social affair. Nourishment takes on its full human meaning only in a context of sharing it with others. But there are circumstances which modify that meaning, sometimes weakening it, sometimes giving it different nuances.

Place

I can take a meal with another outside our homes—in a restaurant, for example. The locale is impersonal, open to every comer. Despite the proprietor's efforts to give the place a feeling of intimacy, I find myself in the anonymous realm of "people." But if I invite the other to my home, the significance of sharing is enriched by that of my house. I receive him into a highly personalized space. I honor him not only with my food but with my intimacy, my "interior." Now there is question not of a simple sharing (a concept which is valid only for the order of things), but of a welcome into my special milieu and, as it were, into myself. Furthermore, when he sits at my table, the other is situated at that point in the world to which hunger brings me back several times every day. In my most vital "here," better than anywhere else, a shared meal is an act of common rebirth. By a kind of reflux of meaning, this special type of visit communicates a more intense sense of aliveness to my home; and when the guests have departed, the table and the house seem to slip back into a lethargy, into the void of unconsciousness.

Time

By a biological necessity the rhythm of working and eating marks the entire life of each person. Meals therefore play a very important role in my subjective duration. There is no need explicitly to recall meals, for my subconscious mind situates me in time with these familiar landmarks as reference points. A meal is the starting point in the morning, the relay station at midday, and in the evening the terminus of the day's efforts and the prelude to a night's rest. If I am in a foreign country where (as in Spain) the hours for eating are quite different from what I am used to at home, my internal duration is thrown into confusion.

The hour at which we share a meal has its own meaning. A lunch eaten in haste with others between the two half-days of work hardly provides for the real exchange of conversation. A meal taken at leisure, especially in the evening, at an hour which fosters intimacy, is marked by a deeper cordiality. All work is finished now; a person is ready to communicate with others and relaxes confidently. The subjective duration of each is attuned to that of the others. The "now" is common to all; all share in the same time as well as in the same meal. Each person feels alive, and the vitality of each enlivens the others. The moment itself is made newly alive, sometimes intensely so, because of the many presences and the united action which fill it. In each home the meal is the privileged "here" and "now" of familial life.[4]

The Material

The nature and source of the food play an important part in the significance of the exchange. If I serve the invited guest my customary food, I associate him with my everyday private life and admit him to share my personal intimacy. Sometimes I choose to honor my guests in a special way, and the meaningfulness of the rare food is brought into play. In serving an unusual dish I say in action that my guests are not ordinary people; I distinguish them from the anonymous crowd by the special character of the food.

We must, however, distinguish various kinds of *rarity*. A man who likes luxury may try to serve exotic dishes. But such prodigality is often inspired by vanity rather than by a desire to honor the guest. History has made Lucullus a model in this respect. Moreover, such opulence is due only to the most impersonal of all possessions: money. The deeper meaning of the action of sharing food thus tends to diminish as elegance becomes extreme. There is, on the other hand, a rarity which reinforces the interpersonal aspects of a meal. In bad times, or when the host is poor, the sharing of food is a sharing of life itself; I give myself to the other in giving him my bread. There is another type of uniqueness which renders the exchange more personal. The more effort I have put into the dishes I serve, the more they become effective signs of the gift of myself. Our earlier analyses shed light here. To a predetermined meal brought by a waiter, I prefer a menu I have composed, of foodstuffs I have chosen and had prepared in my home by others or, better still, with my own hands; such a meal represents intelligence, breeding, and tact. Far from being anonymous, the food carries my name, for it is handmade and homemade! Perhaps I am lucky enough to be able to serve fish I have caught, flesh meat I have hunted, fowl from my poultry-yard, and fruit or vegetables from my garden, and to decorate the table with flowers I have grown. Then through my own work I honor the other in sustaining his life and adding to his joy.

III. COMMUNION

An invitation to dine is always an act of choice: it separates the invited person from the impersonal *crowd*. But guests are not invited simply to *communication* through dialogue. Sharing the table draws them into the deeper unity of *communion* in which each person becomes more himself by giving himself to the other.[5] Between family members living under the same roof mutual love effects the free choice that is always required for communion. Even residents of a boarding house may at times accept with good grace the blind circumstances that brought them together. Then, through sharing food, they can pass from polite neighborliness to friendship. In every instance, communion yields *unanimity* and the *perfect circulation of meaning*.

The Breaking of Bread

Bread is intended to be shared. The golden-crusted loaf on the table awakens my appetite and draws my hands to itself. My hands reach out, take the bread, cut or break it; then separate again to distribute the pieces. In giving the other his share, I withdraw the food from my own body towards which I was instinctively conveying it, for which it was made, and towards which it seemed to come of its own accord, as though my body were a magnet. But now the centripetal movement of radical appropriation is reversed in the centrifugal movement of sharing. I react against the relation of my bread to my body; or, rather, I assert that it cannot be unilateral and exclusive. My food is no longer centered on me alone: I assign it the body and life of another as its terminus and goal.[6]

The same relation which links the food to me now links it to another. I refuse to consider my own life as the only worthwhile life; I recognize the other's as equal or superior in value to mine (depending on how much of a sacrifice I make for him). In sharing my food with another, I share my life; I link my life in a common destiny with that of my guest.

In other words, a shared meal is an act of *communion*. Between my guests and me a new life flows; they are no longer simply individuals placed side by side around my table; rather, in sharing my food with them, I treat them, esteem them, and love them as my own body, as an extension of my body and my entire being. I incorporate my fellows at table into myself and myself into them; I become a single living man with them, my larger body and my larger self. However many we may be, we perform an action which unites us into a single organism. Thus the relation of persons to food brings about a system of living relationships and bonds of love. Each person becomes for me a privileged other person: the one who shares bread (Latin, *panis*, French, *pain*) with me, a "com-panion."

The Distribution

The various ways of distributing food are of major importance, for they are not equally expressive and creative of community. A meal in which each person brings and eats his own food or follows the modern practice of self-service has little unitive power. The individual in such cases keeps his reserve. The eaters are present in the same "here" and the same "now," but they remain simply juxtaposed and do not join in sharing.[7] In other gatherings, however, the pooling of food brought by the members and its distribution without reference to the person who brought it create a genuine community. Each one meets the needs of others and receives from them in turn his own needed food. On still other occasions the circulation of the dishes from guest to guest provides for personal tastes without lessening unity. More unitive still is the distribution of food by the mother or father of the family, for this expresses a common dependence on the one who provides for the household; the action of giving is here attentive to the needs of each, thus recognizing persons and bringing them together as members of a single body.

With the distributed food a fraternal meaning also circulates. A specific kind of social unity is brought into being or confirmed. Community at table enables each person to open out fully in the free gift of himself to the other. Communion is mutual revelation and enrichment, and a covenanting act.

Sharing and Revelation

The table leads men to go beyond the limited kind of communication that is possible when people deliberately remain reserved. Apart from formal dinners which people are obliged to attend, the sharing of bread creates an atmosphere of truthfulness. When the gathering begins, some guests may not know the others or may know them only slightly; social and cultural differences separate them. Each person tends, in the presence of the others, to keep on playing his role, wearing the mask created by his origin, profession, and age. But in the familiar act of eating, a man becomes more natural; he is, after all, proving that he is a man like other men. The basic law according to which we initially understand each other in virtue of our bodily reciprocity comes into play here with special force: the man who has been an unknown to me is eating like me and with me; he is, then, a man like me and with me, a "fellow man" (*Mitmensch*) and a neighbor. Each guest discovers the others through the values they share in common: need, appetite, will to live, the brotherhood of living things. Moreover, it is at the very root of their existential condition as persons at once so precious and so greatly threatened each day, that those at table meet and reveal themselves to one another. Each person senses the invitation to drop his mask; he then reveals himself as a man and as this particular man, and recognizes in the other one who has the same destiny as himself.

Sharing and eating give new meaning to the gathering around the table and to the exchange of thoughts. As soon as each person consents to satisfy his appetite, he is drawn into openness of mind. The common action clears brows and faces; words take on a new simplicity and authenticity; all in all, the space established by the table becomes a field of forces in which mutual frankness is the law. Each individual is more willing to express himself as the drink flows, and he expects the others to do the same. The thoughts spoken at table can doubtless be vastly diverse in quality, from the dullest vulgarity to the sincerest confidences, wittiest banter, or the loftiest philosophical or theological discussion. Plato's *Symposium*, for example, scales the heights of philosophical contemplation. In dialogue the exchange of ideas stimulates each participant. Each speaker finds a complement and an increase of meaning for his own words in the words of others; the dinner-debate brings this kind of mutual challenge into play. Moreover, there is a mysterious interaction between word and food. If the dishes hint in their own way at a particular soil and culture and even at the man who chose, prepared, and served them, the word, in its turn, acquires in the context of a meal its full "nutritive" value; it enters into men, strengthens and assimilates them, and allows itself to be assimilated by them. As spoken and received within the context of people sharing a meal and looking at one another, the word acquires a new power of presence and action.

What is said at table confers, in its turn, a specific meaning on the other elements which mediate presence. Here the hand is not, as in a solitary meal, simply an organ for executing an action; it plays its social role as well, for it accepts, shares, manifests openness and cordiality. As the successive courses arrive, the hand is attentive to the needs of others, showing its prevenient generosity—indifference in this matter is the sign of a closed, self-centered nature. Table manners, moreover—the effort to observe the rules of etiquette and the personal style shown in interpreting them—likewise show the quality of the man. The face becomes more expressive, for the features relax and take on a new animation. Under the influence of the conversation and the sharing in this face-to-face encounter, men reveal more clearly what they are like. There is a quickening in the *circulation of meaning* between word, hand, and face.

To sum up: the table has a *power of epiphany*. There is a sense in which each person gives testimony with regard to himself in terms of the personal qualities he exhibits—whether he is untidy, simple, correct, reserved, or withdrawn; alert or distracted; attentive to others or egoistic; taciturn or talkative; jovial, sprightly, surly, or sad; coarse, urbane, refined, or affected. The common act of meal-taking, in which all the means of expression come into play, is a special occasion for interpersonal manifestation. Then prejudices are overturned: Can this be the man I thought so distant, unapproachable, and stiff? Is it such a simple matter, after all, to meet, understand, respect, and sympathize with one another? In short: Tell me how you eat, and I will tell you what you are. You do not really know someone until you have broken bread with him.[8]

How revelative a shared meal is comes home to us when for some reason those at table are preoccupied and worried or an atmosphere of hostility hangs over the group. The common meal then becomes painfully unmeaningful. The sharing of food ought to draw the participants into a trusting exchange, but instead an inner constraint keeps them apart, silent, and uncommunicative. Bodies are gathered together, but spirits are separated. If someone attempts to start a conversation, it trails off into commonplaces which show each person's desire to avoid any real encounter. If the conversation dies, a heavy silence reigns. Faces and gazes avoid one another. The hands perform only the few actions required by the meal itself. Appetites are ruined, and each participant finishes hurriedly, sometimes even leaving the table before dessert, for the table has failed in its mission of fostering truthfulness and unity. Because no mutual revelation has taken place, it has been impossible to establish any communion.

Sharing and Enrichment

One of the virtues of any communion is that it causes those involved in it to enrich one another. Think of the honor done to guests of lower status when they are invited to sit at the director's or president's table. If the word, hand, and gaze of a great person elevate a partner of lesser standing, much more does sharing a meal have this effect. In partaking of the same food, those at table recognize their equality when it comes to human life itself and the requirements of our fleshly condition. If the important man comes down to my level and accepts me as his fellow, he also raises me up to his own. The shared table creates unity in the depths of the shared human condition.

A meal with equals also is mutually enriching. For the sharing makes each person an end in himself for the others, and an irreplaceable value to which service must be rendered. The enrichment here is not in the line of social status but is entirely personal in character; it is less spectacular, indeed, but it is more deeply meaningful. I recognize the other's dignity as a man; I will him to be for his own sake; I strive that he may continue in existence and continue to be what he is; I nourish him. The implicit wish in every gesture of sharing, from the most ordinary to the most heroic, is that the other should be, and should be a particular kind of person. If the father earns bread for his family by his daily toil, if the mother prepares the family meal several times a day, it is because they want their children to live and to be confirmed in existence. The parents thus prolong into small details their original procreative intention. In short, the sharing signifies that above and beyond any limitations and faults, the person—even an enemy—has a supreme value: "Give him a drink nonetheless, said my father."[9]

This kind of ratification of the person has the special advantage of being immediately effective. I am not content with a wish; I act here and now. Within the limits of my slender means, I make my own the plan which creative Love has for this person. By an act of the will, perhaps quite unemotionally, I re-create him, "re-make" him in the strict sense of the word. The hand that offers bread to another pronounces a kind of existential decree: "Let this man exist!"

Inversely, to exploit the starving individual (or nation), to refuse him needed bread or earnings or assistance—to "take the bread out of his mouth"—is to will his death. One of mankind's oldest dreams is to discover a food of immortality. If we did, the greatest exaltation we can desire would come to pass.

Finally, the meal can and ought to be a means of educational enrichment. Plato regarded the banquet as an integral part of the free man's education.[10] Parents know from experience what effort, patience, and disheartening failures are involved in teaching a child "to behave properly at table." What they are doing, in fact, is to help the small human being emerge from animality; to liberate (*e-ducere*, to lead out) the social being who is as yet the prisoner of instinctual egoism. All the reprimands, advice, and encouragement have as their purpose to enrich the person through apprenticeship in the highest of social acts.

Sharing and Covenant

The hand which visibly breaks and distributes bread remodels invisibly the relationships between the persons involved. All the hands extended to receive and offer food, and to take an active part in the conversation and make the presences more intensely felt, are at work in a field of active forces and in a process of group dynamics; they are creating a living community. They are ready to unite in a common work. Community in eating and community in working call for and strengthen one another. Thus in all civilizations, covenant rites include a sharing in the same food or drink.

A meal often brings men together between two phases in a common task. This is true of the family of farmers or craftsmen, whose life is one of cultivation or commissioned work; of boarding students, and laborers or office workers who take their meal in dining-hall, cafeteria, or even the workshop itself; of sailors on a ship, soldiers in the field, mountain climbers roped together on an ascent, hunters on the trail, and so forth. The brotherhood fostered by the meal is deepened by the shared work. Bread tastes better when we have earned it together. In fact, spiritual unity is often the deeper where there is a common shortage; in giving the little he has, each person draws all the closer to the others. But while the meal brings the past to a climax, it looks to the future as well. Men recoup their strength for the rest of the day or the morrow. In an action that is complex yet one, the community is reborn to itself and acquires new strength. The shared meal is both an act and a promise of brotherhood and mutual love.

We become more aware of this when we see the opposite: the *dispute at table*; it is worse than an embarrassed, hostile, or cautious silence, for it destroys the essential meaning of a meal. The space which the furnishings lay open for the communion of persons becomes a closed field for warring egoisms. The disagreements give the lie to the unity which the gesture of sharing attempts to establish. In each disputing individual, word and hand contradict one another. The circulation of meaning within the individual's action and within the group as a whole is seriously impeded, for *the meaning is divided against itself*. Sometimes the contradiction is great enough to break up the gathering, and the participants separate in an act of mutual excommunication. At other times, the naughty child is sent away, or the disagreeable person leaves In extreme cases, of which literature and history provide well-known examples, betrayal or murder turns disagreement into treachery. The objective meaning of sharing food is perverted by a murderous intent. An action expressing mutual love and faith in life becomes a front for carrying out the work of death. But these are indeed extreme cases. In milder disputes, the unitive power at work in the sharing triumphs over the bitter words spoken. The gesture then effects what it signifies and restores the unity that has been disturbed. When relations have been ruptured, reconciliation can find no more powerful expression than a shared meal.

It is natural, then, that the sign of the shared meal should be part of the activities of very diverse kinds of groups.

The *business dinner* brings together business associates and allows them a more relaxed kind of discussion than would be possible in their offices. Now each party becomes aware of the man hidden behind the professional. In the restaurant, mutual concessions are made and the sale is concluded.

The *marriage feast* is richer in human meaning. At times the marriage rite itself takes the form of sharing the same cup; usually, the rite is accompanied by a meal. The will to share with one another, which is the basis of conjugal life, finds an obvious expression in the breaking and sharing of bread. Moreover, as a sign of gaiety and of hope in life and in man, the meal takes on in these circumstances a plenitude of meaning. The new cell of life which is the home celebrates its birth in the communal action out of which life is daily reborn.

The *anniversary dinner* has a specific meaning of its own. At issue is a commemoration of an event with certain special characteristics: an event sufficiently happy that one can honor it with a joyful rite; a past event but one that still influences the present and the foreseeable future. The meal here offers a privileged opportunity for such a celebration, since, being itself an act of trust in life and mankind and a source of gladness, it proclaims the auspicious character of the event being commemorated. As a complex action in which men express themselves in all the various ways at their disposal, the banquet repeats the past action which has so deeply influenced the lives of those present. The sharing, with its custom-bound ritual, is a symbolic and symbolically effective action, for it renews the mutual relationships between persons and, with society as witness, confirms the bonds once contracted. The meal is richer and more alive than any other memorial, and affirms both the rootedness of men in time and the permanence of their links with one another despite the corrupting influence of time's passage.

Before a sorrowful separation the *farewell meal* acquires a similarly deep meaning. Those at table want to say that whatever the distances, and however definitive, that come between them, their brotherhood and communion will abide. Each will continue to be present to the others in knowledge and love, for interpersonal bonds are not subject to the determinisms exercised by space and time. Even death itself cannot prevent the other from being intentionally present to me if I would have it so. But since it is characteristic of the meal to be repeated daily, even several times a day, it carries within itself, like the visit, a thrust towards future renewal. The farewell meal is charged with the hidden hope of a reunion meal that will be followed by no new separation.

The *funeral meal*, whether ritual or not, is distressingly ambiguous. On the one hand, since every meal is an act of faith in life, a funeral banquet is a kind of challenge issued to death, an upsurge of the will to live. The survivors intend to affirm that they still live. The community that has been robbed of a member closes ranks and seeks a new internal balance, like an organism that has lost a member; life goes on. Yet, at the same time, the joy proper to a shared meal comes into conflict with the suffering felt by the close relatives of the dead person; when they return from the funeral service the home seems vast and empty, even if a crowd of friends is there. There is an empty chair at table; it is "his" place, and no one else may occupy it during the days that follow on his death. The central here-and-now of the family—the shared meal—seems to have been destroyed. During the funeral meal, therefore, a hidden protest is uttered in the hearts of those who are experiencing the deepest grief. To them the arrogance of the will to live that is being manifested—the comfortable feeling in bodies restored by food, the involuntary relaxation of faces and conversation—seems like infidelity to the dead, betrayal, even sacrilege. The relatives, so closely united to the one who has died, find that life has become alien, even hostile; food is tasteless, and they almost feel guilty to be eating. Since the departed can no longer eat, they should not want to, and indeed ought not, eat. Haven't we heard of mothers wasting away and dying of hunger beside the dead body of their child? It is for this reason that in some religions there is a funeral fast, undertaken in fidelity to the departed. This ritual action is full of meaning, for it gives precedence to the sentiments of the heart and fosters communion with the world beyond the grave; but it cannot, of course, be very prolonged. At table more than anywhere else, the mourners are cruelly torn between the world of the living and the world of the dead.

Does life force people, after all, to take earthly food again? Then, since they cannot like the dead man fast forever, nor can they bring him back to the family table, they visit his tomb and bring him food and drink. Through this link which is material, vital, and spiritual, the dead man is still located in the circle of those who share the same table and in the loving communion of his fellow men.

At the other extreme from the funeral meal is the *banquet of reunion* held when a friend or relative returns after a long absence. In the here-and-now of the family the man who was absent takes his own place again; sitting again at table, he visibly joins in the gathering, the conversation, and the living action of the community. Then it becomes clear that all the meals taken during his absence were marked by the expectancy and were a call for and anticipation of his return. Then those present feel that the communion had never ceased but had continued despite all distance, and that to enter once again into the family's life is in fact simply to continue it. Love rejoices to see justice done to its rights. The return is, doubtless, not always idyllic; the years have passed, after all, and seen the members of the family going off in sometimes very divergent directions. But the effort expended on a more than superficial reunion shows that in the hearts of all concerned a communion exists which will not die.

The communion that is essential to every meal is a *source of joy*. Whatever the quality of the food, a certain quality of interpersonal relations is inseparable from the table. The sharing of food is a source of strength against the power of death and loneliness. When a sick person who has long been isolated in his room returns to the family table, all present feel the joy that a resurrection brings. I who am healthy feel at every meal that I am coming to life again and am being confirmed in being by all those present. Society then manifests itself to me as a environment that sustains and nourishes me at every level. I feel that though I may only too often find myself at odds with another, the meal brings us back to the source of our common humanity, and that we are then reborn of one another. Nowhere so much as at table does the other person show his likeness to me; at table, man is amiable to man. That is why I experience more than pleasure there—an interval of repose, the satisfaction of hunger, the good taste of food: I experience joy.

Therefore every meal, even the simplest, is *festive*; and, similarly, there is no festivity without a "feast"—the common etymology testifies to an interchangeable meaning between the things themselves. The community of the table is a celebration, a *feast of humanness:* here social life, which is a communion of incarnate persons freely gathered together, is raised to a higher level. Hence this celebration involves certain necessary rites: conventions of dress, order of courses, the rules of good manners. Every meal also has a *sacred* character. For does not communion give access to that mystery which is most a part of every day, the most immediately at hand, and yet the most unfathomable—man himself?

This central social act can be raised to a higher dignity, transcending any purely human encounter. The history of religions shows that the sharing of a meal adapts itself readily to the form of a *religious rite* in which man opens himself to communion with the deity. By the eating of food offered or victim sacrificed, man is admitted to the intimacy of the gods, sharing their table. He becomes bound to them in a relationship closer than that experienced in the dialogue of prayer: namely, in a community of life. The festive character inherent in every meal finds its climax in a rite which is the bearer of immortality.

NOTES

1. Cf. Heinrich E. Jacob, *Sechstausend Jahre Brot* (Hamburg: Rowohlt, 1954); French tr. by Madeleine Gabelle, *Histoire du pain* (Paris: Éditions du Seuil, 1958).
2. Cf. Claude Lévi-Strauss, *Introduction to a Science of Mythology*: (1) *The Raw and the Cooked* (New York: Harper, 1969); (2) *Du miel aux cendres* (Paris: Plon, 1967); (3) *L'origine des manières de table* (Paris: Plon, 1968). To take an example from France and French culture, it is evident that Brillat-Savarin's famous book, written in 1825, bears the mark of a particular period and a particular society: Jean Anthelme Brillat-Savarin, *The Physiology of Taste, or Meditations on Transcendental Gastronomy*, trans. M.F.K.Fisher (New York: Knopf, 1971).
3. Jean-Jacques Rousseau, *Emile, or Education*, trans. Barbara Foxley (London: Dent, 1911), p. 118; Rousseau adds: "The English are noted for their cruelty"!
4. We will speak later of the events which provide the occasion for the festive meal and modify its meaning.
5. On the various degrees of sociability, cf. Nicolas Berdiaeff, *Cinq méditations sur l'existence* (Paris: Aubier, 1936), pp. 186 ff.; Georges Gurvitch, *La vocation actuelle de la sociologie* 1 (Paris: Presses Universitaires de France, 1957), pp. 143 ff.; and especially Nédoncelle, *La réciprocité des consciences, op. cit.*, pp. 10 ff. and *Love and the Person*, trans. Sr. Ruth Adelaide (New York: Sheed & Ward, 1966). *passim.*
6. Cf. above, Chapter 4, "The Hand as Organ of Giving."
7. We meet here, once again, the recurring conflict between the human and the "rational"!
8. Perhaps it is the revelatory power proper to the table that explains, in part, the claim to draw back the veil from the occult and to make "spirits" speak by means of table turning.
9. Victor Hugo, "Après la bataille," v. 20, in *La légende des siècles*, XLIX, in *Oevres poétiques complètes* (ed. Bouvet), p. 684.
10. Plato, *Laws*, I, 641a-d; ,II, 665b and ff., 672d–674c.

CONCLUSION

By scientific knowledge man discovers, with passionate interest, the intelligibility of the universe. Every new advance in knowledge discloses an objective meaning latent in things, and in a degree which differs from one discipline to another, brings to the datum as experienced a place in a rational order. Thus the mind acquires a growing sense of being "at home" in the world; it tames the world and masters it. But this scientific undertaking is also applied to man. By taking himself as an object of study, the thinking subject is able to give some account of his physical, psychic, moral, religious, and social activity; he comes to see himself as an intelligible universe.

The inventory we have already presented in this book, however, shows that the explanatory method does not exhaust the inquiry into meaning. In the innumerable concrete details of daily life, the subject takes the initiative of creating meanings. And far from remaining inert, these are living, like the consciousness from which they arise, and circulate unceasingly: within the subject himself, between the various ways in which he responds to them; within the system of verbal signs; between the subject and the world and between the subject and other men. These four circles are closely interlocked, and their effects upon each other constitute a living, uninterrupted process of mutual enrichment. By his very presence, moreover, man establishes himself as a source from which meaning is constantly emerging, diffusing itself, and fecundating with its living waters the most distant regions of the experienced world. In a second phase, the meaning man has uttered returns to its author, sometimes invalidated, sometimes confirmed and enriched. Thanks to this perpetual movement of meaning within his experience, man is ceaselessly humanizing himself and humanizing the universe.

This is not to say that the world originates from the Ego and must be absorbed back into it. No interpretation would be more contrary to the findings of the foregoing studies. Indeed there is a problem of meaning, whether in the sphere of knowledge or for the person, only insofar as the data of experience oppose their resistances to the initiative of the thinking subject in a kind of living dialectic. In this respect the body, as mediator between the "I" and the world, saves the subject from total captivity within the system of its representations (as idealism maintains) or the system of linguistic signs (as a certain kind of structuralism maintains). A descriptive account of concrete life, like an attentive study of language, teaches that the person does not allow himself to be reduced to any sort of determinism, though determinisms situate him and support his existence; that to live in a spatial and temporal universe is to experience it and impose a meaning on it; that to utter, to handle, to look at things is to re-create them for himself; that in the encounter with others the significance thus arrived at is affirmed and raised to a higher level; that so many endlessly varied processes in some sense render audible, tangible, and visible the hidden principle, wholly resistant to measurement, from which meaning arises from moment to moment: spirit.

We must never let ourselves think that the empirical meaning imposed on things by the concrete subject or the intelligibility discovered by science exhausts the signifying function. For in his most personal activities man finds himself confronted by an order of ideal values which solicit his freedom of choice. The appeal of the Beautiful, the True, and the Good is that of a meaning above all other meanings which invites him to transcend the empirical but which, in return, transfigures his existence in its details as in its totality. The aesthetic, moral, and religious consciousness is the locus of ideal meanings.

There are, of course, the remaining questions raised by the painful negations of the absurd, and above all the crisis which seems to reduce to nothingness the most amazing of man's conquests of meaning: death. That the person, that civilizations should be destined for death—by this above all is reason scandalized. The silence observed on this point by the various kinds of materialism and positivism indicates at times a resignation of reason from its responsibility, at times a profound indifference with regard to the human person. Indeed, from the human standpoint, all meaning is most radically called into question by death.

One can only admire all the more the obstinacy of mortal man as he takes up the work of science again and again, tirelessly; as he strives to confer an ideal meaning on his concrete existence. Despite all the painful defeats and the efforts which must be made over and over again, man asserts himself as a wrestler, always frustrated, always ardent in the pursuit of meaning. But from the standpoint of an exacting reason, meaning finds its absolute foundation only in God.

BIBLIOGRAPHY

(Only those books are listed here which have been especially useful, whether or not they have been mentioned in the course of this volume.)

Bachelard, Gaston, *The Poetics of Space.* Translated by Marie Jolas. New York: Orion, 1964.

Bergson, Henri, *Creative Evolution.* Translated by Arthur Mitchell. New York: Holt, 1911; Random House, 1944.

——, *Matter and Memory.* Translated by Nancy Margaret Paul and W. Scott Palmer. London: Allen and Unwin, 1911.

——, *Time and Free Will: An Essay on the Immediate Data of Consciousness.* Translated by F. L. Pogson. New York: Macmillan, 1910.

——, *The Two Sources of Morality and Religion.* Translated by R. Ashley Audra and Cloudesley. Brereton, New York: Holt, 1935.

Brun, Jean, *La main et l'esprit.* Paris: Presses Universitaires de France, 1963.

Buytendijk, Frederik J. J., *Attitudes et mouvements: Etude fonctionnelle du mouvement humain.* Translated from Dutch by L. van Haecht. Paris: Desclée de Brouwer, 1957.

Chirpaz, François, *Le corps.* Paris: Presses Universitaires de France, 1963.

De Champeaux, Gérard, and Sterckx, Sébastien. *Introduction au monde des symboles.* Saint-Léger-Vauban: La Pierre-qui-virrrre, 1966.

Dufrenne, Mikel, *Pour l'homme.* Paris: Editions du Seuil, 1968.

Eliade, Mircea, *Images and Symbols: Studies in Religious Symbolism.* Translated by Philip Mairet. New York: Sheed & Ward, 1961.

——, *Myth and Reality.* Translated by Willard R. Trask. New York: Harper and Row, 1963.

——, *Patterns in Comparative Religion.* Translated by Rosemary Sheed. New York: Sheed & Ward, 1958.

——, *The Sacred and the Profane: The Nature of Religion.* Translated by Willard R. Trask. New York: Harcourt, Brace, 1959.

Groethuysen, Bernard, *Anthropologie philosophique.* 6th ed. Paris: Gallimard, 1952.

Gusdorf, Georges, *Speaking (La parole).* Translated by Paul Brockelman. Evanston: Northwestern University Press, 1965.

Heidegger, Martin, *Being and Time.* Translated by John Macquarrie and Edward Robinson. New York: Harper and Row, 1962.

Lavelle, Louis, *Le moi et son destin.* Paris: Aubier, 1936.

——, *Conduite à l'égard d'autrui.* Paris: Albin Michel, 1957.

Lévi-Strauss, Claude, *Introduction to a Science of Mythology:* (1) *The Raw and the Cooked* (New York: Harper 1969); (2) *Du miel aux cendres* (Paris: Plon, 1967); (3) *L'origine des manières de table* (Paris: Plon, 1968).

Marcel, Gabriel, *Being and Having.* Translated by Katharine Farrer. Boston: Beacon, 1951.

——, *Metaphysical Journal.* Translated by Bernard Wall. Chicago: Regnery, 1952.

——, *Problematic Man.* Translated by Brian Thompson. New York: Herder and Herder, 1967.

Merleau-Ponty, Maurice, *Phenomenology of Perception.* Translated by Colin Smith. New York: Humanities Press, 1962.

Minkowski, Eugène, *Le temps vécu: Etudes phénoménologiques et psychopathologiques.* Paris: D'Artrey, 1933.

——, *Vers une cosmologie.* Paris: Aubier, 1936.

Nédoncelle, Maurice, *Love and the Person.* Translated by Sr. Ruth Adelaide. New York: Sheed & Ward, 1966.

——, *La réciprocité des consciences: Essai sur la nature de la personne.* Paris: Aubier, 1942.

Pascal, Blaise, *Pascal's Pensées.* Translated by Martin Turnell. New York: Harper, 1962.

Ponceau, Amédée. *Initation philosophique.* New edition; two volumes. Paris: Rivière, 1964.

Sartre, Jean-Paul, *Being and Nothingness: An Essay on Phenomenological Ontology.* Translated by Hazel E. Barnes. New York: Philosophical Library, 1956.